New Explo

GH00359799

COMPLETE LEAVING CERTI
FOR EXAMINATION IN 2007 AND ONWARDS

EDITED BY
John G. Fahy

CONTRIBUTORS

Carole Scully
John G. Fahy
Marie Dunne
Sean Scully
John McCarthy
Ann Hyland
Mary Shine Thompson

GILL & MACMILLAN

Gill & Macmillan Ltd
Hume Avenue
Park West
Dublin 12
with associated companies throughout the world
www.gillmacmillan.ie

© editorial material John G. Fahy, Carole Scully, Marie Dunne, Sean Scully,
John McCarthy, Ann Hyland, Mary Shine Thompson 2005

0 7171 37635

Print origination by O'K Graphic Design, Dublin

Colour reproduction by Typeform Repro, Dublin

*The paper used in this book is made from the wood pulp of managed forests. For
every tree felled, at least one tree is planted, thereby renewing natural resources.*

Course Overview

Poets Prescribed for Higher Level

JUNE 2007 EXAMINATION	JUNE 2008 EXAMINATION	JUNE 2009 EXAMINATION	JUNE 2010 EXAMINATION
Donne (pages 1–21)	Donne (pages 1–21)	Keats (pages 22–46)	Keats (pages 22–46)
Yeats (pages 47–87)	Frost (pages 88–113)	Bishop (pages 170–200)	Yeats (pages 47–87)
Frost (pages 88–113)	Larkin (pages 201–231)	Larkin (pages 201–231)	Eliot (pages 114–144)
Eliot (pages 114–144)	Montague (pages 232–270)	Montague (pages 232–270)	Kavanagh (pages 145–169)
Kavanagh (pages 145–169)	Rich (pages 271–308)	Rich (pages 271–308)	Rich (pages 271–308)
Bishop (pages 170–200)	Plath (pages 348–376)	Walcott (pages 309–347)	Walcott (pages 309–347)
Montague (pages 232–270)	Mahon (pages 403–431)	Longley (pages 377–402)	Longley (pages 377–402)
Plath (pages 348–376)	Boland (pages 432–458)	Mahon (pages 403–431)	Boland (pages 432–458)

[Ordinary Level: see pages iv–vii]

Poems Prescribed for Ordinary Level
June 2007 Examination

Donne	The Flea (p. 2) Song: Go, and catch a falling star (p. 4)	Vaughan	Peace (p. 467)
		Rossetti	Remember (p. 474)
Yeats	The Lake Isle of Innisfree (p. 49) The Wild Swans at Coole (p. 54) An Irish Airman Foresees his Death (p. 57)	Thomas	Adlestrop (p. 476)
		Auden	Funeral Blues (p. 483)
		Morgan	Strawberries (p. 490)
		Nemerov	Wolves in the Zoo (p. 492)
Frost	'Out, Out –' (p. 102) The Road Not Taken (p. 104) Acquainted With the Night (p. 108)	Levertov	What Were They Like? (p. 499)
		Beer	The Voice (p. 501)
Eliot	Preludes (p. 124) Aunt Helen (p. 128)	Murphy	The Reading Lesson (p. 508)
Kavanagh	Shancoduff (p. 150) A Christmas Childhood (p. 157) On Raglan Road (p. 162)	Adcock	For Heidi with Blue Hair (p. 514)
		Olds	The Present Moment (p. 527)
Bishop	The Fish (p. 173) Filling Station (p. 194)	Durcan	Going Home to Mayo . . . (p. 531)
Montague	The Locket (p. 240) The Cage (p. 244) Like dolmens round my childhood . . . (p. 257)	Bushe	Jasmine (p. 538)
		Muldoon	Anseo (p. 541)
Plath	The Arrival of the Bee Box (p. 372) Child (p. 375)	Duffy	Valentine (p. 548)
		Armitage	It Ain't What You Do . . . (p. 555)

Note: Ordinary level candidates sitting the exam in June 2007 may chose *either* the poems in the left-hand column *or* the poems in the right-hand column

Poems Prescribed for Ordinary Level
June 2008 Examination

Donne	The Flea (p. 2) Song: Go, and catch a falling star (p. 4)	Shakespeare	Fear no more the heat o' the sun (p. 461)
Frost	'Out, Out –' (p. 102) The Road Not Taken (p. 104) Acquainted With the Night (p. 108)	Shelley	Ozymandias (p. 471)
		Rossetti	Remember (p. 474)
		Sassoon	On Passing the New Menin Gate (p. 480)
Larkin	At Grass (p. 205) An Arundel Tomb (p. 212) The Explosion (p. 228)	Wilbur	The Pardon (p. 495)
		Jennings	The Ladybird's Story (p. 504)
Montague	The Cage (p. 244) Like dolmens round my childhood . . . (p. 257)	Murphy	The Reading Lesson (p. 508)
		Angelou	Phenomenal Woman (p. 511)
Rich	Aunt Jennifer's Tigers (p.272) Storm Warnings (p.278) Power (p.305)	McGough	Bearhugs (p. 519)
		Heaney	Postscript (p. 522)
Plath	The Arrival of the Bee Box (p.372) Child (p.375)	Olds	Looking at Them Asleep (p. 529)
Mahon	Grandfather (p.406) After the *Titanic* (p.411) Antarctica (p.427)	Durcan	Going Home to Mayo . . . (p. 531)
		Muldoon	Anseo (p. 541)
Boland	Child of Our Time (p.440) This Moment (p.452)	Hardie	May (p. 544)
		Duffy	Valentine (p. 548)
		Armitage	It Ain't What You Do . . . (p. 555)

Note: Ordinary level candidates sitting the exam in
June 2008 may chose *either* the poems in
the left-hand column *or* the poems in the right-
hand column

Poems Prescribed for Ordinary Level
June 2009 Examination

Keats	On First Looking into Chapman's Homer (p. 26)	Shakespeare	Fear no more the heat o' the sun (p. 461)
	La Belle Dame Sans Merci (p. 30)	Wordsworth	Composed Upon Westminster Bridge (p. 469)
Bishop	The Fish (p. 173)		
	Filling Station (p. 194)	Sassoon	On Passing the New Menin Gate (p. 480)
Larkin	At Grass (p. 205)		
	An Arundel Tomb (p. 212)	Thomas	The Hunchback in the Park (p. 485)
	The Explosion (p. 228)		
Montague	The Locket (p. 240)	Wright	Request to a Year (p. 488)
	The Cage (p. 244)		
	Like dolmens round my childhood . . . (p. 257)	Angelou	Phenomenal Woman (p. 511)
Rich	Aunt Jennifer's Tigers (p. 272)	Heaney	Postscript (p. 522)
	Storm Warnings (p. 278)	Grennan	Taking My Son to School (p. 525)
	Power (p. 305)		
Walcott	To Norline (p. 320)	Olds	Looking at Them Asleep (p. 529)
	Summer Elegies 1 (p. 323)		
Longley	Last Requests (p. 394)	O'Donoghue	Gunpowder (p. 533)
	An Amish Rug (p. 398)		
		Lochhead	Kidspoem/Bairnsang (p. 536)
Mahon	Grandfather (p. 406)		
	After the *Titanic* (p. 411)	Bushe	Midwife (p. 539)
	Antarctica (p. 427)		
		Hardie	May (p. 544)
		O'Callaghan	The Great Blasket Island (p. 546)
		Meehan	Buying Winkles (p. 550)
		Boland	Naming My Daughter (p. 557)

Note: Ordinary level candidates sitting the exam in June 2009 may chose *either* the poems in the left-hand column *or* the poems in the right-hand column

Poems Prescribed for Ordinary Level
June 2010 Examination

Keats	On First Looking into Chapman's Homer (p. 26) La Belle Dame Sans Merci (p. 30)	Milton	When I Consider (p. 465)
Yeats	The Lake Isle of Innisfree (p. 49) The Wild Swans at Coole (p. 54) An Irish Airman Foresees His Death (p. 57)	Vaughan	Peace (p. 467)
		Williams	The Red Wheelbarrow (p. 478)
		Thomas	The Hunchback in the Park (p. 485)
Eliot	Preludes (p. 124) Aunt Helen (p. 128)	Wright	Request to a Year (p. 488)
Kavanagh	Shancoduff (p. 150) A Christmas Childhood (p. 157) On Raglan Road (p. 162)	Nemerov	Wolves in the Zoo (p. 492)
		Jennings	One Flesh (p. 506)
Rich	Aunt Jennifer's Tigers (p. 272) Storm Warnings (p. 278)	Adcock	For Heidi with Blue Hair (p. 514)
		Kennelly	Night Drive (p. 517)
Walcott	To Norline (p. 320) Summer Elegies 1 (p. 323) The Young Wife (p. 331)	McGough	Bearhugs (p. 519)
		Grennan	Taking My Son to School (p. 525)
		O'Donoghue	Gunpowder (p. 533)
Longley	Wounds (p. 382) Last Requests (p. 394) An Amish Rug (p. 398)	Lochhead	Kidspoem/ Bairnsang (p. 536)
		O'Callaghan	The Great Blasket Island (p. 546)
Boland	Child of Our Time (p. 440) This Moment (p. 452)	Meehan	My Father Perceived... (p. 552)
		Boland	Naming My Daughter (p. 557)

Note: Ordinary level candidates sitting the exam in June 2010 may chose *either* the poems in the left-hand column *or* the poems in the right-hand column

CONTENTS

P = poem also prescribed for Ordinary Level

P = poem also prescribed for Ordinary Level

P = poem also prescribed for Ordinary Level

P = poem also prescribed for Ordinary Level

Ordinary Level

Contributors:

Carole Scully
John G. Fahy
Bernard Connolly
John McCarthy
David Keogh

1 *John* DONNE

prescribed for Higher Level exams in 2007 and 2008

John Donne was born in 1572 in Bread Street, London, into a prosperous Catholic family. However, Catholicism was banned by the Anglican Queen Elizabeth I. Many Catholics, including some of Donne's relatives, were either imprisoned or died for their faith. Up until the age of twelve, Donne was educated at home by Catholic tutors. He then attended the University of Oxford. After university, he went to study law at Lincoln's Inn, London, where he discovered the pleasures of London life.

When he inherited a sum of money from his father he spent some time travelling on the Continent, probably in Spain and France. Subsequently, he joined two expeditions, one to attack the Spanish port of Cadiz and the other to the Azores. On his return to England, he became personal secretary to a powerful courtier, Sir Thomas Egerton. At about this time, Donne decided to change to the Anglican religion. At the age of thirty, he eloped with Ann More, Sir Thomas's seventeen-year-old niece, to the intense annoyance of her family. Donne lost his job and was unable to find another. For a long time, he had great difficulty supporting his ever-growing family.

1572–1631

Ann had twelve pregnancies and seven of their children survived.

Donne began to write religious works and the king, James I, was so impressed that he persuaded him to become an Anglican priest. He became famous for his wonderful sermons, some of which are still read today, and was made a royal chaplain to the king. Donne died on 31 March 1631. He was buried in St Paul's Cathedral.

JOHN DONNE   1

The Flea

this poem is also prescribed for Ordinary Level exams in 2007 and 2008

Mark but this flea, and mark in this,
How little that which thou deny'st me is;
Me it sucked first, and now sucks thee,
And in this flea, our two bloods mingled be;
Confess it, this cannot be said   5
A sin, or shame, or loss of maidenhead,
Yet this enjoys before it woo,
And pampered swells with one blood made of two,
And this, alas, is more than we would do.

Oh stay, three lives in one flea spare,   10
Where we almost, nay more than married are.
This flea is you and I, and this
Our marriage bed, and marriage temple is;
Though parents grudge, and you, we are met,
And cloistered in these living walls of jet.   15
Though use make you apt to kill me,
Let not to this, self-murder added be,
And sacrilege, three sins in killing three.

Cruel and sudden, hast thou since
Purpled thy nail, in blood of innocence?   20
In what could this flea guilty be,
Except in that drop which it sucked from thee?
Yet thou triumph'st, and say'st that thou
Find'st not thyself, nor me the weaker now;
'Tis true, then learn how false, fears be;   25
Just so much honour, when thou yield'st to me,
Will waste, as this flea's death took life from thee.

Notes

[6] **maidenhead:** virginity

[7] **woo:** courts

[11] **nay:** even

[16] **apt:** have a tendency

[17] **self-murder:** suicide

Explorations

First reading

1. Discuss your reaction to a flea appearing in a piece of poetry. Try to explain why you react in the way that you do. Does it have something to do with how you view poetry? Consider what turns a passage of writing into a poem.

2. Describe, in your own words, what happens to the flea in each of the three stanzas. Are you amused or disgusted by these descriptions? Perhaps you have another reaction. How would you react if you saw a real flea?

3. Examine each stanza and discuss the way in which Donne uses the flea's fate to express his feelings. How do you feel about this approach? Does it help you to understand more about Donne, or is it simply confusing?

4. Describe the situation in which Donne finds himself.

Second reading

5. Can you suggest the tone of voice that should be used to read this poem? Which words in the poem indicate this tone to you?

6. Choose two phrases from the poem that you found surprising or interesting and discuss Donne's use of language and imagery. Try to understand why they affected you in the way that they did.

7. Look at Donne's attitude to love in this poem. In particular, consider lines 1–4, lines 12–13 and lines 25–27. What is your reaction to his view?

Third reading

8. Do you think that this poem succeeded in persuading Donne's beloved to his point of view? Do you find it a persuasive piece of writing? Why?

9. During the sixteenth century many bawdy love poems were written about the activities of fleas on the female body. Do you feel that Donne simply repeated this formula, or did he take a more individual approach?

10. One famous critic, Sir Arthur Quiller-Couch, described 'The Flea' as 'about the most merely disgusting in our language'. Would you agree or disagree with this statement? Refer closely to the text of the poem to support your answer.

Song: Go, *and catch a falling star*

this poem is also prescribed for Ordinary Level exams in 2007 and 2008

Go, and catch a falling star,
Get with child a mandrake root,
Tell me, where all past years are,
Or who cleft the Devil's foot,
Teach me to hear mermaids singing,   5
Or to keep off envy's stinging,
And find
What wind
Serves to advance an honest mind.

If thou be'est born to strange sights,   10
Things invisible to see,
Ride ten thousand days and nights,
Till age snow white hairs on thee,
Thou, when thou return'st, wilt tell me
All strange wonders that befell thee,   15
And swear
No where
Lives a woman true, and fair.

If thou find'st one, let me know,
Such a pilgrimage were sweet,   20
Yet do not, I would not go,
Though at next door we might meet,
Though she were true, when you met her,
And last, till you write your letter,
Yet she   25
Will be
False, ere I come, to two, or three.

Notes

[2] **mandrake root:** a poisonous plant believed to have human qualities
[4] **cleft:** split
[15] **befell:** happened to

Explorations

First reading

1. List the tasks Donne describes in the three stanzas. Do they have anything in common? Could you suggest a similar list of present-day tasks?
2. What language does Donne use to give a magical or supernatural feeling to the poem? Why do you think he does this?
3. In each stanza Donne uses two very short lines (lines 7–8, 16–17 and 25–26) – what effect does this have on the rhythm of the poem? You may find it helpful to read the poem aloud. Discuss why Donne chose to use this structure.
4. Each of the three stanzas seems to build up to the final line. Do the three final lines help you to understand the theme of this poem? Can you explain the theme in your own words?

Second reading

5. Examine two images from the poem that you feel are particularly effective. Explain how they achieve their effectiveness.
6. Consider the feelings that Donne reveals in the following lines:
   'And swear
   No where

Lives a woman true, and fair.'
What is your reaction to these lines?
7. How would you describe the tone of this poem? Would you consider it to be the same throughout? Pay particular attention to lines 19–20.

Third reading

8. In some manuscripts this poem appears in a group entitled 'Songs which were made to certain airs that were made before'. Would the effect of this poem be changed if it were sung? Try making up a piece of music for the poem.
9. Examine Donne's attitude to women in this poem and compare it to the one expressed in 'The Flea' – discuss your findings. Based on this, how would you describe Donne as a person? Finally, try reading 'The Sun Rising' where Donne expresses another view about women.
10. In the sixteenth century, listing impossible tasks in a poem was a popular device used for emphasis or hyperbole. Do you feel that this device is used successfully in 'Song: Go, and catch a falling star'? What was Donne trying to emphasise?

The Sun Rising

Busy old fool, unruly sun,
Why dost thou thus,
Through windows, and through curtains call on us?
Must to thy motions lovers' seasons run?
Saucy pedantic wretch, go chide   5
Late schoolboys, and sour prentices,
Go tell court-huntsmen, that the King will ride,
Call country ants to harvest offices;
Love, all alike, no season knows, nor clime,
Nor hours, days, months, which are the rags of time.   10

Thy beams, so reverend, and strong
Why shouldst thou think?
I could eclipse and cloud them with a wink,
But that I would not lose her sight so long:
If her eyes have not blinded thine,   15
Look, and tomorrow late, tell me,
Whether both th'Indias of spice and mine
Be where thou left'st them, or lie here with me.
Ask for those kings whom thou saw'st yesterday,
And thou shalt hear, All here in one bed lay.   20

She is all states, and all princes, I,
Nothing else is.
Princes do but play us; compared to this,
All honour's mimic; all wealth alchemy.
Thou sun art half as happy as we,   25
In that the world's contracted thus;
Thine age asks ease, and since thy duties be
To warm the world, that's done in warming us.
Shine here to us, and thou art everywhere;
This bed thy centre is, these walls, thy sphere.   30

Notes

[5] **pedantic:** one who strictly adheres to formal rules

[8] **offices:** duties

[9] **clime:** climate

[17] **mine:** gold mines

[24] **mimic:** imitation

[24] **alchemy:** the science seeking to turn base metal into gold

Explorations

First reading

1. Consider the various reactions you might feel on being awakened by the sunrise. Are any of these reactions echoed by Donne in the way he addresses the sun in the first 8 lines of the poem?
2. Donne indicates the reason for his outburst in the first and second stanzas. Can you explain what it is? Do you have a certain sympathy for his feelings?
3. In the third stanza Donne compares his situation to that of the sun. Is there a change in the tone he uses? Can you explain why this happens?
4. Discuss two images from the poem that you find particularly effective.

Second reading

5. Consider the various emotions that Donne expresses in the poem. Is there a dominant one?
6. Examine the language and imagery Donne uses to communicate the intensity of the love he feels. Does he persuade you of his sincerity?
7. Contrast the rhythm and sounds of lines 1–4 with those used in lines 27–30. How do they help to convey Donne's emotions?

Third reading

8. Discuss the way in which Donne uses concepts of time and space within the poem. Do you find them confusing or do they help you to understand Donne's mood? Would you agree with him that emotions can transcend the confines of time and space?
9. This poem is centred on the conceit of 'Love' and 'Royalty'. Trace the development of this conceit in the poem. Do you find it a successful connection of ideas, or irritatingly clever?
10. Read 'The Flea' again. Which poem would you consider to be the more realistic and vivid?

The Anniversarie

All kings, and all their favourites,
All glory of honours, beauties, wits,
The sun itself, which makes times, as they pass,
Is elder by a year, now, than it was
When thou and I first one another saw: 5
All other things, to their destruction draw,
Only our love hath no decay;
This, no tomorrow hath, nor yesterday,
Running it never runs from us away,
But truly keeps his first, last, everlasting day.   10

Two graves must hide thine and my corse,
If one might, death were no divorce,
Alas, as well as other princes, we,
(Who prince enough in one another be,)
Must leave at last in death, these eyes, and ears,   15
Oft fed with true oaths, and with sweet salt tears;
But souls where nothing dwells but love
(All other thoughts being inmates) then shall prove
This, or a love increased there above,
When bodies to their graves, souls from their graves remove.   20

And then we shall be thoroughly blessed,
But we no more, than all the rest.
Here upon earth, we are kings, and none but we
Can be such kings, nor of such subjects be;
Who is so safe as we? where none can do   25
Treason to us, except one of us two.
True and false fears let us refrain,
Let us love nobly, and live, and add again
Years and years unto years, till we attain
To write threescore, this is the second of our reign.   30

Notes

[11] **corse:** corpse
[27] **refrain:** avoid
[30] **threescore:** sixty

Explorations

First reading

1. Do you find this poem immediately understandable or rather confusing? Did you feel drawn into the poem on the first reading? Is there any aspect of the poem that would encourage you to explore it further?

2. The poem is entitled 'The Anniversarie'; can you explain what type of anniversary Donne is writing about?

3. Consider the way in which Donne conveys a sense of time passing in the poem. Do you find the images depressing?

4. How does Donne describe the love he is celebrating in the poem?

5. Can you express the theme of this poem in a few sentences?

Second reading

6. How would you feel if you received this poem as a gift?

7. Examine Donne's use of images connected with the royal court. Do you find them effective in helping you to understand Donne's feelings?

8. Can you describe Donne's mood in the poem? Is it constant, or can you detect changes as the poem progresses?

Third reading

9. 'True and false fears let us refrain,
    Let us love nobly, and live, and add again
    Years and years unto years, till we attain
    To write threescore, this is the second of our reign.'
    Do you find these lines convincing, coming as they do at the end of this poem? Does the poem successfully support this ending?

10. Imagine that John Donne has asked you to read this poem and give him some advice on how, if necessary, it could be improved. Outline what you would say to him.

Sweetest love, I do not go

Sweetest love, I do not go,
For weariness of thee,
Nor in hope the world can show
A fitter love for me;
But since that I   5
Must die at last, 'tis best,
To use my self in jest
Thus by feigned deaths to die.

Yesternight the sun went hence,
And yet is here today,   10
He hath no desire nor sense,
Nor half so short a way:
Then fear not me,
But believe that I shall make
Speedier journeys, since I take   15
More wings and spurs than he.

O how feeble is man's power,
That if good fortune fall,
Cannot add another hour,
Nor a lost hour recall!   20
But come bad chance,
And we join to it our strength,
And we teach it art and length,
Itself o'er us to advance.

When thou sigh'st, thou sigh'st not wind,   25
But sigh'st my soul away,
When thou weep'st, unkindly kind,
My life's blood doth decay.
It cannot be
That thou lov'st me, as thou say'st,   30
If in thine my life thou waste,
Thou art the best of me.

Let not thy divining heart
Forethink me any ill,

Destiny may take thy part,   35
And may thy fears fulfil;
But think that we
Are but turned aside to sleep;
They who one another keep
Alive, ne'er parted be.   40

 # Explorations

First reading

1. Describe the setting in which Donne places himself. Does the poem make it easy for you to imagine? Discuss the clues that helped you.

2. What tone of voice should be used to speak this poem? Can you choose some words or phrases that you feel indicate this tone?

3. Trace the ways that Donne attempts to reassure his beloved. Would you feel reassured by this poem?

4. What view does Donne convey of death? Why do you think he approaches it in this way?

Second reading

5. Consider the third stanza. Do you find it different in any way from the other stanzas of the poem? Discuss the part that it plays in the overall structure of the poem.

6. What age do you think Donne was when he wrote this? Do you learn anything about his personality? What evidence is there in the poem to support your views?

7. This poem is addressed to Donne's beloved. Do you feel that the emphasis is on Donne's own feelings or on those of his beloved? What does this tell you about their relationship?

Third reading

8. Discuss the rhythm and rhyme used in this poem. Do they add to the overall effect of the piece? Were you aware of them in your reading of this poem?

9. There are some indications that Donne intended this piece to be sung. What aspects of the poem support this? Could you suggest the type of music that might have been used? Would you react differently to the poem if it were a song?

10. Compare Donne's view of death in this poem with the one he communicates in 'The Anniversarie'. Consider the images and language used in each case. Do you think Donne was trying to achieve different effects? If so, why?

A Valediction: Forbidding Mourning

As virtuous men pass mildly away,
And whisper to their souls, to go,
Whilst some of their sad friends do say,
The breath goes now, and some say, no:

So let us melt, and make no noise,   5
No tear-floods, nor sigh-tempests move,
'Twere profanation of our joys
To tell the laity our love.

Moving of th'earth brings harms and fears,
Men reckon what it did and meant,   10
But trepidation of the spheres,
Though greater far, is innocent.

Dull sublunary lovers' love
(Whose soul is sense) cannot admit
Absence, because it doth remove   15
Those things which elemented it.

But we by a love, so much refined,
That our selves know not what it is,
Inter-assured of the mind,
Care less, eyes, lips, and hands to miss.   20

Our two souls therefore, which are one,
Though I must go, endure not yet
A breach, but an expansion,
Like gold to aery thinness beat.

If they be two, they are two so   25
As stiff twin compasses are two,
Thy soul the fixed foot, makes no show
To move, but doth, if th'other do.

And though it in the centre sit,
Yet when the other far doth roam,   30

Valediction: words used to bid farewell

[7] **profanation:** treat a sacred thing with irreverence

[8] **laity:** lay people

[11] **trepidation:** agitation, anxiety

[13] **sublunary:** earthly

[16] **elemented:** physically contributed to

[19] **Inter-assured:** mutually convinced

[31] **hearkens:** listens, yearns

[34] **obliquely:** slanting

It leans, and hearkens after it,
And grows erect, as that comes home.

Such wilt thou be to me, who must
Like th'other foot, obliquely run;
Thy firmness makes my circle just,   35
And makes me end, where I begun.

 # Explorations

First reading

1. Describe the scene that Donne conveys in the first stanza. Do you find it an effective opening to the poem? What are your expectations of the content of the rest of the poem?

2. How does this opening scene lead into the second stanza? What is the quality in the opening scene that Donne uses to illustrate the type of separation he desires? Do you feel that this connection works?

3. 'No tear-floods, nor sigh-tempests move,'
Consider the connection between this line from the second stanza and the images in the third stanza.

4. There is a similar connection between a line in the third stanza and the content of the fourth stanza; can you explain what it is? Is it now possible to trace Donne's line of thought through the first four stanzas?

Second reading

5. In the fourth to the sixth stanzas, Donne assures his beloved that their love is special. Examine the language and images used to convey this. Do you find them persuasive?

6. Donne compares himself and his beloved to a pair of compasses in the final three stanzas of the poem. Explain in your own words how this conceit works. Consider the effectiveness of Donne's description of the compasses.

Third reading

7. Dr Johnson was uncertain 'whether absurdity or ingenuity' underlay Donne's conceit of the lovers and the pair of compasses. Discuss which of the two you feel the conceit represents.

8. What is your reaction to this poem? Did you find the line of thought confusing, or did it

lead you further into the
poem? Were you irritated or
fascinated?
9. Do you feel that Donne
    became so interested in his
    intellectualising that he lost
    track of the emotional content
    of his poem? On the other
    hand, does his intellectualising
enable him to communicate a
depth of emotion?
10. Compare this poem to
    'Sweetest love, I do not go'. If
    you were Donne's beloved,
    which one would you prefer to
    receive? Support your decision
    by close reference to the two
    poems.

The Dreame

Dear love, for nothing less than thee
Would I have broke this happy dream,
It was a theme
For reason, much too strong for phantasy,
Therefore thou waked'st me wisely; yet   5
My dream thou brok'st not, but continued'st it;
Thou art so true, that thoughts of thee suffice,
To make dreams truths, and fables histories;
Enter these arms, for since thou thought'st it best,
Not to dream all my dream, let's act the rest.   10

As lightning, or a taper's light,
Thine eyes, and not thy noise waked me;
Yet I thought thee
(For thou lov'st truth) an angel, at first sight,
But when I saw thou saw'st my heart,   15
And knew'st my thoughts, beyond an angel's art,
When thou knew'st what I dreamed, when thou knew'st when
Excess of joy would wake me, and cam'st then,
I must confess, it could not choose but be
Profane, to think thee anything but thee.   20

Coming and staying showed thee, thee,
But rising makes me doubt, that now,
Thou art not thou.

That love is weak, where fear's as strong as he;
'Tis not all spirit, pure, and brave,   25
If mixture it of fear, shame, honour, have.
Perchance as torches which must ready be,
Men light and put out, so thou deal'st with me,
Thou cam'st to kindle, goest to come; then I
Will dream that hope again, but else would die.   30

Notes

[4] **reason:** reality
[7] **suffice:** are enough
[11] **taper:** slim candle
[20] **profane:** irreverent

 # Explorations

First reading

1. How would you describe the tone of this poem? Compare it with 'The Sun Rising' where Donne is also awakened. What factors contribute to the different tone used by Donne in each of the poems?
2. Trace the narrative line of this poem. Do you feel that it is a convincing incident? How does Donne make the situation seem real?
3. Examine the language and images that Donne uses to describe his beloved. What do they convey about the quality of his love?

Second reading

4. Consider the way in which Donne blends the states of waking and sleeping. Do you find it a successful evocation of a half-waking condition?
5. Is this a particularly revealing poem? Consider how the language Donne uses contributes to the sense of sincerity.

Third reading

6. The final four lines of the poem reveal an anxiety that underlies Donne's love poems, a doubt that he is able to attract true love. Would you agree or disagree?
7. Dryden held the view that Donne 'perplexes the minds of the fair sex with nice speculations of philosophy,

when he should engage their hearts'. Discuss this statement with reference to this poem and two of the other love poems in the course.

8. 'Yet I thought thee
(For thou lov'st truth) an angel, at first sight,'

'This flea is you and I, and this Our marriage bed, and marriage temple is;'

'And swear
No where
Lives a woman true, and fair.'

'She is all states, and all princes, I,
Nothing else is.'

Discuss which of these quotations, if any, reveal Donne's true view of love. Which would you like it to be? Why?

Batter my heart

Batter my heart, three-personed God; for, you
As yet but knock, breathe, shine, and seek to mend;
That I may rise, and stand, o'erthrow me, and bend
Your force, to break, blow, burn, and make me new.
I, like an usurped town, to another due,   5
Labour to admit you, but oh, to no end,
Reason your viceroy in me, me should defend,
But is captived, and proves weak or untrue,
Yet dearly I love you, and would be loved fain,
But am betrothed unto your enemy,   10
Divorce me, untie, or break that knot again,
Take me to you, imprison me, for I
Except you enthral me, never shall be free,
Nor ever chaste, except you ravish me.

Notes

[5] **usurped:** wrongfully seized

[7] **viceroy:** a ruler who exercises authority on behalf of a sovereign

[9] **fain:** gladly

[13] **enthral:** captivate, enslave

[14] **ravish:** rape, enrapture

Explorations

First reading

1. Discuss your initial reaction to this poem. Are you surprised, shocked, overwhelmed? Perhaps you have another reaction?

2. Consider the actual appearance of this poem on the page. What are the differences in the visual impact of this poem and that of 'Song: Go, and catch a falling star'? Does the visual structure of the poems imply anything about their content?

3. Examine the language Donne uses to address God. Choose any words from the poem that you find particularly vivid. How does Donne use the actual sounds of the words to emphasise their effect? What tone of voice do they require?

Second reading

4. Trace the series of images that Donne uses to communicate his relationship with God. Are they what you would expect in a religious poem? Do they help you to understand Donne's feelings?

5. How does Donne convey his inability to commit totally to God? What is the attraction that pulls him away from God? Are you made to believe in his indecision?

6. Consider the rhyme scheme in the poem. How does Donne use it to add impact to his writing? Does it dominate or underpin the sense of emotion?

7. Why do you think Donne wrote this poem? What was he trying to do? Do you feel that it would have helped him?

Third reading

8. 'Take me to you, imprison me, for I
   Except you enthral me, never shall be free,
   Nor ever chaste, except you ravish me.'
   Discuss the effect of Donne's use of the paradox in these lines. Do you find this device helps to communicate the intensity of his feelings, or does it simply get in the way?

9. Robert Graves felt that Donne's opening inspirations frequently wear out after two or three lines and that it is only his wit that moves him forward. Does he 'run out of steam' in this poem? Does he move forward?

10. This poem is one of a group entitled *Divine Meditations*: can you find evidence of either the 'Divine' or the 'Meditation' in it?

At the round earth's imagined corners

At the round earth's imagined corners, blow
Your trumpets, angels, and arise, arise
From death, you numberless infinities
Of souls, and to your scattered bodies go,
All whom the flood did, and fire shall o'erthrow,   5
All whom war, dearth, age, agues, tyrannies,
Despair, law, chance, hath slain, and you whose eyes,
Shall behold God, and never taste death's woe.
But let them sleep, Lord, and me mourn a space,
For, if above all these, my sins abound,   10
'Tis late to ask abundance of thy grace,
When we are there; here on this lowly ground,
Teach me how to repent; for that's as good
As if thou hadst sealed my pardon, with thy blood.

Notes

[3] **infinities:** infinite numbers

[5] **o'erthrow:** overthrow, conquer

[6] **dearth:** scarcity

[6] **agues:** fevers

Explorations

First reading

1. Do you feel that Donne wanted to lead you through this poem or sweep you along? Who was in charge, you or Donne? What was your reaction when you had finished reading the poem?

2. Examine the ways in which Donne communicates the drama of the Day of Judgement in the octet (lines 1–8) of this sonnet. Pay particular attention to the senses that he appeals to in his descriptions.

3. What happens to the focus of the poem in the sestet (lines 9–14)? Is the change gradual or sudden? Were you taken by surprise or did you expect it?

Second reading

4. How would you describe Donne's attitude toward the Day of Judgement? Do you feel that this attitude remains constant or alters in the course of the poem? What do you learn about Donne's emotional state from this?

5. Examine the verbs that Donne uses. Do they help to convey the tone of the poem? Are they reminiscent of any of Donne's other poems?

6. What do you learn about Donne's relationship with (a) God, and (b) his fellow men, from this poem?

Third reading

7. Consider the way in which Donne uses the sounds of words to add depth and pace to his writing. Do you feel that such attention to detail weakens or strengthens the emotional impact of the piece?

8. Are you convinced of Donne's emotional sincerity, or is this simply an intellectual exercise for him? Support your opinion by close reference to the poem.

9. How do you feel about Donne, the man, as he is revealed in this poem? Would you like him as a friend? Did you prefer the man who wrote the love poems? Are they two separate people or aspects of the same man?

10. The critic Mario Praz felt that Donne was more concerned with 'the whole effect' of his writing rather than a search for truth. Choose any three of Donne's poems and discuss this comment.

Thou hast made me

Thou hast made me, and shall thy work decay?
Repair me now, for now mine end doth haste,
I run to death, and death meets me as fast,
And all my pleasures are like yesterday,
I dare not move my dim eyes any way,   5
Despair behind, and death before doth cast
Such terror, and my feeble flesh doth waste
By sin in it, which it towards hell doth weigh;
Only thou art above, and when towards thee
By thy leave I can look, I rise again;   10
But our old subtle foe so tempteth me,
That not one hour I can myself sustain;
Thy Grace may wing me to prevent his art,
And thou like adamant draw mine iron heart.

Note

[14] **adamant:** magnet

Old St Paul's Cathedral, London, where Donne was ordained an Anglican priest in
1615

Explorations

First reading

1. What age do you think Donne was when he wrote this poem? What words convey a sense of his physical condition?

2. Discuss the tone of voice that would be most suitable for this piece. Is there a connection between the sense of Donne's physical state and the tone of the poem?

3. Psychologically, this poem reveals a great deal about the difficulties Donne faced with his religious faith. Can you trace how he communicates the intensity of his mental struggle? Do you feel that this poem enabled him to arrive at a resolution?

Second reading

4. 'And all my pleasures are like yesterday;'
   How do you think the Donne of this poem felt about his earlier love poems?

5. Donne assigns specific roles to God and himself. Can you describe what these are? Compare Donne's approach here with the one he takes in 'Batter my heart'. Is there a poignancy about Donne's role in this poem?

6. The final couplet (rhyming two lines) can be interpreted in different ways. Discuss what these might be and consider which one seems to be most fitting.

Third reading

7. Joan Bennett wrote: 'Metaphysical poetry is written by men for whom the light of day is God's shadow.' Consider Donne's religious poetry in the context of this statement.

8. Donne never intended his poetry for mass publication and during his life most of his works were circulated around a small circle of friends. Do you think that this gave him greater freedom to express himself, or would he have felt more self-conscious? Refer to the poems you have explored.

9. 'Donne is adept at keeping the ball in the air.' (Robert Graves) 'The wheels take fire from the mere rapidity of their motion.' (Coleridge) 'The spell holds for the duration of the poem.' (Michael Schmidt) Was Donne simply a poetic trickster, or did he truly create magic?

10. 'But when I saw thou saw'st my heart,
    And knew'st my thoughts'
    In the poems that you have explored, did you see Donne's heart and know his thoughts? Did Donne see your heart and know your thoughts?

2 John KEATS

prescribed for Higher Level exams in 2009 and 2010

John Keats was born at Finsbury, near London, on 31 October 1795, the eldest child of Frances Jennings Keats and Thomas Keats, a livery-stable keeper.

From 1803 to 1811 he attended Rev. John Clarke's school in an old Georgian country house at Enfield, north London. John Keats was a small boy (fully grown he was only five feet tall) but he was athletic and liked sports, and, though he had a quick temper, he was generally popular.

Clarke's was a liberal, progressive boarding school, which did not allow the flogging or 'fagging' (junior boys acting as servants to the older boys) common at the time. The pupils, who were mostly of middle-class background and destined for the professions, received a well-rounded education. They had their own garden plots to cultivate; interest in music and the visual arts was also encouraged, as well as the usual study of history, geography, arithmetic, grammar, French and Latin. Keats received a particularly good classical Latin education.

Keats left school in 1811 to begin an apprenticeship as a surgeon. This was then the manual side of the medical profession, involving bone-setting, tooth-pulling

1795–1821

John Keats

and amputation, and was considered socially inferior to becoming a physician, which would have entailed expensive university education. After some years as an apprentice, in 1815 Keats registered as a student at Guy's Hospital, London, and attended lectures in anatomy, physiology and chemistry.

In May 1816 the sonnet 'O Solitude' was the first of Keats's poems to be published. In June, Keats wrote 'To One Long in City Pent'. Later that year he composed 'On First Looking into Chapman's Homer'.

He qualified in July 1816 and was licensed to practise as a surgeon and apothecary; but by now he had developed an aversion to surgery (then performed without anaesthetic, in primitive conditions), and he devoted more of his time to writing poetry. His early poems reflect liberal attitudes and a rebellious outlook on life.

Keats began to express his ideas on poetry. He placed great value on the imagination, the importance of feelings, and the central place of beauty in poetry.

Some time in January or February 1818 Keats wrote 'When I have fears that I may cease to be', a sonnet dealing with three major concerns in his life – love, death, and his poetry.

In September 1818 Keats met Fanny Brawne. She became the great love of his life, and they became engaged in the autumn of 1819. 1819 was an extraordinary year, the most productive of Keats's career. He was writing mature poems, sometimes dashing them off at great speed. In April 'La Belle Dame Sans Merci' was written. Between April and May the five great odes were written, also known as the Spring Odes: 'Ode to Psyche', 'Ode to a Nightingale', 'Ode on a Grecian Urn', 'Ode on Melancholy' and 'Ode to Indolence'. Keats's poetic reputation today chiefly rests on these.

In February 1820 Keats suffered a severe lung haemorrhage, the significance of which was apparent to him, as he wrote: 'I know the colour of blood; – it is arterial blood; – I cannot be deceived in that colour; – that drop of blood is my death-warrant.' Indeed, it was the beginning of the end. That summer he spent being cared for by, and falling out with, various friends, and eventually he ended up in the care of Fanny and her mother, who nursed him in their home.

He was advised to avoid the English winter and arrived in Rome in November to stay with friends. Though ably nursed, Keats deteriorated throughout the winter and he died on 23 February 1821, aged twenty-five. He is buried in the Protestant cemetery in Rome, having requested as an inscription for his tombstone: HERE LIES ONE WHOSE NAME WAS WRIT IN WATER.

Fanny Brawne

To One Long in City Pent

To one who has been long in city pent,
   'Tis very sweet to look into the fair
   And open face of heaven, – to breathe a prayer
Full in the smile of the blue firmament.
Who is more happy, when, with heart's content,   5
   Fatigued he sinks into some pleasant lair
   Of wavy grass, and reads a debonair
And gentle tale of love and languishment?
Returning home at evening, with an ear
   Catching the notes of Philomel, – an eye   10
Watching the sailing cloudlet's bright career,
   He mourns that day so soon has glided by:
E'en like the passage of an angel's tear
   That falls through the clear ether silently.

Notes

[1] **To one ...:** the opening line echoes a line of Milton's: 'As one who long in populous city pent' (*Paradise Lost,* book IX, line 445)

[1] **pent:** confined, shut up in a small space

[8] **gentle tale:** presumed to be Leigh Hunt's *The Story of Rimini,* a retelling of a tragic love story from Dante's *Inferno,* which Keats was reading at that time

[10] **Philomel:** the nightingale, from the classical myth of Philomela, who was turned into a nightingale

Explorations

First reading

Examine the poem in two sections.

1. What do you see in the first section, the octave? What words create this picture for you?
2. How does the speaker feel? What words or phrases suggest these feelings? Examine the connotations of these words. Is there any alteration in the mood?
3. Examine the speaker's mood in the sestet. What words, phrases or images suggest this mood?

Second reading

4. What ideas about nature and the lifestyle of human beings are implicit in this poem?
5. What is your reaction to the philosophy of this sonnet? Do you find it convincing? Do you think it should be read by students today?

Third reading

6. Examine this poem as an example of the sonnet form. Do you think it is a good sonnet?

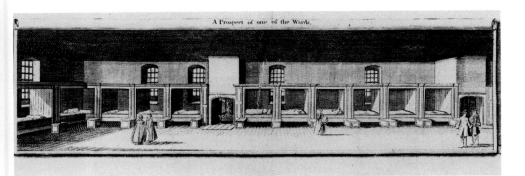

A Prospect of one of the Wards.

A ward in Guy's Hospital, London, c.1800

On First Looking into Chapman's Homer

this poem is also prescribed for Ordinary Level exams in 2009 and 2010

Much have I travell'd in the realms of gold,
   And many goodly states and kingdoms seen;
   Round many western islands have I been
Which bards in fealty to Apollo hold.
Oft of one wide expanse had I been told   5
   That deep-brow'd Homer ruled as his demesne;
   Yet did I never breathe its pure serene
Till I heard Chapman speak out loud and bold:
Then felt I like some watcher of the skies
   When a new planet swims into his ken;   10
Or like stout Cortez when with eagle eyes
   He star'd at the Pacific – and all his men
Look'd at each other with a wild surmise –
   Silent, upon a peak in Darien.

Notes

Chapman: George Chapman (1559–1634), a contemporary of Shakespeare, who wrote successful plays and translated Homer

Homer: Greek epic poet, author of *The Iliad* and *The Odyssey*

[1] **realms of gold:** presumably realms of the poetic imagination; possibly a reference to embossed gold leaf on book covers

[3] **western islands:** Britain and Ireland

[4] **Apollo:** the sun god, also the god of music and poetry, who could foretell the future

[6] **demesne:** dominion

[7] **serene:** air (from the Latin serenum, meaning 'clear sky')

[9] **watcher of the skies:** probably a reference to Herschel's discovery in 1781 of the planet Uranus

[10] **ken:** knowledge, range of vision, sight

[11–14] **Cortez; Pacific:** Keats had read about the conquest of America in J. M. Robertson's History of America. Balboa was in fact the first European to reach the Pacific; in recollection Keats has confused Balboa's first sight of the Pacific with the amazement of Cortés's soldiers on seeing Mexico city.

[14] **Darien:** an older name for the Panamá isthmus

Explorations

First reading

1. Do you think the poet views his own life as an exploration, a journey? Where? How?

2. Do you think he is referring to a purely geographical exploration, or has he something else in mind? Discuss this. What might 'realms of gold' refer to?

Second reading

3. The high point of Keats's experience was reading Chapman's translation of Homer. How does he feel? Examine the metaphorical comparisons he makes in order to convey his feelings. What is suggested by these?

4. How does Keats feel about the reading of poetry in general? Examine in particular the connotations of 'realms of gold', 'goodly states', 'wide expanse', 'deep-brow'd Homer', 'pure serene', 'watcher of the skies', 'wild surmise'. How does he communicate the sense of wonder experienced by readers?

5. Briefly explain the theme of this poem.

6. Read the poem aloud to experience its sonorous quality. What phrases or words make the greatest impression on your ear? Discuss the effects of these.

Third reading

7. The critic Brian Stone said that this poem demonstrated Keats's 'initial mastery of sonnet form'. Would you agree? Consider the poem as a sonnet, and examine (*a*) the sense of unity – trace the development of thought in the poem (*b*) the volta, or change of tone or thought, in the sestet (*c*) the rhyming scheme of the Petrarchan sonnet – do you think this is effective, or does it limit the choice of vocabulary and so produce a strain on the language? (Consider the bookish literary terms, such as 'demesne', 'serene', 'ken'.) Is this a fault? (*d*) the factual error and the extra syllable in line 12 – would you consider these to be serious blemishes, detracting from the perfection of the poem?

8. Do you find that this poem appeals equally to head and heart – in other words, that it has a good balance of thought and feeling, which gives it a sense of completeness? Discuss.

9. The poem celebrates 'not just the private enlightening encounter with Chapman's volume, but rather the human sense of awakening to awe-inspiring beauties and opportunities' (Cedric Watts). Discuss this statement, with reference to the text.

When I Have Fears that I May Cease to Be

When I have fears that I may cease to be
   Before my pen has glean'd my teeming brain,
Before high piled Books in charactery
   Hold like rich garners the full ripen'd grain –
When I behold upon the night's starr'd face   5
   Huge cloudy symbols of a high romance,
And feel that I may never live to trace
   Their shadows with the magic hand of Chance:
And when I feel, fair creature of an hour,
   That I shall never look upon thee more   10
Never have relish in the fairy power
   Of unreflecting Love: then on the Shore
Of the wide world I stand alone and think
Till Love and Fame to Nothingness do sink.

Notes

[2] **teeming:** stocked to overflowing, abundant, prolific
[3] **charactery:** print
[4] **garners:** storehouses for corn, granaries
[9] **fair creature of an hour:** the person referred to has not been identified
This sonnet was written in January 1818.

Explorations

Before reading

1. Read only the title. What might you expect the poem to feature?

First reading

2. What are the poet's main worries? How do they differ from your own projected fears?
3. What is his greatest fear?
4. What is your first impression of his overall mood? What phrases or images seem to be important in this respect?

Second reading

5. Trace the poet's line of thought through each of the quatrains. What exactly is he saying?
6. Examine the images and metaphors that convey these ideas. Do you find them effective? Discuss.
7. What is your considered opinion of the critic Brian Stone's comment that 'its three quatrains are organically separate but logically successive'?

Third reading

8. What can we discern of Keats's views on the poetic process and the poet from this sonnet? Examine in particular lines 4, 6, 7–8, 10, and 12–13.
9. Comment on the notion of love featured here.
10. What aspects of this poem, either of theme or presentation, appeal to you? Explain.

La Belle Dame Sans Merci

this poem is also prescribed for Ordinary Level exams in 2009 and 2010

O what can ail thee knight at arms
    Alone and palely loitering?
The sedge has withered from the Lake
    And no birds sing!

O what can ail thee knight at arms   5
    So haggard and so woe begone?
The squirrel's granary is full
    And the harvest's done.

I see a lily on thy brow
    With anguish moist and fever dew,   10
And on thy cheeks a fading rose
    Fast withereth too –

I met a Lady in the Meads
    Full beautiful, a faery's child
Her hair was long, her foot was light   15
    And her eyes were wild –

I made a Garland for her head,
    And bracelets too, and fragrant Zone:
She look'd at me as she did love
    And made sweet moan –   20

I set her on my pacing steed
    And nothing else saw all day long
For sidelong would she bend and sing
    A faery's song –

She found me roots of relish sweet   25
    And honey wild and manna dew
And sure in language strange she said
    'I love thee true' –

Notes

The poem was composed on 21 April 1819, in Keats's journal letter to George and Georgina. It was published in Hunt's new journal, the *Indicator*, on 10 May 1820. The text used here is the draft in that letter rather than the slightly altered (edited?) published version.

La Belle Dame Sans Merci: the beautiful lady without mercy. The title is taken from a mediaeval ballad composed by Alain Chartier in 1424 and comes from the terminology of courtly love in mediaeval literature. This 'mercy' has been described as 'the sort of gracious kindness which prompts a woman to accept a lover's pleas' (Brian Stone).

[3] **sedge:** coarse grass

[9] **lily:** of a white or pale colour

[13] **meads:** meadows

She took me to her elfin grot
   And there she wept and sigh'd full sore 30
And there I shut her wild wild eyes
   With kisses four.

And there she lulled me asleep
   And there I dream'd – Ah Woe betide!
The latest dream I ever dreamt 35
   On the cold hill side.

I saw pale kings and Princes too
   Pale warriors, death pale were they all;
They cried 'La belle dame sans merci
   Thee hath in thrall.' 40

I saw their starv'd lips in the gloam
   With horrid warning gaped wide
And I awoke and found me here
   On the cold hill's side

And this is why I sojourn here 45
   Alone and palely loitering;
Though the sedge is wither'd from the Lake
   And no birds sing –

[18] **zone:** girdle or ornate belt
[29] **elfin:** fairy (originally referred to diminutive supernatural beings in Arthurian legend)
[29] **grot:** grotto, cave
[40] **in thrall:** enslaved, in her power

 # Explorations

First reading

1. What is your first impression of the atmosphere in this poem? What do you see, hear, and feel? Reread and jot down significant phrases and images.

Second reading

2. Is there a change of speaker in the fourth stanza? Who is speaking from then onwards? Who asked the questions in the first three stanzas?
3. (a) Describe the knight's present condition. (b) What happened to him?
4. What are the indications, as the tale progresses, that the woman is an enchantress?
5. How is the otherworldly atmosphere created in this tale of enchantment? Consider:
   • the lady

- the landscape details and imagery
- the dream
- the archaic language
- the metre.

Third reading

6. What view of love is behind this poem? Read the critical commentary below and discuss it.
7. (a) How do you understand the theme of this poem? (b) Do you think the ballad is an appropriate form of poem for this theme?
8. Do you think the poem is meant to instruct us? If so, comment on the moral.
9. 'The poem has a very simple view of good and evil.' Would you agree with this statement? Explain your views.
10. Which elements of the poem did you consider most effective? Explain.

Fourth reading

11. Consider the following statement: 'If the essence of romantic poetry is to rely on sources of inspiration other than the rational intellect can supply, this poem may be justly considered its quintessence' (Graham Hough).

'La Belle Dame sans Merci', a painting by Sir Frank Dicksee (1853–1928)

Ode to a Nightingale

1

My heart aches, and a drowsy numbness pains
   My sense, as though of hemlock I had drunk,
Or emptied some dull opiate to the drains
   One minute past, and Lethe-wards had sunk:
'Tis not through envy of thy happy lot,   5
   But being too happy in thine happiness, –
      That thou, light-winged Dryad of the trees,
        In some melodious plot
Of beechen green, and shadows numberless,
   Singest of summer in full-throated ease.   10

2

O, for a draught of vintage! that hath been
   Cool'd a long age in the deep-delved earth,
Tasting of Flora and the country green,
   Dance, and Provençal song, and sunburnt mirth!
O for a beaker full of the warm South,   15
   Full of the true, the blushful Hippocrene,
      With beaded bubbles winking at the brim,
        And purple-stained mouth;
That I might drink, and leave the world unseen,
   And with thee fade away into the forest dim: 20

3

Fade far away, dissolve, and quite forget
   What thou among the leaves hast never known,
The weariness, the fever, and the fret
   Here, where men sit and hear each other groan;
Where palsy shakes a few, sad, last gray hairs,   25
   Where youth grows pale, and spectre-thin, and dies;
      Where but to think is to be full of sorrow
        And leaden-eyed despairs,
Where Beauty cannot keep her lustrous eyes,
   Or new Love pine at them beyond tomorrow.   30

4

Away! away! for I will fly to thee,
   Not charioted by Bacchus and his pards,
But on the viewless wings of Poesy,
   Though the dull brain perplexes and retards:

Already with thee! tender is the night,   35
    And haply the Queen-Moon is on her throne,
       Cluster'd around by all her starry Fays;
         But here there is no light,
Save what from heaven is with the breezes blown
    Through verdurous glooms and winding mossy ways. 40

5

I cannot see what flowers are at my feet,
    Nor what soft incense hangs upon the boughs,
But, in embalmed darkness, guess each sweet
    Wherewith the seasonable month endows
The grass, the thicket, and the fruit-tree wild;   45
    White hawthorn, and the pastoral eglantine;
      Fast fading violets cover'd up in leaves;
       And mid-May's eldest child,
The coming musk-rose, full of dewy wine,
    The murmurous haunt of flies on summer eves.   50

6

Darkling I listen; and, for many a time
    I have been half in love with easeful Death,
Call'd him soft names in many a mused rhyme,
    To take into the air my quiet breath;
Now more than ever seems it rich to die,   55
    To cease upon the midnight with no pain,
      While thou art pouring forth thy soul abroad
       In such an ecstasy!
Still wouldst thou sing, and I have ears in vain –
    To thy high requiem become a sod.   60

7

Thou wast not born for death, immortal Bird!
    No hungry generations tread thee down;
The voice I hear this passing night was heard
    In ancient days by emperor and clown:
Perhaps the self-same song that found a path   65
    Through the sad heart of Ruth, when, sick for home,
      She stood in tears amid the alien corn;
       The same that oft-times hath
Charm'd magic casements, opening on the foam
    Of perilous seas, in faery lands forlorn.   70

8

Forlorn! the very word is like a bell
  To toll me back from thee to my sole self!
Adieu! the fancy cannot cheat so well
  As she is fam'd to do, deceiving elf.
Adieu! adieu! thy plaintive anthem fades   75
  Past the near meadows, over the still stream,
      Up the hill-side; and now 'tis buried deep
        In the next valley-glades:
Was it a vision, or a waking dream?
  Fled is that music: – Do I wake or sleep?   80

Notes

[2] **hemlock:** a poison or sedative

[3] **opiate:** a sedative drug

[3] **to the drains:** to the dregs

[4] **Lethe-wards had sunk:** sunk into forgetfulness; in Greek mythology Lethe was one of the rivers that flowed through Hades and whose waters had the power of making the souls of the dead forget their life on earth

[7] **that:** read as 'because'

[7] **Dryad:** wood nymph or spirit of the tree, a poetic reference to the nightingale

[13] **Flora:** in Latin mythology, the goddess of flowers

[14] **Provençal song:** in the Middle Ages travelling singers from Provence, a region in southern France, were famous for their music

[15] **warm South:** southern wine

[16] **Hippocrene:** a fountain on Mount Helicon, sacred to the Muses, usually referred to in connection with poetic inspiration; here Keats uses the term to describe the wine, but it also carries connotations of poetic inspiration

[26] **where youth ...:** carries echoes of his brother Tom's death the previous December, at the age of nineteen, from tuberculosis

[32] **Bacchus:** Roman god of wine

[32] **pards:** leopards

[33] **viewless:** invisible

[36] **Queen-Moon:** Diana, the moon-goddess

[37] **Fays:** fairies

[43] **embalmed:** fragrant

[43] **sweet:** sweetness of taste or of smell

[46] **eglantine:** the sweetbriar, a wild rose

[51] **darkling:** in darkness

[60] **requiem:** funeral music

[60] **become a sod:** the poet, when dead and buried, will no longer be able to hear the nightingale's music

[66] **Ruth:** after the death of her husband, Ruth was driven from her native Moab by famine and went with her mother-in-law, a Jew, to Bethlehem, where she worked in the fields (Ruth 2: 1–3); see also Wordsworth's poem 'The Solitary Reaper' (1807)

[69] **casements:** a type of window

[73] **fancy:** imagination

Explorations

First reading

Read the poem aloud, or close your eyes and listen to a reading of it.

1. What is your first impression of the general atmosphere in this poem? Think of the poet's repeated wishes, the predominant colours, the general sounds of the words.
2. What stanza or image made the greatest impression on you? Why?
3. What aspect of the nightingale is chiefly celebrated here?

Second reading
Stanzas 1 and 2:

4. Do any words or phrases used here surprise or perplex you?
5. What is the poet's mood in the first four lines? Examine it in detail. Why does his heart ache?
6. How do you picture the nightingale and its environment from the detail of this stanza?
7. What does the poet yearn for in stanza 2? Why?
8. What atmosphere is conjured up by stanza 2? Explain how the effect is created by an appeal to the senses.
9. Do you notice any similarities and contrasts between stanzas 1 and 2? Discuss.

Third reading
Stanzas 3, 4, and 5:

10. Explain in detail the poet's view of life that emerges from stanza 3. What is your reaction to this view? What do you think prompts this meditation at this particular point in the poem?
11. What exactly is the poet rejecting and proposing in the first three lines of stanza 4?
12. From midway in stanza 4 ('already with thee ...') to the end of stanza 5 Keats is describing the environment of the nightingale, which he is now sharing. What is your general impression of this world? How did the poet get there? How does he convey its appeal to us?

Fourth reading
Reread stanzas 1–5.

13. What do we learn in fact about the nightingale? Try to picture it. What do we not learn?
14. What do you think the nightingale means to the poet? Can you explain its attraction?
15. In this encounter with the nightingale, what is the poet attempting to achieve? Why does he turn to the 'draught of vintage' (stanza 2) and to

the 'viewless wings of Poesy' (stanza 4)? Explain his motivation.

Fifth reading
Stanzas 6, 7, and 8:

16. Why does the poet find death attractive in stanza 6? Has he really a death wish, or is his motivation more complex? Explain.
17. In what ways does stanza 6 follow an established pattern?
18. Is the introduction of death completely surprising, or has it been prepared for earlier in the poem?
19. What is the poet suggesting about art, as represented by the song of the nightingale, in stanza 7?
20. Why do you think the poet is forlorn in the final stanza? Comment on his philosophical conclusions about art and life, and the general mood in that stanza.

Sixth reading

21. What is the poet writing about in this poem? Consider
    - his attitude to everyday life
    - the place of art in life
    - the value of imagination
    - immortality
    - death.

Read 'Sailing to Byzantium' by W. B. Yeats for similarity of theme.

22. Rereading the poem as an imaginative attempt to share in the artistic life of the nightingale, where do you consider the highs and lows of the experience to be? Examine the changing moods.
23. Trace the argument of the poem.
24. What is your reaction to Keats's claims for the significance of the imagination?
25. This is a very intimate poem in which the reader is allowed to share in the poet's suffering and joy. Examine how this is achieved in the ode.
26. What is the effect of the sensuous imagery?
27. Explore the part played by contrasts and contradictions in this poem.
28. 'In this ode, song is the predominant sound and journey the predominant metaphor.' Discuss.
29. '"Ode to a Nightingale" is a work of pervasive darkness and mystery' (Brian Stone). Discuss this statement.

Ode on a Grecian Urn

1

Thou still unravish'd bride of quietness,
   Thou foster-child of silence and slow time,
Sylvan historian, who canst thus express
   A flowery tale more sweetly than our rhyme:
What leaf-fring'd legend haunts about thy shape   5
   Of deities or mortals, or of both,
      In Tempe or the dales of Arcady?
   What men or gods are these? What maidens loth?
What mad pursuit? What struggle to escape?
      What pipes and timbrels? What wild ecstasy?   10

2

Heard melodies are sweet, but those unheard
   Are sweeter; therefore, ye soft pipes, play on;
Not to the sensual ear, but, more endear'd,
   Pipe to the spirit ditties of no tone:
Fair youth, beneath the trees, thou canst not leave   15
   Thy song, nor ever can those trees be bare;
      Bold Lover, never, never canst thou kiss,
Though winning near the goal – yet, do not grieve;
   She cannot fade, though thou hast not thy bliss,
      For ever wilt thou love, and she be fair!   20

3

Ah, happy, happy boughs! that cannot shed
   Your leaves, nor ever bid the Spring adieu;
And, happy melodist, unwearied,
   For ever piping songs for ever new;
More happy love! more happy, happy love!   25
   For ever warm and still to be enjoy'd,
      For ever panting, and for ever young;
All breathing human passion far above,
   That leaves a heart high-sorrowful and cloy'd,
      A burning forehead, and a parching tongue.   30

4

Who are these coming to the sacrifice?

To what green altar, O mysterious priest,
Lead'st thou that heifer lowing at the skies,
   And all her silken flanks with garlands drest?
What little town by river or sea shore,   35
   Or mountain-built with peaceful citadel,
      Is emptied of this folk, this pious morn?
And, little town, thy streets for evermore
   Will silent be; and not a soul to tell
      Why thou art desolate, can e'er return.   40

5

O Attic shape! Fair attitude! with brede
   Of marble men and maidens overwrought,
With forest branches and the trodden weed;
   Thou, silent form, dost tease us out of thought
As doth eternity: Cold Pastoral!   45
   When old age shall this generation waste,
      Thou shalt remain, in midst of other woe
Than ours, a friend to man, to whom thou say'st,
   'Beauty is truth, truth beauty,' – that is all
      Ye know on earth, and all ye need to know.   50

Notes

This ode was composed in May 1819 and published in *Annals of the Fine Arts* in January 1820 and in the collection *Poems*, 1820. It was probably inspired by more than a single Greek artefact; but there is in existence, in the Keats-Shelley Memorial House in Rome, a drawing made by Keats of the Sosibios Vase, taken from the Musée Napoléon, which may have been partly an inspiration for the poem. The 'heifer lowing at the skies' was very probably inspired by the heifer being led to sacrifice in the south frieze of the Parthenon Marbles.

The Sosibios Vase from Ancient Greece, drawn by Keats

[1] **unravish'd:** untouched, virginal

[3] **sylvan:** of the woods, rural

[7] **Tempe:** a valley in Thessaly, Greece, between Mount Olympus and Mount Ossa, which the gods, especially Apollo, were inclined to favour. In Latin literature the term was used as a general name for any beautiful valley, and so any beautiful rural spot

[7] **Arcady:** from Arcadia, a mountainous district in the Peloponnese, Greece, taken as an ideal region of rural beauty

[8] **loth:** unwilling

[10] **timbrels:** percussion instruments, held in the hand like tambourines

[28] **all breathing human passion ...:** superior to all human passion or love

[29] **cloy'd:** wearied by excess of sweetness, full to surfeit

[37] **pious:** holy

[41] **Attic:** Grecian

[41] **attitude:** disposition of a figure in a statue or painting; posture of the body

[41] **brede:** an archaic poetic expression referring to a frieze or narrow band of ornamentation; braid

[42] **overwrought:** the design of the art work on the surface of the urn; to be overcome emotionally (i.e. the maidens)

[44] **tease:** entice

[45] **Cold Pastoral:** 'pastoral' is literature dealing with the countryside; 'cold' refers to the marble or material of the urn but also suggests lifelessness, death

'Heifer Led to Sacrifice': a frieze from the Parthenon in the British Museum

Explorations

First reading

1. What do you see? How many scenes are depicted? What is your first impression of the mood or moods?

Second reading

2. What qualities of the urn appeal to the poet in the first quatrain? Examine the metaphors used to describe it, and discuss the meaning and connotations of each.

3. What do you understand of the first scene from the urn that is described by the poet? Is this unexpected after Keats's initial description of the urn? Comment.

4. In the second stanza the poet suggests that art is superior to reality ('heard melodies are sweet, but those unheard are sweeter'). How does he develop this idea in stanzas 2 and 3? What reservations has he about the superiority of art in these stanzas?

Third reading

5. In the fourth stanza the poet describes a very different scene. What is the atmosphere here? Why do you think he considers this scene at this particular point, and what is the effect on the direction of the poem?

6. Do you think stanza 5 restates some of the misgivings of stanzas 2 and 3? Explain.

7. In what sense is the urn a 'cold pastoral'?

8. Discuss a number of possible interpretations of the aphorism 'beauty is truth, truth beauty.'

Fourth reading

9. What do you think the poem is about?

10. What values or philosophical attitudes do you think underlie this poem?

11. What conclusion does the poet reach about the value of art?

12. Examine the section 'A reading of the poem' below. Which elements are in accord with your reading? Which elements differ?

13. Re-examine the critical image of the urn. Consider:
    - how it is described
    - the contradictory qualities
    - its symbolic value
    - its particular character.

14. Would you consider this ode to be a significant and coherent statement on the value of the arts to society, or a mess of confused thinking?

15. Where do you find the beauty in this poem?

Fifth reading

16. 'Both "Ode to a Nightingale" and "Ode on a Grecian Urn" deal with the problems of the artist.' Discuss this statement, with appropriate references to the text.

To Autumn

Season of mists and mellow fruitfulness,
Close bosom-friend of the maturing sun;
Conspiring with him how to load and bless
With fruit the vines that round the thatch-eves run;
To bend with apples the moss'd cottage-trees,   5
And fill all fruit with ripeness to the core;
To swell the gourd, and plump the hazel shells
With a sweet kernel; to set budding more,
And still more, later flowers for the bees,
Until they think warm days will never cease,   10
For Summer has o'er-brimm'd their clammy cells.

Who hath not seen thee oft amid thy store?
Sometimes whoever seeks abroad may find
Thee sitting careless on a granary floor,
Thy hair soft-lifted by the winnowing wind;   15
Or on a half-reap'd furrow sound asleep,
Drows'd with the fume of poppies while thy hook
Spares the next swath and all its twined flowers:
And sometimes like a gleaner thou dost keep
Steady thy laden head across a brook;   20
Or by a cyder-press, with patient look,
Thou watchest the last oozings hours by hours.

Where are the songs of Spring? Ay, where are they?
Think not of them, thou hast thy music too, –
While barred clouds bloom the soft-dying day,   25
And touch the stubble-plains with rosy hue;
Then in a wailful choir the small gnats mourn
Among the river sallows, borne aloft
Or sinking as the light wind lives or dies;
And full-grown lambs loud bleat from hilly bourn;   30
Hedge-crickets sing; and now with treble soft
The red-breast whistles from a garden-croft;
And gathering swallows twitter in the skies.

Notes

The ode was written on 19 September 1819. The circumstances of its composition were alluded to briefly in a letter Keats wrote to John Reynolds on 21 September:

'How beautiful the season is now – How fine the air. A temperate sharpness about it. Really, without joking, chaste weather – Dian skies – I never lik'd stubble fields so much as now – Aye better than the chilly green of the spring. Somehow a stubble plain looks warm – in the same way that some pictures look warm – this struck me so much in my Sunday's walk that I composed verses upon it ...'

[7] **gourd:** large fleshy fruit

[15] **winnowing:** the process of separating the grain from the chaff (or covering) at harvest time; the beaten corn was thrown in the air and the wind blew off the lighter chaff

[18] **swath:** a row of corn as it falls when reaped

[19] **gleaner:** person gathering ears of corn left by the reapers

[25] **barred clouds:** clouds patterned in bars

[25] **bloom:** used as a transitive verb and meaning 'to give a glow to'

[28] **sallows:** low-growing willow trees

[30] **bourn:** small stream

[32] **croft:** small agricultural holding

'The Cornfield, 1826', a painting by John Constable (1776–1837)

Explorations

First reading

1. Decide to concentrate either on what you see or on what you hear as you listen to this poem or read it aloud to yourself. What elements of either sights or sounds make an impression on you?

2. On a first reading, what particular qualities of the season are being celebrated?

Second reading

3. What do you think is a key statement in the first stanza? Why?

4. What particular aspect of autumn is depicted in the first stanza?

5. Which of our senses is engaged primarily when we read this first stanza?

Third reading

6. Comment on the mood of the second stanza.

7. What are your impressions of the personifications of autumn in the second stanza? What is suggested about the season, about humankind's relationship with nature, etc.?

8. Why do you think the poet enquires about the songs of spring in the third stanza?

9. Would you describe the mood of this final stanza as nostalgic, depressed, perfect contentment, or what? Examine the mood in detail.

Fourth reading

10. Overall, what aspects of the season appeal to the poet?

11. Comment on the sensuousness of the language used by Keats in this ode.

12. Keats's poetry is preoccupied with the quest for beauty. Explain how this poem can be seen as part of that search. Refer to specific examples.

13. Keats's other great poetic battle was with change and decay. Is there any evidence of that here?

14. Do you find the poet's attitude to life any different here from that displayed in the other odes?

15. Would you consider this a successful nature poem? Comment.

Bright Star

Bright Star, would I were stedfast as thou art –
    Not in lone splendor hung aloft the night,
And watching, with eternal lids apart,
    Like nature's patient, sleepless Eremite,
The moving waters at their priestlike task   5
    Of pure ablution round earth's human shores,
Or gazing on the new soft-fallen masque
    Of snow upon the mountains and the moors –
No – yet still stedfast, still unchangeable
    Pillow'd upon my fair love's ripening breast,   10
To feel for ever its soft swell and fall,
    Awake for ever in a sweet unrest,
Still, still to hear her tender-taken breath,
And so live ever – or else swoon to death –

Notes

[1] **stedfast:** steadfast, constant

[4] **Eremite:** a hermit, recluse

[7] **masque:** mask, as in cover, face mask, or perhaps death mask

[10] **ripening:** maturing

Explorations

First reading

1. What qualities of the star does the poet particularly admire? What quality or characteristic is he less comfortable with?

2. How is the star presented in the octave? What do you think of this presentation? What do you think the star might symbolise for the poet?

Second reading

3. How would you describe the particular atmosphere of the octave? Does this change in the sestet? Explain.

4. What is the central problem the poet is trying to resolve? Discuss this.

5. How do you understand the last line? Do you think it an effective solution?

6. What impression of the author do we get from this poem? Consider:
   • the poet's personality
   • his view of life
   • his ideal of happiness.

Third reading

7. The octave deals with the process of watching, contemplating. If this is a metaphor for poetic vision, what is the poet saying about the mode of poetic contemplation?

8. What particularly attracts the watcher? What is Keats thinking about the subject viewed (the world of nature)? Examine the relationship between nature and mankind as suggested in the poem.

9. One of the characteristics of a Petrarchan sonnet is the contrast between the octave and the sestet. Examine and discuss any contrasts you notice.

10. Do you think the imagery effective? Discuss.

Fourth reading

11. Outline your personal reaction to the poem.

3 W.B. YEATS

prescribed for Higher Level exams in 2007 and 2010

In 1865 William Butler Yeats was born in Dublin to a Co. Sligo family. His grandfather had been rector of the Church of Ireland at Drumcliff. His father, the portrait-painter John Butler Yeats, had married Susan Pollexfen, who belonged to a family of substantial traders and ship-owners from Co. Sligo. His brother, Jack B. Yeats, was to become one of Ireland's best-known painters. William Yeats was educated intermittently at the Godolphin School in London, the High School in Dublin and the Dublin Metropolitan School of Art.

He was interested in mysticism and the supernatural and developed a great curiosity for Irish mythology, history and folklore. It became one of his life's great passions to develop a distinctive, distinguished Irish literature in English. His first long poem, 'The Wanderings of Oisin' (1889), established the tone of what became known as the 'Celtic Twilight'. His early volumes of poetry reflect his interest in mysticism, theosophy and mythology but also deal with his hopeless love affairs, most notably that with Maude Gonne. In 1889 he had met and fallen in love with her; and though she would not marry him, he remained obsessed with her for most of his life. With Lady Gregory of Coole Park, Gort, Co.

1865–1939

Galway and John Millington Synge he founded the Irish Literary Theatre Society in 1899 and later the Abbey Theatre in 1904.

By the end of the century Yeats had changed his decorative, symbolist style of poetry and began to write in a more direct style. From *The Green Helmet* (1910) onwards he shows a more realistic attitude to love and also begins to write about everyday cultural and political affairs. *Responsibilities* (1914) contains satires on the materialism of Dublin's middle class. Among the major themes of his mature years are the need for harmony in life, the search for perfection in life and art, and the mysteries of time and eternity. These are to be found particularly in the poems of the later volumes, *The Tower* (1928), *The Winding Stair* (1933), and *Last Poems* (1936–39).

Yeats was made a senator in 1922 and was very active in public life; he supervised the design of the new coinage in 1926. He was awarded the Nobel Prize for Literature in 1923. He died in Rome in 1939, but his body was not brought back to Ireland until after the war, when it was buried in Drumcliff.

William Butler Yeats as a young man, painted by his father John Butler Yeats (1839–1922)

The Lake Isle of Innisfree

this poem is also prescribed for Ordinary Level exams in 2007 and 2010

I will arise and go now, and go to Innisfree,
And a small cabin build there, of clay and wattles made:
Nine bean-rows will I have there, a hive for the honey-bee,
And live alone in the bee-loud glade.

And I shall have some peace there, for peace comes dropping slow,   5
Dropping from the veils of the morning to where the cricket sings;
There midnight's all a glimmer, and noon a purple glow,
And evening full of the linnet's wings.

I will arise and go now, for always night and day
I hear lake water lapping with low sounds by the shore;   10
While I stand on the roadway, or on the pavements grey,
I hear it in the deep heart's core.

Notes

[1] **I will arise...:** This has echoes of the return of the Prodigal Son in Luke 15: 18 – 'I will arise
and go to my father.' So they were the words of another returning emigrant.

[1] **Innisfree:** (in Irish 'Inisfraoich': Heather Island) – a rocky island on Lough Gill, Co. Sligo

[2] **wattles:** rods interlaced with twigs or branches to make a fence

Explorations

Before reading

1. Read only the title. What comes into your mind when you read the title?

First reading

2. What do you notice about Yeats's island?
3. What sights and sounds will the poet see and hear? List them.
4. Contrast this island with his present surroundings.

Second reading

5. Do you think that the features of the island mentioned by the poet are the usual sights and sounds of everyday life in the country, or will this place be special? Explain your thinking on this.
6. What kind of space or place is the poet attempting to create? What does that indicate about his needs and philosophy of life or values? Refer to the poem to support your theories.
7. What is the poet's attitude to nature as suggested in the poem? Refer to specific lines and phrases.

Third reading

8. The poet seems almost impelled or driven to go and create this ideal place. Where is the sense of compulsion in the poem and how is it created? Explore the style of language he uses, the syntax, the rhythms of his speech and the repeated phrases in order to help you with this.
9. What do you think is the meaning and significance of the last line?

Fourth reading

10. State succinctly what you think the poem is about.
11. What mood do you think the poet creates here and how do the images and the sounds of words contribute to this?
12. Does anything about the poet's vision here appeal to you? Discuss this.

September 1913

What need you, being come to sense,
But fumble in a greasy till
And add the halfpence to the pence
And prayer to shivering prayer, until
You have dried the marrow from the bone?   5
For men were born to pray and save:
Romantic Ireland's dead and gone,
It's with O'Leary in the grave.

Yet they were of a different kind,
The names that stilled your childish play,   10
They have gone about the world like wind,
But little time had they to pray
For whom the hangman's rope was spun,
And what, God help us, could they save?
Romantic Ireland's dead and gone,   15
It's with O'Leary in the grave.

Was it for this the wild geese spread
The grey wing upon every tide;
For this that all that blood was shed,
For this Edward Fitzgerald died,   20
And Robert Emmet and Wolfe Tone,
All that delirium of the brave?
Romantic Ireland's dead and gone,
It's with O'Leary in the grave.

Yet could we turn the years again,   25
And call those exiles as they were
In all their loneliness and pain,
You'd cry, 'Some woman's yellow hair
Has maddened every mother's son':
They weighed so lightly what they gave   30
But let them be, they're dead and gone,
They're with O'Leary in the grave.

Background note

During 1913 Yeats had spent a great deal of energy in support of Lady Gregory's nephew, Sir Hugh Lane. A wealthy art collector, who made a gift to the city of Dublin of an extraordinary collection of modern painting provided the city build a suitable gallery. There was a great deal of dispute about the structure, the location and the cost. Yeats was furious at what seemed a mean-spirited, penny-pinching, anti-cultural response to the project.

Notes

[8] **O'Leary:** John O'Leary (1830–1907) A Fenian who was arrested in 1865 and sentenced to twenty years' imprisonment. After a number of years he was released on condition of exile. Returning to Dublin in 1885 he was greatly influential in Yeats's developing views on Irish nationalism.

[17] **the wild geese:** Irish soldiers who were forced into exile after the Williamite victory of the 1690s. They served in the armies of France, Spain and Austria.

[20] **Edward Fitzgerald:** Lord Edward Fitzgerald (1763–98), one of the leaders of the United Irishmen who died of wounds received while being arrested.

[21] **Robert Emmet:** leader of the rebellion of 1803

[21] **Wolfe Tone:** Theobald Wolfe Tone (1763–98) was leader of the United Irishmen. Captured and sentenced to death, he committed suicide in prison.

 # Explorations

First reading

Stanza 1

1. 'What need you...'. The 'you' here refers to the new Irish, relatively prosperous and Catholic middle classes, whom Yeats is addressing. What does he suggest are their main concerns or needs in life?

2. Explore the connotations of the images used in the first five lines, i.e. what is suggested by each of the pictures. List all the suggestions carried by each of the following and discuss them in groups: 'fumble'; 'greasy till'; 'add the halfpence to the pence'; 'add ... prayer to shivering prayer'; 'dried the marrow from the bone'.

3. As a consequence of your explorations, what do you think is Yeats's attitude to these people? What words do you think best convey the tone?

4. 'For men were born to pray and save:'
   Does the poet really mean this? If not, what? How should it be

---

read? Try reading it aloud.

5. (a) Read aloud the last two lines of the stanza as you think the poet would wish it. (b) How is this refrain different from the earlier lines of the stanza? (c) What do you understand by 'Romantic Ireland' and how does Yeats feel about it?

6. Now read the entire stanza aloud, differentiating between the sections that are sarcastic, bitter, or condemnatory and the lines that are wistful, nostalgic, or plaintive.

Second reading
Stanza 2

7. 'They' – the romantic generations of heroes – had great power and influence in society. How is this suggested? Explore all the possible suggestions carried by lines 10 and 11.

8. How were they different from the present generation?

9. Is there a suggestion that they were fated to act as they did? Examine line 13.

10. In groups, discuss the best possible way of reading this stanza aloud. Then do it.

Third reading
Stanza 3

11. 'for this ... For this ... For this'. Through this repetition Yeats punches out the contrast between past and present. His attitude to the present generation is quite clear by now. But what does this stanza say about his attitude to the heroes of Ireland's past? Explore in detail the suggestions carried by the images.

12. 'All that delirium of the brave'. Discuss what this implies about heroism.

Stanza 4

13. 'All Yeats's sympathy and admiration is with the past generations of heroes.' Discuss this and refer to the text in support of your ideas.

14. 'You'd cry, "Some woman's yellow hair has maddened every mother's son".' What do you think they mean by this?

Fourth reading

15. 'In this poem we find a quite grotesque portrayal of the middle classes in contrast to an unreal and highly romanticised portrayal of past patriots!' Discuss this as an interpretation of the poem.

16. What do you think is the effect of the refrain?

17. Do you think this was a politically risky, even dangerous, poem to publish? Explain.

18. Are you surprised by the passion and strength of feeling here? Outline your reactions.

The Wild Swans at Coole

this poem is also prescribed for Ordinary Level exams in 2007 and 2010

The trees are in their autumn beauty,
The woodland paths are dry,
Under the October twilight the water
Mirrors a still sky;
Upon the brimming water among the stones   5
Are nine-and-fifty swans.

The nineteenth autumn has come upon me
Since I first made my count;
I saw, before I had well finished,
All suddenly mount   10
And scatter wheeling in great broken rings
Upon their clamorous wings.

I have looked upon those brilliant creatures,
And now my heart is sore.
All's changed since I, hearing at twilight,   15
The first time on this shore,
The bell-beat of their wings above my head,
Trod with a lighter tread.

Unwearied still, lover by lover,
They paddle in the cold   20
Companionable streams or climb the air;
Their hearts have not grown old;
Passion or conquest, wander where they will,
Attend upon them still.

But now they drift on the still water,   25
Mysterious, beautiful;
Among what rushes will they build,
By what lake's edge or pool
Delight men's eyes when I awake some day
To find they have flown away?   30

Notes

Coole: Coole Park, outside Gort, Co. Galway and home of Lady Augusta Gregory. She was a friend and benefactor to the poet and collaborated on many of his projects. Yeats regarded Coole Park as a second home and a welcoming refuge and retreat.

[6] **nine-and-fifty swans:** There actually were fifty-nine swans on the lake at Coole Park.

[7] **the nineteenth autumn:** Yeats is referring to the summer and autumn of 1897 which was the first time he stayed for a lengthy period at Coole. At that time he was passionately involved with Maude Gonne and in a state of acute nervous exhaustion.

[18 **Trod with a lighter tread:** It is interesting that the poet chooses to recast 1897 as a hopeful and even carefree period, when this was not the case!

Explorations

First reading

Stanza 1

1. Notice all the details that draw Yeats's eyes and ears to the scene. Visualise them intently, with eyes closed, if you can. If you came upon this scene, what would your thoughts be?

2. How would you describe the atmosphere of this scene? What particular images or sounds contribute to this atmosphere? Explain.

Stanza 2

3. Read the second stanza with energy, aloud if possible, and see if you can make the swans come alive.

4. Examine the description of the swans here. (*a*) What attributes or qualities of these creatures does the poet wish to convey? (*b*) How are these qualities carried by the language? Look at images, verbs, adverbs, the sounds of words and the structure of the long single sentence.

Second reading

5. In the third stanza the poet introduces a personal note. What does he reveal about himself?

6. In stanzas 3 and 4 he explores the contrasts between the life and condition of the swans and his own life and condition. In your own words explain the detail of these contrasts.

7. Do you think the poet envies the swans? If so, what exactly does he envy? Refer to phrases and lines to support your thinking.

8. Is this a logical or a poetic argument? Explain.

Third reading

9. If we read the first four stanzas as lamenting the loss of youth, passion and love, what particular loss frightens him in the final stanza? Explain.

10. What general issues or themes does Yeats deal with in this poem?

11. Do you think there is any sense of resolution of the personal issues raised by Yeats in this poem? Does he come to any definite conclusion? Explain your thinking.

12. Examine how the poem is structured stanza by stanza, moving from that very particular local opening to the general speculation about love in stanza 4, and then opening up into that rather mysterious ending that seeks to look into the future. What is the effect of this?

13. The poem is built upon a series of antitheses: the swans and

the poet; the poet then and the poet now; contrasting moods. Show how these are developed.

14. What do you think the symbolism adds to the poem? Explore the elements of sky and water; trees and paths; great broken rings; and of course the swans themselves.

Fourth reading

15. Would you agree that the poem creates a 'hauntingly evocative description of the swans'? Discuss or write about this.

16. 'Ageing and the diminution of visionary power are bitterly regretted' (Terence Brown). Discuss this view of the poem, referring in detail to the text to substantiate your argument.

Coole Park: the home of Lady Gregory, now demolished

An Irish Airman Foresees his Death

this poem is also prescribed for Ordinary Level exams in 2007 and 2010

I know that I shall meet my fate
Somewhere among the clouds above;
Those that I fight I do not hate,
Those that I guard I do not love;
My country is Kiltartan Cross,   5
My countrymen Kiltartan's poor,
No likely end could bring them loss
Or leave them happier than before.
Nor law, nor duty bade me fight,
Nor public men, nor cheering crowds,   10
A lonely impulse of delight
Drove to this tumult in the clouds;
I balanced all, brought all to mind,
The years to come seemed waste of breath,
A waste of breath the years behind   15
In balance with this life, this death.

Notes

[3] **Those that I fight:** the Germans

[4] **Those that I guard:** the English or possibly the Italians

[5] **Kiltartan Cross:** a crossroads near Robert Gregory's home at Coole Park, Gort, Co. Galway

An Irish Airman: The speaker in the poem is Major Robert Gregory, the only son of Yeats's friend and mentor Lady Augusta Gregory of Coole Park, near Gort, Co. Galway. He was a pilot in the Royal Flying Corps in the First World War and at the time of his death, on 23 January 1918, was on service in Italy. It emerged later that he had been accidentally shot down by the Italian allies.

The entrance to Coole Park today

Explorations

Before reading

1. Read only the title. What do you expect to find in this poem? Imagine what this man's thoughts might be. How might he visualise his death? How might he feel about it? Jot down briefly the thoughts, pictures and feelings you imagine might go through his mind.

First reading

2. Who is the speaker in this poem? If in doubt, consult the note (An Irish Airman) at the end of the poem.

3. Focus on lines 1 and 2. Are you surprised by how definite he is? Can you suggest any reasons why he might be so definite about his coming death? How would you describe his mood?

4. How do you think the speaker would say these first two lines? Experiment with various readings aloud.

5. Taking the first four lines as a unit, are you surprised that they are spoken by a military man, a pilot? In your own words, describe how he views his situation.

Second reading

6. In lines 5–8 the speaker talks about the people of his home area. How does he feel about them? Does he identify with them in any way? Have the people and the speaker anything in common? How does he think his death will affect their lives? Does he feel they will miss him? Do you think his attitude to them is uncaring, or that he feels unable to affect their lives in any way? Discuss these questions and write down the conclusions you come to, together with the evidence from the text.

7. What do you think is the purpose of his mentioning his Kiltartan countrymen in the context of his explanation? How does it fit in with his reasoning?

8. Lines 9 and 10: In your own words, explain these further reasons, which the speaker discounts as having any influence on his decision to volunteer.

9. What is revealed about the character of the speaker in the lines you have explored so far?

Third reading

10. Lines 11 and 12: Here we get to the kernel of his motivation. Examine the language very carefully. 'A lonely impulse of delight': can you understand

why he might feel this sense of delight? Explain how you see it. 'Impulse': what does this tell us about the decision? 'A lonely impulse': what does this suggest about the decision and the man? 'Drove': what does this add to our understanding of how he felt and of his decision? 'Tumult in the clouds': in what other context might the words 'tumult' or 'tumultuous' be used? Suggest a few. What does the sound of the word suggest? What does it suggest about the speaker's view of flying?

11. In the light of what you have discovered so far, and in the voice of the speaker, write a letter home, explaining your decision to volunteer as a pilot. Try to remain true to the speaker's feelings as outlined in the poem.

12. Lines 13–16: 'In spite of his hint of excitement earlier, the speaker did not make a rash and emotional decision.' On the evidence of these lines, would you agree with that statement? Write a paragraph.

13. 'The years to come seemed waste of breath …
    In balance with this life, this death.'
    Yet the speaker seemed to want this kind of life very much. Explore how the use of 'breath' and 'death' as rhyming words help to emphasise this.

Fourth reading

14. Having read this poem, what do you find most interesting about the speaker?

15. What appeals to you about the poem? Do you find anything disturbing about it?

16. Thousands of Irishmen fought and died in the British army during the First World War; others could not bring themselves to join that army while Ireland was governed by England. How does the speaker deal with this issue? Is the title significant?

17. As well as being a rhetorical device, the repetition of words and phrases emphasises certain ideas and issues. List the main ideas thus emphasised.

18. What are the principal themes or issues the poem deals with? Write a number of short paragraphs on this.

19. 'The pictures and images are sparsely used but very effective.' Comment on any two images.

20. To whom is this poem being spoken? Read it aloud. Is the tone more appropriate to a letter or to a public statement or speech? Explain your view with reference to phrases or lines in the text.

Easter 1916

I have met them at close of day
Coming with vivid faces
From counter or desk among grey
Eighteenth-century houses.
I have passed with a nod of the head   5
Or polite meaningless words,
Or have lingered awhile and said
Polite meaningless words,
And thought before I had done
Of a mocking tale or a gibe   10
To please a companion
Around the fire at the club,
Being certain they and I
But lived where motley is worn:
All changed, changed utterly: 15
A terrible beauty is born.

That woman's days were spent
In ignorant good-will,
Her nights in argument
Until her voice grew shrill.   20
What voice more sweet than hers
When, young and beautiful,
She rode to harriers?

Notes

Easter 1916: On Monday 24 April 1916 a force of about 700 republicans, who were members of the Irish Volunteers and the Irish Citizen Army, took over the centre of Dublin in a military revolution and held out for six days against the British army. This was known as the Easter Rising.

[1] **them:** those republicans, in the pre-1916 days

[3] **grey:** built of granite or limestone

[12] **the club:** probably the Arts Club where Yeats was a founder member in 1907

[17] **That woman:** Constance Gore-Booth (1868–1927) of Lissadell, Co. Sligo, who married the Polish Count Markiewicz. She became a fervent Irish Nationalist and was actively involved in the Fianna and the Citizen Army. She was sentenced to death for her part in the Rising but the sentence was later commuted to penal servitude for life – she was released in 1917 under the general amnesty.

This man had kept a school
And rode our wingèd horse;   25
This other his helper and friend
Was coming into his force;
He might have won fame in the end,
So sensitive his nature seemed,
So daring and sweet his thought.   30
This other man I had dreamed
A drunken, vainglorious lout.
He had done most bitter wrong
To some who are near my heart,
Yet I number him in the song;   35
He, too, has resigned his part
In the casual comedy;
He, too, has been changed in his turn,
Transformed utterly:
A terrible beauty is born.   40

Hearts with one purpose alone
Through summer and winter seem
Enchanted to a stone
To trouble the living stream.
The horse that comes from the road,   45
The rider, the birds that range
From cloud to tumbling cloud,
Minute by minute they change;
A shadow of cloud on the stream

[24] **This man:** Padraig Pearse (1879–1916). Barrister, teacher and poet, he was the founder of St Enda's school and editor of *An Claidheamh Soluis*. He believed that a blood sacrifice was necessary to revolutionise Ireland. A member of the revolutionary IRB and the Irish Volunteers he was the Commandant General and President of the Provisional Government during Easter week.

[25] **wingèd horse:** Pegasus, the winged horse, was a symbol of poetic vision.

[26] **This other:** Thomas MacDonagh (1878–1916), poet and academic who taught at University College Dublin

[31] **This other man:** Major John MacBride, who had fought with the Boers against the British in South Africa and in 1903 married Maude Gonne, the woman Yeats loved. He too was executed for his part in the Rising.

[33] **He had done most bitter wrong:** a reference to rumours of family violence and debauchery

[34] **To some who are near my heart:** Maude Gonne and her daughter

[41–43] **Hearts ... stone:** 'Stone' at its simplest is usually taken to be a symbol for the fanatical heart – i.e. those who devote themselves fanatically to a cause, become hardened and lose their humanness as a result.

Changes minute by minute;   50
A horse-hoof slides on the brim,
And a horse plashes within it;
The long-legged moor-hens dive,
And hens to moor-cocks call;
Minute by minute they live: 55
The stone's in the midst of all.

Too long a sacrifice
Can make a stone of the heart.
O when may it suffice?
That is Heaven's part, our part   60
To murmur name upon name,
As a mother names her child
When sleep at last has come
On limbs that had run wild.
What is it but nightfall?   65
No, no, not night but death;
Was it needless death after all?
For England may keep faith
For all that is done and said.
We know their dream; enough   70
To know they dreamed and are dead;
And what if excess of love
Bewildered them till they died?
I write it out in a verse –
MacDonagh and MacBride   75
And Connolly and Pearse
Now and in time to be,
Wherever green is worn,
Are changed, changed utterly:
A terrible beauty is born.   80

[67–68] **needless death ... England may keep faith:** The Bill for Irish Home Rule had
   been passed in the Westminster Parliament. In 1914, however, it was suspended on the
   outbreak of World War I, but with the promise that it would be put into effect after the war.
[76] **Connolly:** James Connolly (1870–1916). Trade Union organiser and founder of the Citizen
   Army, he was military commander of the insurgents in Dublin, Easter 1916.

Explorations

Before reading

1. First reread 'September 1913' and remind yourself how Yeats felt about the Irish middle class of his time.

First reading

SECTION ONE

2. Concentrate on the first fourteen lines. These are the same people who feature in 'September 1913'. Yeats is no longer savagely angry but he certainly has no respect for them. Visualise the encounter he describes – time of day; atmosphere; what the poet does; what he says; how he behaves. Share these ideas.

3. (a) What 'polite meaningless words' might he have said? Invent some dialogue for him. (b) As he speaks these 'polite meaningless words', what is he actually thinking? Script his thoughts and the tale or gibe he might tell later.

4. 'Where motley is worn': what does this tell us about how Yeats regarded Ireland at this time?

5. How would you describe the poet's feelings and mood in this first section?

6. The first fourteen lines are transformed by lines 15 and 16 and given a new context. Framed by use of the perfect tense: 'I have met them. I have passed' the impression is given that that was then, this is now. (a) Reread the first section, from this perspective. (b) Do you think Yeats is ashamed of his earlier treatment of these people? Discuss this with reference to lines or phrases in the poem.

7. 'A terrible beauty is born'. Explore all the suggestions of this phrase.

Second reading

SECTION TWO

8. According to the poet, what are the effects on Constance Markiewicz of fanatical dedication to a political cause?

9. 'This other his helper . . .'. In contrast to the portrait of Constance Markiewicz which is somewhat masculine, this portrait of Thomas MacDonagh is quite feminised. Would you agree? Explain your thinking with reference to words and phrases in the poem.

10. There is great emphasis on change in this section. List all the instances and comment on them.

11. There is a sense that this change or transformation was not something actually effected by these people, but rather

something that happened to them.

'He, too, has been changed in his turn,
Transformed utterly:'

They were changed by death and by executions. Do you think that Yeats is exploring how ordinary people are changed into heroes, and what is he suggesting? Discuss this.

Third reading
SECTION THREE

12. Here Yeats is fascinated by flux and the process of change. (*a*) List all the examples he uses. (*b*) Comment on the atmosphere created here. Is it an appealing picture?

13. In this section he is exploring the paradox that only a stone (the fanatical heart) can alter the flow of a stream, i.e. the course of life. But it can only do this at the expense of losing humanness. What does this indicate about Yeats's thinking on revolutionary politics?

Fourth reading
SECTION FOUR

14. What is your initial impression of the tone of this section? Is the poet weary, worried, confused; giving up; or what? Refer in detail to the text.

15. '… our part
To murmur name upon name'

How does he see the poet's role here?

16. 'sleep … not night but death … needless death … excess of love | Bewildered them…'. The poet is attempting to think through his confusions and uncertainties here. Trace his thoughts in your own words.

17. Finally, at the end of the poem, Yeats lists out the dead, almost as a sacred act. What is the effect of this for the poet, the reader and those who died?

Fifth reading

18. Yeats had been severely disillusioned by the new Irish Catholic middle class but he had to rethink this view after 1916. Explain the process of his rethinking as it happens in the poem.

19. 'Despite his sense of awe and admiration for the change brought about, this poem does not represent a totally unqualified approval of revolutionary politics.' Discuss this view of the poem; support your answer with references to the text.

20. Though written in 1916, Yeats did not have this poem published until October 1920. Speculate on his possible reasons. Do you think they were justified?

Maude Gonne: painting by Sarah Purser

The Second Coming

Turning and turning in the widening gyre
The falcon cannot hear the falconer;
Things fall apart; the centre cannot hold;
Mere anarchy is loosed upon the world,
The blood-dimmed tide is loosed, and everywhere   5
The ceremony of innocence is drowned;
The best lack all conviction, while the worst
Are full of passionate intensity.

Surely some revelation is at hand;
Surely the Second Coming is at hand.   10
The Second Coming! Hardly are those words out
When a vast image out of *Spiritus Mundi*
Troubles my sight: somewhere in sands of the desert
A shape with lion body and the head of a man,
A gaze blank and pitiless as the sun,   15
Is moving its slow thighs, while all about it
Reel shadows of the indignant desert birds.
The darkness drops again; but now I know
That twenty centuries of stony sleep
Were vexed to nightmare by a rocking cradle,   20
And what rough beast, its hour come round at last,
Slouches towards Bethlehem to be born?

Notes

The Second Coming: In its Christian interpretation this refers to the prediction of the second coming of Christ, see Matthew 24. In Yeats's occult and magical philosophy it might also refer to the second birth of the Avatar, or great antithetical spirit, which Yeats and his wife felt certain would be reincarnated as their baby son whose birth was imminent. In fact the child turned out to be a girl, dashing that theory.

[1–2] **Turning ... falconer:** The bird is rising in ever-widening circles and so making the pattern of an inverted cone or gyre. These lines could be read as the trained bird of prey reverting to its wild state or, in a more religious sense, taken to represent Christian civilisation growing further away from Christ (the falconer).

[12] **Spiritus Mundi:** 'The spirit of the world', which Yeats describes as 'a general storehouse of images which have ceased to be a property of any personality or spirit'.

[14] **A shape with lion body and the head of a man:** Instead of the second coming of Christ, Yeats imagines this horrific creature, a sort of Antichrist.

[20] **rocking cradle:** the birth of Christ in Bethlehem began the then two-thousand-year period of Christian history

Explorations

Before reading

1. Read Matthew 24: 1–31 and some of the Book of Revelations, particularly chapters 12, 13, 20 and 21. Discuss these.

First reading

Stanza 1 – Focusing on the Images

2. The trained falcon is released and it circles looking for prey. What do you think might happen if the falcon cannot hear the falconer?

3. What do you see and imagine when you read (a) line 3 and (b) line 4?

4. 'The blood-dimmed tide is loosed'
   What does this picture conjure up for you? Do you find it sinister, frightening, or what?

5. Lines 7 and 8 focus on people. What types of people do you think the poet has in mind? Discuss this.

Second reading

6. Taking the first stanza as a whole, what does it communicate about Yeats's view of civilisation as he saw it at that time?

7. 'The first stanza or section is full of the tension of opposites.' Discuss or write about this.

8. In the second section of the poem Yeats is looking for some sufficiently weighty reason which would explain this collapse of civilisation. What occurs to him first?

9. His first short-lived thought is replaced by this 'vast image' that 'troubles' his sight. Read Yeats's description carefully and (a) Describe what you imagine. (b) What particular qualities are exhibited by this 'rough beast'? (c) What particular images or phrases help create the sense of revulsion?

10. Are you shocked by the association with Bethlehem? What is suggested here? Discuss this.

Third reading

11. Yeats is talking about the end of the Christian era, the end of innocence. This is encapsulated particularly in the horrific image of one of the holiest places in Christianity, Bethlehem, being defiled by this beast. What typically nightmarish elements do you notice in the second section of the poem?

12. In your own words, set out briefly what you think the poem is about.

13. Comment on the power of the imagery.

Sailing to Byzantium

I

That is no country for old men. The young
In one another's arms, birds in the trees
– Those dying generations – at their song,
The salmon-falls, the mackerel-crowded seas,
Fish, flesh, or fowl, commend all summer long   5
Whatever is begotten, born, and dies.
Caught in that sensual music all neglect
Monuments of unageing intellect.

II

An aged man is but a paltry thing,
A tattered coat upon a stick, unless   10
Soul clap its hands and sing, and louder sing
For every tatter in its mortal dress,
Nor is there singing school but studying
Monuments of its own magnificence;
And therefore I have sailed the seas and come   15
To the holy city of Byzantium.

III

O sages standing in God's holy fire
As in the gold mosaic of a wall,
Come from the holy fire, perne in a gyre,
And be the singing-masters of my soul.   20
Consume my heart away; sick with desire
And fastened to a dying animal
It knows not what it is; and gather me
Into the artifice of eternity.

IV

Once out of nature I shall never take   25
My bodily form from any natural thing,
But such a form as Grecian goldsmiths make
Of hammered gold and gold enamelling
To keep a drowsy Emperor awake;
Or set upon a golden bough to sing   30
To lords and ladies of Byzantium
Of what is past, or passing, or to come.

Notes

Byzantium: The Roman emperor Constantine, who became a Christian in A.D. 312, chose Byzantium as his capital city, renaming it Constantinople in 330. Yeats idealised Byzantium, in particular at the end of the fifth century, as the centre of European civilisation – a place where all life was in harmony.

[1] **That:** Ireland

[4] **The salmon-falls, the mackerel-crowded seas:** all images of regeneration, new life, energy and plenty

[5] **commend:** praise, celebrate

[17] **O sages:** probably refers to the depiction of the martyrs being burned in a fire in a mosaic at the church of San Apollinare Nuovo in Ravenna, which Yeats saw in 1907

[19] **perne in a gyre:** When Yeats was a child in Sligo he was told that 'pern' was another name for spool or bobbin on which the thread was wound. So the idea of circular movement is carried in the word 'perne' which Yeats constructs here as a verb. A 'gyre' is a revolving cone of time, in Yeats's cosmology. Here, Yeats is asking the sages to journey through the cone of time, to come to him and teach him perfection, teach his soul to sing.

[24] **artifice of eternity:** Artifice is something constructed, created – here a work of art. The word can also have connotations of trickery or sleight of hand. In a certain sense art is outside time and has a sort of eternal quality about it. Yeats asks the sages to gather him into the eternity of art.

[27] **such a form:** Yeats wrote that he had read somewhere that there existed in the Emperors' Palace in Byzantium 'a tree made of gold and silver, and artificial birds that sang'. Here the golden bird is used as a metaphor for art which is beautiful, perfect and unchanging.

[32] **Of what is past, or passing, or to come:** Though Yeats wished to escape out of the stream of time into the eternity of art, ironically, the golden bird's song is about time.

Explorations

First reading
Stanza 1

1. Read the first stanza carefully for yourself, as many times as you feel necessary. In groups, try out different ways of reading aloud the first sentence. Why do you think it should be read in that way?

2. Notice the perspective. The poet has already left Ireland, either in reality or imagination, and is looking back. (a) What does he remember about the country? (b) Why is it 'no country' for old men?

3. The first stanza portrays the sensuality of life very vividly. Explore how the poet does this. Consider the imagery; the sounds of words; repeated letters, the crowded syntax; the repetitions and rhythms of the sentence, etc.

4. How do you think the poet feels about this teeming fertility? Ostensibly he is renouncing the world of the senses, but do you think he dwells on these scenes a little too much if he dislikes or hates them? Consider phrases such as 'The young | In one another's arms, birds in the trees'; 'commend all summer long'; 'Caught in that sensual music'. Do you think there might be a hint of nostalgia

and a sense of loss here? Discuss the tone of the stanza.

5. Yet in the midst of all this energy and life there are the seeds of death. Explain the paradox and word punning in 'dying generations'. Where else, in the first stanza, is there an awareness of time?

6. What does the poet value that he feels is neglected in Ireland?

7. Reread the stanza and list all the reasons you can find for Yeats's departure or withdrawal.

8. Now read aloud the first sentence as you think the poet intended it.

Second reading
Stanza 2

9. In this stanza Yeats asserts that only the soul gives meaning to the human being. (a) Explore the contrast between body and soul here. (b) Do you think that the imagery used is effective? Explain.

10. 'Nor is there ... own magnificence': (a) Tease out the possible meanings of these two lines. Explore the following reading: the only way the spirit learns to sing (achieves perfection) is by studying monuments created by and for itself, i.e. works of art. In other words, art enriches the soul.

(b) Explain why the poet has come to Byzantium.

Third reading
Stanza 3

11. In the third stanza Yeats entreats the sages of the timeless city to teach his soul to sing, i.e. perfect his spirit. But perfection cannot be achieved without pain and sacrifice. Where in the stanza is this notion dealt with?
12. What is the poet's ultimate goal as expressed in the stanza?
13. Byzantium was renowned as the city of religion, philosophy and a highly formalised art. Where are these elements reflected in the second and third stanzas?

Fourth reading

14. In the fourth stanza he wishes that his spirit be transformed into the perfect work of art and so live on, ageless and incorruptible. What do you notice about this piece of art?
15. Do you think Yeats achieves the yearned-for escape from the flux of time into the 'immortality' of art? Consider carefully the irony of the final line.
16. Essentially, what is Yeats writing about in this poem?
17. 'This poem is built around essential contrasts and polarities.' Discuss this with reference to relevant phrases and lines.
18. Can you appreciate Yeats's dilemma as experienced here, as well as his deep yearning?

Mosaic from the church of San Apollinare Nuovo in Ravenna showing a procession of saints carrying crowns, symbols of martyrs. (See the note referring to line 17 in the poem 'Sailing to Byzantium'.)

The Stare's Nest By My Window

Section VI
From 'Meditations in Time of Civil War'

The bees build in the crevices
Of loosening masonry, and there
The mother birds bring grubs and flies.
My wall is loosening; honey-bees,
Come build in the empty house of the stare.   5

We are closed in, and the key is turned
On our uncertainty; somewhere
A man is killed, or a house burned,
Yet no clear fact to be discerned:
Come build in the empty house of the stare.   10

A barricade of stone or of wood;
Some fourteen days of civil war;
Last night they trundled down the road
That dead young soldier in his blood:
Come build in the empty house of the stare.   15

We had fed the heart on fantasies,
The heart's grown brutal from the fare;
More substance in our enmities
Than in our love; O honey-bees,
Come build in the empty house of the stare.   20

Notes

Stare's Nest: 'Stare' is the term sometimes used in the West of Ireland for a starling.

Meditations in Time of Civil War: This is quite a lengthy poem structured in seven sections. Apart from the first, composed in England in 1921, the other sections were written in Ireland during the Civil War of 1922–23.

[1] **The bees:** There is a possible echo of the bees who were sent by the gods to perform certain tasks in Porphyry's mystical writing. At any rate they may symbolise patient creative endeavour, as distinct from the destructive forces all around.

[14] **That dead young soldier:** This is based on an occurrence that reputedly took place beside Yeats's Galway house, Thoor Ballylee, in which a young soldier was dragged down a road, his body so badly battered and mutilated that his mother could only recover his head.

Explorations

Before reading

1. Read only the title. What might you expect to find in this poem?

First reading

Stanzas 1–3

2. Examine the detail of the first three lines of stanza 1. Write about what you see: the details, the sounds, the atmosphere.

3. In the actual historical context many big houses of the establishment class were abandoned or evacuated for fear of reprisals. What do you imagine might have been the poet's thoughts when he first came upon this scene by the window?

4. There are two references to 'loosening' masonry or walls in the first stanza. Do you think these might be significant? Explain.

5. Read the second stanza carefully. What is the atmosphere in the house and what details contribute to this?

6. What single word do you find most powerful in the third stanza? Write about it.

Second reading

7. Tease out the meaning of the fourth stanza, in your own words.

8. Comment on the tones you find in the final stanza and suggest how these are created.

9. How do you think the repeated refrain should be read? Try it.

Third reading

10. Would you agree that Yeats is torn between a bitter disappointment and a desperate hope here? Discuss this.

11. 'The poem captures the atmosphere of war with vivid realism.' Discuss this statement with reference to the text.

12. Explore the music of this piece: the onomatopoeia of words; the effect of the rhyming; the haunting refrain, etc.

13. 'This poem is really a prayer.' Discuss.

Fourth reading

14. 'This poem could be read as a metaphor for the situation of the poet's traditional class, the Anglo-Irish ascendancy.' Discuss this.

15. How did this poem affect you? Write about it.

In Memory of Eva Gore-Booth and Con Markiewicz

The light of evening, Lissadell,
Great windows open to the south,
Two girls in silk kimonos, both
Beautiful, one a gazelle.
But a raving autumn shears   5
Blossom from the summer's wreath;
The older is condemned to death,
Pardoned, drags out lonely years
Conspiring among the ignorant.
I know not what the younger dreams –   10
Some vague Utopia – and she seems,
When withered old and skeleton-gaunt,
An image of such politics.
Many a time I think to seek
One or the other out and speak   15
Of that old Georgian mansion, mix
Pictures of the mind, recall
That table and the talk of youth,
Two girls in silk kimonos, both
Beautiful, one a gazelle.   20

Dear shadows, now you know it all,
All the folly of a fight
With a common wrong or right.
The innocent and the beautiful
Have no enemy but time;   25
Arise and bid me strike a match
And strike another till time catch;
Should the conflagration climb,
Run till all the sages know.
We the great gazebo built,   30
They convicted us of guilt;
Bid me strike a match and blow.

Background note

Eva Gore-Booth (1870–1926) was a poet and a reader of Eastern Philosophy. She became involved in social work for the poor and was a member of the women's suffrage movement.

Constance Gore-Booth (1868–1927) married a Polish poet and landowner, Count Casimir Markiewicz. A committed socialist republican, she became involved in Irish revolutionary movements and joined the Citizen Army. For her part in the Easter Rising she was sentenced to death, but the sentence was commuted to life imprisonment and she was released in the general amnesty of 1917. She was appointed Minister for Labour in the first Dail Eireann of 1919, the first Irish woman government minister. She took the anti-treaty side in the Civil War.

Notes

[1] **Lissadell:** The Co. Sligo Georgian mansion referred to below, built in the early part of the nineteenth century and home of the Gore-Booth family. Yeats visited in 1894–95.

[3] **kimonos:** traditional Japanese long robes

[4] **gazelle:** A small delicately formed antelope. The reference is to Eva Gore-Booth.

[7] **The older:** Constance

[8] **lonely years:** Her husband returned to his lands in the Ukraine and she was separated from her children.

[16] **old Georgian mansion:** Lissadell, an image of aristocratic elegance and good taste for Yeats

[21] **Dear shadows:** Both women were dead at the time of writing.

[30] **gazebo:** The scholar A.N. Jeffares gives three possible meanings: (a) a summer house (b) a vantage point and (c) to make a fool of oneself or be conspicuous (in Hibernian English).

 # Explorations

First reading

Lines 1–4

1. Picture the scene in the first four lines – notice all the details. What do you learn about the lifestyle?

2. What questions are you prompted to ask by these lines? Formulate at least three.

Share your questions.

3. (a) Do you think Yeats treasured this memory? (b) What do the lines reveal about what Yeats valued or considered important in life?

Lines 5–6

4. Do you think these lines are an

---

effective metaphor for the passage of time or a rather tired one? Discuss this.

Lines 7–13

5. Read these lines, consult the notes and then state briefly, in your own words, how the life paths or careers of these two women have developed.

6. Do you think that Yeats approved of their careers? Explain your view with reference to words and phrases in the text.

Second reading

7. 'Two girls in silk kimonos, both Beautiful, one a gazelle'
These lines are repeated at the end of the first section. Do you think the refrain here should be spoken in the same tone as lines 3 and 4, or have intervening lines coloured the poet's feeling? Explain your opinion on this. Read aloud the first section as you think Yeats would want it read.

8. Lines 20–25 carry the kernel of the poet's insight, which he feels certain the spirits ('Dear shadows') of the two sisters will understand. (a) What is this wisdom or insight? (b) Is there a certain weariness of tone here? Explain.

9. What do you understand by Yeats's animated wish to light a bonfire at the end of the poem?

Third reading

10. What are the main issues or themes that Yeats deals with in this poem? Support your view with detailed reference.

11. What could one discern about the poet's philosophy of life from a reading of this poem? Again refer to the detail of the text.

12. Yeats felt that the Anglo-Irish ascendancy class with their great houses and wealth had a duty to set an example of graciousness and cultured living. (a) Do you think he felt that Eva and Con had let the side down? Where and how might this be suggested? (b) Do you think he may have considered their activities un-feminine?

13. 'The off-rhymes that Yeats employs from time to time gives the poem a conversational naturalism and reinforce the theme of imperfection.' Discuss this with reference to the details of the poem.

14. Many of Yeats's poems are about time structured on quite violent contrasts. Do you think this an effective device here? Comment.

15. Think or talk about your personal reactions to this poem. What did it make you think about? What insights did it give you?

Eva Gore-Booth (left) and her sister Constance (Con Markiewicz)

Swift's Epitaph

Swift has sailed into his rest;
Savage indignation there
Cannot lacerate his breast.
Imitate him if you dare,
World-besotted traveller; he
Served human liberty.

Background note

Jonathan Swift (1667–1745) was the most famous Dean of St Patrick's Cathedral, Dublin. Poet, political pamphleteer and satirist, he was the author of such well-known works as: The Drapier Letters; A Modest Proposal; A Tale of a Tub and Gulliver's Travels. Politically conservative, Swift voiced the concerns and values of protestant Ireland with an independence of mind and a courage that Yeats admired.

This poem is a translation, with some alterations, of the Latin epitaph on Swift's burial stone in St Patrick's, Cathedral, Dublin. Yeats changed the first line and added the adjective 'World-besotted' in the penultimate line.

The original epitaph, which is in Latin, runs as follows:

> Here is laid the Body of
> JONATHAN SWIFT
> Doctor of Divinity,
> Dean of this Cathedral Church,
> Where savage indignation
> can no longer
> Rend his heart,
> Go traveller, and imitate,
> if you can,
> This earnest and dedicated
> Champion of Liberty.
> He died on the 19th day of Oct.,
> 1745 A.D. aged 78 years.

Explorations

First reading

1. What does the first line suggest about Swift's death?
2. What can we learn about Swift's life from this epitaph?
3. What qualities of Swift's do you think Yeats admired?
4. Comment on the tone of the epitaph. Do you think it is unusual? Refer in detail to words and phrases.

Second reading

5. How do Yeats's alterations in lines 1 and 5 (see question 2) change the epitaph?
6. Contrast Swift's original epitaph with Yeats's own epitaph. (p. 87)

W.B. Yeats in his later years

An Acre of Grass

Picture and book remain,
An acre of green grass
For air and exercise,
Now strength of body goes;
Midnight, an old house   5
Where nothing stirs but a mouse.

My temptation is quiet.
Here at life's end
Neither loose imagination,
Nor the mill of the mind   10
Consuming its rag and bone,
Can make the truth known.

Grant me an old man's frenzy,
Myself must I remake
Till I am Timon and Lear   15
Or that William Blake
Who beat upon the wall
Till Truth obeyed his call;

A mind Michael Angelo knew
That can pierce the clouds,   20
Or inspired by frenzy
Shake the dead in their shrouds;
Forgotten else by mankind,
An old man's eagle mind.

Notes

[2–5] **An acre of green grass ... an old house:** The reference is to Riversdale, a farmhouse with orchards and fruit gardens at the foot of the Dublin mountains in Rathfarnham which Yeats leased in 1932 for thirteen years.

[9] **loose imagination:** unstructured imagination

[11] **rag and bone:** The left-over, discarded bric-à-brac of life. Lines 10–11 might refer to the imagination's everyday, casual focus on the bric-à-brac of life.

[15] **Timon:** An Athenian, died in 399 B.C., who was satirised by the comic writers of his time for his marked misanthropy or strong dislike of humanity. Shakespeare dramatised the story in Timon of Athens.

[15] **Lear:** Shakespeare's King Lear who couldn't accept old age gracefully, lost his reason and lived wild on the heath.

[16] **William Blake:** (1757–1827) By profession an engraver, Blake is best known for his more accessible poems 'Songs of Innocence' and 'Songs of Experience'. Lesser known is a great body and range of work which shows him as a mystic, apocalyptic visionary, writer of rude verses and an independent thinker who challenged the accepted philosophies and values of his age. He was considered mad by his contemporaries. Yeats admired him greatly and co-edited his *Prophetic Books* in 1893. He also wrote an interpretation of Blake's mythology.

[19] **Michael Angelo:** Michelangelo Buonarroti (1475–1564) was one of the premier figures of the Italian Renaissance – sculptor, architect, painter and poet. Among his most famous creations are the statue of David and the ceiling of the Sistine Chapel in Rome.

Explorations

First reading

1. Explore the images and sounds of the first stanza. (*a*) What do we learn about the condition of the poet? (*b*) How would you describe the atmosphere created in this stanza? What words and sound contribute most to that?

2. In the second stanza, despite his age the poet is still thinking of poetry. In your own words, describe his dilemma.

3. Examine the metaphor for the mind used in lines 10 and 11. What do you think of it?

4. Comment on the tones found in stanzas 1 and 2. Do you think there is a sense of emptiness at the end of the second stanza? Explore how the sounds of the words contribute to this.

Second reading

5. 'Grant me an old man's frenzy' This is a very unusual prayer. Does the remainder of stanza 3 help to explain this intercession? Consult the textual notes and try to outline in your own words what Yeats is actually praying for.

6. What is the connection that Yeats is making between poetry, madness and truth?

7. There is evidence of a new energy in both language and imagery in stanzas 3 and 4. Comment in detail on this.

8. This extraordinary change or metamorphosis culminates in the final image of 'An old man's eagle mind.' Trace how this conceit (or startling comparison) has been prepared for earlier in the fourth stanza.

Third reading

9. Would you agree that this poem is a most unusual response to the theme of old age?

10. Yeats's theories of creativity (partly inspired by the works of the German philosopher Nietzsche) included the need for continual transformation of the self. Trace the transformation that occurs here.

Politics

'In our time the destiny of man presents its
meanings in political terms'
(Thomas Mann)

How can I, that girl standing there,
My attention fix
On Roman or on Russian
Or on Spanish politics?
Yet here's a travelled man that knows   5
What he talks about,
And there's a politician
That has read and thought,
And maybe what they say is true
Of war and war's alarms,   10
But O that I were young again
And held her in my arms.

Background note

Written in May 1938 the poem was composed as an answer to an article about Yeats, which had
praised his public language but suggested that he should use it on political subjects.

Note

Thomas Mann: (1875–1955) a German novelist

Explorations

First reading

1. In your own words, state the dilemma or conflict that Yeats is experiencing here.
2. 'And maybe what they say is true | Of war'
   From the context of the poem, what do you suppose they say? Examine Thomas Mann's epigraph for suggestions.
3. 'That girl standing there'
   To whom or to what do you think he might be referring?

Second reading

4. Write about the essential conflicts that are set up here: politics versus love; public life versus private; public devotion versus private satisfaction, etc.
5. 'For all its simplicity of language. This is a very well crafted poem.' Discuss this statement with reference to the text.
6. State what you think this poem is about.
7. 'The vision in this poem is that of an old man.' Argue about this.

From 'Under Ben Bulben'

V

Irish poets, learn your trade,
Sing whatever is well made,
Scorn the sort now growing up
All out of shape from toe to top,
Their unremembering hearts and heads   5
Base-born products of base beds.
Sing the peasantry, and then
Hard-riding country gentlemen,
The holiness of monks, and after
Porter-drinkers' randy laughter;   10
Sing the lords and ladies gay
That were beaten into the clay
Through seven heroic centuries;
Cast your mind on other days
That we in coming days may be   15
Still the indomitable Irishry.

VI

Under bare Ben Bulben's head
In Drumcliff churchyard Yeats is laid.
An ancestor was rector there
Long years ago, a church stands near,   20
By the road an ancient cross.
No marble, no conventional phrase;
On limestone quarried near the spot
By his command these words are cut:
Cast a cold eye   25
On life, on death.
Horseman, pass by!

September 4, 1938

Background note

The final draft of this poem is dated 4 September 1938, about five months before the poet's death. Parts of it were published in 1939. 'Under Ben Bulben' as a whole can be seen as Yeats's poetic testimony, an elegy for himself, defining his convictions and the poetic and social philosophies that motivated his life's work.

Section V: Yeats urges all artists, poets, painters, sculptors to promote the necessary heroic images that nourish civilisation.

Section VI: rounds his life to its close and moves from the mythologies associated with the top of Ben Bulben to the real earth at its foot, in Drumcliff churchyard.

Notes

Section V

[2] **whatever is well made:** note [14] comments on the great tradition of art and letters

[3–6] **Scorn the sort ... products of base beds:** Yeats had joined the Eugenics Society in London in 1936 and became very interested in its literature and in research on intelligence testing. ('Eugenics' is the science of improving the human race through selective breeding.)

[11–12] **Sing the lords ... beaten into the clay:** refers to the Cromwellian settlement of 1652 which evicted the majority of Irish landowners to Clare and Connaught to make room for new English settlers

[13] **centuries:** the centuries since the Norman Invasions

[14] **other days:** A reference to the great tradition in European art and letters valued by Yeats. But it could also be a reference to Ireland's literary tradition, particularly of the eighteenth century.

Section VI

[17] **Ben Bulben:** a mountain north of Sligo connected with Irish mythology

[18] **Drumcliff:** At the foot of Ben Bulben, it was the site of a sixth century monastery founded by St Colmcille.

[19] **ancestor was rector there:** The Revd John Yeats (1774–1846), Yeats's grandfather, was rector there and is buried in the graveyard.

[20–21] **a church stands near ... ancient cross:** As well as the remains of a round tower, there is a high cross and part of an older cross in the churchyard.

[27] **horseman:** has echoes of the fairy horseman of folk belief, but might also have associations with the Irish Ascendancy class

Explorations

First reading

1. Yeats's advice to Irish poets to write about the aesthetically pleasing ('whatever is well made') is quite understandable but what do you think of his advice on what they should scorn? Consult the textual notes. (*a*) What exactly is he saying? (*b*) What is your reaction to this rant?

2. In your own words, what does Yeats consider to be the proper subjects for poetry?

3. What image of 'Irishry' does Yeats wish to celebrate? Do you think he is being elitist and superior?

Second reading

4. Would you agree that this section exhibits an abhorrence for the present at the expense of a romanticised past? Explain your opinion with reference to the details of the verse.

5. This reads like an incantation. What features of poetic technique do you think contribute to this? Consider: the metre; the rhyming scheme; choice of diction, etc.

6. Write about the poet's attitude of mind as you detect it from these lines.

7. Professor Terence Brown has written of 'Under Ben Bulben':

'Skill (i.e. poetic) here is complicit with a repulsive politics and a deficient ethical sense.' On the evidence of the extract, would you agree with this?

Section VI

First reading

1. Yeats visualised the details of his last resting place very carefully. Without checking back, what details of the churchyard can you remember?

2. How would you describe the atmosphere of the churchyard? What details in the verse contribute particularly to this?

Second reading

3. What do these lines reveal about the poet, how he sees himself and wishes to be remembered?

4. Discuss the epitaph in the last three lines. How does it differ from most epitaphs you have read?

5. The scholar A.N. Jeffares felt that the epitaph embodied Yeats's essential attitude to life and death 'which he thought must be faced with bravery, with heroic indifference and with the aristocratic disdain of the horseman'. Consider this as a possible reading of the lines and write a response to it.

Ben Bulben

Cast a cold Eye
On Life, on Death.
Horseman, pass by!

W. B. YEATS

June 13th 1865
January 28th 1939

Yeats's grave in Drumcliff churchyard

4 Robert FROST

prescribed for Higher Level exams in 2007 and 2008

Robert Lee Frost was born in San Francisco on 26 March 1874. Following his father's death in 1885, he moved with his younger sister Jeanie and his mother to Lawrence, Massachusetts, where his grandparents lived. Robert entered Lawrence High School in 1888. There he studied Latin, Greek, ancient and European history and mathematics. From high school he went to Dartmouth College and Harvard but left the two colleges without graduating. On 19 December 1895 he married Elinor White, a former classmate. For health reasons he took up farming. In later years he recalled that his favourite activities were 'mowing with a scythe, chopping with an axe and writing with a pen'. He supplemented his income by teaching and lecturing. Frost devoted his free time to reading the major poets in order to perfect his own writing. Shakespeare, the English Romantics (Wordsworth, Keats and Shelley) and the Victorian poets (Hardy, Kipling and Browning) all influenced his work. The many biblical references in his poems reflect his scripture studies while his classical education enabled him to write with confidence in traditional forms. He followed the

1874–1963

principles laid down in Wordsworth's 'Preface to the Lyrical Ballads', basing his poetry on incidents from common life described in 'language really used by men'.

Frost and his family emigrated to England in 1912. There he published two collections *A Boy's Will* (1913) and *North of Boston* (1914). The books were well received and he was introduced into the literary circles in London, where he met W.B. Yeats. After the outbreak of World War I Frost returned to America and wrote his next collection *Mountain Interval*. This book contains some of his best-known poems including 'Birches', 'Out, Out –' and 'The Road Not Taken', with their characteristic themes of isolation, fear, violence and death. Frost bought another farm in Franconia, New Hampshire and supported his family by college teaching, readings, lectures, book royalties and reprint fees. In January 1917 he became Professor of English at Amherst, Massachusetts. By 1920 he could afford to move to Vermont and devote himself to apple-farming and writing poetry. In recognition of his work he won the Pulitzer Prize four times, in 1924, 1931, 1937 and 1943.

Unlike his public life, Frost's personal life was dogged by tragedy. His sister Jeanie was committed to a mental asylum. His daughter Lesley had an emotionally disturbed life and blamed her father for her problems. His favourite child, Majorie, had a nervous breakdown, developed tuberculosis and died in 1934 aged twenty-nine. Irma, his third daughter, suffered from mental illness throughout her adult life. Elinor, his wife, died of a heart attack on 20 March 1938 and his only son Carol committed suicide in 1940. Frost survived the turbulence of these years with the support of his friend, secretary and manager, Kay Morrison. In his final years, Frost enjoyed public acclaim. He recited 'The Gift Outright' at John F. Kennedy's inauguration, watched on television by over sixty million Americans. He travelled as a celebrated visitor from Brazil to Ireland and Russia. On his eighty-eighth birthday he received the Congressional Gold Medal from President Kennedy and in the same year, 1962, published his final volume *In The Clearing*. On 29 January 1963, two months before his eighty-ninth birthday, Robert Frost died peacefully in a Boston hospital.

Robert Frost

The Tuft of Flowers

I went to turn the grass once after one
Who mowed it in the dew before the sun.

The dew was gone that made his blade so keen
Before I came to view the levelled scene.
I looked for him behind an isle of trees;   5
I listened for his whetstone on the breeze.

But he had gone his way, the grass all mown,
And I must be, as he had been, – alone,

'As all must be,' I said within my heart,
'Whether they work together or apart.'   10

But as I said it, swift there passed me by
On noiseless wing a bewildered butterfly,

Seeking with memories grown dim o'er night
Some resting flower of yesterday's delight.

And once I marked his flight go round and round,   15
As where some flower lay withering on the ground.

And then he flew as far as eye could see,
And then on tremulous wing came back to me.

I thought of questions that have no reply,
And would have turned to toss the grass to dry;   20

But he turned first, and led my eye to look
At a tall tuft of flowers beside a brook,

A leaping tongue of bloom the scythe had spared
Beside a reedy brook the scythe had bared.

I left my place to know them by their name,   25
Finding them butterfly weed when I came.

Notes

[1] **to turn the grass:** to toss the grass so that it will dry

[3] **keen:** sharp-edged, eager

[6] **whetstone:** a stone used for sharpening edged tools by friction

[23] **scythe:** a long, curving, sharp-edged blade for mowing grass

The mower in the dew had loved them thus,
By leaving them to flourish, not for us,

Nor yet to draw one thought of ours to him,
But from sheer morning gladness at the brim.   30

The butterfly and I had lit upon,
Nevertheless, a message from the dawn,
That made me hear the wakening birds around,
And hear his long scythe whispering to the ground,

And feel a spirit kindred to my own;   35
So that henceforth I worked no more alone;

But glad with him, I worked as with his aid,
And weary, sought at noon with him the shade;

And dreaming, as it were, held brotherly speech
With one whose thought I had not hoped to reach. 40

'Men work together,' I told him from the heart,
'Whether they work together or apart.'

Explorations

First reading

1. Describe the scene in the first five couplets. What do you see? Who is present? What is he doing?
2. Explore the mood in these opening lines. How does the speaker feel? Do you think you would feel the same way?
3. How does the speaker feel after he discovers the butterfly weed? What words or phrases suggest a change in his mood?
4. According to the poem, why did the mower not cut these flowers?
5. What image or phrases caught your attention, on a first reading? Why?

Second reading

6. In your opinion, what is the 'message from the dawn'?
7. What do you think the poet means when he says 'henceforth I worked no more alone'.

Third reading

8. Briefly outline the themes of this poem.
9. Shifts of mood and tone are marked by the word 'but'. Trace these changes in the poem.
10. The speaker describes the mower as a 'spirit kindred to my own'. In what sense is this true?

Fourth reading

11. Three times Frost introduces the concept of 'turning', in the poem. Examine the changes that occur with each of them.
12. Follow the development of the main ideas. Examine the images that convey these ideas and state whether or not you find them effective.
13. 'Frost rejects ornate, poetic diction preferring a language that is conversational and relaxed.' Examine Frost's use of language in the poem.
14. 'Frost's decision to write in conventional forms, using traditional rhythms and rhymes and syntax, reflects his belief that poetry should be accessible to the ordinary man.' Assess this poem in the light of the above statement.

Harvesting: painting by Julien Dupré (1851–1910)

Mending Wall

Something there is that doesn't love a wall,
That sends the frozen-ground-swell under it,
And spills the upper boulders in the sun;
And makes gaps even two can pass abreast.
The work of hunters is another thing: 5
I have come after them and made repair
Where they have left not one stone on a stone,
But they would have the rabbit out of hiding,
To please the yelping dogs. The gaps I mean,
No one has seen them made or heard them made,   10
But at spring mending-time we find them there.
I let my neighbour know beyond the hill;
And on a day we meet to walk the line
And set the wall between us once again.
We keep the wall between us as we go.   15
To each the boulders that have fallen to each.
And some are loaves and some so nearly balls
We have to use a spell to make them balance:
'Stay where you are until our backs are turned!'
We wear our fingers rough with handling them.   20
Oh, just another kind of out-door game,
One on a side. It comes to little more:
There where it is we do not need the wall:
He is all pine and I am apple orchard.
My apple trees will never get across   25
And eat the cones under his pines, I tell him.
He only says, 'Good fences make good neighbours.'
Spring is the mischief in me, and I wonder
If I could put a notion in his head:
'*Why* do they make good neighbours? Isn't it   30
Where there are cows? But here there are no cows.
Before I built a wall I'd ask to know
What I was walling in or walling out,
And to whom I was like to give offence.
Something there is that doesn't love a wall,   35
That wants it down.' I could say 'Elves' to him,
But it's not elves exactly, and I'd rather
He said it for himself. I see him there

Bringing a stone grasped firmly by the top
In each hand, like an old-stone savage armed.   40
He moves in darkness as it seems to me,
Not of woods only and the shade of trees.
He will not go behind his father's saying,
And he likes having thought of it so well
He says again, 'Good fences make good neighbours.'   45

 # Explorations

First reading

1. You have been asked to paint a picture based on this poem. Where would you place the wall and the two men? What are the men doing? Are they looking at each other? Describe their postures and their facial expressions. What other details would you include?

2. How are the gaps in the wall created?

3. What do you think the poet means when he describes wall-building as 'just another kind of outdoor game'?

4. Outline the arguments Frost uses against building walls.

Second reading

5. In what sense is the neighbour 'all pine and I am apple orchard'?

6. 'He moves in darkness ...' What forms of darkness overshadow the neighbour?

7. Describe as clearly as possible your image of the neighbour as Frost portrays him.

Third reading

8. Walls unite and divide. How is this illustrated within the poem?

9. 'Good fences make good neighbours.' Do you think the speaker agrees with this proverb? Explain your answer.

10. The neighbour repeats the proverb because 'he likes having thought of it so well'. Why is this comment ironic?

11. What do we learn about the narrator's personality in the poem?

Fourth reading

12. What themes and issues are raised in this poem?

13. How does Frost achieve a sense of mystery in the poem?

Are any of the images
mysterious or magical? What
effect do they have on the
poem?

14. Follow the development of the
main ideas. Examine the
images that convey these ideas
and state whether or not you
find them effective.

15. This poem is concerned with
unity and division,
communication and isolation,
hope and disappointment. Do
you agree? Where are these
tensions most obvious? Are
they resolved at the end?

16. 'Human nature, not Mother
Nature, is the main concern in
Frost's poetry.' Would you
agree with this statement,
based on your reading of this
poem?

After Apple-Picking

My long two-pointed ladder's sticking through a tree
Toward heaven still,
And there's a barrel that I didn't fill
Beside it, and there may be two or three
Apples I didn't pick upon some bough.   5
But I am done with apple-picking now.
Essence of winter sleep is on the night,
The scent of apples: I am drowsing off.
I cannot rub the strangeness from my sight
I got from looking through a pane of glass   10
I skimmed this morning from the drinking trough
And held against the world of hoary grass.
It melted, and I let it fall and break.
But I was well
Upon my way to sleep before it fell,   15
And I could tell
What form my dreaming was about to take.
Magnified apples appear and disappear,
Stem end and blossom end,
And every fleck of russet showing clear.   20
My instep arch not only keeps the ache,
It keeps the pressure of a ladder-round.
I feel the ladder sway as the boughs bend.

Notes

[7] **Essence:** scent
[12] **hoary:** white
with age
(hoarfrost: white
particles of
frozen dew)
[40] **woodchuck:**
a burrowing
rodent or
groundhog
which hibernates
for half the year

And I keep hearing from the cellar bin
The rumbling sound   25
Of load on load of apples coming in.
For I have had too much
Of apple-picking: I am overtired
Of the great harvest I myself desired.
There were ten thousand thousand fruit to touch,   30
Cherish in hand, lift down, and not let fall.
For all
That struck the earth,
No matter if not bruised or spiked with stubble,
Went surely to the cider-apple heap   35
As of no worth.
One can see what will trouble
This sleep of mine, whatever sleep it is.
Were he not gone,
The woodchuck could say whether it's like his   40
Long sleep, as I describe its coming on,
Or just some human sleep.

Apple Trees and Poplars in the setting sun: painting by Camille Pissaro (1831–1903)

Explorations

First reading

1. Imagine the orchard as Frost describes it in the opening lines. What details does he include? How would you describe the scene now the apple-picking is over?
2. Explain in your own words what happened at the drinking trough in the morning.
3. Why had the apple-picker to be so careful with the apples?
4. What connects the woodchuck and the harvester?

Second reading

5. The fruit has been harvested. How does the speaker feel now?
6. What is it that will trouble his sleep?
7. Select your favourite image in the poem and explain your choice.
8. Does the poet successfully capture the sensations of picking apples? Examine his use of images and the language used.

Third reading

9. There are moments of confusion in the poem. Is this deliberate? Why? Refer closely to the text in your answer.
10. In the poem, autumn is seen as a season of abundance rather than a time of decay. How does the poet recreate for the reader the richness of the harvest?
11. A dream-like quality pervades the poem. How is this achieved? Consider the language used, the imagery, descriptions, metre and rhyme.

Fourth reading

12. Frost's language is sensuously evocative and rich in imagery. Discuss his use of tactile, visual and auditory imagery in the poem as a whole.
13. What part do sounds and rhythm play in the creation of the mood in the poem?
14. Briefly explain your personal reaction to 'After Apple-Picking'.

Birches

When I see birches bend to left and right
Across the lines of straighter darker trees,
I like to think some boy's been swinging them.
But swinging doesn't bend them down to stay.
Ice-storms do that. Often you must have seen them   5
Loaded with ice a sunny winter morning
After a rain. They click upon themselves
As the breeze rises, and turn many-colored
As the stir cracks and crazes their enamel.
Soon the sun's warmth makes them shed crystal shells   10
Shattering and avalanching on the snow-crust –
Such heaps of broken glass to sweep away
You'd think the inner dome of heaven had fallen.
They are dragged to the withered bracken by the load,
And they seem not to break; though once they are bowed   15
So low for long, they never right themselves:
You may see their trunks arching in the woods
Years afterwards, trailing their leaves on the ground
Like girls on hands and knees that throw their hair
Before them over their heads to dry in the sun.   20
But I was going to say when Truth broke in
With all her matter-of-fact about the ice-storm
I should prefer to have some boy bend them
As he went out and in to fetch the cows –
Some boy too far from town to learn baseball,   25
Whose only play was what he found himself,
Summer or winter, and could play alone.
One by one he subdued his father's trees
By riding them down over and over again
Until he took the stiffness out of them,   30
And not one but hung limp, not one was left
For him to conquer. He learned all there was
To learn about not launching out too soon
And so not carrying the tree away
Clear to the ground. He always kept his poise   35
To the top branches, climbing carefully
With the same pains you use to fill a cup
Up to the brim, and even above the brim.

Then he flung outward, feet first, with a swish,
Kicking his way down through the air to the ground.   40
So was I once myself a swinger of birches.
And so I dream of going back to be.
It's when I'm weary of considerations,
And life is too much like a pathless wood
Where your face burns and tickles with the cobwebs   45
Broken across it, and one eye is weeping
From a twig's having lashed across it open.
I'd like to get away from earth awhile
And then come back to it and begin over.
May no fate willfully misunderstand me   50
And half grant what I wish and snatch me away
Not to return. Earth's the right place for love:
I don't know where it's likely to go better.
I'd like to go by climbing a birch tree,
And climb black branches up a snow-white trunk   55
Toward heaven, till the tree could bear no more,
But dipped its top and set me down again.
That would be good both going and coming back.
One could do worse than be a swinger of birches.

A Road through Belvedere, Vermont:
painting by Thomas W. Whittredge
(1820–1910)

Explorations

Before reading

1. Have you ever climbed a tree? Discuss your experience, explaining where you were, how difficult it was and what skills you needed to climb up and down.

First reading

2. On a first reading, what do you see? Visualise the trees, the ice, the sky and the boy. What sounds can you hear? Are there any other details you should include?
3. What images caught your imagination?
4. How would you describe the general mood of the poem?

Second reading

5. Based on the details given by Frost, describe the character of the boy.
6. Would you agree that the boy is a skilled climber? What details support this point of view?
7. Do you think that the speaker really intends to climb trees again? What makes him long to be a 'swinger of birches' once more?
8. What do you understand by the line 'And life is too much like a pathless wood'?
9. Is the speaker's wish to escape from earth a death wish?

Explain your answer.

10. Explain clearly what you think Frost means in the last eight lines of the poem.

Third reading

11. Frost uses the image of girls drying their hair in the sun. Why? How effective is this image?
12. 'One could do worse than be a swinger of birches'. Does the poet present a convincing argument in support of this claim?
13. How does Frost achieve a conversational tone in the poem? Why does he adopt this voice?

Fourth reading

14. In what way do the boy's actions resemble those of a poet?
15. How does the music in the poem – sounds, metre, etc. – contribute to the atmosphere?
16. Comment on the poet's contrasting use of light and darkness.
17. 'Though much of Frost's poetry is concerned with suffering, he is also capable of capturing moments of unearthly beauty and joy in his work.' Comment on the poem in the light of this statement.

'Out, Out –'

this poem is also prescribed for Ordinary Level exams in 2007 and 2008

The buzz-saw snarled and rattled in the yard
And made dust and dropped stove-length sticks of wood,
Sweet-scented stuff when the breeze drew across it.
And from there those that lifted eyes could count
Five mountain ranges one behind the other   5
Under the sunset far into Vermont.
And the saw snarled and rattled, snarled and rattled,
As it ran light, or had to bear a load.
And nothing happened: day was all but done.
Call it a day, I wish they might have said   10
To please the boy by giving him the half hour
That a boy counts so much when saved from work.
His sister stood beside them in her apron
To tell them 'Supper'. At the word, the saw,
As if to prove saws knew what supper meant,   15
Leaped out at the boy's hand, or seemed to leap –
He must have given the hand. However it was,
Neither refused the meeting. But the hand!
The boy's first outcry was a rueful laugh,
As he swung toward them holding up the hand   20
Half in appeal, but half as if to keep
The life from spilling. Then the boy saw all –
Since he was old enough to know, big boy
Doing a man's work, though a child at heart –
He saw all spoiled. 'Don't let him cut my hand off –   25
The doctor, when he comes. Don't let him, sister!'
So. But the hand was gone already.
The doctor put him in the dark of ether.
He lay and puffed him lips out with his breath.
And then – the watcher at his pulse took fright.   30
No one believed. They listened at his heart.
Little – less – nothing! – and that ended it.
No more to build on there. And they, since they
Were not the one dead, turned to their affairs.

Notes

'Out, Out –': The title is taken from William Shakespeare's famous tragedy *Macbeth*. 'Out, Out brief candle; life's but a walking shadow, a poor player that struts and frets his hour upon the stage, and then is heard no more: it is a tale told by an idiot, full of sound and fury, signifying nothing.'

[28] **ether:** an anaesthetic

Explorations

First reading

1. Read the poem aloud. What words and phrases made the greatest impact on your ear? What animals are suggested in the opening line? How are these animals evoked?

2. Why does Frost describe the scenery?

3. Frost refers repeatedly to 'they' and 'them'. Who do you think these people are? What is your impression of them?

4. The poem turns on the word 'supper'. What happens? Is it an appropriate word in the context?

5. 'He saw all spoiled'. In what sense is all spoiled?

6. What is the boy's immediate fear? Refer to the poem to support your answer.

Second reading

7. Trace the narrative line in this poem. Were you surprised by the ending? Do you think it is an effective conclusion?

8. Comment on the title. Is it a suitable one? Could you suggest another?

9. 'Little – less – nothing!' Read this line aloud and comment on the rhythm. What is the effect of the exclamation mark?

Third reading

10. How effectively does the poet evoke the terror felt by the boy? Examine the techniques used by Frost in your answer.

11. Would you describe the poet as a detached or a sympathetic observer? Is he angered by the incident? How do we know? Comment on the tone.

12. How does the poet engage the reader's sympathies for the boy? Examine the details given, the use of emotive language and the comments made throughout the poem.

Fourth reading

13. What themes and issues are explored in the poem?

14. Sound plays an important role in the poem. Examine the use of assonance, alliteration and onomatopoeia in 'Out, Out –'.

15. 'In his poetry, Frost confronts the reader with the harsh realities of life.' Discuss this statement, in the light of your reading of this poem.

16. Identify and discuss some of the distinctive qualities of Frost's style that are evident in this poem.

The Road Not Taken

this poem is also prescribed for Ordinary Level exams in 2007 and 2008

Two roads diverged in a yellow wood,
And sorry I could not travel both
And be one traveler, long I stood
And looked down one as far as I could
To where it bent in the undergrowth;   5

Then took the other, as just as fair,
And having perhaps the better claim,
Because it was grassy and wanted wear;
Though as for that the passing there
Had worn them really about the same,   10

And both that morning equally lay
In leaves no step had trodden black.
Oh, I kept the first for another day!
Yet knowing how way leads on to way,
I doubted if I should ever come back.   15

I shall be telling this with a sigh
Somewhere ages and ages hence:
Two roads diverged in a wood, and I –
I took the one less traveled by,
And that has made all the difference.   20

Explorations

First reading

1. On a first reading, what do you notice about the setting of the poem? What details made the deepest impression on you? Explain.

2. What is the main focus of the speaker's attention throughout the poem?

3. Why does he choose the second road? Are his reasons convincing?

4. Why will the speaker talk about this moment 'ages and ages hence'?

5. What is the difference referred to by Frost in the last line?

Second reading

6. Comment on the title of the poem. What does it lead you to expect? Does the poem fulfil your expectations?

7. On a surface level the speaker is faced with a choice between two paths. On a deeper level what do the roads symbolise?

8. What is the dominant mood of the poem? What words, phrases and images suggest this mood?

Third reading

9. What images create an autumnal atmosphere in the poem? Why did Frost choose this time of year?

10. What themes or issues can you identify in 'The Road Not Taken'?

11. Do you find the imagery in this poem effective in conveying the theme? Refer to specific images in your answer.

12. The poem opens and closes on a note of regret. Trace the development of thought and mood throughout the poem.

Fourth reading

13. Doubt is replaced by certainty in this poem. Examine the movement from one state to the other.

14. What appeals to you about this poem? Consider the theme, images, sounds, and particular words or phrases, in your answer.

Spring Pools

These pools that, though in forests, still reflect
The total sky almost without defect,
And like the flowers beside them, chill and shiver,
Will like the flowers beside them soon be gone,
And yet not out by any brook or river,   5
But up by roots to bring dark foliage on.

The trees that have it in their pent-up buds
To darken nature and be summer woods –
Let them think twice before they use their powers
To blot out and drink up and sweep away   10
These flowery waters and these watery flowers
From snow that melted only yesterday.

Note

[6] **foliage:** the leaves of a tree or plant

Explorations

First reading

1. What have the pools and the flowers got in common?
2. What do you notice about the trees? What characteristic of the trees does the poet focus on, especially in the second stanza? Why?
3. Why should the trees think twice before they drain the pools and overshadow the flowers?

Second reading

4. Outline the argument of the poem. Would you agree that it is condensed with considerable skill? What is the effect of this on the reader?
5. What image made the greatest impression on you? Explain your choice.
6. How important are the sounds of words in creating the atmosphere in this poem?

Third reading

7. What mood is evoked by this scene? How is this mood created?
8. The beauty of this poem lies in the aptness of the descriptions and the clarity of the language. Do you agree? Explain your answer.

Fourth reading

9. Fragility and strength are contrasted in the poem. Where is this contrast most evident? What is the effect? How is this effect achieved?
10. Discuss the techniques Frost uses in this poem to depict the changing nature of the world. Support your answer by quotation or reference.
11. 'Frost is a master of the lyric form, his images are sensuous, his language clear and his tone controlled.' Examine 'Spring Pools' in the light of this statement.
12. Give your personal reaction to the poem.

Acquainted With the Night

this poem is also prescribed for Ordinary Level exams in 2007 and 2008

I have been one acquainted with the night.
I have walked out in rain – and back in rain.
I have outwalked the furthest city light.

I have looked down the saddest city lane.
I have passed by the watchman on his beat   5
And dropped my eyes, unwilling to explain.

I have stood still and stopped the sound of feet
When far away an interrupted cry
Came over houses from another street,

But not to call me back or say good-bye;   10
And further still at an unearthly height,
One luminary clock against the sky

Proclaimed the time was neither wrong nor right.
I have been one acquainted with the night.

Note

[12] **luminary:** something that gives light, especially a heavenly body

Explorations

First reading

1. Describe the scene in your own words.
2. Examine the images used. What have they got in common? Do they provide an insight as to the central idea of the poem?
3. How would you describe the poet's mood?

Second reading

4. What do you think is the main theme of the poem? Explain your answer.
5. Do you think the imagery used is effective in illustrating the theme? Which images are most appropriate, in your opinion?
6. What feelings does the poem arouse in you? How does it do this?

Third reading

7. What do you notice about the verbs in the poem? In what tense is it written? What purpose might this serve?
8. This poem can be read at more than one level. Suggest another reading of 'Acquainted With the Night'.

Fourth reading

9. Note the repetitions in the poem. What effect do they have?
10. How does Frost evoke the atmosphere of the urban landscape?
11. There is a deep sense of isolation in this poem. Do you agree? Where is it most evident, in your opinion?
12. ' "Acquainted With the Night" is a tribute to the triumph of the human spirit in the face of adversity, rather than a record of the defeat of the soul at its darkest hour.' Discuss the poem in the light of this statement.

Design

I found a dimpled spider, fat and white,
On a white heal-all, holding up a moth
Like a white piece of rigid satin cloth –
Assorted characters of death and blight
Mixed ready to begin the morning right,   5
Like the ingredients of a witches' broth –
A snow-drop spider, a flower like a froth,
And dead wings carried like a paper kite.

What had that flower to do with being white,
The wayside blue and innocent heal-all?   10
What brought the kindred spider to that height,
Then steered the white moth thither in the night?
What but design of darkness to appall? –
If design govern in a thing so small.

Note

[2] **heal-all:** a common flower, used for medicinal purposes, usually blue or violet in colour

Explorations

First reading

1. What do you normally associate with the word 'dimpled'?
2. What images in the octave captured your attention? What do they suggest about the subject matter of the poem?
3. The poet raises several issues in the sestet. What are these issues and what conclusion, if any, does he reach?
4. Jot down the words or phrases that best describe your response to this poem on a first reading.

Second reading

5. How does the octet–sestet division mark the development of thought in the poem.
6. Describe the poet's mood in the sestet.
7. What is the effect of the scene on the speaker? Does he find it repulsive, horrifying, interesting, puzzling? Refer to the text to support your answer.

Third reading

8. Briefly outline the main argument in this poem.
9. Discuss the poet's use of colour.
10. Would you describe this as a nature poem? Explain your answer.

Fourth reading

11. What view of life and death is expressed in the poem? Where is this most evident?
12. Comment on the way the imagery in the poem forges the link between evil and beauty, innocence and death.
13. What is your own reaction to 'Design'?
14. Briefly compare the portrayal of nature in this poem with its portrayal in another poem by Frost, on your course.

Provide, Provide

The witch that came (the withered hag)
To wash the steps with pail and rag
Was once the beauty Abishag,

The picture pride of Hollywood.
Too many fall from great and good   5
For you to doubt the likelihood.

Die early and avoid the fate.
Or if predestined to die late,
Make up your mind to die in state.

Make whole stock exchange your own!   10
If need be occupy a throne,
Where nobody can call *you* crone.

Some have relied on what they knew,
Others on being simply true.
What worked for them might work for you.   15

No memory of having starred
Atones for later disregard
Or keeps the end from being hard.

Better to go down dignified
With boughten friendship at your side   20
Than none at all. Provide, provide!

Notes

[1]   **hag:** an ugly old woman, a witch
[3]   **Abishag:** (1 Kings 1: 2–4) 'Having searched for a beautiful girl throughout
      the territory of Israel, they found Abishag of Shunem and brought her to the
      king. The girl was of great beauty. She looked after the king and waited on
      him...'
[12] **crone:** a withered old woman

Explorations

Before reading

1. Read the title only. Jot down what you imagine the poem is about before reading the poem itself.

First reading

2. The idea that youth rapidly fades is introduced in the opening stanza. What images convey this?
3. What advice does Frost offer as to how to avoid the worst aspects of old age?
4. How can one avoid being called a 'crone'?
5. Imagine you are the old woman in the poem. Write your response to 'Provide, Provide'.

Second reading

6. Can memories offer comfort to the old?
7. Has 'boughten friendship' any advantages according to the poet? What is his tone here?

8. What do you think is meant by the title of the poem?

Third reading

9. Is the poem intended to teach us a lesson? Comment on the moral.
10. Do you think Frost is being serious or humorous here? Examine the tone throughout the poem.

Fourth reading

11. Do your think there is an important theme in the poem? Explain your answer.
12. Examine the contrasts in the poem. State what they are and whether or not you think they are effective.
13. Did you enjoy this poem? Why?
14. 'Realism rather than pessimism is a hallmark of Frost's poetry.' Discuss this statement in the light of your reading of this poem.

5 T.S. ELIOT

prescribed for Higher Level exams in 2007 and 2010

Thomas Stearns Eliot was born on 26 September 1888 in St Louis, Missouri, US. He was the youngest of seven children. His father, Henry, was a brick manufacturer and his mother, Charlotte, was a teacher who also wrote poetry and supported social reform.

His father's ancestors had emigrated from East Coker, near Yeovil, in Somerset, England to Boston, Massachusetts in the late seventeenth century. T.S. Eliot's grandfather, William, moved to St Louis after he graduated from Harvard University in the 1830s. William became a prominent figure in St Louis, speaking out against slavery and promoting women's rights. There, he also established the first Unitarian Church. T.S. Eliot's mother encouraged her son's reverence for his grandfather and it is perhaps this influence which adds the almost missionary zeal to some of his poetry, seeking to bring a message to Western civilisation, which he saw as a moral and cultural wasteland. The family's contact with Boston and the New England coast was maintained through summer visits. These were happy times for the young T.S. Eliot and it is not surprising that sea imagery and themes are prominent throughout his poetry.

1888–1965

Eliot entered Harvard University on 26 September 1906, his eighteenth birthday. There he published frequently in the *Harvard Advocate*, an undergraduate literary magazine, of which he also became editor. In Harvard, Professor Irving Babbit influenced Eliot through his classicism and emphasis upon tradition; George Santayana, the Spanish-born philosopher, awakened a love of philosophy in Eliot which led to Eliot's own study of the British philosopher, Bradley, who exercised considerable influence on Eliot's thoughts. He also studied the Italian poet Dante, who remained a lifelong source of inspiration. Eliot spent the academic year 1910–11 in Paris, where he studied in the Sorbonne. During this time Eliot became fascinated with the sordid squalor of much of urban life. This was to become part of his poetic trademark. He also came under the influence of the French symbolist poets, in particular Baudelaire (1821–67). Intending to study in Germany in 1914, the outbreak of World War I forced him instead to go to England. There he met the American poet Ezra Pound, who would exert a considerable influence over his work and his literary career. At the insistence of Pound, the editor of the magazine *Poetry* agreed to publish 'The Love Song of J. Alfred Prufrock', from which one can date the beginning of modern poetry in English. This poem became the central piece of *Prufrock and other Observations*, published in 1917.

In 1915, Eliot married Vivienne Haigh-Wood. The marriage was to be difficult, leading to the nervous breakdown of both and the permanent illness of Vivienne. (In 1933 Eliot legally separated from her.) Eliot worked as a teacher for a year, 1915–16, leaving teaching to work in Lloyd's Bank until 1925 when he joined the publishing firm now known as Faber & Faber. 'The Wasteland' was published in 1922 and was immediately denounced as impenetrable and incoherent by conservative critics, but its depiction of a sordid society, empty of spiritual values, appealed to the poetry-reading public. The spiritual questing that informed this poem and others such as 'Journey of the Magi' led in 1927 to Eliot's baptism into the Anglican Church, whose Anglo-Catholicism satisfied his spiritual and emotional needs. Religious themes became increasingly important to him leading to the publication of, among others, the poetic drama 'Murder in the Cathedral' (1935), which deals with the assassination of St Thomas à Becket, and to the 'Four Quartets', a philosophic sequence dealing with issues of spiritual renewal and of time. These sufficiently consolidated his reputation to the extent that he was awarded the Nobel Prize for Literature in 1948. Following his wife's death, Eliot married his secretary at Faber & Faber, which brought him great personal happiness. He died on 4 January 1965, after several years of declining health, from emphysema. His ashes are buried in East Coker in Somerset, England.

Eliot's importance to twentieth-century poetry can hardly be over-stated. Through his critical essays and especially through his own poetic practice he played a very considerable role in establishing the modern conception of poetry – impersonal but packed with powerful reserves of private emotions, learned, allusive and organised by associative connections. On a lighter note, his lifelong love of cats lead to his publication of *Old Possum's Book of Practical Cats* (1939), which was the basis for *Cats*, a spectacular musical comedy of the 1980s.

The Love Song of J. Alfred Prufrock

S'io credessi che mia risposta fosse
a persona che mai tornasse al mondo,
questa fiamma staria senza più scosse.
Ma per ciò che giammai di questo fondo
non tornò vivo alcun, s'i'odo il vero,
senza tema d'infamia ti rispondo.

Let us go then, you and I,
When the evening is spread out against the sky
Like a patient etherised upon a table;
Let us go, through certain half-deserted streets,
The muttering retreats   5
Of restless nights in one-night cheap hotels
And sawdust restaurants with oyster-shells:
Streets that follow like a tedious argument
Of insidious intent
To lead you to an overwhelming question . . .   10
Oh, do not ask, 'What is it?'
Let us go and make our visit.

In the room the women come and go
Talking of Michelangelo.

The yellow fog that rubs its back upon the window-panes,   15
The yellow smoke that rubs its muzzle on the window-panes,
Licked its tongue into the corners of the evening,
Lingered upon the pools that stand in drains,
Let fall upon its back the soot that falls from chimneys,

Notes

S'io credessi ...: from Dante (*Inferno* XXVII, 61–6), spoken by the warrior Count Guido da Montefeltro, in Hell for the false advice he gave to the Pope. It reads in English: 'If I believed that my reply would be to one who would return to the world, this flame would tremble no more; but as no one ever returns alive from this depth, if what I hear is true, without fear of disgrace I answer you.'

[14] **Michelangelo:** the Italian painter and sculptor; a heroic contrast to Prufrock

Slipped by the terrace, made a sudden leap,   20
And seeing that it was a soft October night,
Curled once about the house, and fell asleep.

And indeed there will be time
For the yellow smoke that slides along the street
Rubbing its back upon the window-panes;   25
There will be time, there will be time
To prepare a face to meet the faces that you meet;
There will be time to murder and create,
And time for all the works and days of hands
That lift and drop a question on your plate;   30
Time for you and time for me,
And time yet for a hundred indecisions,
And for a hundred visions and revisions,
Before the taking of a toast and tea.

In the room the women come and go   35
Talking of Michelangelo.

And indeed there will be time
To wonder, 'Do I dare?' and, 'Do I dare?'
Time to turn back and descend the stair,
With a bald spot in the middle of my hair –   40
(They will say: 'How his hair is growing thin!')
My morning coat, my collar mounting firmly to the chin,
My necktie rich and modest, but asserted by a simple pin –
(They will say: 'But how his arms and legs are thin!')
Do I dare   45
Disturb the universe?
In a minute there is time
For decisions and revisions which a minute will reverse.

[23] **And indeed there will be time ...:** echoes the Old Testament, Ecclesiastes 3: 1–8
[29] **works and days:** the title of a didactic poem by the Greek writer Hesiod, eighth century
    B.C.

For I have known them all already, known them all –
Have known the evenings, mornings, afternoons,   50
I have measured out my life with coffee spoons;
I know the voices dying with a dying fall
Beneath the music from a farther room.
So how should I presume?

And I have known the eyes already, known them all –   55
The eyes that fix you in a formulated phrase,
And when I am formulated, sprawling on a pin,
When I am pinned and wriggling on the wall,
Then how should I begin
To spit out all the butt-ends of my days and ways?   60
And how should I presume?

And I have known the arms already, known them all –
Arms that are braceleted and white and bare
(But in the lamplight, downed with light brown hair!)
Is it perfume from a dress   65
That makes me so digress?
Arms that lie along a table, or wrap about a shawl.
And should I then presume?
And how should I begin?

Shall I say, I have gone at dusk through narrow streets   70
And watched the smoke that rises from the pipes
Of lonely men in shirt-sleeves, leaning out of windows?...

I should have been a pair of ragged claws
Scuttling across the floors of silent seas.

And the afternoon, the evening, sleeps so peacefully!   75
Smoothed by long fingers,
Asleep ... tired ... or it malingers,
Stretched on the floor, here beside you and me.
Should I, after tea and cakes and ices,
Have the strength to force the moment to its crisis?   80

[52] **a dying fall:** the description of a piece of music by Duke Orsino in Shakespeare's *Twelfth Night*

But though I have wept and fasted, wept and prayed,
Though I have seen my head (grown slightly bald)
brought in upon a platter,
I am no prophet – and here's no great matter;
I have seen the moment of my greatness flicker,   85
And I have seen the eternal Footman hold my coat, and
snicker,
And in short, I was afraid.

And would it have been worth it, after all,
After the cups, the marmalade, the tea,   90
Among the porcelain, among some talk of you and me,
Would it have been worth while,
To have bitten off the matter with a smile,
To have squeezed the universe into a ball
To roll it towards some overwhelming question,   95
To say: 'I am Lazarus, come from the dead,
Come back to tell you all, I shall tell you all' –
If one, settling a pillow by her head,
Should say: 'That is not what I meant at all.
That is not it, at all.'   100
And would it have been worth it, after all,
Would it have been worth while,
After the sunsets and the dooryards and the sprinkled
streets,
After the novels, after the teacups, after the skirts that   105
trail along the floor –
And this, and so much more? –
It is impossible to say just what I mean!
But as if a magic lantern threw the nerves in patterns on a
screen: 110
Would it have been worth while

[82] **My head … platter:** Matthew's Gospel 14: 3–11. The head of John the Baptist was
brought thus to Salome, as a reward for her dancing in front of Herod.

[86] **eternal Footman:** a personification of death; see John Bunyan's *The Pilgrim's Progress*
(1678)

[94] **squeezed … ball:** a reference to Andrew Marvell's (1621–78) poem of seduction 'To His
Coy Mistress'

[96] **Lazarus:** the dead man whom Jesus raised from the dead; see St John's Gospel 11: 1–44

If one, settling a pillow or throwing off a shawl,
And turning toward the window, should say:
'That is not it at all,
That is not what I meant at all.'   115

No! I am not Prince Hamlet, nor was meant to be;
Am an attendant lord, one that will do
To swell a progress, start a scene or two,
Advise the prince; no doubt, an easy tool,
Deferential, glad to be of use,   120
Politic, cautious, and meticulous;
Full of high sentence, but a bit obtuse;
At times, indeed, almost ridiculous –
Almost, at times, the Fool.

I grow old . . . I grow old . . .   125
I shall wear the bottoms of my trousers rolled.

Shall I part my hair behind? Do I dare to eat a peach?
I shall wear white flannel trousers, and walk upon the beach.
I have heard the mermaids singing, each to each.

I do not think that they will sing to me.   130

I have seen them riding seaward on the waves
Combing the white hair of the waves blown back
When the wind blows the water white and black.

We have lingered in the chambers of the sea
By sea-girls wreathed with seaweed red and brown   135
Till human voices wake us, and we drown.

[116] **Prince Hamlet:** In Shakespeare's play of the same name, Hamlet agonizes about being
   indecisive.
[118] **To swell a progress:** in Elizabethan times a state or royal journey
[122] **Full of high sentence:** a description of the talk of the Clerk in Chaucer's (1343–1400)
   The Canterbury Tales
[124] **the Fool:** the court jester in Shakespeare's *King Lear*, a sort of idiot savant
[129] **mermaids singing:** A reference to John Donne's (1576–1631) poem 'Song'; also in
   contrast to the sirens of Greek legend who lead sailors to their deaths.

Explorations

First reading

1. The 'J. Alfred Prufrock' of the title is the speaker in the poem. Knowing this, how do you visualise him? What words or phrases make images for you? Is he the sort of person you would expect to sing a love song?

2. What is the mood of the speaker in the poem? Anger, despair, regret or fear?

3. Would you agree that Prufrock is trying to come to some decision? What do you think this is? What, if anything, has Prufrock to look forward to?

Second reading

4. The Italian epigraph comes from Dante's *The Divine Comedy*. It is spoken by one of the damned souls in the Inferno. What sort of expectations does this arouse for you?

5. Who do you think is the 'you' of the first line? Is it the reader or is it another side of Prufrock's personality?

6. Would you agree that the dramatic scene outlined from lines 1–12 suggests some inner sickness or sordid lifestyle? How does the language used here add to this understanding?

7. In lines 13–14 what does the naming of Michelangelo mean to you? What do the rhythm and rhyme of these lines suggest to you? Why are they repeated later?

8. Would you agree that the image of the fog in lines 15–22 also suggests a cat? With what have cats been traditionally associated? What does the rhyming of 'leap' and 'sleep' suggest to you?

9. The motif of time is particularly strong in lines 23–4. Where else does it occur in the poem? What does 'To prepare a face to meet the faces that you meet,' mean to you?

10. Prufrock seems particularly self-conscious and indecisive in lines 37–48. Is there an incongruity between this and his apparent wish to 'disturb the universe'?

11. Would you agree that Prufrock is more disillusioned than angry at the meaninglessness of his life, as described in lines 49–54?

12. What fears are expressed by Prufrock in lines 55–69? Does Prufrock show simultaneous attraction for and revulsion of women? How is this shown?

13. Do you agree that the question raised in lines 70–74 adds to our understanding of

The Balcony: painting by Edouard Manet (1832–1883)

Prufrock's predicament? What does the image of 'ragged claws scuttling' tell us about his state of mind? What is the tone here? Embarrassment? Distress? Self-irony? How does the language used add to the tone?

14. Some of the major themes of the poem come together in lines 75–88. What images suggest these themes? Would you agree that this section marks a turning point, where Prufrock accepts his inadequacy?

15. What does the reference to Lazarus in the lines 89–110 mean to you? Is it fear of rejection alone that makes Prufrock indecisive?

16. What does the line 'But as if a magic lantern threw the nerves in patterns on a screen' suggest to you?

17. How does Prufrock see himself in lines 111–19? Explain the references to 'Prince Hamlet' and 'the Fool'. Is there a tone of resignation here?

18. In lines 120–31, Prufrock seems to be making some decisions at last. What is the quality of these decisions?

19. Would you agree that the

reference to the sea and mermaids is an escape into a dream world? What brings him back to reality?

Third reading

20. What do you think is the 'overwhelming question' of the poem?

21. Show how the distrustful attitude of Prufrock towards others is seen in the ironical transitions in the poem.

22. Discuss the view that Prufrock's confusion and self-doubt are reflected in the apparent incoherence of the poem.

Fourth reading

23. 'Eliot's main concern in his poetry is the human condition in the modern world.' Discuss this view with references to both 'The Love Song of J. Alfred Prufrock' and 'A Game of Chess'.

24. The poet Ezra Pound called Prufrock a portrait of failure and futility. Would you agree?

25. Discuss the possibilities of dramatising this poem, either on stage or on film. What difficulties would it present? How could these be overcome?

Preludes

this poem is also prescribed for Ordinary Level exams in 2007 and 2010

I

The winter evening settles down
With smell of steaks in passageways.
Six o'clock.
The burnt-out ends of smoky days.
And now a gusty shower wraps   5
The grimy scraps
Of withered leaves about your feet
And newspapers from vacant lots;
The showers beat
On broken blinds and chimney-pots,   10
And at the corner of the street
A lonely cab-horse steams and stamps.

And then the lighting of the lamps.

II

The morning comes to consciousness
Of faint stale smells of beer   15
From the sawdust-trampled street
With all its muddy feet that press
To early coffee-stands.

With the other masquerades
That time resumes,   20
One thinks of all the hands
That are raising dingy shades
In a thousand furnished rooms.

III

You tossed a blanket from the bed,
You lay upon your back, and waited;   25
You dozed, and watched the night revealing
The thousand sordid images
Of which your soul was constituted;
They flickered against the ceiling.
And when all the world came back   30
And the light crept up between the shutters,

And you heard the sparrows in the gutters,
You had such a vision of the street
As the street hardly understands;
Sitting along the bed's edge, where   35
You curled the papers from your hair,
Or clasped the yellow soles of feet
In the palms of both soiled hands.

                    IV
His soul stretched tight across the skies
That fade behind a city block,   40
Or trampled by insistent feet
At four and five and six o'clock;
And short square fingers stuffing pipes,
And evening newspapers, and eyes
Assured of certain certainties,   45
The conscience of a blackened street
Impatient to assume the world.

I am moved by fancies that are curled
Around these images, and cling:
The notion of some infinitely gentle   50
Infinitely suffering thing.

Wipe your hand across your mouth, and laugh;
The worlds revolve like ancient women
Gathering fuel in vacant lots.

Notes

[19] **masquerades:** false pretences, disguise

[22] **shades:** window blinds

[36] **curled the papers from your hair:** paper was used to curl hair before the
     arrival of manufactured curlers

[54] **vacant lots:** empty building sites

Explorations

First reading

1. The four poems here are snapshots of modern urban life, where the observer is like a camera moving through the streets. Imagine yourself as that observer, what do you see, hear and smell as you read the poem?
2. Did anything unexpected strike you?

Second reading

FIRST PRELUDE

3. In the First Prelude, would you agree that the image of 'The burnt-out ends of smoky days' (line 4) evokes a feeling of disgust at a useless end to a useless day? What other words and phrases emphasise the speaker's sense of staleness?
4. How is the sense of cramped conditions indoors evoked?
5. Lines 11–12 picture a lonely cab-horse, who is obviously also impatient and uncomfortable. Can this be seen as symbolic of urban life?
6. 'And then the lighting of the lamps' suggests perhaps an introduction to some dramatic events, but these possibilities are not fulfilled. Would you agree that the irony here contributes to the speaker's sense of aimless endurance?

SECOND PRELUDE

7. Would you agree that the atmosphere of the Second Prelude is oppressive and empty of charm? How is the morning rush hour conveyed?
8. The same sense of cramped indoor conditions seen in the First Prelude is continued here. What images suggest these?
9. For the speaker the rush of urban life is a 'masquerade'. It is a performance put on to give life an apparent meaning and purpose. Does anything lie behind this performance, or is the speaker suggesting that the performance is all there is to life?

THIRD PRELUDE

10. The Third Prelude begins with the image of a woman whose sluggish, half-conscious mind projects her interior being. What impression of the woman do we get here and later in this Prelude as she prepares for life's 'masquerade'? What vision of the street does she have? Can morning be seen almost as an intruder? Would you agree that the proper reaction to what is portrayed is disgust?

FOURTH PRELUDE

11. In the Fourth Prelude the street is personified. Its soul and the souls of the passers-by are

fused. How is the suffering of both conveyed? Is the speaker being ironic when he says? 'and eyes | Assured of certain certainties'?

12. The speaker is momentarily moved to pity in the face of human suffering when he says 'I am moved ... thing' Are you shocked by his immediate turn to cynicism when he says 'Wipe your hand across your mouth, and laugh'? Does he mean us to laugh at the plight of the 'ancient women gathering fuel'? Or is he suggesting that in face of the meaninglessness and suffering of life, pity is too easy an emotion?

Third reading

13. Discuss how Eliot depersonalises character by talking about bodily members in the poem. How does he depersonalise the observer/speaker?
14. What vital impulses, if any, animate the lives of the characters in the poems?
15. Compare the imagery Eliot uses here with that which he uses in 'The Love Song of J. Alfred Prufrock'.
16. In the art of music, a 'Prelude' is a short introductory piece. Examine the musical effects of the poems, particularly the use of rhythm and rhyme.

The Street: painting by George Grosz (1893–1959) representing the dysfunctional urban landscape described by Eliot

Aunt Helen

this poem is also prescribed for Ordinary Level exams in 2007 and 2010

Miss Helen Slingsby was my maiden aunt,
And lived in a small house near a fashionable square
Cared for by servants to the number of four.
Now when she died there was silence in heaven
And silence at her end of the street. 5
The shutters were drawn and the undertaker wiped his feet –
He was aware that this sort of thing had occurred before.
The dogs were handsomely provided for,
But shortly afterwards the parrot died too.
The Dresden clock continued ticking on the mantelpiece, 10
And the footman sat upon the dining-table
Holding the second housemaid on his knees –
Who had always been so careful while her mistress lived.

Note

[10] **Dresden:** German city famous for its production of fine china

Explorations

First reading

1. What do you notice about the setting of the poem? List the things that made an immediate impression on you.

Second reading

2. What is the reaction to Aunt Helen's death? Does anyone mourn her? Does the poet mourn her?
3. Would the footman and housemaid have behaved as described in lines 11–12 when she was alive? Why are they behaving like this now?
4. Would you agree that Aunt Helen had a rather false sense of values? If so, how is this shown? Would you like her lifestyle?

Third reading

5. This poem is seen as a mockery of conventional middle-class life in the early twentieth century. Do you think Eliot is mocking the person of his aunt or is he rather satirising the external realities which surround her? Would you agree that her world is one of lifeless artifice, symbolised by a Dresden clock?
6. Eliot's poetic technique included presenting us with a gallery of comic types where (a) places and people are suggested in a few strokes but (b) gain their final tone and significance from the poem as a whole. Comment on his descriptions of the characters in the poem under these headings.
7. Do you find any trace of the personality or the feelings of the poet in this poem?
8. Do you think that there is anything in the structure of the poem which mimics the speech or tone of Aunt Helen?

A Game of Chess (extract from The Waste Land II)

The Chair she sat in, like a burnished throne,
Glowed on the marble, where the glass
Held up by standards wrought with fruited vines
From which a golden Cupidon peeped out
(Another hid his eyes behind his wing)   5
Doubled the names of sevenbranched candelabra
Reflecting light upon the table as
The glitter of her jewels rose to meet it,
From satin cases poured in rich profusion.
In vials of ivory and coloured glass   10
Unstoppered, lurked her strange synthetic perfumes,
Unguent, powdered, or liquid – troubled, confused
And drowned the sense in odours; stirred by the air
That freshened from the window, these ascended
In fattening the prolonged candle-flames,   15
Flung their smoke into the laquearia,
Stirring the pattern on the coffered ceiling.
Huge sea-wood fed with copper
Burned green and orange, framed by the coloured stone,
In which sad light a carvèd dolphin swam.   20

Notes

A Game of Chess: The title alludes to two plays by Thomas Middleton (1570–1627) i.e. *A Game of Chess* and *Women Beware Women*. Both of these involve sexual intrigue. In the latter play, a young woman is raped while her mother, quite unaware, plays a game of chess downstairs. The allusion refers to the theme of lust without love. The title could also refer to Shakespeare's play *The Tempest*, in which two lovers play a game of chess which is associated with fertility and genuine love. *The Tempest* is referred to again later in the poem.

[1] **The Chair she sat in, like a burnished throne:** This refers to Shakespeare's *Antony and Cleopatra*, Act II, Scene II, recalling Enorbarbus's long description of Cleopatra's first meeting with Antony.

[4] **Cupidon:** a 'beau' or 'Adonis', a handsome young man; also has echoes of Cupid

[12] **Unguent:** in ointment form

[16] **laquearia:** meaning a panelled ceiling; taken from the Roman poet Virgil's 'Aeneid' where he describes the banquet given by Dido, queen of Carthage, for Aeneas, with whom she fell in love

Above the antique mantel was displayed
As though a window gave upon the sylvan scene
The change of Philomel, by the barbarous king
So rudely forced; yet there the nightingale
Filled all the desert with inviolable voice   25
And still she cried, and still the world pursues,
'Jug Jug' to dirty ears.
And other withered stumps of time
Were told upon the walls; staring forms
Leaned out, leaning, hushing the room enclosed.   30
Footsteps shuffled on the stair.
Under the firelight, under the brush, her hair
Spread out in fiery points
Glowed into words, then would be savagely still.

'My nerves are bad to-night. Yes, bad. Stay with me. 35
Speak to me. Why do you never speak? Speak.
What are you thinking of? What thinking? What?
I never know what you are thinking. Think.'

I think we are in rats' alley
Where the dead men lost their bones.   40

'What is that noise?'
The wind under the door.
'What is that noise now? What is the wind doing?'
Nothing again nothing.

---

[22] **sylvan scene:** This is taken from Milton's *Paradise Lost*, IV, 140. The phrase occurs in the description of the Garden of Eden as Satan looks at it for the first time.

[23] **Philomel:** A Greek legend recalled in the Roman writer Ovid's *Metamorphoses VI*. Philomel was raped by her sister Procne's husband, Tereus, King of Thrace, who also cut off Philomel's tongue to prevent her telling. Philomel wove her story into a garment to inform Procne, who in revenge, killed Tereus's son and served him as a dish to Tereus at a banquet. The sisters fled pursued by Tereus, but the gods changed all three into birds; Tereus became a hawk, Procne a swallow and Philomel a nightingale. Poets often refer to a nightingale as 'Philomel'. The reference to the legend here may be to underscore secret or hidden lustful practices.

[42] **The wind under the door:** a reference to John Webster's (1578–1632) play *The Devil's Law Case*, a tragi-comedy

'Do   45
You know nothing? Do you see nothing? Do you remember
'Nothing? '

I remember
Those are pearls that were his eyes.
'Are you alive, or not? Is there nothing in your head?'   50
But
O O O O that Shakespeherian Rag –
It's so elegant
So intelligent
'What shall I do now? What shall I do?   55
I shall rush out as I am, and walk the street
With my hair down, so. What shall we do tomorrow?

What shall we ever do?'
The hot water at ten.
And if it rains, a closed car at four.   60
And we shall play a game of chess,
Pressing lidless eyes and waiting for a knock upon the door.

When Lil's husband got demobbed, I said –
I didn't mince my words, I said to her myself,
HURRY UP PLEASE ITS TIME   65
Now Albert's coming back, make yourself a bit smart.
He'll want to know what you done with that money he gave
you
To get yourself some teeth. He did, I was there.
You have them all out, Lil, and get a nice set,   70
He said, I swear, I can't bear to look at you.
And no more can't I, I said, and think of poor Albert,
He's been in the army four years, he wants a good time,
And if you don't give it him, there's others will, I said.
Oh is there, she said. Something o' that, I said.   75
Then I'll know who to thank, she said, and give me a straight
look.

[49] **Those are pearls that were his eyes:** from Shakespeare's *The Tempest*; Ariel's song that
   speaks of drowning
[62] **Pressing lidless eyes ... the door:** a reference to the game of chess in Middleton's play
   Women Beware Women

HURRY UP PLEASE ITS TIME
If you don't like it you can get on with it, I said.
Others can pick and choose if you can't.   80
But if Albert makes off, it won't be for lack of telling.
You ought to be ashamed, I said, to look so antique.
(And her only thirty-one.)
I can't help it, she said, pulling a long face,
It's them pills I took, to bring it off, she said.   85
(She's had five already, and nearly died of young George.)
The chemist said it would be all right, but I've never been
the same.
You *are* a proper fool, I said.
Well, if Albert won't leave you alone, there it is, I said,   90
What you get married for if you don't want children?
HURRY UP PLEASE ITS TIME
Well, that Sunday Albert was home, they had a hot
gammon,
And they asked me in to dinner, to get the beauty of it hot –   95
HURRY UP PLEASE ITS TIME
HURRY UP PLEASE ITS TIME
Goonight Bill. Goonight Lou. Goonight May. Goonight.
Ta ta. Goonight. Goonight.
Good night, ladies, good night, sweet ladies, good night,   100
good night.

[100] **Good night, ladies ... good night:** The last words spoken by Ophelia, heroine of
Shakespeare's play *Hamlet*, who drowned, driven mad by love and by a time that is out of
joint.

Background note

This poem is Section II of *The Waste Land*, published in 1922. *The Waste Land* summed up the
disillusionment and disgust of the post-World War I generation, who saw the standardised civilisation
that was developing as barren and who saw twentieth-century man as condemned to a living death.
Such attitudes can also be seen in 'Preludes' and in 'The Love Song of J. Alfred Prufrock'. At the
centre of this living death lay an inability to love and a confusion between love and lust. 'A Game of
Chess' depicts the stunting effects of lust mistaken for love. In the poem we see people as pawns
moving about in two games that end not in checkmate but in stalemate.

Explorations

First reading

1. The first scene of the poem is set in a wealthy lady's boudoir (lines 1–62). What strikes you immediately about this scene?

2. The second scene (lines 63–101) is set in a public house. Try reading this scene aloud in a 'Cockney' or 'Scouser' accent. What impression of the women do you get?

Second reading

3. The opening section of the poem has been called a scene of splendid clutter. List some of these cluttering items. Would you find these attractive?

4. The immediate opening section, picturing the lady seated at her dressing table, is a reference to Cleopatra. Why do you think the poet makes this reference?

5. What does the description of the 'cupidons' suggest to you? Is there any hint of the lady's behaviour here?

6. Examine the description of the lady's perfumes. Is the poet suggesting her ability to seduce or is he describing by implication a deeply disturbed person? Look in particular at the choice of verbs.

7. Would you agree that the description of the ceiling adds a claustrophobic atmosphere to this decadent and sensuous scene?

8. Lines 21–24 refer to the Greek legend of Philomel who was changed into a nightingale, following her rape. How does this fit into the overall theme of the poem?

9. What does the description of the lady brushing her hair mean to you?

10. Lines 35–62 constitute a 'dialogue' between the lady and an apparently silent male protagonist. Would you agree that she is seen as quite neurotic here? What in the language used suggests this? Would you agree that his situation is as desperate as hers? Is the reference to Shakespeare elegant?

11. This setting closes with a deep feeling of purposelessness. What images particularly contribute to this theme of sterility?

12. The second scene (lines 63–101), narrated by an unidentified lower-class lady in a pub at closing time, is overheard by the protagonist. Tell the story narrated by the lady in your own words. Would you regard this story as gossip?

13. In what ways are the themes of sterility, emptiness and lust continued here?
14. The barman's words have an immediate meaning but they also have longer-term implications. What are these, do you think?
15. The last line is taken from Shakespeare's Hamlet and is spoken by Ophelia, whom many see as having died for love. Why do you think it is included here?

Third reading
16. Examine the poem as a piece of social satire. What has it to teach us?
17. Discuss the interweaving of past and present in the poem. How do the references to classical literature, legend, etc. add to our understanding of the poem?

18. Examine the use of rhythm and repetition in the poem. Would you describe the poem as musical?
19. Would you agree that both settings in the poem have all the elements of good drama?

Fourth reading
20. Explore the relationship between sensuality and culture in this poem.
21. 'Eliot is the poet of psychological turmoil, cultural decay and moral degeneracy.' Discuss this view in reference to this poem. Where else in Eliot's poetry can this be seen?
22. 'The lives of Eliot's characters are ultimately sterile.' Discuss this statement with reference to this poem and to others.

Journey of the Magi

'A cold coming we had of it,
Just the worst time of the year
For a journey, and such a long journey:
The ways deep and the weather sharp,
The very dead of winter.'   5
And the camels galled, sore-footed, refractory,
Lying down in the melting snow.
There were times we regretted
The summer palaces on slopes, the terraces,
And the silken girls bringing sherbet.   10
Then the camel men cursing and grumbling
And running away, and wanting their liquor and women,
And the night-fires going out, and the lack of shelters,
And the cities hostile and the towns unfriendly
And the villages dirty and charging high prices: 15
A hard time we had of it.
At the end we preferred to travel all night,
Sleeping in snatches,
With the voices singing in our ears, saying
That this was all folly.   20

Then at dawn we came down to a temperate valley,
Wet, below the snow line, smelling of vegetation,
With a running stream and a water-mill beating the dark-
ness,
And three trees on the low sky.   25
And an old white horse galloped away in the meadow.
Then we came to a tavern with vine-leaves over the lintel,
Six hands at an open door dicing for pieces of silver,
And feet kicking the empty wine-skins.
But there was no information, and so we continued   30
And arrived at evening, not a moment too soon
Finding the place; it was (you may say) satisfactory.

All this was a long time ago, I remember,
And I would do it again, but set down
This set down   35
This: were we led all that way for
Birth or Death? There was a Birth, certainly,

We had evidence and no doubt. I had seen birth and death,
But had thought they were different; this Birth was
Hard and bitter agony for us, like Death, our death.   40
We returned to our places, these Kingdoms,
But no longer at ease here, in the old dispensation,
With an alien people clutching their gods.
I should be glad of another death.

Notes

Magus: singular of Magi, the three wise men who brought gifts to the Infant Jesus

[1–5] **A cold … of winter:** taken from the 1622 Christmas Day sermon of Bishop Launcelot
Andrewes

[42] **the old dispensation:** life pre-Christ

 # Explorations

Before reading

1. The Magi are the Three Wise Men or Kings who visited the Infant Jesus at his birth in Bethlehem. Knowing this, what does the title of the poem lead you to expect?

First reading

2. Were any of your expectations met on reading the poem?

Second reading

3. The poem is the monologue of an old man reviewing the past. With what did he and the others have to struggle in making this journey? What forsaken luxuries did they still yearn for? Where does it suggest that they had deep doubts about their desire to witness a Birth?

4. At the end of the second section of the poem, the Magi arrive at Christ's birthplace after some fruitless searching. Could the imagery at the beginning of this section symbolise a birth or a new beginning? These are followed by symbols surrounding Christ's death. Can you identify these?

5. In the last book of the Bible, Revelations 19: 11, Christ is seen riding a white horse in glory. Is there anything

glorious about the image of the white horse here?

6. Would you agree that the last line of the second section is something of an anticlimax? Why is there no sense of awe or celebration?

7. In the final section the magus philosophically reflects on the significance of what he had seen. Birth (capitalised) is the birth of Christ which also brought a Death. What is this Death? – Christ's Death or the Death of an old way of life, or both? Is this why the Magi were no longer at ease in their own Kingdoms? Why should the magus be glad of another death?

Third reading

8. Eliot's theme is that death is the way to rebirth. Is this a paradox? Examine how the cycle of birth and death are suggested throughout the poem.

9. The poem can also be seen as representing Eliot's own spiritual journey from agnosticism to faith. He wrote it at the time of his baptism into the Anglican Church in 1927. Does the poem suggest a readiness to believe, an assertion of belief or indeed a sense of being conditioned by fate as much as faith?

10. How would you describe the tone of this poem?

Usk (extract from Landscapes III)

Do not suddenly break the branch, or
Hope to find
The white hart behind the white well.
Glance aside, not for lance, do not spell
Old enchantments. Let them sleep.   5
'Gently dip, but not too deep',
Lift your eyes
Where the roads dip and where the roads rise
Seek only there
Where the grey light meets the green air   10
The hermit's chapel, the pilgrim's prayer.

Usk: an area in Wales, about nine miles north of Newport

[3] **hart:** a male deer or stag

[6] **Gently dip, but not too deep:** from a song by George Peele (1558–96) – appropriate because of the song's suggestion of folk rituals

[11] **hermit:** one who chooses to live a life of isolation and prayer

[11] **pilgrim:** one who goes on a spiritual journey

 # Explorations

First reading

1. From a set of poems called *Landscapes*, Eliot wrote this following a holiday in Wales in 1935. In it, the poet evokes some images of the past. What are these images? To what period do they refer?

2. There is also a sense of movement in the poem. What images give the poem that sense?

Second reading

3. The first line exhorts the viewer not to break the peace of the scene, yet the next few lines forbid him to dwell on resurrecting the past. Is this a contradiction? Would you agree that the quoted line (line 6) shows the poet's true intention toward the past?

4. The last five lines suggest a more active journey. Towards what will it lead? What kind of journey is this for the poet?

5. 'Where the grey light meets the green air'. Examine this line. Could this symbolize a moment of clarification for the poet? What do the colours mean to you?

Third reading

6. Is there a sense of transition in this poem?

7. Comment on the use of colour in the poem. Does it help to enliven the atmosphere or indeed the sense of poet as painter?

8. Examine the lyrical qualities of the poem. How do they contribute to the energy which surrounds this poem?

9. Compare and contrast this poem with 'Rannoch, by Glencoe'.

Rannoch, by Glencoe (extract from Landscapes IV)

Here the crow starves, here the patient stag
Breeds for the rifle. Between the soft moor
And the soft sky, scarcely room
To leap or soar. Substance crumbles, in the thin air
Moon cold or moon hot. The road winds in   5
Listlessness of ancient war,
Languor of broken steel,
Clamour of confused wrong, apt
In silence. Memory is strong
Beyond the bone. Pride snapped,   10
Shadow of pride is long, in the long pass
No concurrence of bone.

Note

Rannoch, by Glencoe: An area of the Scottish Highlands south of Fort William. This poem, like 'Usk', is from a set of poems called *Landscapes*.

Through Glencoe: painting by Louis B. Hurt (1856–1929)

Explorations

Before reading

1. What are your visions of the Scottish Highlands? What do they symbolise for you?

First reading

2. Were your views confirmed by this poem?
3. List the images of violence and death you see here. Are these images from the past or the present?
4. What sounds does the poet evoke?

Second reading

5. In the first few lines of the poem, how does Eliot suggest a sense of barrenness and oppressiveness?
6. The road appears to wander with no purpose. What words in particular evoke this lack of energy? Is the poet suggesting that a depressing sense of history is causing it? Compare the road here to that in 'Usk'.
7. The memory of past rivalries and wrongs are strong in this landscape. What is the poet's attitude to these? Is he suggesting that pride is that which keeps old rivalries from being resolved? Is this what he also means by 'no concurrence of bone'?

Third reading

8. Examine how Eliot creates a feeling of place in this poem. Would you agree that he creates a landscape which, paradoxically, is both austere and rich? How does he do this? What other paradoxes do you see in the poem?
9. We get little, if any, sense of the poet's presence in the poem. Why does he have this sense of detachment, do you think?
10. Discuss the feelings of constriction evident here. Examine where else in Eliot's poetry such feelings exist.
11. Would you consider this to be a lyrical poem?
12. Discuss this poem and 'Usk' under the heading 'Life and Death'.

East Coker IV (extract from The Four Quartets)

The wounded surgeon plies the steel
That questions the distempered part;
Beneath the bleeding hands we feel
The sharp compassion of the healer's art
Resolving the enigma of the fever chart.   5

Our only health is the disease
If we obey the dying nurse
Whose constant care is not to please
But to remind of our, and Adam's curse,
And that, to be restored, our sickness must grow worse.   10

The whole earth is our hospital
Endowed by the ruined millionaire,
Wherein, if we do well, we shall
Die of the absolute paternal care
That will not leave us, but prevents us everywhere.   15

The chill ascends from feet to knees,
The fever sings in mental wires.
If to be warmed, then I must freeze
And quake in frigid purgatorial fires
Of which the flame is roses, and the smoke is briars.   20

The dripping blood our only drink,
The bloody flesh our only food:
In spite of which we like to think
That we are sound, substantial flesh and blood –
Again, in spite of that, we call this Friday good.   25

Background note

'East Coker', from which this poem is taken, is in turn one of The Four Quartets written between 1935 and 1942. The main theme of 'East Coker' is that true wisdom is humility and that at a certain stage in its spiritual progress, the soul must put itself in the hands of God and die in order to be reborn. This is best exemplified by Jesus's death on the Cross. This theme of death and rebirth is also seen in 'The Journey of the Magi' and 'Usk'. In order to achieve one's rebirth, or full spiritual potential, one must first endure the 'Dark Night of the Soul', a time of emptiness and suffering but also of heightened awareness, so called by St John of the Cross, to whom Eliot is indebted.

Notes

East Coker: A village near Yeovil in Somerset, England, from which Eliot's direct ancestor, Andrew Eliot, left for the New World around 1699. T.S. Eliot's ashes were buried there after his death in 1965.

[1] **steel:** the surgeon's scalpel, similar to the 'dart of love' described by St John of the Cross in the 'Living Flame of Love'

[15] **prevents:** used here in the seventeeth-century sense of to go before with spiritual guidance or to predispose to repentance

[19] **purgatorial fires:** Purgatory is a temporary state or place where the soul is purified by punishment.

 # Explorations

First reading

1. Have you ever wondered why we call Good Friday 'good', when on that day Jesus was tortured horribly and killed? Is this a paradox? Think about this for a while.

2. The poem is full of paradoxes. List these. Do they help us to understand the notion of 'necessary evil', a perhaps temporary evil which will be to our ultimate good?

Second reading

3. The 'wounded surgeon' in the first stanza is Jesus. To what extent is He being compared to a physical surgeon? Why is His compassion 'sharp'? Why is the fever chart described as an 'enigma'?

4. The image of a hospital is continued in the second stanza, where the nurse is the church. In what sense is she dying? What is her role? What was

the curse put on Adam as he left the Garden of Eden?

5. The 'ruined millionaire' of the third stanza is Adam. Why is he called this? What was his legacy to the world? What is the desired outcome of doing well in this 'hospital'? If God is the provider of 'paternal care' what is His role?

6. The fourth stanza suggests a process of purgation. Is this the 'Dark Night of the Soul', i.e. a period of black despair before Life is rediscovered? How complete is this process? Is there any sense in which this purgation leads to healing?

7. The fifth stanza refers to both the Crucifixion and the Eucharist. In what ways is the imagery linked to the idea that suffering is the basis of our cure, seen throughout the poem? Is this why we call Good Friday good?

Third reading

8. Look again at Question 2 above and your list of paradoxes. Would you agree that physical suffering can lead to a spiritual good?

9. Examine the lyrical qualities of the poem. To what extent do these aid the devotional tone of the poem?

10. Would you consider this to be an emotional or intellectual poem?

11. The style of this poem reflects the style of seventeeth-century metaphysical poetry, such as that of Donne, Herbert or Marvell. Research the features of this style of poetry and indicate to what extent Eliot is using such a style here.

Crucifixion: painting by Diego Velásquez (1599–1660)

6 *Patrick* KAVANAGH

prescribed for Higher Level exams in 2007 and 2010

Patrick Kavanagh was born on 21 October 1904. He was the fourth child and the eldest son of James and Bridget (née Quinn) born in the townland of Mucker, Inniskeen parish, Co. Monaghan. From the age of twelve Kavanagh started writing verse and collected it in a copybook. His brother Peter later published this juvenilia in his *Collected Poems*. Kavanagh was keen to use the things around him in his poems no matter how mundane they may seem to others. Regular trips to Dundalk brought him into contact with literature, especially with the literary journals of the time such as *Poetry* and *The Irish Statesman*. He entered the joint trades of cobbler and small farmer like his father before him, but also began to see himself as someone different from the regular farmers. He now began to see himself as a poet.

His first volume of poetry *Ploughman and Other Poems* was published in 1936. It contained many of the ideas that would remain central to his poetry for the rest of his life. His poetry in this book examined not only his surrounding area but also poetry itself, *the nature of the poet and the creative act*. In 1939, Kavanagh made a major change to his life by giving up farming and decided to concentrate

1904–1967

on writing as a career, moving to live in Dublin in the process. He wrote a number of regular columns as well as book and film reviews at the time. As well as his poetry he also produced a novel, *Tarry Flynn*. He also ventured into publishing a newspaper called *Kavanagh's Weekly* in 1952. Its stated purpose 'was to introduce the critical constructive note into Irish thought'. Kavanagh put every aspect of Irish life under scrutiny. It was either loved or hated at the time. Kavanagh himself was put under scrutiny later that year. An article in *The Leader* criticised his work. He sued *The Leader* for libel but lost. Soon after this period, he entered the Rialto hospital with lung cancer. Against great odds, he made a heroic recovery and spent the summer of 1955 regaining his strength on the banks of the Grand Canal in Dublin. He described this period as his 'rebirth'. Kavanagh's health began to decline again in the late 1950s. He returned to journalism. On 19 April 1967 he married Katherine Moloney, whom he had known for a number of years;. on 30 November in that year he died at the age of sixty-three.

Inniskeen Road: July Evening

The bicycles go by in twos and threes –
There's a dance in Billy Brennan's barn tonight,
And there's the half-talk code of mysteries
And the wink-and-elbow language of delight.
Half-past eight and there is not a spot   5
Upon a mile of road, no shadow thrown
That might turn out a man or woman, not
A footfall tapping secrecies of stone.

I have what every poet hates in spite
Of all the solemn talk of contemplation.   10
Oh, Alexander Selkirk knew the plight
Of being king and government and nation.
A road, a mile of kingdom, I am king
Of banks and stones and every blooming thing.

Note   [11] **Alexander Selkirk:** A Scottish sailor who was
abandoned on an uninhabited island. Daniel
Defoe's *Robinson Crusoe* was based on his life.

Billy Brennan's barn, Inniskeen, Co. Monaghan

Explorations

First reading

1. What does the 'wink-and-elbow language of delight' mean? Do you think this is an appropriate phrase? Why?
2. Write a dialogue between some of the inhabitants of Billy Brennan's barn.
3. The poet names specific places and people in the poem. What effect does this have?
4. Who was Alexander Selkirk? Why does the poet compare himself to him?
5. Do you think that Kavanagh would forgo being a poet in order to fit in with the crowd? Discuss this.

Second reading

6. The poet uses a good deal of alliteration in the first quatrain. What is the effect of this?
7. Do you see any changes in the language used in the three sections? Would you agree that there are different voices in the poem? Who is the focus of each section?
8. The word 'blooming' has two meanings in the poem. What are they?

Third reading

9. Compare the rhythm of the first quatrain with that of the second. Do you see any major changes? What effect does this have on the development of the poem?
10. Compare the rhythm of the first quatrain with that of the second. Do you see any major changes? How do the vowel sounds contribute to this?
11. Trace the development of thought in the poem over the first and second quatrains and the sestet.

Fourth reading

12. Imagine that the last line of this poem had never been written. How would it change your reading of the whole poem?
13. What is your image of the typical poet? Does Kavanagh, in this poem, fit this?
14. Would you agree with the assertion that 'Kavanagh is a whingeing self-pitying introvert who wants to have his cake and eat it'?

Epic

I have lived in important places, times
When great events were decided: who owned
That half a rood of rock, a no-man's land
Surrounded by our pitchfork-armed claims.
I heard the Duffys shouting 'Damn your soul'   5
And old McCabe stripped to the waist, seen
Step the plot defying blue cast-steel –
'Here is the march along these iron stones'
That was the year of the Munich bother. Which
Was most important? I inclined   10
To lose my faith in Ballyrush and Gortin
Till Homer's ghost came whispering to my mind
He said: I made the *Iliad* from such
A local row. Gods make their own importance.

Notes

[8] **march:** boundary

[9] **Munich bother:** 1939

[11] **Ballyrush and Gortin:** townlands in Co. Monaghan

[12] **Homer:** a Greek poet

[13] **Iliad:** an 'epic' poem by Homer

Patrick Kavanagh

Explorations

Before reading

1. Think about the title. What is an epic? What might you expect the poem to deal with?

First reading

2. What is the argument about? Does it seem important to you? Can you see how it could be important to others?
3. Do the people who are arguing seem to be reasonable? Describe what you imagine them to look like. Write a dialogue that either side might have among themselves.
4. Write a newspaper report on the argument.
5. What does Kavanagh mean by the 'Munich bother'? What does his attitude toward it seem to be?
6. What is his attitude towards the people of the village?

Second reading

7. The first line sounds very portentous. Do you think it is effective?
8. Examine the 'war' imagery that he uses. What does it suggest to you? Write about this.
9. The narrator changes his mind halfway through the poem. What do you notice about this change?

Third reading

10. Comment on the poet's use of irony.

Fourth reading

11. Do you think that the last line summarises the whole poem? In your own words, write about the theme.
12. In an epic poem there is often a hero. Is there one in this poem? Discuss this.

Shancoduff

this poem is also prescribed for Ordinary Level exams in 2007 and 2010

My black hills have never seen the sun rising,
Eternally they look north towards Armagh.
Lot's wife would not be salt if she had been
Incurious as my black hills that are happy
When dawn whitens Glassdrummond chapel.   5

My hills hoard the bright shillings of March
While the sun searches in every pocket.
They are my Alps and I have climbed the Matterhorn
With a sheaf of hay for three perishing calves
In the field under the Big Forth of Rocksavage.   10

The sleety winds fondle the rushy beards of Shancoduff
While the cattle-drovers sheltering in the Featherna Bush
Look up and say: 'Who owns them hungry hills
That the water-hen and snipe must have forsaken?
A poet? Then by heavens he must be poor.'   15
I hear and is my heart not badly shaken?

Notes

[10] **Rocksavage:**
[11] **Shancoduff:**   ⎤ places in County Monaghan near the poet's father's farm
[12] **Featherna Bush:** ⎦

Explorations

First reading

1. The title of the poem is taken from the name of the place where Kavanagh's family had a farm. It is derived from two Irish words; 'Sean' and 'Dubh'. Do you know what these words mean? If not, find out. What sort of a place would you expect from such a name?

Second reading

2. How does Kavanagh describe this place? Draw a picture or describe the scene in your own words as you imagine it.
3. What is the cattle-drover's attitude to the hills?
4. What is the poet's reaction to this?

Third reading

5. He personifies the place. How does he do this? What effect does it have?
6. He names a lot of specific places in the poem e.g. Glassdrummond, Featherna, Rocksavage. Why does he do this?
7. He repeatedly uses the possessive 'my' when talking about the hills. What does it tell us about the narrator?
8. Do you think the cattle drovers place any value on poetry? Examine their words carefully.

Fourth reading

9. In an earlier version of the poem, Kavanagh used the word 'faith' instead of the word 'heart' in the last line of the poem. Why do you think he made that change? What effect does it have? Do you think that it was a good change to make?
10. In another poem Kavanagh says that 'Naming a thing is the love act and the pledge'. Relate that statement to 'Shancoduff'.
11. 'Shancoduff is a love poem.' Do you agree?

The Great Hunger

I

Clay is the word and clay is the flesh
Where the potato-gatherers like mechanized scare-crows
    move
Along the side-fall of the hill – Maguire and his men.
If we watch them an hour is there anything we can
    prove
Of life as it is broken-backed over the Book   5
Of Death? Here crows gabble over worms and frogs
And the gulls like old newspapers are blown clear of the
    hedges, luckily.
Is there some light of imagination in these wet clods?
Or why do we stand here shivering?
                       Which of these men   10
Loved the light and the queen
Too long virgin? Yesterday was summer. Who was it
    promised marriage to himself
Before apples were hung from the ceilings for Hallowe'en?
We will wait and watch the tragedy to the last curtain
Till the last soul passively like a bag of wet clay   15
Rolls down the side of the hill, diverted by the angles
Where the plough missed or a spade stands, straitening
    the way.

A dog lying on a torn jacket under a heeled-up cart,
A horse nosing along the posied headland, trailing
A rusty plough. Three heads hanging between wide-
    apart   20
Legs. October playing a symphony on a slack wire paling.
Maguire watches the drills flattened out
And the flints that lit a candle for him on a June altar
Flameless. The drills slipped by and the days slipped by
And he trembled his head away and ran free from the
    world's halter,   25
And thought himself wiser than any man in the townland
When he laughed over pints of porter
Of how he came free from every net spread
In the gaps of experience. He shook a knowing head
And pretended to his soul   30

That children are tedious in hurrying fields of April
Where men are spanging across wide furrows.
Lost in the passion that never needs a wife –
The pricks that pricked were the pointed pins of harrows.
Children scream so loud that the crows could bring   35
The seed of an acre away with crow-rude jeers.
Patrick Maguire, he called his dog and he flung a stone in
       the air
And hallooed the birds away that were the birds of the years.
Turn over the weedy clods and tease out the tangled skeins.
What is he looking for there?   40
He thinks it is a potato, but we know better
Than his mud-gloved fingers probe in this insensitive hair.

'Move forward the basket and balance it steady
In this hollow. Pull down the shafts of that cart, Joe,
And straddle the horse,' Maguire calls.   45
'The wind's over Brannagan's, now that means rain.
Graip up some withered stalks and see that no potato falls
Over the tail-board going down the ruckety pass –
And *that's* a job we'll have to do in December,
Gravel it and build a kerb on the bog-side. Is that
       Cassidy's ass   50
Out in my clover? Curse o' God –
Where is that dog?
Never where he's wanted.' Maguire grunts and spits
Through a clay-wattled moustache and stares about him
       from the height.
His dream changes again like the cloud-swung wind   55
And he is not so sure now if his mother was right
When she praised the man who made a field his bride.

Watch him, watch him, that man on a hill whose spirit
Is a wet sack flapping about the knees of time.
He lives that his little fields may stay fertile when his
       own body   60

Notes
[32] **spanging:** long fast steps
[34] **harrows:** spiked frame for smoothing land

Is spread in the bottom of a ditch under two coulters
        crossed in Christ's Name.

He was suspicious in his youth as a rat near strange bread
When girls laughed; when they screamed he knew that
        meant
The cry of fillies in season. He could not walk
The easy road to his destiny. He dreamt   65
The innocence of young brambles to hooked treachery.

O the grip, O the grip of irregular fields! No man escapes.
It could not be that back of the hills love was free
And ditches straight.
No monster hand lifted up children and put down apes   70
As here
                        'O God if I had been wiser!'
That was his sigh like the brown breeze in the thistles.
He looks towards his house and haggard. 'O God if I
        had been wiser!'
But now a crumpled leaf from the whitethorn bushes   75
Darts like a frightened robin, and the fence
Shows the green of after-grass through a little window,
And he knows that his own heart is calling his mother a liar.
God's truth is life – even the grotesque shapes of its
        foulest fire.

The horse lifts its head and crashes   80
Through the whins and stones
To lip late passion in the crawling clover.
In the gap there's a bush weighted with boulders like
        morality,
The fools of life bleed if they climb over.

The wind leans from Brady's, and the coltsfoot leaves
        are holed with rust,   85
Rain fills the cart-tracks and the sole-plate grooves;
A yellow sun reflects in Donaghmoyne
The poignant light in light in puddles shaped by hooves.

Notes   [61] **coulter:** the iron cutter at the front of a ploughshare
[87] **Donaghmoyne:** a townland in Co. Monaghan

Come with me, Imagination, into this iron house
And we will watch from the doorway the years run
    back,   90
And we will know that a peasant's left hand wrote on
    the page.
Be easy, October. No cackle hen, horse neigh, tree sough,
    duck quack.

Explorations

Before reading

1. What do you think of the title of the poem? Comment on the poet's use of the word 'Great'.

First reading

2. From reading the poem, how do you visualise Patrick Maguire? What age do you think he might be? What do you think he looks like? How does he live, etc.?
3. Write a diary for one day in the life of Patrick Maguire.
4. The poem describes a man and his physical environment. What is the relationship between the two? Describe his environment in your own words.
5. Can you find any indications in the poem of Maguire's attitude to women?
6. Maguire complains about children in the poem. Do you think that this represents his complete attitude toward children?
7. To what extent does Maguire attempt justification for his current position?

Second reading

8. What do you think of the poem's narrator? Is he sympathetic? Is he biased? Is he patronising, etc.?
9. In the fourth verse of the poem, Maguire speaks. Compare the impression that we get of him here with the impression we get from the narrator.
10. 'There is a difference between the life lived and the life wished for.' Do you think that this statement is true for Patrick Maguire? How is this conveyed to us?

Third reading

11. Late autumn is mentioned a number of times throughout the poem. What do you think is the significance of this image?
12. There are religious metaphors used in the poem – explain what each one refers to. What is their overall effect?
13. At the beginning of the poem, the sounds of the words are very harsh. Comment on some of the sounds and words used to give this harsh tone.

Fourth reading

14. Do you think that the poem as a whole could be an allegory for 1930s and 1940s Ireland? Explain your answer.
15. If a similar poem was being written about contemporary Ireland, do you think its concerns would be the same? What would its concerns be? What type of imagery would it use?
16. Do you think that the phrase 'God's truth is life' could be an apt summary of the whole poem?
17. Kavanagh paints a portrait of Patrick Maguire. It has been said that he does not paint a still life but rather uses a 'cinematic technique'. Using examples from the poem, explain what you think is meant by this.

Fifth reading

18. This is part one of a longer poem. Where do you think the poem will go from here?

A Christmas Childhood

this poem is also prescribed for Ordinary Level exams in 2007 and 2010

I

One side of the potato-pits was white with frost –
How wonderful that was, how wonderful!
And when we put our ears to the paling-post
The music that came out was magical.

The light between the ricks of hay and straw   5
Was a hole in Heaven's gable. An apple tree
With its December-glinting fruit we saw –
O you, Eve, were the world that tempted me

To eat the knowledge that grew in clay
And death the germ within it! Now and then   10
I can remember something of the gay
Garden that was childhood's. Again

The tracks of cattle to a drinking-place,
A green stone lying sideways in a ditch
Or any common sight the transfigured face   15
Of a beauty that the world did not touch.

II

My father played the melodion
Outside at our gate;
There were stars in the morning east
And they danced to his music.   20

Across the wild bogs his melodion called
To Lennons and Callans.
As I pulled on my trousers in a hurry
I knew some strange thing had happened.

Outside in the cow-house my mother   25
Made the music of milking;
The light of her stable-lamp was a star
And the frost of Bethlehem made it twinkle.

A water-hen screeched in the bog,
Mass-going feet   30
Crunched the wafer-ice on the pot-holes,
Somebody wistfully twisted the bellows wheel.

My child poet picked out the letters
On the grey stone,
In silver the wonder of a Christmas townland,   35
The winking glitter of a frosty dawn.

Cassiopeia was over
Cassidy's hanging hill,
I looked and three whin bushes rode across
The horizon – the Three Wise Kings.   40

An old man passing said:
'Can't he make it talk' –
The melodion. I hid in the doorway
And tightened the belt of my box-pleated coat.

I nicked six nicks on the door-post   45
With my penknife's big blade –
There was a little one for cutting tobacco.
And I was six Christmases of age.

My father played the melodion,
My mother milked the cows,   50
And I had a prayer like a white rose pinned
On the Virgin Mary's blouse.

Notes

[17,21,43, 49]   **melodion:** a small accordion
[37]   **Cassiopeia:** a northern constellation

Explorations

Before reading

1. The first part of the poem is an evocation of the poet's memories of his own childhood. What are your memories of Christmas-time when you were young?

First reading

2. Do you think that the narrator had a happy childhood? What are his happiest memories?

3. What type of a child do you think he was, according to the evidence in this poem? Discuss this.

4. Why does the narrator compare his village with Bethlehem?

5. What is the relationship between the narrator and nature?

Second reading

6. Show how Kavanagh uses religious imagery throughout the poem. What effect does it have? Does the imagery change as the poem progresses?

7. What type of voice does the narrator use: an adult voice, child voice or what? Read it aloud.

8. There is awe for the innocence of the past in this poem. Where and how is this conveyed?

Third reading

9. How does Kavanagh make the ordinary seem wondrous and extraordinary?

Fourth reading

10. What is the narrator's standing in relation to everybody else in the poem?

11. What does this poem say about childhood?

Advent

We have tested and tasted too much, lover –
Through a chink too wide there comes in no wonder.
But here in this Advent-darkened room
Where the dry black bread and the sugarless tea
Of penance will charm back the luxury   5
Of a child's soul, we'll return to Doom
The knowledge we stole but could not use.

And the newness that was in every stale thing
When we looked at it as children: the spirit-shocking
Wonder in a black slanting Ulster hill   10
Or the prophetic astonishment in the tedious talking
Of an old fool will awake for us and bring
You and me to the yard gate to watch the whins
And the bog-holes, cart-tracks, old stables where Time
    begins.

O after Christmas we'll have no need to go searching   15
For the difference that sets an old phrase burning –
We'll hear it in the whispered argument of a churning
Or in the streets where the village boys are lurching.
And we'll hear it among simple decent men too
Who barrow dung in gardens under trees,   20
Wherever life pours ordinary plenty.
Won't we be rich, my love and I, and please
God we shall not ask for reason's payment,
The why of heart-breaking strangeness in dreeping
    hedges
Nor analyse God's breath in common statement.   25
We have thrown into the dust-bin the clay-minted
    wages
Or pleasure, knowledge and the conscious hour –
And Christ comes with a January flower.

Explorations

Before reading

1. What do you know about 'Advent'? Share ideas.

First reading

2. The first line would suggest that the speaker has experienced a great many of the pleasures of the world. What is the disadvantage of this, as he outlines it in the second line? Explain this in your own words.

3. What is the speaker's personal plan for Advent and what is its purpose? Explore lines 2–6. What phrase do you think best sums up his goal? Discuss these.

4. What change does the speaker hope or expect will follow from this period of penance? Read the remainder of the poem again and list the main changes.

5. What is your understanding of the effect of 'penance'? Is the speaker's understanding different? Discuss this.

6. Who do you think the lover is? What leads you to this conclusion?

Second reading

7. Comment on the religious imagery used in the poem.

8. The poem is made up of two sonnets. Is the tone in each different? How?

9. The poet talks about money throughout the poem. What is wealth to him?

Third reading

10. What does the image of a January flower represent for you?

11. Write about the other images and sounds that the poet finds exciting. Do they have anything in common?

12. What is the poet's attitude to God?

Fourth reading

13. ' 'Advent' expresses a belief that poetry depends on the poet's attitude to the world.' Do you agree?

14. Picasso said that all artists should strive to reach a state of 'childlikeness'. Based on this poem, do you think Kavanagh would agree?

15. 'This poem is really Kavanagh's manifesto for his own poetry.' Do you agree? Where is this evident?

16. The poem was originally entitled 'Renewal'. Which title do you prefer? Which is the more appropriate?

On Raglan Road

this poem is also prescribed for Ordinary Level exams in 2007 and 2010

(Air: 'The Dawning of the Day')

On Raglan Road on an autumn day I met her first and
    knew
That her dark hair would weave a snare that I might
    one day rue;
I saw the danger, yet I walked along the enchanted way,
And I said, let grief be a fallen leaf at the dawning of
    the day.

On Grafton Street in November we tripped lightly along
    the ledge   5
Of the deep ravine where can be seen the worth of
    passion's pledge,
The Queen of Hearts still making tarts and I not making
    hay –
O I loved too much and by such by such is happiness
    thrown away.

I gave her gifts of the mind I gave her the secret sign
    that's known
To the artists who have known the true gods of sound
    and stone   10
And word and tint. I did not stint for I gave her poems
    to say
With her own name there and her own dark hair like
    clouds over fields of May.

On a quiet street where old ghosts meet I see her walking
    now
Away from me so hurriedly my reason must allow
That I had wooed not as I should a creature made of
    clay –   15
When the angel woos the clay he'd lose his wings at the
    dawn of day.

Note [1] **Raglan Road:** a street off Pembroke Road in Ballsbridge, Dublin. Kavanagh lived
on Pembroke Road from 1946 to 1958. After that he lived at 19 Raglan Road.

Explorations

First reading

1. What is the relationship between the poet and the dark-haired woman? What was their relationship?
2. What is the poet's attitude to love and courtship?
3. Was there an equal relationship?
4. How does he think he scared her off? What do you think?

Second reading

5. This poem is also a popular song. Are there any elements of the poem that make this obvious?

Third reading

6. Do you think that he's telling the truth when he says that he 'loved too much'?
7. Trace the images of nature in the poem.
8. What effect does he have by putting rhymes in the middle of lines?
9. What part does time play in the poem?

Fourth reading

10. Do you think that the phrase 'it takes two to tango' ever occurred to Kavanagh?
11. Is the poet a misogynist?

'On Raglan Road on an autumn day'

The Hospital

A year ago I fell in love with the functional ward
Of a chest hospital: square cubicles in a row
Plain concrete, wash basins – an art lover's woe,
Not counting how the fellow in the next bed snored.
But nothing whatever is by love debarred,   5
The common and banal her heat can know.
The corridor led to a stairway and below
Was the inexhaustible adventure of a gravelled yard.

This is what love does to things: the Rialto Bridge,
The main gate that was bent by a heavy lorry,   10
The seat at the back of a shed that was a suntrap.
Naming these things is the love-act and its pledge;
For we must record love's mystery without claptrap,
Snatch out of time the passionate transitory.

Note

[2] **hospital:** the Rialto Hospital, Dublin

Rialto Hospital

Explorations

Before reading

1. What feelings surface when you hear the word 'Hospital'? Now what is your immediate reaction to the first line and a half?

First reading

2. What does he find beautiful about the hospital?
3. Try to sketch out where things in the poem are in relation to each other physically.
4. The poet thinks that adventure in a 'gravelled yard' could be inexhaustible. Do you agree with him?
5. What do you think the poet means in lines 5 and 6? Discuss your interpretation.

Second reading

6. The tone of the poem is dominated by broad vowel sounds. What effect does this have?

7. What effect do the sounds at the end of the poem have? Describe these sounds.

Third reading

8. According to this poem, what does love do to things?
9. How does the poet use the conventions of the sonnet to make the points that he wants to make?

Fourth reading

10. Do you think that this poem actually does 'record love's mystery without claptrap'?
11. Is Kavanagh's poetic manifesto as shown in this poem put into practice in any of his other poems? If so, where?
12. Is the poet at ease with himself? Share your views on this.

Canal Bank Walk

Leafy-with-love banks and the green water of the canal
Pouring redemption for me, that I do
The will of God, wallow in the habitual, the banal
Grow with nature again as before I grew.
The bright stick trapped, the breeze adding a third   5
Party to the couple kissing on an old seat,
And a bird gathering materials for the nest for the Word
Eloquently new and abandoned to its delirious beat.
O unworn world enrapture me, encapture me in a web
Of fabulous grass and eternal voices by a beech,   10
Feed the gaping need of my senses, give me ad lib
To pray unselfconsciously with overflowing speech
For this soul needs to be honoured with a new dress
        woven
From green and blue things and arguments that cannot
        be proven.

Note

Canal Bank Walk: the Grand Canal near Baggot St. Bridge, Dublin

Walk by the Grand Canal: oil painting by Helen Mulkerns

Explorations

First reading

1. How does he set the scene?
2. What does Kavanagh want from God?

Second reading

3. How does Kavanagh use sound to express his mood in the first quatrain?
4. What is the relationship between nature and humans in the poem?
5. How important is the image of water in the poem?
6. What tense is the poem set in? Why is this important?
7. How does he use internal rhyme to set his mood and theme?
8. Go through the images by the canal bank; the twig, the couple, etc. and show how they could relate to the poet's own state.

Third reading

9. The sestet has been described as a hymn. Explain how someone could come to this conclusion.
10. How does the narrator see himself?
11. In order to make sense the reader must often continue on from the end of one line into the next. What is the effect of these 'run-on' lines?
12. Where is God in the poem? How does the poet understand God and His place in the world?

Lines Written on a Seat on the Grand Canal, Dublin

'Erected to the Memory of Mrs Dermot O'Brien'

O commemorate me where there is water,
Canal water preferably, so stilly
Greeny at the heart of summer. Brother
Commemorate me thus beautifully
Where by a lock niagarously roars   5
The falls for those who sit in the tremendous silence
Of mid-July. No one will speak in prose
Who finds his way to these Parnassian islands.
A swan goes by head low with many apologies,
Fantastic light looks through the eyes of bridges –   10
And look! a barge comes bringing from Athy
And other far-flung towns mythologies.
O commemorate me with no hero-courageous
Tomb – just a canal-bank seat for the passer-by.

Notes

[8] **Parnassian:** of Parnassus; a mountain in Greece sacred to Apollo and the muses

[11] **Athy:** a town in the Midlands

Patrick Kavanagh's Memorial Seat, Grand Canal, Dublin

Explorations

First reading

1. Where exactly is this poem situated? What kind of place do you think it is, from what we are shown in the poem? What makes it so attractive?

2. What mood is the poet in? What words or phrases suggest this?

Second reading

3. There is both movement and stillness in the poem. How does the poet reconcile these?

4. Do you think that Kavanagh is very much aware of his own mortality in this poem? Discuss this.

5. Why does he not want a tomb?

6. What does his preferred form of commemoration suggest about the poet?

Third reading

7. Where does the poet use alliteration and what is its effect?

8. Explore his use of hyperbole. What atmosphere does it help to create in this poem?

9. In the first quatrain he uses 'y' sounds frequently. What do you think is the effect of this?

10. Kavanagh tends to use half-rhymes rather than full rhymes in this poem. Examine these and say what you think is the effect of this technique.

Fourth reading

11. In the poem how does Kavanagh see the place and function of the poet?

12. Do poets deserve commemoration? Does Kavanagh?

7 Elizabeth BISHOP

prescribed for Higher Level exams in 2007 and 2009

Elizabeth Bishop was born on 8 February 1911 in Worcester, Massachusetts. Her father died when she was eight months old. Her mother never recovered from the shock and for the next five years was in and out of mental hospitals. In 1916 she was institutionalised and separated from her daughter, whom she was never to see again – she died in 1934. Elizabeth was reared for the most part by her grandparents in Great Village, Nova Scotia. The elegy 'First Death in Nova Scotia' draws on some childhood memories. 'Sestina' too evokes the sadness of this period. Yet her recollections of her Nova Scotia childhood were essentially positive and she had great affection for her maternal grandparents, aunts and uncles in this small agricultural village.

She went to boarding-school and then attended Vassar College, a private university in New York, from 1930–34. She graduated in English literature (but also took Greek and music), always retaining a particular appreciation for Renaissance lyric poetry and for the works of Gerard Manley Hopkins. It was at Vassar that she first began to publish stories and poems in national magazines and where she met the poet Marianne Moore, who became an important influence on her career as

1911–1979

a poet and with whom she maintained a lifelong friendship and correspondence. It was also at Vassar that she formed her first lesbian relationship, and here too, on her own admission, the lifelong problem with alcohol addiction began.

In 1939 she moved to Key West, Florida, a place she had fallen in love with over the previous years. 'The Fish' reflects her enjoyment of the sport of fishing at that time. Key West became a sort of refuge and base for Bishop over the next fifteen years. In 1945 she won the

'Cabin with Porthole', a watercolour by Elizabeth Bishop

Elizabeth Bishop standing with a bicycle in Key West, Florida, c.1940

Houghton Mifflin Poetry Award. In 1946 her first book of poetry, *North and South*, was published and was well received by the critics. 'The Fish' is among its thirty poems.

The years 1945–51, when her life was centred on New York, were very unsettled. She felt under extreme pressure in a very competitive literary circle and drank heavily. 'The Bight' and 'The Prodigal' reflect this dissolute period of her life.

In 1951 she left for South America on the first stage of a writer's trip round the world. She was fascinated by Brazil and by Lota Soares, on old acquaintance with whom she began a relationship that was to last until the latter's death in 1967. 'Questions of Travel' and 'The Armadillo' reflect this period of her life. In 1970 she was appointed poet in residence at Harvard, where she taught advanced verse writing and studies in modern poetry for her first year and, later, poets and their letters. She began to do a good many public readings of her poetry to earn a living. She continued to do public readings, punctuated by spells in hospital with asthma, alcoholism and depression. She died suddenly of a brain aneurysm on 6 October 1979.

The Fish

this poem is also prescribed for Ordinary Level exams in 2007 and 2009

I caught a tremendous fish
and held him beside the boat
half out of water, with my hook
fast in a corner of his mouth.
He didn't fight.   5
He hadn't fought at all.
He hung a grunting weight,
battered and venerable
and homely. Here and there
his brown skin hung in strips   10
like ancient wallpaper,
and its pattern of darker brown
was like wallpaper:
shapes like full-blown roses
stained and lost through age.   15
He was speckled with barnacles,
fine rosettes of lime,
and infested
with tiny white sea-lice,
and underneath two or three   20
rags of green weed hung down.
While his gills were breathing in
the terrible oxygen
– the frightening gills,
fresh and crisp with blood,   25
that can cut so badly –
I thought of the coarse white flesh
packed in like feathers,
the big bones and the little bones,
the dramatic reds and blacks   30
of his shiny entrails,
and the pink swim-bladder
like a big peony.
I looked into his eyes
which were far larger than mine   35
but shallower, and yellowed,
the irises backed and packed
with tarnished tinfoil

seen through the lenses
of old scratched isinglass.   40
They shifted a little, but not
to return my stare.
– It was more like the tipping
of an object toward the light.
I admired his sullen face,   45
the mechanism of his jaw,
and then I saw
that from his lower lip
– if you could call it a lip –
grim, wet, and weaponlike,   50
hung five old pieces of fish-line,
or four and a wire leader
with the swivel still attached,
with all their five big hooks
grown firmly in his mouth.   55
A green line, frayed at the end
where he broke it, two heavier lines,
and a fine black thread
still crimped from the strain and snap
when it broke and he got away.   60
Like medals with their ribbons
frayed and wavering,
a five-haired beard of wisdom
trailing from his aching jaw.
I stared and stared   65
and victory filled up
the little rented boat,
from the pool of bilge
where oil had spread a rainbow
around the rusted engine   70
to the bailer rusted orange,
the sun-cracked thwarts,
the oarlocks on their strings,
the gunnels – until everything
was rainbow, rainbow, rainbow!   75
And I let the fish go.

Note

[40] **isinglass:** a semi-transparent form of gelatine extracted from certain fish
and used in making jellies, glue, etc.

Explorations

First reading

1. How do you visualise the fish? Think of it as a painting or a picture. What details strike you on a first reading?
2. What is your initial impression of the speaker in this poem?

Second reading

3. Consider in detail the description of the fish. Which elements of the description could be considered objective or factual? Which elements could be seen as purely subjective on the part of the poet? Which are imagined or aesthetic elements in the description?
4. Do you think the poet's re-creation of the fish is a good one? Explain your views.

Third reading

5. Explore the attitude of the speaker towards the fish, over the entire length of the poem. What changes do you notice, and where?
6. Why do you think she released the fish? Explore the text for possible reasons.
7. Do you think this is an important moment for the poet? What does she learn or discover? Where, in the text, is this suggested?
8. Is the poet excited by this experience? Where, in the text, is this suggested? Comment on the tone of the poem.

Fourth reading

9. What issues does this poem raise? Consider what the poem has to say about:
   • our relationship with the natural world
   • the nature of creativity
   • moments of insight and decision
   • other themes hinted at.
10. Do you think the imagery is effective in getting across a real understanding of the fish and an awareness of the poet's mood? Explore any two relevant images and explain how they function.
11. This is quite a dramatic poem. Explain how the dramatic effect is created. Consider such elements as the way the narrative builds to a climax; the ending; the effect of the short enjambed lines; and the speaker's interior debate.
12. What did you like about this poem?

The Bight

(On my birthday)

At low tide like this how sheer the water is.
White, crumbling ribs of marl protrude and glare
and the boats are dry, the pilings dry as matches.
Absorbing, rather than being absorbed,
the water in the bight doesn't wet anything,   5
the color of the gas flame turned as low as possible.
One can smell it turning to gas; if one were Baudelaire
one could probably hear it turning to marimba music.
The little ocher dredge at work off the end of the dock
already plays the dry perfectly off-beat claves.   10
The birds are outsize. Pelicans crash
into this peculiar gas unnecessarily hard,
it seem to me, like pickaxes,
rarely coming up with anything to show for it,
and going off with humorous elbowings.   15
Black-and-white man-of-war birds soar
on impalpable drafts
and open their tails like scissors on the curves
or tense them like wishbones, till they tremble.
The frowsy sponge boats keep coming in   20
with the obliging air of retrievers,
bristling with jackstraw gaffs and hooks
and decorated with bobbles of sponges.
There is a fence of chicken wire along the dock
where, glinting like little plowshares,   25
the blue-gray shark tails are hung up to dry
for the Chinese-restaurant trade.
Some of the little white boats are still piled up
against each other, or lie on their sides, stove in,
and not yet salvaged, if they ever will be, from the last bad storm, 30
like torn-open, unanswered letters.
The bight is littered with old correspondences.
Click. Click. Goes the dredge,
and brings up a dripping jawful of marl.
All the untidy activity continues,   35
awful but cheerful.

Notes

Bight: recess of coast, bay

[2] **marl:** soil composed of clay and lime, sometimes used as fertiliser

[3] **pilings:** heavy beams driven into the sea-bed as support for a jetty or dock

[7] **Baudelaire:** Charles-Pierre Baudelaire (1821–67), French lyric poet, author of *Les Fleurs du Mal*

[8] **marimba:** type of xylophone used in African or South American music

[9] **ocher [ochre]:** orange-brown colour

[10] **claves [clefs?]:** symbols of musical notation; there are three clefs, C, G, and F, which, when placed on a particular line of a stave of music, show the pitch of the notes

[17] **impalpable:** not easily grasped; imperceptible to touch

[20] **frowsy:** slovenly, unkempt

 # Explorations

First reading

1. Think of the poem as a painting. Describe it as you see it laid out: background, foreground, centre, left side, right side.

2. What mood is suggested by the scene? Explain.

Second reading

3. In what ways do you think it differs from a chocolate-box painting?

4. Is the reader-viewer encouraged to view the scene in a new and fresh way? Where and how does this happen? Examine the details of the descriptions. What is unusual about them?

Third reading

5. What do you think is the impact of the subtitle, 'On my birthday'? Might it be significant that she marks her birthday in this way, viewing this scene? How might she identify with the scene? From the evidence of the text, what do you think her mood is?

Fourth reading

6. Consider the style of the versification. Concentrate on such aspects as metre, rhyme or the lack of it, the organisation of sentence or sense units, etc. What does the form of the poem contribute to its effectiveness?

7. Would you consider it accurate to suggest that the poem moves along in bursts of poetic intensity, punctuated by more prosaic reflections? Discuss.

At the Fishhouses

Although it is a cold evening,
down by one of the fishhouses
an old man sits netting,
his net, in the gloaming almost invisible,
a dark purple-brown,   5
and his shuttle worn and polished.
The air smells so strong of codfish
it makes one's nose run and one's eyes water.
The five fishhouses have steeply peaked roofs
and narrow, cleated gangplanks slant up   10
to storerooms in the gables
for the wheelbarrows to be pushed up and down on.
All is silver: the heavy surface of the sea,
swelling slowly as if considering spilling over,
is opaque, but the silver of the benches,   15
the lobster pots, and masts, scattered
among the wild jagged rocks,
is of an apparent translucence
like the small old buildings with an emerald moss
growing on their shoreward walls.   20
The big fish tubs are completely lined
with layers of beautiful herring scales
and the wheelbarrows are similarly plastered
with creamy iridescent coats of mail,
with small iridescent flies crawling on them.   25
Up on the little slope behind the houses,
set in the sparse bright sprinkle of grass,
is an ancient wooden capstan,
cracked, with two long bleached handles
and some melancholy stains, like dried blood,   30
where the ironwork has rusted.
The old man accepts a Lucky Strike.
He was a friend of my grandfather.
We talk of the decline in the population
and of codfish and herring   35
while he waits for a herring boat to come in.
There are sequins on his vest and on his thumb.

He has scraped the scales, the principal beauty,
from unnumbered fish with that black old knife,
the blade of which is almost worn away.   40

Down at the water's edge, at the place
where they haul up the boats, up the long ramp
descending into the water, thin silver
tree trunks are laid horizontally
across the gray stones, down and down   45
at intervals of four or five feet.

Cold dark deep and absolutely clear,
element bearable to no mortal,
to fish and to seals ... One seal particularly
I have seen here evening after evening.   50
He was curious about me. He was interested in music;
like me a believer in total immersion,
so I used to sing him Baptist hymns.
I also sang 'A Mighty Fortress Is Our God'.
He stood up in the water and regarded me   55
steadily, moving his head a little.
Then he would disappear, then suddenly emerge
almost in the same spot, with a sort of shrug
as if it were against his better judgment.
Cold dark deep and absolutely clear,   60
the clear gray icy water ... Back, behind us,
the dignified tall firs begin.
Bluish, associating with their shadows,
a million Christmas trees stand
waiting for Christmas. The water seems suspended   65
above the rounded gray and blue-gray stones.
I have seen it over and over, the same sea, the same,
slightly, indifferently swinging above the stones,
icily free above the stones,
above the stones and then the world.   70
If you should dip your hand in,
your wrist would ache immediately,
your bones would begin to ache and your hand would burn
as if the water were a transmutation of fire
that feeds on stones and burns with a dark gray flame.   75

If you tasted it, it would first taste bitter,
then briny, then surely burn your tongue.
It is like what we imagine knowledge to be:
dark, salt, clear, moving, utterly free,
drawn from the cold hard mouth   80
of the world, derived from the rocky breasts
forever, flowing and drawn, and since
our knowledge is historical, flowing, and flown.

'Nova Scotia Landscape', a watercolour by Elizabeth Bishop

Explorations

First reading

1. On a first reading, what do you notice about the setting of the poem? List the things that make an immediate impression on you.
2. Examine in detail what is being described in the first section. What is your impression of the atmosphere of the place?
3. What do you suppose is the writer's attitude to that scene in the first section? Does she find it repulsive, or awe-inspiring, or is she completely unaffected by it? Comment, with reference to the text.
4. What aspect of the scene draws the poet's main focus of attention during the entire poem?

Second reading

5. List all the characteristics or facets of the sea alluded to, or reflected on, by the poet throughout the poem.
6. Do you think she manages to evoke effectively the mysterious power of the sea? Comment.

Third reading

7. Bishop's poetic technique involved (a) detailed description and (b) making the familiar strange or unusual so that we see it afresh. Comment on her description of the sea, under these headings.
8. How would you assess the mood of this poem? Take into consideration both the landscape and the poet.
9. The poem is written in free verse. What does this contribute to the effect of the poem? What else do you notice about the technique of this poem?

Fourth reading

10. The poem builds to a moment of insight for the poet. Where is this, and what is the insight? Describe, in as much depth as you can, what she comes to learn from the sea.
11. Outline the main issues raised by this poem.
12. Do you find any trace of the personality or feelings of the poet in this poem? Comment.

The Prodigal

The brown enormous odor he lived by
was too close, with its breathing and thick hair,
for him to judge. The floor was rotten; the sty
was plastered halfway up with glass-smooth dung.
Light-lashed, self-righteous, above moving snouts,   5
the pigs' eyes followed him, a cheerful stare –
even to the sow that always ate her young –
till, sickening, he leaned to scratch her head.
But sometimes mornings after drinking bouts
(he hid the pints behind a two-by-four),   10
the sunrise glazed the barnyard mud with red;
the burning puddles seemed to reassure.
And then he thought he almost might endure
his exile yet another year or more.

But evenings the first star came to warn.   15
The farmer whom he worked for came at dark
to shut the cows and horses in the barn
beneath their overhanging clouds of hay,
with pitchforks, faint forked lightnings, catching light,
safe and companionable as in the Ark.   20
The pigs stuck out their little feet and snored.
The lantern – like the sun, going away –
laid on the mud a pacing aureole.
Carrying a bucket along a slimy board,
he felt the bats' uncertain staggering flight,   25
his shuddering insights, beyond his control,
touching him. But it took him a long time
finally to make his mind up to go home.

Note

[23] **aureole:** a halo of light around the sun or moon

Explorations

Before reading

1. What does the title of the poem lead you to expect?

First reading

2. Were any of your expectations met on reading the poem?
3. How do you see the character in this poem?
   - What is he doing? How does he live?
   - Why is he there?
   - Does he find any satisfaction in his work?
   - What helps him endure his exile?
4. What details of the scene affected you most?

Second reading

5. Examine the final five lines. What do you think the 'shuddering insights, beyond his control' might be? Re-create his thoughts as you imagine them here.
6. Bishop appeals to a range of senses – smell, sight, sound, touch – to re-create the atmosphere of the place. Examine a sample of each type of image and discuss the effect.
7. How would you describe the atmosphere of the place? Is it one of unrelieved misery, or is there some contentment in it? Refer to the text.
8. Examine the poet's attitude to the prodigal. Do you think she is condemnatory, sympathetic, or neutral? Discuss, with reference to the text.
9. What is your own attitude to the prodigal?

Third reading

10. What are the main human issues raised by this poem?
11. Briefly express the theme of the poem.
12. Bishop's poetic technique involved really looking at the detail of her subject matter. Where do you think this works best in 'The Prodigal'?

Questions of Travel

There are too many waterfalls here; the crowded streams
hurry too rapidly down to the sea,
and the pressure of so many clouds on the mountaintops
makes them spill over the sides in soft slow-motion,
turning to waterfalls under our very eyes.   5
– For if those streaks, those mile-long, shiny, tearstains,
aren't waterfalls yet,
in a quick age or so, as ages go here,
they probably will be.
But if the streams and clouds keep travelling, travelling,   10
the mountains look like the hulls of capsized ships,
slime-hung and barnacled.

Think of the long trip home.
Should we have stayed at home and thought of here?
Where should we be today?   15
Is it right to be watching strangers in a play
in this strangest of theatres?
What childishness is it that while there's a breath of life
in our bodies, we are determined to rush
to see the sun the other way around?   20
The tiniest green hummingbird in the world?
To stare at some inexplicable old stonework,
inexplicable and impenetrable,
at any view,
instantly seen and always, always delightful?   25
Oh, must we dream our dreams
and have them, too?
And have we room
for one more folded sunset, still quite warm?

But surely it would have been a pity   30
not to have seen the trees along this road,
really exaggerated in their beauty,
not to have seen them gesturing
like noble pantomimists, robed in pink.
– Not to have had to stop for gas and heard   35
the sad, two-noted, wooden tune

of disparate wooden clogs
carelessly clacking over
a grease-stained filling-station floor.
(In another country the clogs would all be tested.   40
Each pair there would have identical pitch.)
– A pity not to have heard
the other, less primitive music of the fat brown bird
who sings above the broken gasoline pump
in a bamboo church of Jesuit baroque: 45
three towers, five silver crosses.
– Yes, a pity not to have pondered,
blurr'dly and inconclusively,
on what connection can exist for centuries
between the crudest wooden footwear   50
and, careful and finicky,
the whittled fantasies of wooden cages.
– Never to have studied history in
the weak calligraphy of songbirds' cages.
– And never to have had to listen to rain   55
so much like politicians' speeches:
two hours of unrelenting oratory
and then a sudden golden silence
in which the traveller takes a notebook, writes:

'Is it lack of imagination that makes us come   60
to imagined places, not just stay at home?
Or could Pascal have been not entirely right
about just sitting quietly in one's room?

Continent, city, country, society:
the choice is never wide and never free.   65
And here, or there ... No. Should we have stayed at home,
wherever that may be?'

Notes

[45] **baroque:** the style of art that developed in the seventeenth century after the
Renaissance, characterised by massive, complex and ornate design

[62] **Pascal:** Blaise Pascal (1623–62), French mathematician, physicist and
philosopher, author of *Pensées*, who commented: 'I have discovered that all human
evil comes from this, man's being unable to sit still in a room.'

Explorations

First reading

1. This is a travel poem with a difference. What are the elements found here that one would normally expect of a travel poem, and what elements do you find different or unusual?

2. Follow the traveller's eye. What does she notice in particular about the geography and culture of Brazil?

3. What impression of Brazilian culture do you get? Examine the references in detail.

Second reading

4. Do you think the poet feels comfortable in this place? What is her attitude to what she sees? Do you think she is just the usual tired, grumpy traveller, or what?

5. One critic has said that Bishop is essentially a poet of the domestic, because she feels estranged in the greater world. Comment on that statement, in the light of your reading of this poem.

6. What bothers her about travel? Jot down your ideas on this.

Third reading

7. List the main issues raised in this poem.

8. What do you notice about the style in which the poem is written? Comment critically on it.

'Brazilian Landscape', a watercolour by Elizabeth Bishop

The Armadillo

For Robert Lowell

This is the time of year
when almost every night
the frail, illegal fire balloons appear.
Climbing the mountain height,

rising toward a saint   5
still honored in these parts,
the paper chambers flush and fill with light
that comes and goes, like hearts.

Once up against the sky it's hard
to tell them from the stars –   10
planets, that is – the tinted ones:
Venus going down, or Mars,

or the pale green one. With a wind,
they flare and falter, wobble and toss;
but if it's still they steer between   15
the kite sticks of the Southern Cross,

receding, dwindling, solemnly
and steadily forsaking us,
or, in the downdraft from a peak,
suddenly turning dangerous.   20

Last night another big one fell.
It splattered like an egg of fire
against the cliff behind the house.
The flame ran down. We saw the pair

of owls who nest there flying up   25
and up, their whirling black-and-white
stained bright pink underneath, until
they shrieked up out of sight.

The ancient owls' nest must have burned.
Hastily, all alone,   30

Notes

[3] **fire balloons:** St John's Day (24 June) was celebrated by releasing these fire balloons in a type of local religious worship. Air currents took them up the mountainside, where they sometimes became a hazard to houses. Bishop's partner, Lota Soares, had a sprinkler system installed on the roof to counter the danger.

[16] **Southern Cross:** a constellation of stars in the Southern Hemisphere

a glistening armadillo left the scene,
rose-flecked, head down, tail down,

and then a baby rabbit jumped out,
short-eared, to our surprise.
So soft! – a handful of intangible ash   35
with fixed, ignited eyes.

Too pretty, dreamlike mimicry!
O falling fire and piercing cry
and panic, and a weak mailed fist
clenched ignorant against the sky!   40

Explorations

First reading

1. Trace the sequence of events in the poem.
2. What images strike you most forcibly?
3. What is your first impression of the location in this poem? How do you imagine it?

Second reading

4. Do you think it would be correct to say that the poet is ambivalent in her attitude to the fire balloons? Discuss.
5. Trace the development of the fire imagery throughout the poem. How does the poet link it with the natural world?
6. Where do you think the poet's sympathies lie in this poem? Explain.

Third reading

7. Examine the poet's outlook on life here. What image of the local people is presented? What view of humanity in general informs this poem? Can you discern a philosophy of life behind it? Note your impressions, however tentative. Then formulate your thoughts in a more organised way.
8. Would you say the poet is uncharacteristically emotional here? Explain your views.
9. What else do you notice about the style of this poem?

Fourth reading

10. Why do you think this might be considered an important poem?

Sestina

September rain falls on the house.
In the failing light, the old grandmother
sits in the kitchen with the child
beside the Little Marvel Stove,
reading the jokes from the almanac,   5
laughing and talking to hide her tears.

She thinks that her equinoctial tears
and the rain that beats on the roof of the house
were both foretold by the almanac,
but only known to a grandmother.   10
The iron kettle sings on the stove.
She cuts some bread and says to the child,

It's time for tea now; but the child
is watching the teakettle's small hard tears
dance like mad on the hot black stove,   15
the way the rain must dance on the house.
Tidying up, the old grandmother
hangs up the clever almanac

on its string. Birdlike, the almanac
hovers half open above the child,   20
hovers above the old grandmother
and her teacup full of dark brown tears.
She shivers and says she thinks the house
feels chilly, and puts more wood in the stove.

It was to be, says the Marvel Stove.   25
I know what I know, says the almanac.
With crayons the child draws a rigid house
and a winding pathway. Then the child
puts in a man with buttons like tears
and shows it proudly to the grandmother   30

But secretly, while the grandmother
busies herself about the stove,
the little moons fall down like tears
from between the pages of the almanac

into the flower bed the child   35
has carefully placed in the front of the house.

Time to plant tears, says the almanac.
The grandmother sings to the marvellous stove
and the child draws another inscrutable house.

 # Explorations

First reading

1. What is the prevailing atmosphere in this poem? What elements chiefly contribute to this?
2. What are the recurring elements in this poem?

Second reading

3. How do you see the grandmother?
4. How do you see the child here?
5. Is the child completely unhappy? Are there any alleviating soft elements in her life?
6. What do you think is absent from the child's picture of life?

Third reading

7. Do you understand how the poem is constructed? Explain briefly.
8. Trace the progression of the tear imagery throughout the poem, from the reference to September rain in the first stanza. How do you interpret this, in the context of the statement the poet is making about her childhood?
9. Examine the references to her drawings of the house. What do they suggest to you about the child and her environment?

Fourth reading

10. What thoughts does this poem spark off about childhood and about domestic relationships?
11. Do you think Bishop has made a successful re-creation of a child's world? Examine, in particular, the actions and the diction.
12. Would you consider this to be a sentimental poem? The term 'sentimental' can be read neutrally as 'emotional thought expressed in literature' or more negatively as 'showing emotional weakness, mawkish tenderness'. Which, if either, description applies? Discuss.

First Death in Nova Scotia

In the cold, cold parlor
my mother laid out Arthur
beneath the chromographs:
Edward, Prince of Wales,
with Princess Alexandra,   5
and King George with Queen Mary.
Below them on the table
stood a stuffed loon
shot and stuffed by Uncle
Arthur, Arthur's father.   10

Since Uncle Arthur fired
a bullet into him,
he hadn't said a word.
He kept his own counsel
on his white, frozen lake,   15
the marble-topped table.
His breast was deep and white,
cold and caressable;
his eyes were red glass,
much to be desired.   20

'Come,' said my mother,
'Come and say good-bye
to your little cousin Arthur.'
I was lifted up and given
one lily of the valley   25
to put in Arthur's hand.
Arthur's coffin was
a little frosted cake,
and the red-eyed loon eyed it
from his white, frozen lake.   30

Arthur was very small.
He was all white, like a doll
that hadn't been painted yet.
Jack Frost had started to paint him

Notes

[3] **chromograph:** printed reproduction of a colour photograph

[8] **loon:** a diver, a kind of bird, noted for its clumsy gait on land

[36] **Maple Leaf:** national emblem of Canada

[42] **ermine:** white fur with black spots, from a type of stoat, used in monarchs' robes

the way he always painted
the Maple Leaf (Forever).
He had just begun on his hair,
a few red strokes, and then
Jack Frost had dropped the brush   35
and left him white, forever.   40

The gracious royal couples
were warm in red and ermine;
their feet were well wrapped up
in the ladies' ermine trains.
They invited Arthur to be   45
the smallest page at court.
But how could Arthur go,
clutching his tiny lily,
with his eyes shut up so tight
and the roads deep in snow?   50

 # Explorations

First reading

1. First decide who is speaking. Where and when was the event depicted, and what age is the speaker?
2. What do you find unusual or confusing on a first reading?
3. If we consider the speaker to be a young child, does this help you come to grips with the poem? Reread.

Second reading

4. What is most noticeable about the scene here?
5. What is the atmosphere in the parlour?
6. How do you think the child speaker feels? Discuss.

Third reading

7. Examine the title. Why 'first death'? Discuss the many possible connotations of this.
8. Comment on the use of colour in the poem.
9. Comment on the versification.

Fourth reading

10. Do you think the poet has managed to re-create successfully the young child's experience?
11. Contrast this poem with Séamus Heaney's 'Mid-Term Break'.
12. What did you learn about Elizabeth Bishop from a reading of this poem?

Filling Station

this poem is also prescribed for Ordinary Level exams in 2007 and 2009

Notes

Oh, but it is dirty!
– this little filling station,
oil-soaked, oil-permeated
to a disturbing, over-all
black translucency.   5
Be careful with that match!

Father wears a dirty,
oil-soaked monkey suit
that cuts him under the arms,
and several quick and saucy   10
and greasy sons assist him
(it's a family filling station),
all quite thoroughly dirty.

Do they live in the station?
It has a cement porch   15
behind the pumps, and on it
a set of crushed and grease –
impregnated wickerwork;
on the wicker sofa
a dirty dog, quite comfy.   20

Some comic books provide
the only note of color –
of certain color. They lie
upon a big dim doily
draping a taboret   25
(part of the set), beside
a big hirsute begonia.

Why the extraneous plant?
Why the taboret?
Why, oh why, the doily?   30
(Embroidered in daisy stitch
with marguerites, I think,
and heavy with gray crochet.)

Notes

[24] **doily:** small ornamental table-napkin
[25] **taboret:** a type of stool
[32] **marguerites:** daisies

Somebody embroidered the doily.
Somebody waters the plant,   35
or oils it, maybe. Somebody
arranges the rows of cans
so that they softly say:
ESSO—SO—SO—SO
to high-strung automobiles.   40
Somebody loves us all.

Edward Hopper: Gas (1940) (Museum of Modern Art, New York)

Explorations

Before reading

1. Think about the title. What do you see?

First reading

2. Describe the atmosphere this poem creates for you. What details appear to you to be significant in creating this? Discuss them.

Second reading

3. Plan the shots you would use if you were making a film of this scene. Describe what you see in each shot, and explain your choice of detail.

4. Is there any progression, development of complexity, etc. in this film? How do you understand it?

5. What do the doily, the taboret and the begonia add to the atmosphere?

Third reading

6. What is it about this scene that fascinates the poet: the forecourt, the domestic details, or something else? Discuss.

7. How do you understand the 'somebody' in stanza 6?

Fourth reading

8. Do you think the poet is discovering a truth, and making a statement about life? If so, what? Discuss this.

9. Write up your own notes on the theme of the poem, the poet's philosophy of life, her poetic method, and the style and tone of the poem.

10. 'The details of Bishop's poems are always compelling but never the whole point.' Discuss, with reference to the text.

11. 'This is a poem that manages to create poignancy and wit simultaneously.' Discuss.

In the Waiting Room

In Worcester, Massachusetts,
I went with Aunt Consuelo
to keep her dentist's appointment
and sat and waited for her
in the dentist's waiting room.   5
It was winter. It got dark
early. The waiting room
was full of grown-up people,
arctics and overcoats,
lamps and magazines.   10
My aunt was inside
what seemed like a long time
and while I waited I read
the *National Geographic*
(I could read) and carefully   15
studied the photographs:
the inside of a volcano,
black, and full of ashes;
then it was spilling over
in rivulets of fire.   20
Osa and Martin Johnson
dressed in riding breeches,
laced boots, and pith helmets.
A dead man slung on a pole
– 'Long Pig', the caption said.   25
Babies with pointed heads
wound round and round with string;
black, naked women with necks
wound round and round with wire
like the necks of light bulbs.   30
Their breasts were horrifying.
I read it right straight through.
I was too shy to stop.
And then I looked at the cover:
the yellow margins, the date.   35

Suddenly, from inside,
came an *oh!* of pain
– Aunt Consuelo's voice –

Note

[21] **Osa and Martin Johnson:** American photographers and explorers; Bishop first saw the Johnsons' jungle film *Baboons* in the winter of 1935

not very loud or long.
I wasn't at all surprised;   40
even then I knew she was
a foolish, timid woman.
I might have been embarrassed,
but wasn't. What took me
completely by surprise   45
was that it was *me*:
my voice, in my mouth.
Without thinking at all
I was my foolish aunt,
I – we – were falling, falling,   50
our eyes glued to the cover
of the *National Geographic*,
February, 1918.

I said to myself: three days
and you'll be seven years old.   55
I was saying it to stop
the sensation of falling off
the round, turning world
into cold, blue-black space.
But I felt: you are an I̲,   60
you are an *Elizabeth*,
you are one of *them*.
Why should you be one, too?
I scarcely dared to look
to see what it was I was.   65
I gave a sidelong glance
– I couldn't look any higher –
at shadowy gray knees,
trousers and skirts and boots
and different pairs of hands   70
lying under the lamps.
I knew that nothing stranger
had ever happened, that nothing
stranger could ever happen.
Why should I be my aunt,   75
or me, or anyone?
What similarities –
boots, hands, the family voice

I felt in my throat, or even
the *National Geographic*   80
and those awful hanging breasts –
held us all together
or made us all just one?
How – I didn't know any
word for it – how 'unlikely' ...   85
How had I come to be here,
like them, and overhear
a cry of pain that could have
got loud and worse but hadn't?

The waiting room was bright   90
and too hot. It was sliding
beneath a big black wave,
another, and another.

Then I was back in it.
The War was on. Outside,   95
in Worcester, Massachusetts,
were night and slush and cold,
and it was still the fifth
of February, 1918.

Date of the poem

It was probably written about 1970 and was published in the *New Yorker* on 17 July 1971. It is the opening poem of her collection *Geography III*, published in 1976.

Explorations

Before reading

1. What might you expect from this title?
2. Do you remember what it was like as a child to sit in a dentist's waiting-room? Re-create such an experience. Make brief notes for yourself.

First reading

3. In the poem, what elements of the waiting-room experience are all too familiar to you?
4. Who is the speaker in this poem? Assemble as much information, factual and impressionistic, as you can.

Second reading

5. After the familiar, what is encountered by the child?
6. Which event most unnerves her? Can you suggest why she is unnerved?
7. What is the child's reaction to this experience?

Third reading

8. What is your understanding of the experience described in this poem? Comment briefly.
9. What view of woman does Bishop project in this poem?

10. Comment on the experience of childhood reflected here.

Fourth reading

11. What themes or issues are raised by this poem? Explain how the poet deals with some of the following:
    - a child's realisation of selfhood
    - the poet's uncomfortable connection with the rest of humanity
    - the variety and strangeness of the world of which one is a part
    - that we are always at risk of being ambushed by the unfamiliar, even in the security of the domestic
    - that the chief lessons of childhood are learning to deal with pain and mortality, and accepting unity in spite of difference
    - any others.
12. What is your own reaction to this poem? Structure your thoughts in the form of questions.
13. Comment on the structure of the poem (five sections) and the type of verse used.

8 *Philip* LARKIN

prescribed for Higher Level exams in 2008 and 2009

Philip Arthur Larkin was born in Coventry in 1922, the son of Eva Larkin and Sydney Larkin, the city treasurer. He attended King Henry VIII High School, where he was an avid reader and had some poems and humorous prose printed in the school magazine. In 1940 he went to study English at St John's College, Oxford. He is remembered as a shy, introverted person with a speech impediment. He was a prominent member of the Jazz Club and the English Society. As it was wartime, Larkin expected to be called up, but he failed his medical and so managed to spend a full three years at Oxford. Among his contemporaries were John Wain and Kingsley Amis.

In 1943 Larkin was awarded a first-class degree in English language and literature and the same year had three poems included in *Oxford Poetry, 1942–43*. From 1943 to 1946 he was librarian at Wellington, Shropshire, where he reorganised the library and managed to write a good deal. It was here that he first became involved in a relationship with Ruth Bowman.

Some of his poems were included in the anthology *Poetry from Oxford in Wartime*, published in 1945 by Fortune Press, which

1922–1985

also brought out Larkin's first collection, *The North Ship*, the same year. In 1946 his first novel, *Jill*, was published. In September that year he took up a position as assistant librarian at the University College of Leicester. There he met Monica Jones, a lecturer in the English Department, with whom he began a relationship that was to last, on and off, for the rest of his life.

His second novel, *A Girl in Winter*, was published in 1947. In 1948 his father died, and Larkin went back to live with his mother. He became engaged to Ruth Bowman, but the engagement was broken off in 1950. In that year Larkin went to Belfast to become the sub-librarian at Queen's University. He enjoyed living in Belfast, and he wrote a good deal.

In April 1951 Larkin had twenty of his early poems privately printed as *XX Poems*. These included 'Wedding-Wind' and 'At Grass' (both included in his later volume *The Less Deceived*). His emotional life became a bit of a tangle. He developed particular relationships with Patsy Strang and Winifred Arnott, who worked in the library.

And Monica Jones came to visit.

In 1955 his collection *The Less Deceived* was published. This included the poem 'Toads', a protest against the daily grind of work. Going for interview for the job of librarian at the University of Hull later that year, Larkin feared the board would have seen his poem as representative of his attitude to his job; but he was appointed and, with brief absences, he spent the rest of his life in this position. Here he met Maeve Brennan.

In 1964 *The Whitsun Weddings* was published, and in 1965 Larkin was awarded the Queen's Gold Medal for Poetry. *All That Jazz*, a selection of his jazz reviews, was published in 1970. He was a visiting fellow at All Souls College, Oxford, for the academic year 1970/71, and he edited *The Oxford Book of Twentieth-Century Verse* (1973).

In 1974 *High Windows* was published, and Larkin bought his first house, opposite the university, where he lived for the rest of his life. His mother died in 1977. In

1982 Monica Jones became ill, and Larkin brought her to live at his home.

Required Writing: Miscellaneous Pieces, 1955–82 was published in 1982. In 1984 Larkin refused the offer of appointment as Poet Laureate. He died on 2 December 1985.

Wedding-Wind

The wind blew all my wedding-day,
And my wedding-night was the night of the high wind;
And a stable door was banging, again and again,
That he must go and shut it, leaving me
Stupid in candlelight, hearing rain,   5
Seeing my face in the twisted candlestick,
Yet seeing nothing. When he came back
He said the horses were restless, and I was sad
That any man or beast that night should lack
The happiness I had.   10
                        Now in the day
All's ravelled under the sun by the wind's blowing.
He has gone to look at the floods, and I
Carry a chipped pail to the chicken-run,
Set it down, and stare. All is the wind   15
Hunting through clouds and forests, thrashing
My apron and the hanging cloths on the line.
Can it be borne, this bodying-forth by wind
Of joy my actions turn on, like a thread
Carrying beads? Shall I be let to sleep   20
Now this perpetual morning shares my bed?
Can even death dry up
These new delighted lakes, conclude
Our kneeling as cattle by all-generous waters?

Explorations

First reading

1. List what you notice on a first reading of this poem.
2. Who is the speaker?
3. What scene is the speaker describing (a) in the first stanza and (b) in the second stanza?

Second reading

4. How is the woman feeling in the first stanza? What words and phrases indicate her feelings? Explore in detail the nuances and changes of the speaker's mood in the first stanza.
5. What is revealed about her lifestyle in the second stanza? What unanswered questions have you about her and about her circumstances?
6. What is her mood and what are her feelings in the second stanza? How do we know? Does she always express them explicitly, or are we left to interpret her feelings through other means? Explain.
7. Do you think her mood is one of unqualified optimism? Explain.

Third reading

8. Briefly outline Larkin's view of marriage and love as you understand it from this poem.
9. Do you think he is successful at interpreting the woman's viewpoint in this poem? Explain.
10. Do you find the setting appropriate to this theme? Comment.
11. Examine the effectiveness of the imagery. Consider in particular the symbolism of storm and of floods. Explore also what the other images contribute to this poem.

At Grass

This poem is also prescribed for Ordinary Level exams in 2008 and 2009

The eye can hardly pick them out
From the cold shade they shelter in,
Till wind distresses tail and mane;
Then one crops grass, and moves about
– The other seeming to look on –   5
And stands anonymous again.

Yet fifteen years ago, perhaps
Two dozen distances sufficed
To fable them: faint afternoons
Of Cups and Stakes and Handicaps,   10
Whereby their names were artificed
To inlay faded, classic Junes –

Silks at the start: against the sky
Numbers and parasols: outside,
Squadrons of empty cars, and heat,   15
And littered grass: then the long cry
Hanging unhushed till it subside
To stop-press columns on the street.

Do memories plague their ears like flies?
They shake their heads. Dusk brims the shadows. 20
Summer by summer all stole away,
The starting-gates, the crowds and cries –
All but the unmolesting meadows.
Almanacked, their names live; they

Have slipped their names, and stand at ease,   25
Or gallop for what must be joy,
And not a fieldglass sees them home,
Or curious stop-watch prophesies:
Only the groom, and the groom's boy,
With bridles in the evening come.   30

Note

[24] **Almanacked:** listed in an almanac, or official register

A stud farm in England, c. 1950

 # Explorations

race meeting do you think are well caught in stanzas 2 and 3?

Third reading

6. It is as if this scene is viewed from a distance by the poet. Explore how the sense of distance is created in the first three stanzas. What effect has this on the tone of the poem?

7. Explore the poetic use of language in the fourth stanza. (a) What atmosphere do you think is evoked by line 2? (b) Technically, how is the sense of easeful and untraumatic departure communicated in line 3? Examine the sounds of the words. (c) What is suggested to you by 'the unmolesting meadows'? Do you find this phrase in any way startling or slightly disturbing? (d) What part does rhyme play in the creation of atmosphere? (e) Consider the phrase 'their names live; they ...' What do you think is the effect of the punctuation of that phrase and of its particular place in the stanza?

8. How would you describe the atmosphere in stanza 5? Consider the phrases 'have slipped their names' and 'not a fieldglass sees them home' in this context. What is the effect of the poet's presumption that they gallop 'for what must be joy'?

9. Examine the natural, homely, undistressing evocation of death in the last two lines. It comes not as the Grim Reaper but as the unthreatening and completely familiar 'groom' and 'groom's boy'. The long vowels of these words are soothing, and semantically they suggest care, comfort, feeding. Yet the finality of it is not disguised. The inverted word order of the final line emphasises that all activity ends in that final verb. Do you think this portrayal of death is effective and suitable in the context of the poem?

Fourth reading

10. Would you agree that the tone of this poem is unemotional and detached? How is this achieved? Consider the speaking voice (first person, third person, or what?), the sense of distance or perspective, and the effect of the style of description (a succession of brief pictures, often unconnected, like a series of untitled photographs).

11. Comment on the sources and effectiveness of the imagery.

12. What do you particularly like about this poem? Or what do you find less than satisfactory?

Church Going

Once I am sure there's nothing going on
I step inside, letting the door thud shut.
Another church: matting, seats, and stone,
And little books; sprawlings of flowers, cut
For Sunday, brownish now; some brass and stuff   5
Up at the holy end; the small neat organ;
And a tense, musty, unignorable silence,
Brewed God knows how long. Hatless, I take off
My cycle-clips in awkward reverence,

Move forward, run my hand around the font.   10
From where I stand, the roof looks almost new –
Cleaned, or restored? Someone would know: I don't.
Mounting the lectern, I peruse a few
Hectoring large-scale verses, and pronounce
'Here endeth' much more loudly than I'd meant.   15
The echoes snigger briefly. Back at the door
I sign the book, donate an Irish sixpence,
Reflect the place was not worth stopping for.

Yet stop I did: in fact I often do,
And always end much at a loss like this,   20
Wondering what to look for; wondering, too,
When churches fall completely out of use
What we shall turn them into, if we shall keep
A few cathedrals chronically on show,
Their parchment, plate and pyx in locked cases,   25

Notes

[10] **font:** ornate container, usually of marble or stone and raised on a pedestal, that holds the baptismal water

[13] **lectern:** raised podium or desk from which the reading is done in a church

[15] **'here endeth':** from the archaic phrase 'Here endeth the Lesson,' used at the end of scripture readings

[25] **parchment:** literally animal skin prepared for writing on, here used to signify all church paper, books, and records

[25] **plate:** silver and gold vessels

[25] **pyx:** a container for the consecrated Communion wafers

And let the rest rent-free to rain and sheep.
Shall we avoid them as unlucky places?

Or, after dark, will dubious women come
To make their children touch a particular stone;
Pick simples for a cancer; or on some   30
Advised night see walking a dead one?
Power of some sort or other will go on
In games, in riddles, seemingly at random;
But superstition, like belief, must die,
And what remains when disbelief has gone?   35
Grass, weedy pavement, brambles, buttress, sky,
A shape less recognisable each week,
A purpose more obscure. I wonder who
Will be the last, the very last, to seek
This place for what it was; one of the crew   40
That tap and jot and know what rood-lofts were?
Some ruin-bibber, randy for antique,
Or Christmas-addict, counting on a whiff
Of gown-and-bands and organ-pipes and myrrh?
Or will he be my representative,   45

Bored, uninformed, knowing the ghostly silt
Dispersed, yet tending to this cross of ground
Through suburb scrub because it held unspilt
So long and equably what since is found
Only in separation – marriage, and birth,   50
And death, and thoughts of these – for which was built
This special shell? For, though I've no idea
What this accoutred frowsty barn is worth,
It pleases me to stand in silence here;

---

[30] **simples:** an archaic word for herbs

[41] **tap:** perhaps to strike gently, or to bore a hole containing an internal screw thread

[41] **jot:** to write brief notes; can also mean to bump or jolt. He may be using both 'tap' and 'jot' in their meaning 'to strike gently', referring to the tapping done by experts who examine timbers in old buildings.

[41] **roof-lofts:** screened galleries separating the nave of a church from the choir

[44] **myrrh:** a perfumed gum-resin used in incense

[53] **accoutred:** richly attired

[56] **blent:** archaic form of 'blended'

A serious house on serious earth it is,   55
In whose blent air all our compulsions meet,
Are recognised, and robed as destinies.
And that much never can be obsolete,
Since someone will forever be surprising
A hunger in himself to be more serious,   60
And gravitating with it to this ground,
Which, he once heard, was proper to grow wise in,
If only that so many dead lie round.

 # Explorations

First reading
STANZAS 1 AND 2
1. This is a first-person narrative poem, so follow the incident with the speaker. See it through his eyes. Step inside the church with him. What is to be seen in the first two stanzas? List everything you notice. What picture of the church do you get? Is it in use, is it well cared for, etc.?
2. What do you notice about the speaker – dress, actions, attitude to the place? What sort of character is he? How does he see himself? What words and phrases do you think are most revealing about the character of the speaker? Explain.

Second reading
STANZAS 3, 4, AND 5
3. Is there a change of tone and attitude on the part of the speaker in stanza 3? Explain.
4. Is there a change of style or mode of telling with stanza 3? Explain what you notice.
5. In your own words, trace the speaker's thoughts through stanzas 3, 4, and 5.

STANZAS 6 AND 7
6. What value does the speaker see in the institution of the church? Why does he still find himself 'tending to this cross of ground'? Examine the speaker's thought in stanza 6.
7. 'A serious house on serious earth it is' (stanza 7). What do you think the speaker means by 'serious', in the context of this stanza and of the poem as a whole?

Third reading
8. Trace the speaker's shifting

attitudes to religion and to the church throughout this poem.

9. Can you state briefly what the poem is about?
10. What appeals to you about it?
11. Comment on Larkin's philosophy as it is revealed in this poem.

Fourth reading

12. Andrew Motion talks about the 'self-mocking, detail-collecting, conversational manner' of this poem. Examine these three aspects of Larkin's style in the poem.

An Arundel Tomb

this poem is also prescribed for Ordinary Level exams in 2008 and 2009

Side by side, their faces blurred,
The earl and countess lie in stone,
Their proper habits vaguely shown
As jointed armour, stiffened pleat,
And that faint hint of the absurd –   5
The little dogs under their feet.

Such plainness of the pre-baroque
Hardly involves the eye, until
It meets his left-hand gauntlet, still
Clasped empty in the other; and   10
One sees, with a sharp tender shock,
His hand withdrawn, holding her hand.

They would not think to lie so long.
Such faithfulness in effigy
Was just a detail friends would see: 15
A sculptor's sweet commissioned grace
Thrown off in helping to prolong
The Latin names around the base.

They would not guess how early in
Their supine stationary voyage   20
The air would change to soundless damage,
Turn the old tenantry away;
How soon succeeding eyes begin
To look, not read. Rigidly they

Persisted, linked, through lengths and breadths   25
Of time. Snow fell, undated. Light
Each summer thronged the glass. A bright
Litter of birdcalls strewed the same
Bone-riddled ground. And up the paths
The endless altered people came,   30

Washing at their identity.
Now, helpless in the hollow of

An unarmorial age, a trough
Of smoke in slow suspended skeins
Above their scrap of history,   35
Only an attitude remains:

Time has transfigured them into
Untruth. The stone fidelity
They hardly meant has come to be
Their final blazon, and to prove   40
Our almost-instinct almost true:
What will survive of us is love.

Notes

Arundel Tomb: the monument to the Earl and Countess of Arundel in Chichester Cathedral
[7] **pre-baroque:** the baroque was a style in art predominant about 1600–1720, characterised
     by massive, complex and ornate design. 'Pre-baroque' suggests a more simple design.
[40] **blazon:** coat of arms

Arundel monument, Chichester Cathedral

Explorations

Before reading

1. When did you last visit a graveyard, an old church, or a commemorative monument of any kind? Perhaps it was a famous monument like Kilmainham Jail, or just an old church. Visualise it and write brief notes on what you remember; or

2. Discuss your experiences or compose a diary extract on your visit.

First reading

3. If possible, listen to the poem read aloud. Close your eyes. What do you see in the poem? In discussion, share what you particularly noticed.

STANZAS 1 AND 2

4. What is the poet looking at? What absorbs his attention?

5. What specific details attract his attention in stanza 2? How does he feel on seeing this? What words or phrases suggest this?

6. How do you react to this detail? Do you share his attitude?

Second reading

STANZA 3

7. Examine stanza 3. If they could see it, how do you think the earl and countess would view this pose and the detail of the effigy?

8. What does the poet think was the original reason for the detail of the hands? Examine the last two lines of stanza 3.

STANZA 4

9. How is the passage of time evoked in stanza 4? Is it violent or gently insidious? Has the passage of time any social and cultural implications here? Explain.

10. Explore the connotations of 'supine stationary voyage'. What does it suggest to you?

11. If the earl and countess were aware of what has happened up to now and could somehow communicate, what would they say to a visitor to Chichester Cathedral? Choose the view of either figure.

12. Reread stanzas 1 to 4. What do you think is the underlying issue that preoccupies the poet here?

Third reading

STANZAS 5, 6, AND 7

13. What pictures or images do you notice in particular in stanza 5? What is the effect of these images?

14. Examine from 'rigidly they' to 'washing at their identity'. If

you had a camera to film this section as a sequence of shots, how would you do it? Do you think that shots of contrasting images would create an atmosphere true to the verse? Outline the sequence.

15. What words in stanza 6 best describe the predicament of the earl and countess? Explain.

16. What attitude to life and human enterprise underpins stanza 6, in your opinion?

17. Read the section 'Background' in the Critical Notes. Does this throw any light on your understanding of stanza 7? Attempt to restate the message of stanza 7 in your own words.

Fourth reading

18. Compose extracts from an imaginary diary that Larkin might have written about this event and that show how he was affected by this experience.

19. Briefly, what are the main themes or issues raised by the poem?

20. Larkin concludes with a seemingly positive statement: 'What will survive of us is love.' Is this sentiment justified by the poem as a whole? Review the evidence throughout the poem.

21. How does this poem make you feel, and how does it do that?

22. Briefly compare Larkin's treatment of the possible survival of love against the ravages of time with other poems of a similar theme.

The Whitsun Weddings

That Whitsun, I was late getting away:
 Not till about
One-twenty on the sunlit Saturday
Did my three-quarters-empty train pull out,
All windows down, all cushions hot, all sense   5
Of being in a hurry gone. We ran
Behind the backs of houses, crossed a street
Of blinding windscreens, smelt the fish-dock; thence
The river's level drifting breadth began,
Where sky and Lincolnshire and water meet.   10

All afternoon, through the tall heat that slept
 For miles inland,
A slow and stopping curve southwards we kept.
Wide farms went by, short-shadowed cattle, and
Canals with floatings of industrial froth;   15
A hothouse flashed uniquely: hedges dipped
And rose: and now and then a smell of grass
Displaced the reek of buttoned carriage-cloth
Until the next town, new and nondescript,
Approached with acres of dismantled cars.   20

At first, I didn't notice what a noise
 The weddings made
Each station that we stopped at: sun destroys
The interest of what's happening in the shade,
And down the long cool platforms whoops and skirls   25
I took for porters larking with the mails,
And went on reading. Once we started, though,
We passed them, grinning and pomaded, girls
In parodies of fashion, heels and veils,
All posed irresolutely, watching us go,   30
As if out on the end of an event
 Waving goodbye
To something that survived it. Struck, I leant
More promptly out next time, more curiously,
And saw it all again in different terms: 35
The fathers with broad belts under their suits

And seamy foreheads; mothers loud and fat,
An uncle shouting smut; and then the perms,
The nylon gloves and jewellery-substitutes,
The lemons, mauves, and olive-ochres that   40

Marked off the girls unreally from the rest.
   Yes, from cafés
And banquet-halls up yards, and bunting-dressed
Coach-party annexes, the wedding-days
Were coming to an end. All down the line   45
Fresh couples climbed aboard: the rest stood round;
The last confetti and advice were thrown,
And, as we moved, each face seemed to define
Just what it saw departing: children frowned
At something dull; fathers had never known   50

Success so huge and wholly farcical;
   The women shared
The secret like a happy funeral;
While girls, gripping their handbags tighter, stared
At a religious wounding. Free at last,   55
And loaded with the sum of all they saw,
We hurried towards London, shuffling gouts of steam.
Now fields were building-plots, and poplars cast
Long shadows over major roads, and for
Some fifty minutes, that in time would seem   60

Just long enough to settle hats and say
   I nearly died,
A dozen marriages got under way.
They watched the landscape, sitting side by side
 – An Odeon went past, a cooling tower,   65
And someone running up to bowl – and none
Thought of the others they would never meet
Or how their lives would all contain this hour.
I thought of London spread out in the sun,
Its postal districts packed like squares of wheat: 70

There we were aimed. And as we raced across
   Bright knots of rail
Past standing Pullmans, walls of blackened moss

Came close, and it was nearly done, this frail
Travelling coincidence; and what it held   75
Stood ready to be loosed with all the power
That being changed can give. We slowed again,
And as the tightened brakes took hold, there swelled
A sense of falling, like an arrow-shower
Sent out of sight, somewhere becoming rain.   80

 # Explorations

Before reading

In a television interview in 1981 Larkin explained the genesis of this poem. It had its origins in a journey from Hull to London on Whit Saturday 1955, when Larkin took:

> a very slow train that stopped at every station and I hadn't realised that, of course, this was the train that all the wedding couples would get on and go to London for their honeymoon; it was an eye-opener for me. Every part was different but the same somehow. They all looked different but they were all doing the same things and sort of feeling the same things. I suppose the train stopped at about four, five, six stations between Hull and London and there was a sense of gathering emotional momentum. Every time you stopped, fresh emotion climbed aboard. And finally, between Peterborough and London when you hurtle on, you felt the whole thing was being aimed like a bullet – at the heart of things, you know. All this fresh, open life. Incredible experience. I've never forgotten it.

[Quoted by Andrew Motion in *Philip Larkin: A Writer's Life*.]

First reading

1. Where is the speaker in this poem?
2. What is happening?
3. What images or pictures particularly catch your eye?

Second reading

4. Get on the train with the poet and observe what he sees on the journey. List the kinds of things he notices (categories rather than individual sights) and the order in which he sees them.
5. Note the sections you do not understand.
6. What mood is the speaker in at the start of the journey (stanzas 1 and 2)? What words or phrases lead you to this view?

Third reading

7. Is the poet immediately fascinated by the happenings on the station platforms? What is Larkin's initial attitude to the wedding guests? What details strike him in stanzas 3 to 6?
8. When does he make an effort to understand them, to get inside their thinking? Does his attitude change then? Explain.
9. What is his attitude to the couples? What words or phrases lead you to this conclusion?
10. What do you think is the significance of the weddings for the poet?

Fourth reading

11. From your reading of this poem, what do you conclude about Larkin's views on weddings and marriage?
12. What picture of England emerges from the poem? Examine stanzas 1, 2, 6 and 7 in particular.
13. What has a reading of this poem added to your understanding of Philip Larkin, man and poet?
14. What questions have you about this poem?

MCMXIV

Those long uneven lines
Standing as patiently
As if they were stretched outside
The Oval or Villa Park,
The crowns of hats, the sun   5
On moustached archaic faces
Grinning as if it were all
An August Bank Holiday lark;

And the shut shops, the bleached
Established names on the sunblinds,   10
The farthings and sovereigns,
And dark-clothed children at play
Called after kings and queens,
The tin advertisements
For cocoa and twist, and the pubs   15
Wide open all day;

And the countryside not caring:
The place-names all hazed over
With flowering grasses, and fields
Shadowing Domesday lines   20
Under wheat's restless silence;
The differently-dressed servants
With tiny rooms in huge houses,
The dust behind limousines;

Never such innocence, 25
Never before or since,
As changed itself to past
Without a word – the men
Leaving the gardens tidy,
The thousands of marriages   30
Lasting a little while longer:
Never such innocence again.

Notes

MCMXIV: 1914

[15] **twist:** probably a twist of tobacco, i.e. tobacco sold in a rope-shaped piece

[20] **Domesday** [pronounced 'doomsday']: The Domesday Book was the record of the great survey of the lands of England ordered by William the Conqueror in 1086; so this reference communicates an awareness of the country's history and a sense of continuity with the past.

September 1914: A band leads volunteers enlisting in the British army near Waterloo Station, London

 # Explorations

First reading

1. It might be helpful if you were to think of this poem as a picture:
   Centre and foreground: stanza 1
   Right side: stanza 2
   Left side: stanza 3
   Background: stanza 4
   Describe what you see in each part of the picture.
2. Describe the atmosphere in each part of this picture. What words or phrases suggest it?

Second reading

3. Concentrate on stanzas 1 and 4, the central line of the picture. What image of humanity comes across from these sections?
4. Jot down words or phrases that you think best describe the atmosphere in the entire picture (all four stanzas).
5. What questions could you ask about any of the events or scenes in the poem? Do you think the style of the poem encourages you to question and speculate? Explain.

Third reading

6. Examine the attitude or tone of voice of the poet during this poem. Would you describe him as a detached observer, a sympathetic viewer, cynical, nostalgic, or what? Do you think his attitude changes during the course of the poem? Explain your opinion, with reference to the text.

7. What point or points do you think the poet is making in the poem?

8. Compose a new title for the poem and justify it with reference to the body of the text.

9. Do you know any other poems dealing with a similar theme? Which poem do you prefer, and why?

10. Do you find this poem different in any way from the other Larkin poems you have read? Explain, with reference to particular lines or details of poems.

11. 'The grim reality of human suffering and the transience of all things is hidden behind a veneer of nostalgia in "MCMXIV".' Discuss this view of the poem, with suitable reference to the text.

12. 'Despite a naïve, idealistic view of humankind, Larkin shows some awareness of social problems in "MCMXIV".' Explore this opinion of the poem.

13. When asked to select two of his poems for an anthology in 1973, Larkin opted for 'MCMXIV' and 'Send No Money', saying:
    They might be taken as representative examples of the two kinds of poem I sometimes think I write: the beautiful and the true ... I think a poem usually starts off either from the feeling 'How beautiful that is' or from the feeling 'How true that is.' One of the jobs of the poem is to make the beautiful seem true and the true beautiful, but in fact the disguise can usually be penetrated.
    [James Gibson (editor), *Let the Poet Choose*.]

    (a) In what ways do you think 'MCMXIV' might be considered to exemplify the beautiful?

    (b) Do you think it makes the beautiful seem true and the true beautiful? Discuss this, with reference to the text.

Ambulances

Closed like confessionals, they thread
Loud noons of cities, giving back
None of the glances they absorb.
Light glossy grey, arms on a plaque,
They come to rest at any kerb: 5
All streets in time are visited.

Then children strewn on steps or road,
Or women coming from the shops
Past smells of different dinners, see
A wild white face that overtops   10
Red stretcher-blankets momently
As it is carried in and stowed,

And sense the solving emptiness
That lies just under all we do,
And for a second get it whole,   15
So permanent and blank and true.
The fastened doors recede. Poor soul,
They whisper at their own distress;

For borne away in deadened air
May go the sudden shut of loss   20
Round something nearly at an end,
And what cohered in it across
The years, the unique random blend
Of families and fashions, there

At last begin to loosen. Far   25
From the exchange of love to lie
Unreachable inside a room
The traffic parts to let go by
Brings closer what is left to come,
And dulls to distance all we are.   30

Explorations

First reading

1. What is happening in this poem?
2. Follow the ambulance through the streets. Describe what you see.
3. What is the reaction of the onlookers?

Second reading

4. Read the first stanza carefully. What is suggested about the ambulances? Consider in particular the connotations of each of the following phrases: 'Closed like confessionals,' 'they thread', 'giving back | None of the glances', 'come to rest', 'All streets in time are visited.'
5. Read the second stanza carefully. What do we learn about the victims? Consider the connotations of 'children strewn', 'a wild white face', 'stowed'.
6. In the third stanza the victims are frightened because they sense the answer to the question of the meaning 'That lies just under all we do.' What is the answer sensed here?
7. In the first three lines of stanza 4, what words or phrases indicate the seriousness of the situation?
8. What does the use of 'something' and 'it' suggest to you when used to describe the victim?
9. In what sense does the phrase 'begin to loosen' describe death in the poem?
10. The syntax of the last stanza is deliberately scrambled. Why do you think this might be? If you read 'a room | The traffic parts to let go by' as a metaphorical rendering of 'an ambulance', does the sense become clearer?

Third reading

11. What view of death comes from this poem? Support your opinion with reference to the text.
12. How would you describe the poet's attitude to death?
13. What view of life is intimated in this poem?
14. Explain your own response to the poem's philosophy and its view of death.

Fourth reading

15. 'The awful ordinariness of death is one of Larkin's chief preoccupations in this poem.' Discuss this statement, with reference to the text.
16. 'The poem becomes a celebration of the values of consciousness' (Andrew Motion). Examine the poem from this perspective.

The Trees

The trees are coming into leaf
Like something almost being said;
The recent buds relax and spread,
Their greenness is a kind of grief.

Is it that they are born again   5
And we grow old? No, they die too.
Their yearly trick of looking new
Is written down in rings of grain.

Yet still the unresting castles thresh
In fullgrown thickness every May.   10
Last year is dead, they seem to say,
Begin afresh, afresh, afresh.

Explorations

First reading

1. What do you notice about the trees on a first reading of this poem?
2. What phrases do you find perplexing?
3. Is it your first impression that this is a predominantly sad or a predominantly happy poem?

Second reading

4. What aspect or quality of the trees does the poet focus on throughout these verses? Explain, with reference to specific words or phrases, etc.
5. 'The trees are coming into leaf | Like something almost being said ...'
   What does this simile suggest about the process of foliation? From your own experience, do you think this is an accurate observation? Explain.
6. 'Their greenness is a kind of grief.' How could this be? Do you think the 'grief' applies to the trees or to the poet? How do you interpret the line?
7. What have the trees in common with humanity? Is this a source of comfort or of despair to the poet? Explain.
8. What is your reaction to the description of the trees as 'unresting castles'?
9. Trace the poet's mood in each of the stanzas. What words or phrases carry this mood?

Third reading

10. Explore the relationship between the poet and nature in this poem.
11. What do you think is the essential wisdom or truth of this poem?
12. Would you agree that Larkin's attitude here is one of 'grudging optimism'? Explain your views, with reference to the poem.
13. Read 'The Trees' in conjunction with 'Ambulances'. Do you find the outlook on life in both poems similar or different? Explain. Which poem, in your opinion, exhibits more of a longing for life? Explain.

The Explosion

this poem is also prescribed for Ordinary Level exams in 2008 and 2009

On the day of the explosion
Shadows pointed towards the pithead:
In the sun the slagheap slept.

Down the lane came men in pitboots
Coughing oath-edged talk and pipe-smoke,   5
Shouldering off the freshened silence.

One chased after rabbits; lost them;
Came back with a nest of lark's eggs;
Showed them; lodged them in the grasses.

So they passed in beards and moleskins,   10
Fathers, brothers, nicknames, laughter,
Through the tall gates standing open.

At noon, there came a tremor; cows
Stopped chewing for a second; sun,
Scarfed as in a heat-haze, dimmed.   15

The dead go on before us, they
Are sitting in God's house in comfort,
We shall see them face to face –

Plain as lettering in the chapels
It was said, and for a second   20
Wives saw men of the explosion

Larger than in life they managed –
Gold as on a coin, or walking
Somehow from the sun towards them,

One showing the eggs unbroken.   25

 # Explorations

First reading

1. On a first reading, what details made most impression on you?
2. What happens in the poem?

Second reading

3. What do you notice about the village? Examine all details carefully.
4. What information are we given about the miners? Explore details of dress, habit, manner, mood, philosophy, etc.

5. Are there any hints, either in the imagery or the method of narration, that a tragedy was about to happen? Examine stanzas 1 to 4 for any signs of the ominous.
6. Do you think the poet's description of the explosion is effective? Explain your thinking on this.
7. The fifth stanza marks a division between two quite different halves in this poem. How do the last ten lines differ from the first four

stanzas? How would you
describe the atmosphere in
the last ten lines? What words
or phrases contribute to this?

8. What is suggested in stanza
8? What is the effect of the
imagery in this stanza?

9. What do you think is the
effect of the last line?

Third reading

10. What does the poet want us
to feel in this poem, and how
does he achieve this?

11. What statement about life,
society and people do you
think the poet is making here?
Refer to details in the poem.

12. Is this a poem you might
remember five years from
now? Why?

Cut Grass

Cut grass lies frail:
Brief is the breath
Mown stalks exhale.
Long, long the death

It dies in the white hours   5
Of young-leafed June
With chestnut flowers,
With hedges snowlike strewn,

White lilac bowed,
Lost lanes of Queen Anne's lace,   10
And that high-builded cloud
Moving at summer's pace.

Notes

Queen Anne's lace: wild carrot, a plant sometimes used in herbal medicine
and reputed to have contraceptive properties

Explorations

Before reading

1. From your own experiences, list what you have noticed about a June day in the countryside.

First reading

2. What elements of nature's activity does the poet focus on?

3. Do you find the poet's attitude to the cut grass particularly sensitive? Explain.

4. What is suggested by the image of the 'white hours' of young-leafed June?

5. 'Lost lanes of Queen Anne's lace'. What do you see when you read this line? What atmosphere does it conjure up?

Second reading

6. What exactly is Larkin's main idea about the season, as communicated in this poem? State it briefly in your own words.

7. What part do the sounds of words play in the creation of atmosphere in the poem?

8. 'While the main focus may be on the exuberance of nature in June, we are also aware of the transience of life, the swift passage of time and the changing seasons in this poem.' Comment.

Third reading

9. Do you think this poem is effective? Explain your own reaction to it.

9 *John* MONTAGUE

prescribed for Higher level exams in 2007, 2008 and 2009

John Montague was born on 28 February 1929 into a family struggling to survive in a turbulent world.

His father James, a Catholic Nationalist, was unable to find work in the new state of Northern Ireland. So, he decided to follow his brother and other members of the Montague family to New York in an effort to provide for his family. His wife, Molly, and his two sons remained in Co. Tyrone until 1928 when they were finally able to join him in New York. The following year, John Montague was born in St Catherine's Hospital, Brooklyn: a new child for a new beginning for the Montague family.

Sadly, this new beginning was destined to fail. The times proved to be just as turbulent in America as they had been in Ireland. Some eight months after John's birth, in October 1929, the New York stock market collapsed and the Great Depression hit America. John's father lost his job and his mother became ill. The family relied on the support of John's uncle, who ran two 'speakeasies' – illegal drinking dens. When John's uncle died, any hope of a new beginning disappeared and the Montague family separated once again.

At the age of four, John left his

1929–

mother and father in Brooklyn and travelled with his two older brothers to a new life in Co. Tyrone. While his brothers went to live with his maternal grandmother, John was sent to the Garvaghey home of his father's two unmarried sisters. He would never again live with his mother, father and brothers as a family unit under one roof. His mother returned to Northern Ireland when John was seven, but did not reclaim him. Instead, she lived some eight miles away and the pair met only infrequently. His father did not come home until some years later.

John proved to be a very able student and read History and English at UCD, where he achieved a double First. He continued his studies in America and lived in France before returning to Ireland.

Resolving not to rely on poetry for his income, John Montague has worked in a variety of areas: as a journalist, a critic and a teacher at Berkeley, UCD and UCC amongst others, whilst publishing a substantial body of writing. His contribution to the world of letters has been widely recognised and he has won a number of awards.

He retired from teaching in 1988 and now divides his time between France and Ireland. He continues to work with words.

Killing the Pig

The noise.

He was pulled out, squealing,
an iron cleek sunk in the roof
of his mouth.

(Don't say they are not intelligent: 5
they know the hour has come
and they want none of it;
they dig in their little trotters,
will not go dumb or singing
to the slaughter.)   10

That high pitched final effort,
no single sound could match it –

a big plane roaring off,
a *diva* soaring towards her last note,
the brain-chilling persistence of an electric saw,   15
scrap being crushed.

Piercing & absolute,
only high heaven ignores it.

Then a full stop.
Mickey Boyle plants   20
a solid thump of the mallet
flat between the ears.

Swiftly the knife seeks the throat;
swiftly the other cleavers work
till the carcass is hung up   25
shining and eviscerated as
a surgeon's coat.

A child is given
the bladder to play with.
But the walls of the farmyard   30
still hold that scream,
are built around it.

Notes

[3] **cleek:** hook
[14] ***diva:*** a famous woman singer
[24] **cleavers:** heavy chopping tools often used by butchers
[26] **eviscerated:** intestines and bowels removed

Explorations

First reading

1. (i) What is your reaction to this poem? (ii) Do you feel that the killing of a pig is a suitable subject for a poem? Why?

2. A. *Class Discussion*: Montague begins the poem with two words 'The noise'. (i) In your own words, describe the noise. (ii) How does his use of metaphors help you to imagine the noise?

   B. *Individual Writing*: Using the points that arose in the discussion, answer the following question. How does Montague convey the noise the pig makes as he is dragged to the slaughter?

3. 'Then a full stop.' (i) Why does the 'squealing' noise stop? (ii) What sounds take its place? (iii) Which sound do you find the most disturbing? Why?

4. A. *Paired Discussion*: (i) How does Montague describe the killing of the pig? (ii) What is your reaction to the image of 'a surgeon's coat'?

   B. *Individual Writing*: Using the points that arose in the discussion, answer the following question. Do you find it easy or difficult to read lines 19–27? Give reasons for your answer.

Second reading

5. A. *Group Discussion*: (i) What are your feelings for the pig when you read the line 'they dig in their little trotters'? (ii) Does the gift of the pig's bladder to the child as a plaything tell you anything about the people's attitude to the pig's death?

   B. *Individual Writing*: Using the points that were discussed, answer the following question. How do you feel about the way that the people in the poem react to the pig's death?

6. 'But the walls of the farmyard still hold that scream are built around it.' (i) Can you explain what Montague means by these lines? (ii) Would you agree that suffering and death are indeed part of farming?

7. A. *Class Discussion*: Is this poem simply about a particular incident, the killing of a pig, or does it have a reference to life in general?

   B. *Individual Writing*: Using the points that arose in the discussion, answer the following question. What do you think the theme of this poem is?

Third reading

8. Sounds play a big part in this

The Trout

for Barrie Cooke

CD Track 2

Flat on the bank I parted
Rushes to ease my hands
In the water without a ripple
And tilt them slowly downstream
To where he lay, tendril-light,   5
In his fluid sensual dream.

Bodiless lord of creation,
I hung briefly above him
Savouring my own absence,
Senses expanding in the slow   10
Motion, the photographic calm
That grows before action.

As the curve of my hands
Swung under his body
He surged, with visible pleasure.   15
I was so preternaturally close
I could count every stipple
But still cast no shadow, until

The two palms crossed in a cage
Under the lightly pulsing gills.   20
Then (entering my own enlarged
Shape, which rode on the water)
I gripped. To this day I can
Taste his terror on my hands.

Notes

Barrie Cooke: Artist living in Ireland who uses Nature as the subject matter for many of his paintings

[5] **tendril:** a slender, leafless shoot, a fine curl of hair

[16] **preternatural:** supernatural, outside the normal range of nature

Explorations

Pre-reading

1. Have you ever sat looking into water, watching fish swimming, or tried to catch a fish? Take a moment to think about your experience, and then try writing a short passage recreating it.

First reading

2. *Group Discussion*: Compare Montague's description with your own piece. Were there any similarities or differences?

3. (i) In your own words, give a description of the fish. (ii) How does Montague want us to feel about the fish? (iii) What words or phrases does he use to make us feel this way?

4. 'Bodiless lord of creation, I hung briefly above him Savouring my own absence,' (i) What do these lines tell you about the boy's feelings? (ii) Can you suggest why he feels like this?

5. A. *Paired Discussion*: 'I gripped. To this day I can Taste his terror on my hands.' (i) How do the boy's feelings change when he catches the fish? (ii) Are you surprised by this change? B. *Individual Writing*: Using the points that arose in the discussion, answer the following question. Do you find Montague's description of the boy catching the fish realistic? Give reasons for your answer.

6. (i) Describe the mood that is conveyed in each of the four stanzas. (ii) In each case, choose one line or phrase that you feel communicates the mood.

Second reading

7. A. *Group Discussion*: (i) What senses does Montague appeal to in his descriptions in order to make the scene in this poem come alive? (ii) 'Taste his terror on my hands': can you explain what Montague is trying to suggest in this line? B. *Individual Writing*: Discuss how Montague's use of sensory images helps the reader to become involved in this poem. Use references to support your view.

8. A. *Class Discussion*: (i) The first two stanzas are really two long sentences with very little punctuation. Read these two stanzas aloud and discuss the effect that this structure has on the rhythm and tone of the reading. (ii) The third

and fourth stanzas are written in shorter sentences. Can you suggest why there is this change?

B. Individual Writing: Using the points that arose in the discussion, answer the following question. How does Montague's use of punctuation help to convey what happens in the poem?

9. How do the sounds of the words contribute to the effectiveness of the poem? You might like to include the poet's use of assonance and alliteration, vowels and consonants in your consideration.

Third reading

10. *A. Class Discussion*: In an interview with Dennis O'Driscoll, John Montague commented on the way he wrote poetry: '. . . from time to time a poem will start to arrive and I try to get it all out. The metaphor I've used for years has been fishing, trying to get the fish out on to the bank.' Do you think that fishing is a good metaphor for writing a poem? Why?

B. Individual Writing: Trace how 'The Trout' could be a metaphor for the creative process.

11. Robert Welch admires John Montague's poetry because of 'the brilliant suddenness of its responses to the touch, feel, look and shock of the actual'. Discuss this statement with regard to 'Killing the Pig' and 'The Trout'.

Barrie Cook: 'Portrait of John Montague'

The Locket

this poem is also prescribed for Ordinary Level exams in 2007 and 2009

Sing a last song
for the lady who has gone,
fertile source of guilt and pain.
The worst birth in the annals of Brooklyn,
that was my cue to come on,   5
my first claim to fame.

Naturally, she longed for a girl,
and all my infant curls of brown
couldn't excuse my double blunder
coming out, both the wrong sex,   10
and the wrong way around.
Not readily forgiven,

So you never nursed me
and when all my father's songs
couldn't sweeten the lack of money,   15
'when poverty comes through the door
love flies up the chimney',
your favourite saying,

Then you gave me away,
might never have known me,   20
if I had not cycled down
to court you like a young man,
teasingly untying your apron,
drinking by the fire, yarning

Of your wild, young days   25
which didn't last long, for you,
lovely Molly, the belle of your small town,
landed up mournful and chill
as the constant rain that lashes it
wound into your cocoon of pain.   30

Standing in that same hallway,
'Don't come again,' you say, roughly,

Notes
[24] **yarning:**
telling
stories

'I start to get fond of you, John,
and then you are up and gone';
the harsh logic of a forlorn woman   35
resigned to being alone.

And still, mysterious blessing,
I never knew, until you were gone,
that, always around your neck
you wore an oval locket   40
with an old picture in it,
of a child in Brooklyn.

Edward Hopper: 'Automat'

Explorations

Pre-reading

1. John Montague said that the song 'The Tri-coloured Ribbon' was in his mind when he wrote this poem. Listen to this song, or read the lyrics if possible.

First reading

2. *Class Discussion*: (i) How did you feel when you had finished reading this poem? (ii) Choose **two images** that you found emotionally affecting and explain how and why they touched you.

3. Examine the first three stanzas. (i) What reasons does Montague give for his mother's rejection of him when he was born? (ii) Do you feel that they were valid reasons for her behaviour, or is he simply trying to find excuses?

4. 'fertile source of guilt and pain.'
   (i) Why would Montague's mother be the source of 'guilt and pain' for him? (ii) Would you feel 'guilt and pain' if you were Montague?

Second reading

5. A. *Paired Discussion*: In the fourth stanza, Montague describes the efforts he made to form some sort of relationship with his mother. Does he use words that you would normally associate with a mother–child relationship? (ii) Is there a connection between this stanza and his use of the word 'lady' in the second line of the poem?
   B. *Individual Writing*: Using the points that arose in the discussion, answer the following question. How does Montague describe his relationship with his mother when he was older and went to visit her?

6. A. *Paired Discussion*: (i) The fifth and sixth stanzas tell us more about the poet's mother. (ii) Do you feel more sympathetic towards her having read these stanzas? Do they help you to understand her actions better, or do you feel that Montague is once again trying to excuse her?
   B. *Individual Writing*: Imagine that you are Montague's mother. Write the story in this poem in the way she might see it.

7. A. *Class Discussion*: (i) Did the final stanza surprise you? Why? (ii) Consider how the phrase 'mysterious blessing' might be interpreted.

B. Individual Writing: Using the points that arose in the discussion, answer the following question. Do you find the seventh stanza a successful conclusion to the poem? Give reasons for your opinion.

Third reading

8. Montague uses a conversational style to recount his relationship with his mother. (i) What effect does it have on the impact of the poem? (ii) Is this style as simple as it appears?

9. *A. Group Discussion*: (i) John Montague has said that he tends not to read this poem aloud to an audience because he feels that it is too private. Do you understand his feelings? (ii) Would you find it easier to write something emotional rather than to say it?

B. Class Debate: Write and present a short speech either for or against the following motion: 'Emotions are better expressed through the spoken word than through the written word.'

10. 'For a man, the death of a mother can be quite central . . . the death of the woman who gave you birth is a very deep experience.' In the light of these comments by John Montague, consider how effectively this poem expresses his 'very deep experience' of his mother's death.

11. The song 'The Tri-Coloured Ribbon' tells of a girl losing her lover in the fight for Ireland's freedom. Consider the ways in which the political situation in Ireland affected the relationship between Montague and his mother.

The Cage

this poem is also prescribed for Ordinary level exams in 2007, 2008 and 2009

My father, the least happy
man I have known. His face
retained the pallor
of those who work underground:
the lost years in Brooklyn   5
listening to a subway
shudder the earth.

But a traditional Irishman
who (released from his grille
in the Clark Street I.R.T.)   10
drank neat whiskey until
he reached the only element
he felt at home in
any longer: brute oblivion.

And yet picked himself   15
up, most mornings,
to march down the street
extending his smile
to all sides of the good,
(all-white) neighbourhood   20
belled by St Teresa's church.

When he came back
we walked together
across fields of Garvaghey
to see hawthorn on the summer   25
hedges, as though
he had never left;
a bend of the road

which still sheltered
primroses. But we   30
did not smile in
the shared complicity
of a dream, for when

weary Odysseus returns   35
Telemachus should leave.

Often as I descend
into subway or underground
I see his bald head behind
the bars of the small booth;
the mark of an old car   40
accident beating on his
ghostly forehead.

Notes

[3] **pallor:** paleness

[10] **I.R.T.:** Interborough Rapid Transit Subway Company, first subway company in New York

[34] **Odysseus:** The hero of the 'Odyssey'. Married Penelope, the cousin of Helen of Troy.
Fought bravely in the Trojan War. After many adventures, lasting some twenty years, finally
returned home to Penelope.

[35] **Telemachus:** son of Odysseus and Penelope. He was a baby when Odysseus left to fight
in the Trojan War. When Odysseus returned after twenty years he sent Telemachus into
exile, because he had been warned that he should not trust his son. Unfortunately, the
warning referred to another of Odysseus' sons, who later accidentally killed Odysseus.
Telemachus then returned and became king.

Max Ferguson: 'My Father in the Subway 11'

Explorations

First reading

1. Imagine that you are phoning someone to arrange to have John Montague's father collected at the airport. Using the details given in the poem, write a short passage outlining the description you would give to ensure that the right person is met.

2. *Paired Discussion*: (i) How did Montague's father earn his living in Brooklyn? (ii) From the descriptions in the poem, do you think he worked in a pleasant place?

3. *A. Class Discussion*: (i) What was 'the only element I he felt at home in'? (ii) Look up the words 'brute' and 'oblivion' in the dictionary. Do the meanings of these words suggest that he really 'felt at home' or found comfort there? (iii) This was a man who had been actively involved in Republican activities when he was young; how do you think he would have felt about the way his life had developed?
   B. Individual Writing: Using the points that were discussed, answer the following question. Imagine that you meet Montague's father and you ask him to talk about his life. Write a passage to express what you think he would say. You will find your work on Questions 2 and 3 helpful.

4. '. . . the good (all-white) neighbourhood belled by St. Teresa's church.' (i) What sort of a neighbourhood did Montague's father live in? (ii) Can you suggest why Montague put the words 'all-white' in brackets? You might find it helpful to think about the position of black people in America in the first half of the twentieth century.

5. From his description, do you think that Montague enjoyed the walk with his father? Use quotations from the poem to support your view

Second reading

6. *A. Paired Discussion*: (i) Images of being below and above ground fill this poem. Examine the way that Montague describes each place. (ii) What effects did each place have on his father?
   B. Individual Writing: Using the points that arose in the discussion, answer the following question. How do you feel about Montague's father when you read about his life in Brooklyn?

7. *A. Class Discussion*: (i) The

cage mentioned in the title appears twice in the poem itself. What impression do you get of this cage from these descriptions? (ii) Consider what cages are used for. For instance, do they protect or do they trap? (iii) Might there be a connection between the cage and being underground?

B. *Individual Writing*: Using the points that arose in the discussion, answer the following question. Do you think that 'The Cage' is a suitable title for this poem? Why?

Third reading

8. A. *Class Discussion*: Montague once referred to his father as 'my poor old battered father', and he ends the poem with the memory of the scar on his father's head. Is this the only type of injury that this man suffered?

B. *Presentation to the Class*: Using the points that arose in the discussion, answer the following question. Write and present a short speech on the following topic: 'In his poetry, John Montague shows us that psychological wounds can often be more damaging than physical ones.' Support your argument with quotations from relevant poems.

9. It is clear that Montague confronts some very personal issues in 'The Cage' and in 'The Locket'. (i) How does he describe his relationship with (a) his mother and (b) his relationship with his father? (ii) Consider the implications of his use of imagery based on Courtly Love when writing about (a) his mother, and (b) Classical Literature in connection with his father. (iii) Do you think Montague develops an understanding of the reasons for his parents' behaviour? Why?

10. 'Montague uses his own family situation as a metaphor for the suffering brought about by the political turmoil in Northern Ireland.' Discuss, with reference to 'The Cage' and 'The Locket'.

Windharp

CD Track 5

for Patrick Collins

The sounds of Ireland,
that restless whispering
you never get away
from, seeping out of
low bushes and grass,   5
heatherbells and fern,
wrinkling bog pools,
scraping tree branches,
light hunting cloud,
sound hounding sight,   10
a hand ceaselessly
combing and stroking
the landscape, till
the valley gleams
like the pile upon   15
a mountain pony's coat.

Notes

Windharp: an open box with strings stretched across it, played by the wind

Patrick Collins: 1910–94. Painter whose work seeks to evoke misty Celtic landscapes

[6] **heatherbells:** heather with bell-shaped flowers

[11] **ceaselessly:** without end

[15] **pile:** a velvet-like surface

Patrick Collins: 'Bird Flying in the Wood'

Explorations

Pre-reading

1. Make an audio tape of the wind and listen to it before reading this poem. (i) Write a list of the words that occur to you as you listen to the tape. (ii) What does the list reveal about your thoughts on the wind? (iii) Do you see it as a positive or negative force, a constructive or destructive energy?

First reading

2. A. *Class Discussion*: (i) What do you notice about the punctuation of this poem? (ii) Read the poem aloud, then change all the commas to full stops and read the poem aloud again. What effect did the change in punctuation have on the way that the poem was read? (iii) Can you suggest why Montague chose to punctuate his poem in this way?
   B. *Individual Writing*: Using the points that arose in the discussion, answer the following question. How does Montague use punctuation to help convey his impression of the wind?

3. A. *Paired Discussion*: (i) Given that the wind cannot be seen, how does Montague set about creating a visual 'pen picture'

of it? (ii) What aspect of the wind does he concentrate on? (iii) Pick out **two lines** that you find particularly effective.
   B. *Individual Writing*: Using the points that were discussed, answer the following question. Do you find Montague's description of the wind successful? Refer to the poem in your answer.

4. Apart from showing us the visual effects of the wind, Montague also helps us to 'hear' the wind. Examine the way that he suggests the changing speed of the wind by his use of (i) sibilant (hissing) 's'; alliteration; assonance and internal rhyme (ii) the rhythm of the lines.

5. (i) What type of words does Montague use in lines 7–12 to suggest the sensation of feeling the wind blowing? (ii) Would you say it is a pleasant or unpleasant feeling? Why?

Second reading

6. A. *Individual Writing*: 'light hunting cloud, I sound hounding sight,'.
   (i) Write a passage describing what you imagine when you read these lines. (ii) How is Montague's style of writing different from yours? (iii) Can you think of three words to describe his style?

7. A. *Group Discussion*: Montague met the American poet William Carlos Williams and the two became friends. (i) Read 'The Red Wheelbarrow' by William Carlos Williams (also in this Anthology) and discuss how both 'The Red Wheelbarrow' and 'Windharp' seek to make the ordinary more noticeable.
B. *Magazine Article*: Using the points that arose in the discussion, answer the following question. Using references from **two poems** by Montague, write an article for a literary magazine, entitled: 'John Montague's poetry makes me see my world in a new light.'

8. A. *Class Discussion*: (i) What did you think when you saw the title of this poem? (ii) How does the wind interact with a windharp? (iii) How does the wind interact with the Irish landscape? (iv) Can you suggest a connection between the two?
B. *Paired Writing*: Using the points that were discussed, answer the following question. Imagine that John Montague has just read this poem to you and tells you that he is thinking of calling it 'Windharp'. With one of you writing as Montague and one of you as yourself, write out the conversation that the two of you have – beginning with:
JM: So I was thinking that I'd call this poem 'Windharp'. What do you think?
You: Well, John, I think that . . .

Third reading

9. As always with John Montague, this poem has many layers. In your own words, explain the themes of 'Windharp'. You may find it helpful to refer back to Questions 7 and 8.

10. Montague regarded himself as a 'bewildered boy [who] had lost and refound himself in nature'. With reference to 'Killing the Pig', 'The Trout' and 'Windharp', discuss how nature helps Montague to make important discoveries that help him to understand his world.

11. *Group Discussion*: Look at the list of words that you made as you listened to the tape of the wind. (i) Having worked on the poem, do you want to change the list in any way, either by adding or deleting words, in order to more fully express your thoughts on the wind? (ii) Can you explain the reasons for your changes?

All Legendary Obstacles

CD Track 6

All legendary obstacles lay between
Us, the long imaginary plain,
The monstrous ruck of mountains
And, swinging across the night,
Flooding the Sacramento, San Joaquin,   5
The hissing drift of winter rain.

All day I waited, shifting
Nervously from station to bar
As I saw another train sail
By, the San Francisco Chief or   10
Golden Gate, water dripping
From great flanged wheels.

At midnight you came, pale
Above the negro porter's lamp.
I was too blind with rain   15
And doubt to speak, but
Reached from the platform
Until our chilled hands met.

You had been travelling for days
With an old lady, who marked   20
A neat circle on the glass
With her glove, to watch us
Move into the wet darkness
Kissing, still unable to speak.

Notes

[1] **legendary:** having a
connection with legends/myths

[1] **obstacles:** something or
someone that blocks progress

[3] **ruck:** a crease or a wrinkle

[5] **the Sacramento:** longest river
in California

[5] **San Joaquin:** second longest
river in California

[12] **flanged:** having a projecting
rim

Explorations

Pre-reading

1. Think back to a time when you were looking forward to meeting someone. Try to remember how you felt as you were waiting. Were you excited, anxious, impatient? Perhaps you felt a mixture of emotions.

First reading

2. A. *Class Discussion*: (i) Does the first stanza of this poem make a successful opening? Why? (ii) Choose the words or phrases that you feel play a key part in the first stanza.
   B. *Individual Writing*: Using the points that were discussed, answer the following question. Write a short piece beginning with the following words: 'When I read the first stanza of "All Legendary Obstacles" I felt . . .'. You might like to share some of your thoughts with the class.

3. (i) How does Montague feel in the second stanza, as he waits for his lover to arrive? (ii) What are the clues that convey his feelings?

4. A. *Paired Discussion*: (i) Describe what Montague does when his lover finally arrives. Use quotations to support your description. (ii) Are you surprised by his behaviour? Why?
   B. *Individual Writing*: Using the points that arose in the discussion, answer the following question. What do you think Montague is trying to say about Love in this stanza?

5. A. *Group Discussion*: (i) Who is introduced into the scene in the final stanza? (ii) Are there any clues given as to the type of person she is? (iii) Do you think she would have made a good travelling companion 'for days'? (iv) Would you be comfortable being watched by her? Why?
   B. *Individual Writing*: Using the points that were discussed, answer the following question. Imagine that you are the old lady. Describe the journey and the meeting of the two lovers from your point of view.

Second reading

6. 'All legendary obstacles lay between
   Us,'.
   Describe, in your own words, all the obstacles that the lovers face.

7. 'The monstrous ruck of mountains'; 'The hissing drift of winter rain'. How does Montague's use of sound in

these lines help you to
visualise what is being
described?

8. *Class Discussion*:
'Move into the wet darkness
Kissing, still unable to speak.'
(i) Do you think that these
lines indicate a happy ending
for the couple? (ii) Does the
poem support a happy
ending, or is it less certain?
(iii) Can you arrive at a
majority decision?

Third reading

9. Montague has commented
that the story of Orpheus and
Eurydice lies behind this
poem. Orpheus doomed
Eurydice to death and the
Underworld when he looked
back at her despite being
warned not to by Hades, the
god of the Underworld. What
implications does this story
have for Montague's feelings
about his relationship?

10. 'This poem begins with a
specific incident in a
particular relationship, but
ends by revealing something
of the nature of Love itself.'
Discuss.

11. Montague said of 'All
Legendary Obstacles', 'It's a
complicated poem.' Write a
letter to John Montague
explaining why you agree or
disagree with his assessment.

The Same Gesture

There is a secret room
of golden light where
everything – love, violence,
hatred is possible;
and, again, love.   5

Such intimacy of hand
and mind is achieved
under its healing light
that the shifting of
hands is a rite   10

like court music.
We barely know our
selves there though
it is what we always were –
most nakedly are –   15

and must remember
when we leave, re-
suming our habits
with our clothes:
work, phone, drive   20

through late traffic
changing gears with
the same gesture as
eased your snowbound
heart and flesh.   25

Note

[10] **rite:** a religious or solemn action

Explorations

First reading

1. Begin a sentence with 'I found this poem . . .' and add in your response to this poem, then follow it with 'because . . .' and explain what it was in the poem that made you respond in this way. You might like to share your response with the class.

2. 'There is a secret room of golden light'
'under its healing light'
A. *Paired Discussion*: (i) What do the words 'secret', 'golden', 'healing' and 'light' suggest about this room? (ii) Do these words tell you anything about the nature of the relationship that takes place in this room?
B. *Individual Writing*: Using the points that arose in the discussion, answer the following question.
Describe, in your own words, how you imagine the 'secret room'.

Second reading

3. *Class Discussion*: In the first stanza, Montague lists the emotions that the couple experience in this room. (i) Are you surprised by the emotions that are grouped together? Why? (ii) Can you see any connection between the three 'love, violence, |

hatred'? Are they the emotions you would expect to occur in the room that you imagined?

4. (i) How does Montague convey the close intimacy of their relationship in the second stanza? (ii) Is it simply a physical relationship or does it have a deeper quality? (iii) What do you think Montague is trying to convey about their relationship by using the word 'rite'?

5. A. *Group Discussion*:
'We barely know our
selves there though
it is what we always were –
most nakedly are – '.
(i) When Montague uses the word 'nakedly' does he just mean a physical nakedness?
B. *Individual Writing*: Using the points that arose in the discussion, answer the following question.
How does Montague portray the love that is shared by the lovers in the **first three stanzas** of the poem? Use quotations to support your view. You will find it helpful to refer back to your work on Questions 3 and 4.

6. *Group Discussion*: (i) How do the couple prepare to leave the room?)ii) Can you suggest a connection between

the 'clothes' image and the image of 'nakedness' that you considered in Question 5? (iii) What happens to the intimacy that the couple shared when they leave the room?

7. Using your work on Question 6, can you explain the theme of this poem in your own words?

8. With reference to lines 6–15 and lines 16–25, examine how Montague uses the pace and rhythm of his writing to suggest the different ways that the lovers feel in (i) the 'secret room' and (ii) the outside world.

Third reading

9. *Class Discussion*: (i) Compare Montague's description of two lovers in an intimate setting with that of John Donne in his poem 'The Sun Rising' (also in the Anthology). (ii) Which one do you prefer? Why?

10. 'In his poems "All Legendary Obstacles" and "The Same Gesture", Montague reveals Truths about Love that challenge us to reassess our expectations of what "being in love" truly means.' Discuss, using quotations from both poems to support your answer.

Like dolmens round my childhood...

this poem is also prescribed for Ordinary Level exams in 2007, 2008 and 2009

Like dolmens round my childhood, the old people.

Jamie MacCrystal sang to himself,
A broken song without tune, without words;
He tipped me a penny every pension day,
Fed kindly crusts to winter birds.   5
When he died, his cottage was robbed,
Mattress and money-box torn and searched.
Only the corpse they didn't disturb.

Maggie Owens was surrounded by animals,
A mongrel bitch and shivering pups,   10
Even in her bedroom a she-goat cried.
She was a well of gossip defiled,
Fanged chronicler of a whole countryside;
Reputed a witch, all I could find
Was her lonely need to deride.   15

The Nialls lived along a mountain lane
Where heather bells bloomed, clumps of foxglove.
All were blind, with Blind Pension and Wireless.
Dead eyes serpent-flickered as one entered
To shelter from a downpour of mountain rain.   20
Crickets chirped under the rocking hearthstone
Until the muddy sun shone out again.

Mary Moore lived in a crumbling gatehouse,
Famous as Pisa for its leaning gable.
Bag-apron and boots, she tramped the fields   25
Driving lean cattle from a miry stable.
A by-word for fierceness, she fell asleep
Over love stories, *Red Star* and *Red Circle*,
Dreamed of gypsy love-rites, by firelight sealed.

Wild Billy Eagleson married a Catholic servant girl   30
When all his Loyal family passed on:

We danced around him shouting 'To hell with King Billy',
And dodged from the arc of his flailing blackthorn.
Forsaken by both creeds, he showed little concern
Until the Orange drums banged past in the summer   35
And bowler and sash aggressively shone.

Curate and doctor trudged to attend them,
Through knee-deep snow, through summer heat,
From main road to lane to broken path,
Gulping the mountain air with painful breath.   40
Sometimes they were found by neighbours,
Silent keepers of a smokeless hearth,
Suddenly cast in the mould of death.

Ancient Ireland, indeed! I was reared by her bedside,
The rune and the chant, evil eye and averted head,   45
Fomorian fierceness of family and local feud.
Gaunt figures of fear and of friendliness,
For years they trespassed on my dreams,
Until once, in a standing circle of stones,
I felt their shadows pass   50

Into that dark permanence of ancient forms.

Notes

[1] **dolmens:** megalithic tombs consisting of upright stones capped by a large
     flat stone
[12] **defiled:** corrupted, dirtied, polluted
[13] **fanged:** with sharp, large wolf- or doglike teeth
[13] **chronicler:** a person who keeps track of, or records events
[14] **reputed:** generally considered
[15] **deride:** ridicule, make fun of
[18] **Wireless:** a radio
[21] **hearthstone:** the area in front of the fireplace
[26] **miry:** muddy, dirty
[31] **Loyal:** Loyalists, owing allegiance to the sovereign
[33] **flailing:** swinging wildly

[33] **blackthorn:** a stick made from the wood of the blackthorn shrub

[45] **rune:** early Germanic alphabet often believed to have magical significance

[45] **chant:** piece spoken in sing-song voice

[45] **evil eye:** a gaze believed to be able to cause harm

[45] **averted:** turned away

[46] **Fomorian:** in Irish mythology a gruesome and disfigured race who inhabited Ireland. They lived in the sea and had Tory island as their base.

[47] **gaunt:** lean and exhausted-looking

Markey Robinson: 'Country Road'

Explorations

Pre-reading

1. Have you ever seen a dolmen? Describe what it looked like. Or have you visited any of Ireland's ancient heritage sites, such as Newgrange or Carrowmore? How did you feel when you were there? Did you feel closer to the past?

First reading

2. *Individual Writing*: Imagine that you are writing for a local newspaper. Choose one of the people described in stanzas 1 to 5 and write an obituary (death notice) for him/her. Give an honest account of what he/she was like and how he/she lived.
3. Which of the five people do you least like? Explain the reasons behind your choice, using quotations to support your views.
4. *Paired Discussion*: (i) Does Montague tell us everything about 'the old people'?(ii) Why do you think that he chose to use only a few details in his descriptions?
5. *A. Group Discussion*: (i) Which of the following words would you use to sum up the old people's lifestyles: lonely; contented; isolated; harsh; peaceful? (ii) How do you feel about the way that they lived? *B. Individual Writing*: Using the points that were discussed, answer the following question. How do Montague's descriptions make us believe that 'the old people' were real people with real lives? Refer to the poem to support your opinions.

You will find your work on this question and Question 4 helpful.

Second reading

6. (i) What images does Montague use in the final stanza to convey Ancient Ireland? (ii) Based on these images, how do you imagine Ancient Ireland? (iii) What sort of people would have survived in such a world?
7. *Class Discussion*:
'Ancient Ireland, indeed!
I was reared by her bedside,'
(i) What do you think that Montague is saying here about the connection between his life in the present and Ireland's past? (ii) How does Montague's attitude to 'the old people' change in the final four lines of the poem? Is this change in his view of 'the old people' related to how he sees the connection between the past and the present?

8. *A Short Presentation to the Class*: Using your work for Questions 5 and 6, write a short piece for presentation to the class beginning with the sentence: 'Montague thinks that "the old people" are like dolmens because . . .'. After the class has listened to the pieces, you might like to arrive at an agreed explanation of the connection.

Third reading

9. Do you think that Montague wrote this poem when he was a child, or did he write it as an adult remembering back to his childhood? Refer to the poem to support your decision.

10. 'In Montague's poetry, we can always hear the voice of his four-year-old abandoned self asking the question, "Where do I belong?"' Discuss with reference to **at least three poems** by Montague that you have studied.

11. 'With Montague, personal experience is inextricably interwoven with national politics and the Truths of our human existence.' Consider this statement, using quotations from the poems you have studied to support your view.

The Wild Dog Rose

1

I go to say goodbye to the *cailleach*,
that terrible figure who haunted my childhood
but no longer harsh, a human being
merely, hurt by event.
        The cottage,   5
circled by trees, weathered to admonitory
shapes of desolation by the mountain winds,
straggles into view. The rank thistles
and leathery bracken of untilled fields
stretch behind with – a final outcrop –   10
the hooped figure by the roadside,
its retinue of dogs
               which give tongue
as I approach, with savage, whingeing cries
so that she slowly turns, a moving nest   15
of shawls and rags, to view, to stare
the stranger down.
            And I feel again
that ancient awe, the terror of a child
before the great hooked nose, the cheeks   20
dewlapped with dirt, the staring blue
of the sunken eyes, the mottled claws
clutching a stick

Notes

[1] **cailleach:** from the Celtic, originally meant 'the veiled one'. A number of interpretations
    including: an old woman
    a Hag (a Celtic teacher of Wisdom)
    a Witch (someone who practises magic)
[6] **admonitory:** reproving, rebuking
[12] **retinue:** a group of attendants attending to an important person
[21] **dewlapped:** a dewlap is a loose fold of skin hanging from an animal's throat
[22] **mottled:** marked with spots or patches

                    but now hold
and return her gaze, to greet her,   25
as she greets me, in friendliness.
Memories have wrought reconciliation
between us, we talk in ease at last,
like old friends, lovers almost,
sharing secrets   30
                    of neighbours
she quarrelled with, who now lie
in Garvaghey graveyard, beyond all hatred;
of my family and hers, how she never married,
though a man came asking in her youth.   35
'You would be loath to leave your own,'
she sighs, 'and go among strangers'–
his parish ten miles off.
                    For sixty years
since, she has lived alone, in one place.   40
Obscurely honoured by such confidences,
I idle by the summer roadside, listening,
while the monologue falters, continues,
rehearsing the small events of her life.
The only true madness is loneliness,   45
the monotonous voice in the skull
that never stops
                    because never heard.

                    2

                    And there
where the dog rose shines in the hedge   50
she tells me a story so terrible
that I try to push it away,
my bones melting.

[27] **wrought:** beaten out, hammered into shape

[36] **loath:** reluctant

[41] **obscurely:** not easily understood, vaguely

[43] **monologue:** a person speaking alone

                    Late at night
a drunk came beating at her door   55
to break it in, the bolt snapping
from the soft wood, the thin mongrels
rushing to cut, but yelping as
he whirls with his farm boots
to crush their skulls.   60
                    In the darkness
they wrestle, two creatures crazed
with loneliness, the smell of the
decaying cottage in his nostrils
like a drug, his body heavy on hers,   65
the tasteless trunk of a seventy-year-
old virgin, which he rummages while
she battles for life
                    bony fingers
reaching desperately to push   70
against his bull neck. 'I prayed
to the Blessed Virgin herself
for help and after a time
I broke his grip.'
                    He rolls   75
to the floor, snores asleep,
while she cowers until dawn
and the dogs' whimpering starts
him awake, to lurch back across
the wet bog.   80

                    3

                    And still
the dog rose shines in the hedge.
Petals beaten wide by rain, it
sways slightly, at the tip of a
slender, tangled, arching branch   85
which, with her stick, she gathers
into us.

[77] **cowers:** shrinks back or crouches in fear

N.P. Rasmussen: 'Dog Roses in Flower'

                              'The wild rose
is the only rose without thorns,'
she says, holding a wet blossom   90
for a second, in a hand knotted
as the knob of her stick.
'Whenever I see it, I remember
the Holy Mother of God and
all she suffered.'   95
                         Briefly
the air is strong with the smell
of that weak flower, offering
its crumbling yellow cup
and pale bleeding lips   100
fading to white
                    at the rim
of each bruised and heart-
shaped petal.

Explorations

First reading

1. *Class Discussion*: Having read 'The Wild Dog Rose', read 'Like dolmens round my childhood . . .'. Are there any similarities that immediately strike you between the descriptions of the old people in 'Like dolmens round my childhood . . .' and the description of the old woman in Section 1 of 'The Wild Dog Rose'?

2. (i) Describe, in your own words, where the old woman lives. (ii) Can you suggest reasons why she continued living in such an environment, on her own, for over sixty years? (iii) Does her rejection of the marriage offer because she was loath to leave her own tell you anything about her attitude to the wider world?

3. *Paired Discussion*:
'– a final outcrop –
the hooped figure by the roadside'.
(i) What does Montague's use of the phrase 'a final outcrop' suggest to you about the old

woman's appearance? (ii) Are there any other words or phrases in Section 1 that help you to imagine how she looked?

Individual Writing: Using the points that arose in the discussion, answer the following question. Imagine that you pass by the old woman as she waits for Montague. Write a description of what you think of her.

4. Do you, like the poet, find Section 2 of the poem 'a story so terrible'? Why?

Second reading

5. *Class Discussion*: Montague wrote that 'Ireland has often been seen as feminine, . . . and her colonisation has aspects of rape – becoming even more complicated when colonial England became Protestant and Ireland remained Roman Catholic, attached to the medieval ethos of the Virgin Mary.' (i) How does this statement affect your approach to the poem? (ii) Examine the old woman's attitude to the Virgin Mary in Section 2 and discuss what she feels when she thinks about Her.

6. The wild dog rose is described in Section 3. (i) How does it compare to the surrounding vegetation that Montague

described in lines 5–9 of Section 1? (ii) What do you think the word 'shines' conveys about the wild rose? Is it really a 'weak' flower, or has it an unexpected strength?

7. *Class Discussion*: Consider the image of the old woman gaining the strength to resist her attacker from her belief in the Virgin Mary and the image of the wild dog rose. (i) What do you think these two images suggest about Montague's attitude to England's colonisation of Ireland? (ii) Do you feel that the poem ends on a positive or a negative tone?

Third reading

8. 'The only true madness is loneliness,'.
   Discuss Montague's depiction of loneliness and the effects it has on those who endure it in 'Like dolmens round my childhood . . .' and 'The Wild Dog Rose'.

9. Write an article for a literary magazine entitled: 'Women in John Montague's Poetry'. Use references from relevant poems by John Montague on your course.

10. 'a human being merely, hurt by event.' Consider these lines with reference to **three** of Montague's poems.

A Welcoming Party

CD Track 10

Wie war das möglich?

That final newsreel of the war:
A welcoming party of almost shades
Met us at the cinema door
Clicking what remained of their heels.

From nests of bodies like hatching eggs   5
Flickered insectlike hands and legs
And rose an ululation, terrible, shy;
Children conjugating the verb 'to die'.

One clamoured mutely of love
From a mouth like a burnt glove;   10
Others upheld hands bleak as begging bowls
Claiming the small change of our souls.

Some smiled at us as protectors.
Can those bones live?
Our parochial brand of innocence   15
Was all we had to give.

To be always at the periphery of incident
Gave my childhood its Irish dimension; drama of unevent:
Yet doves of mercy, as doves of air,
Can falter here as anywhere.   20

That long dead Sunday in Armagh
I learnt one meaning of total war
And went home to my Christian school
To belt a football through the air.

Notes

Wie war das moglich?: How was it possible?

[1] **newsreel:** a short film of news items

[2] **shades:** ghosts

[7] **ululation:** wailing

[8] **conjugating:** giving different forms of a verb

[9] **clamoured:** shouted loudly

[9] **mutely:** silently

[15] **parochial:** local, narrow

[17] **periphery:** outer region

Explorations

Pre-reading

1. How do you feel when you see images of war on television news programmes? Do you think that some images should be censored or should all images be shown? Can viewers become accustomed to images of war, so that what they once considered shocking becomes ordinary? Does showing these pictures actually have any effect?

First reading

2. (i) Can you suggest why Montague begins this poem with a question in German? (ii) Do you think it makes a good opening for the poem? Why?

3. *Class Discussion*: How old do you think the poet and his friends were when this incident occurred? From your reading of the first stanza, describe how you imagine the boys acted as they watched these images in the cinema.

4. *Individual Writing*: How, in the second and third stanzas, does Montague convey the horror of the scenes in the newsreel? Choose **two images** that you find especially effective and explain why you chose them.

5. 'Claiming the small change of our souls.' (i) Does this line suggest a response in terms of money or emotions? (ii) What do you think the 'almost shades' were 'begging' for?

6. *A. Class Discussion*: (i) What does the boys' question, 'Can those bones live?' indicate about their reaction to what they were seeing? (ii) When Montague returned to his school he played football. Why do you think he did this?

   B. Individual Writing: Using your work on Questions 2–5, write the conversation that you imagine Montague and his friends had after they left the cinema and were on their way back to school.

Second reading

7. *Group Discussion*:
   'To be always at the periphery of incident
   Gave my childhood its Irish dimension; drama of unevent:'.
   (i) What reason does Montague give, in these lines, for the boys' limited reaction to the newsreel? (ii) In your opinion, has Ireland become more involved with world affairs since Montague was

young, during the 1940s? Do
you think that young people
nowadays would have a
different response to a similar
newsreel?
B. *Class Debate*: Write a
speech for presentation to the
class for or against the
motion: 'The Ireland that
John Montague describes is
dead and gone.'

8. 'Yet doves of mercy, as doves
of air,
Can falter here as anywhere.'
(i) Try to explain these lines
in your own words. What
might the 'doves of mercy'
be? (ii) How are they
connected to the boys? (iii)
Does the fact that the 'doves
of mercy' 'falter' have
anything to do with the boys
playing football in the final
line of the poem?

Third reading

9. 'For Montague, the
experiences of childhood have
resonances in the world of the
adult.' Discuss with reference
to **at least three poems** by
Montague that you have
studied.

10. 'I learnt one meaning'.
Montague sees poetry as the
learning and acceptance of
meaning, no matter how
difficult that meaning may be.
Consider how this concept
informs Montague's work,
supporting your argument by
quotations from the
Montague poems on your
course.

11. 'John Montague's poetry acts
like a prism, revealing the
layers of universal Truths
contained in the individual's
experience of ordinary life.'
Discuss, with reference to the
poems that you have studied.

prescribed for Higher Level exams in 2008, 2009 and 2010

A drienne Rich was born in Baltimore, USA, on 16 May 1929, the elder of two daughters. Her father, Arnold, was a doctor and a pathology professor at Johns Hopkins University, while her mother, Helen, had been a talented pianist and composer before devoting herself to raising her two daughters.

Adrienne was a bright child and was educated at home by her parents prior to entering the school system. It was her father who was to have the greater influence on her. Indeed, it was under his guidance that she began to write poetry. As she developed, Rich was to experience a sense of conflict as she tried to break away from her father's influence both in her writing and in her life.

In 1951 Adrienne graduated from Radcliffe College with an excellent degree. In the same year she received the Yale Younger Poets award for her first book of poetry. In 1953 she married a Harvard economist, Alfred Conrad, and had three sons. Adrienne continued to write, but she felt increasingly unhappy with the direction of her life. The 1960s were a time of great political upheaval in the United States and both Rich and her husband became involved with movements for social justice, with

1929–

her interest focusing on the women's movement.

Her experiences as a lesbian and a feminist led her to develop an empathy with all those groups in society who are considered less equal, and her poetry became increasingly politicised as she sought to give a voice to those who are not normally heard. Although Rich has won many prizes for her writing, in 1997 she declined the National Medal for the Arts from the then President, Bill Clinton, saying, 'A president cannot meaningfully honour certain token artists while the people at large are so dishonoured.'

Adrienne Rich published her latest book of poems, 'Midnight Salvage', in 1999, at the age of seventy.

Aunt Jennifer's Tigers

this poem is also prescribed for Ordinary Level exams in 2008, 2009 and 2010

Aunt Jennifer's tigers prance across a screen,
Bright topaz denizens of a world of green.
They do not fear the men beneath the tree;
They pace in sleek chivalric certainty.

Aunt Jennifer's fingers fluttering through her wool   5
Find even the ivory needle hard to pull.
The massive weight of Uncle's wedding band
Sits heavily upon Aunt Jennifer's hand.

When Aunt is dead, her terrified hands will lie
Still ringed with ordeals she was mastered by.   10
The tigers in the panel that she made
Will go on prancing, proud and unafraid.

Frances Broomfield: 'Tyger/Tyger'

Notes

[1] **prance:** to spring forward on back legs with front legs raised; to walk arrogantly

[2] **topaz:** a yellow/gold gem

[2] **denizens:** inhabitants

[4] **chivalric:** courtly, knightly

[10] **ordeals:** painful or horrifying experiences

 # Explorations

First reading

1. Imagine that you are a director preparing to film this scene. Using the clues given in the poem, write the instructions that you would give to (i) the set designer, regarding how the sets should look; and (ii) the cameraman, describing the camera shots that he should use.

2. Divide a copy page into two short columns. Put the heading 'Tigers' at the top of one column and 'Aunt Jennifer' at the top of the second. Put the answers to the following questions side by side in the relevant columns. Leave a one-line gap after each pair of answers: (i) What verbs are associated with the tigers in the first and third stanzas? What verbs are associated with Aunt Jennifer in the second and third stanzas? (ii) What colours are associated with the tigers in the first stanza? What colours are associated with Aunt Jennifer in the second stanza? (iii) What emotions are associated with the tigers in the first and third stanzas? What emotions are associated with Aunt Jennifer in the second and third stanzas?

3. *Class Discussion:* (i) Discuss the differences between the two lists of verbs in Question 2. (ii) Is there a feeling of power in one list and powerlessness in the other? (iii) Can you decide who was having more fun in life – the tigers or Aunt Jennifer? Give reasons for your decision.

4. *A. Paired Discussion:* The colour yellow/gold is suggested in connection with the tigers and Aunt Jennifer. Using the list you made in Question 2 (ii), discuss the following questions: (i) Are there any differences in the way the colour is used with

the tigers and with Aunt Jennifer? (ii) Consider the colours that appear alongside the yellow/gold in each case. Do they change how you see the yellow/gold?

B. *Individual Writing*: Using the points that arose in the discussion, answer the following question. How does Rich use colour to convey that the tigers have very different lives from Aunt Jennifer's?

5. *Group Discussion*: (i) Using your lists of emotions from Question 2, discuss the mood created in the images of the tigers and the mood created in the descriptions of Aunt Jennifer. (ii) Would you rather be with the tigers or with Aunt Jennifer? Why?

Second reading

6. A. *Paired Discussion*: (i) Do you find it surprising that Aunt Jennifer was the creator of the tiger screen? Why? (ii) Can you suggest what might have driven Aunt Jennifer to make this screen? (iii) What do you think she was trying to say?

B. *Paired Writing*: With one of you as Aunt Jennifer and one as a reporter, write an interview with Aunt Jennifer about her tiger screen.

7. A. *Class Discussion*: (i) Discuss the different ways in which the male figures interact with the tigers and with Aunt Jennifer. (ii) What is the poet's attitude to the male figures in the poem? (iii) Do you think that this is a fair attitude, bearing in mind that Rich wrote this poem as a woman living in the early 1950s?

B. *Individual Writing*: Using the points that arose in the discussion, answer the following question. How are men portrayed in this poem?

Third reading

8. (i) Can you explain the theme of the poem? (ii) Do you agree or disagree with the attitude expressed in the theme? Give reasons for your answer.

9. Physically, the tigers are suggested as whole bodies, while Aunt Jennifer is represented only by her hands. How does Rich use this method to reveal the differing lives of Aunt Jennifer and the tigers?

10. 'Power lies at the heart of this poem.' Discuss this statement, using references from the poem to support your views.

The Uncle Speaks in the Drawing Room

I have seen the mob of late
Standing sullen in the square,
Gazing with a sullen stare
At window, balcony, and gate.
Some have talked in bitter tones,   5
Some have held and fingered stones.

These are follies that subside.
Let us consider, none the less,
Certain frailties of glass
Which, it cannot be denied,   10
Lead in times like these to fear
For crystal vase and chandelier.

Not that missiles will be cast;
None as yet dare lift an arm.
But the scene recalls a storm   15
When our grandsire stood aghast
To see his antique ruby bowl
Shivered in a thunder-roll.

Let us only bear in mind
How these treasures handed down   20
From a calmer age passed on
Are in the keeping of our kind.
We stand between the dead glass-blowers
And murmurings of missile-throwers.

Notes

[7] **follies:** foolish activities
[16] **aghast:** dismayed

Explorations

First reading

1. *Class Discussion*: (i) What image does the word 'mob' suggest to you? (ii) How would you describe the mood of the mob in the first stanza? (iii) Pick out **two words** that really help you to understand their mood.

2. 'These are follies that subside.' (i) What does this line tell you about the uncle's attitude to the mob?
'Not that missiles will be cast;'. (ii) Do you think that the uncle truly believes what he is saying? (iii) Is he really as calm and confident as the two quotations in this question suggest? Refer to the second and third stanzas to support your view.

3. *A. Group Discussion*: The uncle is concerned about the 'crystal vase and chandelier.' Would you be concerned about items such as these if your house were under threat of attack?
B. Individual Writing: Using the points that arose in the discussion, answer the following question. What do the uncle's reactions reveal about the type of person that he is?

4. *A. Paired Discussion*: (i) Is it significant that the uncle speaks in 'the drawing room'? (ii) Would the effect have been the same if the uncle were in the kitchen or the bedroom? Why?
B. Individual Writing: Using the points that were discussed, answer the following question. Imagine that you were visiting the house when this incident occurred. Write a letter to your friend describing what happened and how you felt about it all.

Second reading

5. (i) What do the 'crystal vase and chandelier' and the 'ruby bowl' suggest about the uncle's lifestyle? (ii) Pick out any other words in the poem that give further clues about the type of house that the uncle lives in. (iii) How do you think the mob feel about the way that he lives?

6. *Class Discussion*: (i) What qualities do 'the mob' in the first stanza and the 'thunder-roll' in the third stanza have in common? (ii) Might they have similar effects on the glass objects? (iii) How are the 'glass-blowers' in the final stanza different from them?

7. (i) What does the final stanza tell us about the uncle's attitude to the glass objects? (ii) Pick out the key phrases that you feel reveal his

attitude. (iii) Do you agree with his opinion? Why?

Third reading

8. *Individual Writing*: (i) This poem comes from Rich's book entitled 'A Change of World'. How could this poem be seen as representing a possible 'change of world'? (ii) What could (a) the uncle, (b) the glass objects and (c) the mob represent in this context? You might like to share your thoughts with the class when you have finished.

9. *A. Group Discussion*: Where do you think Rich's sympathies lie: with the uncle or with the mob? Refer to the poem to support your viewpoint.

B. Individual Writing: Using the points that were discussed, answer the following question. How does the poem reveal Rich's loyalties?

10. 'In "The Uncle Speaks in the Drawing Room" and "Aunt Jennifer's Tigers", Rich skilfully uses everyday language to create poems that are both elegant and vivid.' Discuss this statement with regard to her use of (i) rhyme and rhythm, alliteration, assonance and onomatopoeia; (ii) clear and effective images.

C. Johnson-Wahl: 'Sunset, Waverly Place'

Storm Warnings

this poem is also prescribed for Ordinary Level exams in 2008, 2009 and 2010

The glass has been falling all the afternoon,
And knowing better than the instrument
What winds are walking overhead, what zone
Of gray unrest is moving across the land,
I leave the book upon a pillowed chair   5
And walk from window to closed window, watching
Boughs strain against the sky

And think again, as often when the air
Moves inward toward a silent core of waiting,
How with a single purpose time has traveled   10
By secret currents of the undiscerned
Into this polar realm. Weather abroad
And weather in the heart alike come on
Regardless of prediction.

Between foreseeing and averting change   15
Lies all the mastery of elements
Which clocks and weatherglasses cannot alter.
Time in the hand is not control of time,
Nor shattered fragments of an instrument
A proof against the wind; the wind will rise,   20
We can only close the shutters.

I draw the curtains as the sky goes black
And set a match to candles sheathed in glass
Against the keyhole draught, the insistent whine
Of weather through the unsealed aperture.   25
This is our sole defense against the season;
These are the things that we have learned to do
Who live in troubled regions

Notes

[11] **undiscerned:** unperceived by thought or senses

[14] **prediction:** forecast

[15] **averting:** preventing

[23] **sheathed:** enclosed, protected by

[25] **aperture:** gap

K.F. Nordstrom: 'Storm Clouds'

Explorations

Pre-reading

1. How do you feel about
   storms: the wind, rain,
   thunder and lightning? Are
   you afraid of them or do you
   feel exhilarated by them?
   Take 1 minute and write a list
   of all the words that come
   into your head when you
   think of the word 'Storms'.
   Don't try to control the
   words or leave out words that
   seem to have no sensible
   connection. When the minute
   is up, review your list. You
   could use it as a basis for a
   short descriptive piece of
   writing, either in prose or
   poetry, about your perception
   of 'Storms'.

First reading

2. *Group Discussion*: (i) What
   do you think of Rich's
   description of a developing
   storm? (ii) Are there any
   similarities between her poem
   and your written piece? (iii)
   Did any of her images or
   phrases express something of
   what you felt about storms? If
   so, try to explain what she
   was able to express for you.
3. 'Weather abroad
   And weather in the heart
   alike come on
   Regardless of prediction.'
   (i) What thoughts does the

impending storm trigger in
Rich? (ii) Do you feel that the
connection she makes actually
works? Why?

4. *Class Discussion*: The third
   stanza outlines the level of
   power that we humans have
   in the face of impending
   storms, be they emotional or
   meteorological. How effective
   does Rich think our power is?
   Choose **one phrase or one
   image** from this stanza that
   you feel clearly conveys this
   view.
5. *Individual Writing*: (i) In your
   own words, outline the
   actions that Rich takes in the
   final stanza. (ii) Do these
   actions actually succeed in
   keeping the storm out of her
   house?

Second reading

6. Examine the structure of this
   poem and compare it to 'Aunt
   Jennifer's Tigers' and 'The
   Uncle Speaks in the Drawing
   Room'. (i) What similarities
   do you notice between the
   three poems? (ii) What would
   you consider to be the main
   difference? (iii) Can you
   suggest why Rich altered her
   approach to structure in this
   way?
7. *Class Discussion*: (i) What
   does the weather suggest to

you about Rich's emotions?
(ii) How do you interpret her actions of closing the curtains and lighting the candle? (iii) Can you think of another poem by Rich where a woman contains her emotions?

Third reading

8. 'Rich uses language in this poem with the skill of a sculptor. Rhythm and metre; metaphor; assonance and alliteration have all been chiselled into a smoothly flowing form.' Discuss this statement using quotations to illustrate your points.

9. A lyric poem is one in which a single speaker communicates a mood, an attitude or a state of mind to the reader. A lyric poem does not seek to tell a story, but rather to express an individual feeling or thought. Consider whether 'Storm Warnings' could be described as a lyric. Support your arguments with relevant quotations and references.

10. 'These are the things that we have learned to do
Who live in troubled regions.'
Taking any **three** of Rich's poems, discuss how she conveys her view that women have learned to do certain 'things' in order to 'live in troubled regions'.

11. Review the short descriptive piece that you wrote on 'Storms'. (i) Does it suggest anything about your emotional state? (ii) Having read Rich's poem, would you like to add anything to it or are you happy with your work?

Living in Sin

She had thought the studio would keep itself;
no dust upon the furniture of love.
Half heresy, to wish the taps less vocal,
the panes relieved of grime. A plate of pears,
a piano with a Persian Shawl, a cat   5
stalking the picturesque amusing mouse
had risen at his urging
Not that at five each separate stair would writhe
under the milkman's tramp; that morning light
so coldly would delineate the scraps   10
of last night's cheese and three sepulchral bottles;
that on the kitchen shelf among the saucers
a pair of beetle-eyes would fix her own –
envoy from some village in the moldings . . .
Meanwhile, he, with a yawn,   15
sounded a dozen notes upon the keyboard,
declared it out of tune, shrugged at the mirror,
rubbed at his beard, went out for cigarettes;
while she, jeered by the minor demons,
pulled back the sheets and made the bed and found   20
a towel to dust the table-top,
and let the coffee-pot boil over on the stove.
By evening she was back in love again,
though not so wholly but throughout the night
she woke sometimes to feel the daylight coming   25
like a relentless milkman up the stairs.

Notes

[1] **studio:** studio flat/apartment: a flat with a room used as an artist's
     studio, a one-roomed flat
[3] **heresy:** contrary to doctrine or what is normally accepted
[6] **picturesque:** beautiful, as in a picture
[10} **delineate:** draw
[11] **sepulchral:** like a tomb, gloomy
[14] **moldings:** mouldings, strips of decorative wood
[26] **relentless:** persistent

'Lovers' by Robert Colquhoun (1914–62)

Explorations

First reading

1. *Class Discussion*: (i) Have you ever heard the phrase 'Living in Sin' used before? (ii) What do you understand it to mean? (iii) In the 1950s and 1960s this phrase suggested a relationship that was rather shocking, yet exciting, because the couple were not married. Do you think that the phrase has lost its impact nowadays?

2. *A. Paired Discussion*: (i) What picture of the studio does the girl have in her imagination in lines 4–7? (ii) What is the studio like in reality?
   B. Individual Writing: Using the points that arose in the discussion, answer the following question. Imagine that you are the girl in the poem. Describe how you feel about the studio in which you are living.

3. Consider the description of the man in lines 15–18. (i) Does he seem like a man who would tempt a woman to 'live in sin'? Why? (ii) From the clues in these lines, describe him in your own words.

4. *Group Discussion*: (i) How does the woman spend her time when she first gets up? (ii) Consider the phrase 'jeered by the minor demons'. Does it help you to understand what urges the woman to do these things?

5. *A. Class Discussion*: (i) Why do you think that it is she who tidies up the 'studio' while he does not? (ii) Do you think that this is a realistic portrayal of male/female behaviour? Why?
   B. Presentation to the Class: Using the points that were discussed, answer the following question. Write and present a short speech on the following topic: 'Women are too concerned with housework, while men are not concerned enough.'

6. 'By evening she was back in love again,'.
   (i) Can you suggest what might make the woman fall back in love with the man as the day progresses? (ii) This line implies a happy ending to the poem. Do you think that there is, indeed, a happy ending? Why?

Second reading

7. *Paired Writing*: Imagine that **either the man or the woman** writes to a 'Problem Page' in a magazine about their relationship. With one of you writing as the man/woman and the other writing as the

'Agony Aunt/Uncle', write the letters that you think would pass between the two. You might like to read your work out to the class so as to see the different approaches to the situation.

8. What do you think that Rich is trying to communicate about Love in the poem? Do you agree with her? Refer to the poem in your answer.

Third reading

9. A. *Group Discussion*: (i) The woman's decision to tidy the 'studio' is a significant one. How could it be seen as a metaphor for women in society? (ii) Is Rich suggesting that women are trained, or forced, by society to behave in a certain way?

B. *Individual Writing*: Using the points that arose in the discussion, answer the following question. In your own words, explain the themes of this poem. Use quotations to support your points.

10. Rich wrote this poem in the 1950s. Do you think that the message the poem carries is relevant in the twenty-first century?

The Roofwalker

– for Denise Levertov

Over the half-finished houses
night comes. The builders
stand on the roof. It is
quiet after the hammers,
the pulleys hang slack.   5
Giants, the roofwalkers,
on a listing deck, the wave
of darkness about to break
on their heads. The sky
is a torn sail where figures   10
pass magnified, shadows
on a burning deck.

I feel like them up there:
exposed, larger than life,
and due to break my neck.

                                          15

Was it worth while to lay –
with infinite exertion –
a roof I can't live under?
– All those blueprints,
closings of gaps,   20
measurings, calculations?
A life I didn't choose
chose me: even
my tools are the wrong ones
for what I have to do.   25
I'm naked, ignorant,
a naked man fleeing
across the roofs
who could with a shade of difference
be sitting in the lamplight   30
against the cream wallpaper
reading – not with indifference –
about a naked man
fleeing across the roofs.

Note

**Denise
Levertov:**
1923–97. Poet
born in England
but who moved to
America after her
marriage.
Feminism and
Activism became
important elements
in her writing.
Developed a style
where the thinking
process was
reflected in line
and image.

Explorations

Pre-reading

1. Have you ever walked along a high narrow wall, or a narrow track on a hillside, or across a bridge where you felt uncomfortable about your situation? Take a moment to remember, then write a short passage describing your feelings.

First reading

2. A. *Class Discussion*: (i) What mood is created in the first section of the poem? (ii) How do you think the builders feel about being up on the roof?
   B. *Individual Writing*: Using the points that were discussed, answer the following question. Imagine that you are one of the builders. Using the information in the first section of the poem, describe in your own words your thoughts and feelings at this time.

3. A. *Paired Discussion*: 'Giants, the roofwalkers, on a listing deck,'.
   (i) The speaker imagines the builders on something other than a roof. Can you explain what it is? (ii) What does this imagery tell you about the speaker's attitude to the builders?
   B. *Individual Writing*: Using

the points that were discussed, answer the following question. Choose **one image** that you find particularly vivid from the first section and explain in your own words what it helps you to 'see'.

4. 'I feel like them up there: exposed, larger than life, and due to break my neck.'
   (i) In what way do these lines signal a change in the speaker's attitude towards the roofwalkers? (ii) Do you think that she is afraid, or worried, or both?

5. *Class Discussion*: (i) How does the speaker feel about her life? (ii) Pick out **one image or phrase** that you think clearly suggests these feelings. (iii) Do you think she has put a lot of effort into trying to make this life work? Why?

6. *Individual Writing*: Remembering the piece that you wrote before reading this poem, and using your work for Questions 3 and 4, write a short piece expressing what you would say to this woman if you were to meet her.

Second reading

7. 'I'm naked, ignorant, a naked man fleeing across the roofs'.

(i) What emotions do you feel when you read these lines? (ii) What do you think the word 'fleeing' suggests about the man's actions? (iii) Does this image help you to understand how the speaker feels, or do you find it confusing?

8. *Class Discussion*: Read lines 30–34. (i) What mood is created in this final image? (ii) Do you find the mood surprising, given the feelings that the speaker expressed earlier on in the poem? (iii) Is the speaker actually 'sitting in the lamplight', or is she just imagining the scene?

9. A. *Class Discussion*: (i) Do you think that the speaker would be truly happy if she could manage to change and sit in a room with 'cream wallpaper'? (ii) Which phrases or images reveal her realisation that, even by changing, she would not be happy in such a situation?
B. *Individual Writing*: Using your work on Questions 7, 8 and 9, answer the following: (i) Can you explain the **final 13 lines** of this poem in your own words? (ii) Do you find

the **final 13 lines** of this poem a successful conclusion to the piece? Give reasons for your viewpoint.

Third reading

10. A. *Group Discussion*: (i) How is the appearance of this poem different from poems such as 'Aunt Jennifer's Tigers' and 'Storm Warnings'? (ii) What effect does this appearance have on the way you read the poem? (iii) Can you suggest why Rich decided to try a new approach with this poem?
B. *Individual Writing*: Using the points that were discussed, answer the following question. 'When we read "The Roofwalker", it is as if we are inside Rich's head listening to her thoughts.' Discuss, with reference to the poem.

11. Choose **two poems** that you feel show Rich's efforts to use her 'tools' of writing to the best of her ability. In your answer, examine her use of everyday language, images, rhyme, rhythm, assonance and alliteration.

Our Whole Life

Our whole life a translation
the permissible fibs

and now a knot of lies
eating at itself to get undone

Words bitten thru words   5

meanings burnt-off like paint
under the blowtorch

All those dead letters
rendered into the oppressor's language

Trying to tell the doctor where it hurts   10
like the Algerian
who has walked from his village, burning

his whole body a cloud of pain
and there are no words for this

except himself   15

Notes

[2] **permissible:** allowable

[8] **dead letters:** undelivered letters

[9] **oppressor:** one who governs harshly and cruelly

Explorations

Pre-reading

1. Have you ever been somewhere where you and your family did not speak the language and had difficulty making yourself understood? Or did you find the first days in Irish College very difficult because you could not understand or be understood? Recount your experience to the class.

First Reading

2. Did this poem remind you in any way of the experiences that were described in the Pre-reading exercise?

3. *A. Class Discussion*: Rich uses the word 'translation' in the opening line of the poem. (i) Look it up in a dictionary and write down the definitions given. (ii) Suggest situations where you might be involved in translating words. (iii) How are the 'fibs', 'lies' and 'meanings' connected to the act of 'translation'?
    B. Individual Writing: Using the points that arose in the discussion, answer the following question. What aspects of language is Rich concerned with in lines 1–7 of this poem?

4. *A. Group Discussion*: 'All those dead letters rendered into the oppressor's language'.
    (i) Imagine that you had sent letters to someone and they had never been delivered; how would you feel? (ii) Do you think that Rich is suggesting similar emotions by using the phrase 'dead letters' here? (iii) Think back to Ireland's past. How did the Irish people feel when they were forced to speak English? (iv) Do you think that Rich uses the phrase 'the oppressor's language' to convey similar feelings?
    B. Individual Writing: Using the points that were discussed, answer the following question. In your own words, describe the emotions that Rich is trying to communicate in the two lines quoted above.

5. Imagine that you are the Algerian in lines 10–15. Write a short passage expressing your feelings and thoughts as you go through the experience that Rich describes. You might like to share your work with the class.

6. *Class Discussion*: Using your work for Questions 3, 4 and 5, discuss the following: (i) Can

you see any connections between your three answers? (ii) Do you think that Rich is happy with the language she uses? (iii) What clues in the poem lead you to your conclusion?

Second Reading

7. A. *Class Discussion*: Rich uses the phrase 'the oppressor's language'. (i) Has the 'oppressor' figure appeared in any of Rich's other poems that you have studied? (ii) Can you sum up how this 'oppressor' figure is portrayed? (iii) In the light of this, whom do you think the 'Our' in the first line of the poem refers to?

    B. *Individual Writing*: Using the points that arose in the discussion, answer the following question. What is Rich trying to say in this poem about the language that women use?

8. *A Class Debate*: Write a short speech either for or against the motion: 'The English language is a male-centred language.'

9. *Individual Writing*: (i) In your own words, explain the theme of this poem. (ii) What is your reaction to this theme?

Third Reading

10. How do you feel about the way that Adrienne Rich portrays the male figure in her poetry? Use references from **at least four of her poems** to support your viewpoint.

11. Rich uses the 'stream of consciousness' approach in this poem to suggest the way in which her thoughts and feelings spontaneously develop. Using references **from this poem** and **one other poem** by Rich, discuss the advantages and disadvantages of such an approach.

Trying to Talk with a Man

Out in this desert we are testing bombs,
that's why we came here.

Sometimes I feel an underground river
forcing its way between deformed cliffs
an acute angle of understanding   5
moving itself like a locus of the sun
into this condemned scenery.

What we've had to give up to get here –
whole LP collections, films we starred in
playing in the neighborhoods, bakery windows   10
full of dry, chocolate-filled Jewish cookies,
the language of love-letters, of suicide notes,
afternoons on the riverbank
pretending to be children

Coming out to this desert   15
we meant to change the face of
driving among dull green succulents
walking at noon in the ghost town
surrounded by a silence

that sounds like the silence of the place   20
except that it came with us
and is familiar
and everything we were saying until now
was an effort to blot it out –
coming out here we are up against it   25

Out here I feel more helpless
with you than without you
You mention the danger
and list the equipment
we talk of people caring for each other   30
in emergencies – laceration, thirst –
but you look at me like an emergency
Your dry heat feels like power

your eyes are stars of a different magnitude
they reflect lights that spell out: EXIT   35
when you get up and pace the floor

talking of the danger
as if it were not ourselves
as if we were testing anything else.

Notes

[4] **deformed:** misshapen
[5] **acute angle:** an angle less than 90°
[6] **locus:** the defined motion of a point
[17] **succulents:** thick and fleshy plants
[31] **laceration:** torn flesh

James Doolin: 'The Indian Shafts Valley'

Explorations

First reading

1. (i) What is your reaction to the opening two lines of the poem? (ii) Did they make you want to read the rest of the poem? Why?

2. *Individual Writing*: (i) In your own words, describe the scene that you imagine from the clues in lines 1–7 and lines 15–19. (ii) How would you feel in such an environment? You might like to share your thoughts with the class.

3. *Class Discussion*: (i) What sort of environment did the people live in before they came to the desert? (ii) Are there any indications in the poem as to why they left this world for the desert?

4. A. *Group Discussion*: (i) Examine lines 1–7 and 15–19, where Rich describes the desert. What do you notice about her use of punctuation in these lines? (ii) Now look at lines 8–14. What do you notice about the punctuation in these lines? (iii) Why do you think she changes her use of punctuation?

   B. *Individual Writing*: Using the points that were discussed, answer the following question. How does Rich use punctuation to strengthen her descriptions in this poem?

Second reading

5. *Paired Discussion*:
   'surrounded by a silence
   that sounds like the silence of the place
   except that it came with us'.
   (i) Can you explain the two types of silence that Rich is referring to here? (ii) Why do you think there is silence between the two people?

6. *Class Discussion*: (i) What do the couple do in response to the silence? (ii) Why do you think they react in this way? *Individual Writing*: Based on the behaviour that you have considered in Questions 5 and 6, do you think that the couple are happy or unhappy together? Use quotations from the poem to prove your viewpoint.

7. 'Out here I feel more helpless with you than without you'. (i) What do these lines tell you about the way that the speaker feels when she is with her partner? (ii) Does the title of the poem make it easier for you to understand why she feels 'helpless'? (iii) Can you now suggest what the theme of this poem is?

8. A. *Class Discussion*: (i) Do the last 12 lines of the poem indicate a happy or unhappy ending for the couple?
   B. *Individual Writing*: Using

the points that were discussed, answer the following question. Do you find the conclusion to the poem a satisfactory one? Support your opinion by reference to the poem.

Third Reading

9. This poem is based on two areas of imagery: (a) the testing of bombs in the desert; (b) the nature of the couple's relationship. Trace how Rich weaves the two together in order to convey the theme of this poem. Before you answer this question you might find it helpful to set out the relevant points in two columns, following the method we used for 'Aunt Jennifer's Tigers'.

10. The lyric poem is one in which a single speaker communicates a mood, an attitude or a state of mind to the reader. Discuss the following statement with reference to 'Trying to Talk with a Man' **and one other poem**: 'Rich takes the lyric poem and gives it a political twist so that the single speaker communicates not only about herself, but also about the society that she lives in.'

Diving into the Wreck

First having read the book of myths,
and loaded the camera,
and checked the edge of the knife-blade,
I put on
the body-armor of black rubber   5
the absurd flippers
the grave and awkward mask.
I am having to do this
not like Cousteau with his
assiduous team   10
aboard the sun-flooded schooner
but here alone.

There is a ladder.
The ladder is always there
hanging innocently   15
close to the side of the schooner.
We know what it is for,
we who have used it.
Otherwise
it's a piece of maritime floss   20
some sundry equipment.

I go down.
Rung after rung and still
the oxygen immerses me
the blue light   25
the clear atoms
of our human air.
I go down.
My flippers cripple me,
I crawl like an insect down the ladder   30
and there is no one
to tell me when the ocean
will begin.

First the air is blue and then
it is bluer and then green and then   35

black I am blacking out and yet
my mask is powerful
it pumps my blood with power
the sea is another story
the sea is not a question of power   40
I have to learn alone
to turn my body without force
in the deep element.

And now: it is easy to forget
what I came for   45
among so many who have always
lived here
swaying their crenellated fans
between the reefs
and besides   50
you breathe differently down here.

I came to explore the wreck.
The words are purposes.
The words are maps.
I came to see the damage that was done   55
and the treasures that prevail.
I stroke the beam of my lamp
slowly along the flank
of something more permanent
than fish or weed   60

the thing I came for:
the wreck and not the story of the wreck
the thing itself and not the myth
the drowned face always staring
toward the sun   65
the evidence of damage
worn by salt and sway into this threadbare beauty
the ribs of the disaster
curving their assertion
among the tentative haunters.   70

This is the place.
And I am here, the mermaid whose dark hair

streams black, the merman in his armored body
We circle silently
about the wreck   75
we dive into the hold.
I am she: I am he

whose drowned face sleeps with open eyes
whose breasts still bear the stress
whose silver, copper, vermeil cargo lies   80
obscurely inside barrels
half-wedged and left to rot
we are the half-destroyed instruments
that once held to a course
the water-eaten log   85
the fouled compass

We are, I am, you are
by cowardice or courage
the one who find our way
back to this scene   90
carrying a knife, a camera
a book of myths
in which
our names do not appear.

Notes

[1] **myths:** legends, folklore
[9] **Cousteau:** Jacques-Yves Cousteau - Famous for his underwater films and TV programmes. Worked tirelessly to increase public awareness of the oceans.
[10] **assiduous:** hard-working
[11] **schooner:** a type of ship
[20] **maritime:** connected with the sea
[20] **floss:** thread
[21] **sundry:** various pieces
[48] **crenellated:** lacy, with irregular edges
[56] **prevail:** triumph, exist
[67] **threadbare:** worn, ragged
[69] **assertion:** statement
[70] **tentative:** cautious, uncertain
[80] **vermeil:** a bright, beautiful red, as in vermilion

Explorations

Pre-reading

1. Rich's poems work on a number of interwoven levels and this can sometimes cause confusion, particularly in a longer poem such as this. For this poem, use an A4 or double copy page. Rule out five equal columns. Use the following five headings: 'Setting'; 'Activity'; 'Emotional Setting'; 'Emotional Activity'; 'Political Messages'. As you answer the questions, fill in the appropriate columns with points summarising your thinking. In this way, the interrelationship between the layers should become clearer.

First reading

2. A. *Class Discussion*: This discussion will help you to fill in the 'Setting' and 'Activity' Columns. (i) Where is this poem set? (ii) What is the speaker going to do? (iii) What preparations does she make? (iv) What does she use to move down to the water? (v) Is her journey down the ladder an easy one or does it take a lot of effort? (vi) Is there anyone with her?
B. *Individual Writing*: Using the answers that arose out of your discussion, begin to fill in the columns headed 'Setting' and 'Activity' in point form.

3. A. *Class Discussion*: Again, this discussion will help you to fill in the 'Setting' and 'Activity' columns. (i) What does the diver have to learn to do in the water? (ii) Why does she go to the wreck? (iii) How do you imagine the wreck from the description in the poem? (iv) Who does the diver meet at the wreck?
B. *Individual Writing*: Using the answers that you discussed, finish filling in the columns headed 'Setting' and 'Activity' in point form.

Second Reading

4. A. *Class Discussion*: This discussion will help you to fill in the 'Emotional Setting' column. (i) How do you think the diver feels as she prepares for the dive? (ii) Consider what her checking of the knife edge and putting on the 'body-armor' convey about the emotional setting for the poem. (iii) Read lines 22–37 and consider her emotions during these experiences.
B. *Individual Writing*: Using the answers that arose out of your discussion, fill in the column headed 'Emotional Setting' in point form.

5. *Class Discussion*: This discussion will help you to fill in the 'Emotional Activity' column. (i) How does the diver's mood change when she learns how to move in 'the deep element'? (ii) What are her feelings when she reaches the wreck? (iii) How does she feel when she meets the mermaid and merman? (iv) What is her mood in the final eight lines of the poem, when she becomes one with the mermaid and merman?

   B. *Individual Writing*: Using the answers that arose out of your discussion, fill in the column headed 'Emotional Activity' in point form.

6. *Class Discussion*: This discussion will help you to fill in the final column: 'Political Messages'. This poem tells of a heroic quest for treasure in an old wreck and the transformation that occurs to the heroine when she succeeds in her quest. (i) Consider what the quest represents: is the diver trying to learn something about being a woman, or is she questioning 'the book of myths' that contain all the accepted inequalities of our society? (ii) What do you think the treasure represents: is it self-knowledge, or knowledge about why men have most of the power in society? (iii) What might the wreck represent: the diver's own unsatisfactory life as a woman, or the outdated rules of society that reinforce inequality? (iv) What could her transformation into an androgynous figure (partly male, partly female) represent: the achievement of true personal power through surviving all the injustices, or could it stand for society, doomed to destruction because it is based on inequality?

   B. *Individual Writing*: Using the answers that arose out of your discussion, fill in the column 'Political Messages' in point form.

Third Reading

7. A. *Paired Discussion*: Referring back to the relevant columns should prove helpful. (i) How does the physical setting at the beginning of the poem influence the diver's emotional setting? (ii) What effects do the physical activities that the diver engages in have on her emotional activities?

   B. *Individual Writing*: Using the answers that arose out of your discussion, answer the following question. Trace how the diver's emotions change as she goes through the different experiences described in the poem. Use quotations to support your

From a Survivor

The pact that we made was the ordinary pact
of men & women in those days

I don't know who we thought we were
that our personalities
could resist the failures of the race   5

Lucky or unlucky, we didn't know
the race had failures of that order
and that we were going to share them

Like everybody else, we thought of ourselves as special

Your body is as vivid to me   10
as it ever was: even more

since my feeling for it is clearer:
I know what it could and could not do

it is no longer
the body of a god   15

or anything with power over my life
Next year it would have been 20 years
and you are wastefully dead
who might have made the leap
we talked, too late, of making   20

which I live now
not as a leap
but a succession of brief, amazing movements

each one making possible the next

Note

Rich wrote this poem to her husband, Alfred Conrad, who committed suicide in 1970.

Edward Hopper: 'Hotel by the Railroad'

Explorations

Pre-reading

1. Have you ever been a bridesmaid or a groomsman at a wedding? What can you remember about the day? How did the couple who were getting married feel about their wedding? Did the experience make you feel positively or negatively about getting married?

First Reading

2. (i) From your first reading of the poem, can you suggest a phrase that sums up Rich's feelings for her late husband? (ii) Do you find some of the feelings expressed in this poem surprising when set against the other poems on your course? Why?

3. A. *Class Discussion*: (i) Can you explain what the 'ordinary pact' was that Rich made with her husband? (ii) Look up the word 'pact' in the dictionary and note the definitions of the word. (iii) Do you think that it is a good word to describe the marriage of a man and a woman? Why?

   B. *Individual Writing*: Using the points that were discussed, answer the following question. What does Rich's use of the word 'pact' to describe marriage suggest about her attitude to this connection between men and women?

4. A. *Class Discussion*: (i) What do you think she means by the phrase 'the failures of the race'? (ii) Can you suggest a connection between the 'pact' and these 'failures'?

   B. *Individual Writing*: Using the points that arose in the discussion, answer the following question. How did Rich and her husband feel about getting married?

5. (i) How does Rich's attitude towards her husband's body change during their marriage? (ii) Do you think that such a change is natural in a long-term relationship? Why? (iii) In your opinion, would such a change make the couple's love stronger or weaker? Give reasons for your answer.

6. A. *Paired Discussion*: (i) Do you think that Rich's husband was a supportive husband when he was alive? (ii) What leads you to this conclusion?

   B. *Individual Writing*: Using the points that arose in the discussion, answer the following question. Using your work on this question and Question 5, describe in your own words the type of relationship that Rich and her husband shared.

Second Reading

7. *Class Discussion*: (i) Can you suggest what the 'leap' in lines 19 and 22 might represent? (ii) Do Rich's other poems give you any indication of what this 'leap' might involve?

8. 'but a succession of brief, amazing movements
   each one making possible the next'
   (i) Why do you think that Rich does not use a full stop at the end of the poem? (ii) What do these final lines suggest to you about Rich's attitude to her life? (iii) Is there a connection between these lines and the poem's title?

Third Reading

9. *Group Discussion*: Rich uses very little punctuation in this poem. (i) Read the poem aloud as it is and listen to it carefully. (ii) Put in the correct punctuation and read the poem again. (iii) What effect does the added punctuation have on the way the poem is read? (iv) Which version do you prefer, the unpunctuated or the punctuated one? Why?

10. *Class Presentation*: Prepare a piece for presentation to the class either agreeing or disagreeing with the following statement: 'Rich has a depressingly negative view of male/female relationships.' Use quotations from **at least three of her poems** to support your argument.

11. Survival is an important concept in Rich's poetry. With reference to **two of her poems featuring women who are successful survivors** and **two of her poems featuring women who are unsuccessful survivors**, explain the factors that Rich believes make women successful or unsuccessful survivors.

Power

this poem is also prescribed for Ordinary Level exams in 2008 and 2009

Living   in the earth-deposits   of our history

Today a backhoe divulged   out of a crumbling flank of earth
one bottle   amber   perfect   a hundred-year-old
cure for fever   or melancholy   a tonic
for living on this earth   in the winters of this climate   5

Today I was reading about Marie Curie:
she must have known she suffered   from radiation sickness
her body bombarded for years   by the element
she had purified
It seems she denied to the end   10
the source of the cataracts on her eyes
the cracked and suppurating skin   of her finger-ends
till she could no longer hold   a test-tube or a pencil

She died   a famous woman   denying
her wounds   15
denying
her wounds   came   from the same source as her power

Notes

[2] **backhoe:** a mechanical digger
[2] **flank:** side of the body between ribcage and hip
[4] **melancholy:** a thoughtful sadness
[6] **Marie Curie:** 1867–1934. Discovered the radioactive elements plutonium and radium
     that are used in medicine today. First person to win two Nobel prizes. Died of leukaemia
     caused by exposure to high levels of radiation.
[11] **cataracts:** condition where the lens of the eye becomes opaque so that light cannot pass
     through
[12] **suppurating:** oozing pus

ABONNEMENTS

Trois mois Six mois Un an
FRANCE & COLONIES
4 fr.   7 fr. 50 14 fr
UNION POSTALE
5 fr.   10 fr.   20 fr.

Le Petit Journal
illustré

PARAISSANT LE DIMANCHE

32ᵉ Année - Nᵒ 1595

On s'abonne dans tous
les bureaux de poste

Les Manuscrits ne sont pas rendus

Mᵐᵉ CURIE dans son Laboratoire

Après les jours glorieux qu'elle vient de vivre en Amérique, où elle a reçu, avec mille témoignages d'admiration, le gramme de radium offert par les Femmes américaines, l'illustre chimiste a repris son existence laborieuse dans la paix de son Laboratoire.

Marie Curie depicted in a French magazine in 1921

Explorations

First reading

1. *Class Discussion*: (i) What is your reaction to the way that this poem is arranged on the page? (ii) Did this arrangement encourage or discourage you from reading the poem? Why?

2. A. *Paired Discussion*: (i) What is the discovery that triggers the poet's thoughts? (ii) What senses does Rich appeal to in her description of this discovery in lines 2–5? (iii) Why do you think that the bottle was thrown away with its contents apparently unused?

   B. *Paired Writing*: Using the points that were discussed, answer the following question. You are visiting Rich when she discovers the bottle. With one of you writing as Rich and the other as yourself, write out the conversation that you have.

3. Do you find the first five lines of this poem interesting or confusing? Give reasons for your opinion.

Second reading

4. The poet's thoughts move on to the woman scientist Marie Curie. (i) What effects did Curie's work have on her life? (ii) Would you like to live a life such as Marie Curie's? Why?

5. A. *Class Discussion*: (i) How does Marie Curie react to the 'radiation sickness'? (ii) Can you suggest any reasons for her behaviour? (iii) As a woman, Curie was very unusual in the male-dominated scientific world. Do you think that this factor played a part in her denial of her sickness?

   B. *Individual Writing*: Using the points that arose in the discussion, answer the following question. Imagine that you are interviewing Marie Curie for a newspaper. Using your work on this question and Question 4, write out the questions that you would ask her and the answers that she might give.

6. *Group Discussion*: (i) Do you find the movement of the poem from describing the discovery of the 'bottle' to writing about Marie Curie confusing? (ii) Might the idea of a 'cure' connect the two images in some way?

Third reading

7. (i) Obviously, Curie had physical wounds from the radiation sickness, but could she have also been 'wounded'

by the society in which she lived? In what ways? (ii) Why would Rich be unhappy about Curie denying the fact that, as a woman, society inflicted 'wounds' on her?

8. Do you find Rich's use of the 'stream of consciousness' method successful in 'Power', or is it all rather confusing? Use quotations from the poem to support your opinion.

9. Compare 'Power' with 'Aunt Jennifer's Tigers'. Which poem do you prefer? Give reasons for your preference.

10. Consider how Rich explores the concept of 'Power' in **three** of the poems that you have studied. Use quotations to support your answer.

11 *Derek* WALCOTT

prescribed for Higher Level exams in 2009 and 2010

Derek Walcott and his twin brother were born on 23 January 1930 on St Lucia, an isolated island in the Lesser Antilles in the Caribbean. The family, who were relatively prosperous, lived in Castries, the capital of the island. Sadly, Walcott's early life was not without tragedy. His father, a civil servant and amateur painter, died when Derek was only one year old. Then a fire burned Castries down and the capital had to be rebuilt. Walcott's mother, however, remained a stable and stimulating influence. A respected Methodist teacher, she encouraged her boys to read widely.

Until 1979 St Lucia was part of the British Empire, having previously been under French control. This chequered history produced a cultural mix of British and French influences with a large measure of the native West Indian. Indeed, Walcott's personal heritage – 'I have Dutch, nigger and English in me' – reflects the diversity of the cultures on the island. As a result, the theme of trying to find an identity that acknowledges the two cultures, African and European, occurs frequently in Walcott's work.

At home he was surrounded by the sounds of the local Creole language, while at school – St Mary's College – he spoke English, the

1930–

language of the Empire. Interestingly, this part of his life provides a link between Walcott and Ireland. In 1947, the Presentation Brothers of Cork took over St Mary's. Walcott, then seventeen, became friendly with one of the brothers, Brother Liam, who spoke enthusiastically of Irish history and literature to the boys on a small volcanic island in a warm, blue sea. At the age of eighteen, he published his first book of poetry and left St Lucia for Jamaica to attend university, where he studied French, Latin and Spanish.

From his earliest years, Walcott has written both poetry and drama, and he regards the two as being of equal importance. Indeed, many of his poems contain dramatic passages of dialogue. Similarly, Walcott is also an accomplished artist and his poetry frequently has a strong visual element.

Derek Walcott won the Nobel Prize for Literature in 1992. He now divides most of his time between Trinidad and the USA. His work with poetry and drama continues.

A Letter from Brooklyn

An old lady writes me in a spidery style,
Each character trembling, and I see a veined hand
Pellucid as paper, travelling on a skein
Of such frail thoughts its thread is often broken;
Or else the filament from which a phrase is hung   5
Dims to my sense, but caught, it shines like steel,
As touch a line and the whole web will feel.
She describes my father, yet I forget her face
More easily than my father's yearly dying;
Of her I remember small, buttoned boots and the place   10
She kept in our wooden church on those Sundays
Whenever her strength allowed;
Grey-haired, thin-voiced, perpetually bowed.

'I am Mable Rawlins,' she writes, 'and know both your parents';
He is dead, Miss Rawlins, but God bless your tense: 15
'Your father was a dutiful, honest,
Faithful, and useful person.'
For such plain praise what fame is recompense?
'A horn-painter, he painted delicately on horn,
He used to sit around the table and paint pictures.'   20
The peace of God needs nothing to adorn
It, nor glory nor ambition.
'He is twenty-eight years buried,' she writes, 'he was called home,
And is, I am sure, doing greater work.'
The strength of one frail hand in a dim room   25
Somewhere in Brooklyn, patient and assured,
Restores my sacred duty to the Word.
'Home, home,' she can write, with such short time to live,
Alone as she spins the blessings of her years;

Not withered of beauty if she can bring such tears,   30
Nor withdrawn from the world that breaks its lovers so;
Heaven is to her the place where painters go,
All who bring beauty on frail shell or horn,
There was all made, thence their *lux-mundi* drawn,
Drawn, drawn, till the thread is resilient steel,   35
Lost though it seems in darkening periods,
And there they return to do work that is God's.

So this old lady writes, and again I believe.
I believe it all, and for no man's death I grieve.

Notes

[3] **pellucid:** transparent
[3] **skein:** a loose bundle of wool or thread
[5] **filament:** a slender thread
[18] **recompense:** reward
[34] **thence:** from that place
[34] **lux-mundi:** the light of the world, often associated with Christ
[35] **resilient:** able to spring back to original shape

Derek Walcott: 'Domino Players'

Explorations

Pre-reading

1. Have you ever received a letter, note, card or text message that cheered you up? Did you keep it? Why?

First reading

2. *Class Discussion*: (i) Did this letter have a positive or negative effect on Walcott? (ii) What do you think he did with this letter?

3. 'An old lady writes me in a spidery style,
   Each character trembling'
   (i) Copy down these lines in your normal handwriting. (ii) Now try writing them in the way that is suggested by the words 'spidery' and 'trembling'.

4. (i) Using the clues given in lines 1–13 write out a physical description of the old lady. (ii) Can you think of three words to sum up her physical appearance?

5. (i) From her description, do you think that Mable liked Walcott's father? Why? (ii) What do you think she means by the phrase 'he was called home'?

Second reading

6. *A. Group Discussion*: (i) How would you describe Walcott's reactions to what the old lady writes in lines 14–22? (ii) How does his reaction change from line 23? (iii) Can you suggest why he feels differently after this line?
   B. Individual Writing: Using the points that arose in the discussion, answer the following question. In your own words, describe the changes that take place in Walcott's attitude towards the old lady in the course of this poem.

7. (i) Which of the following words do you think could be used to describe the old lady's faith: simple, devout, rigid, firm, strong, human? (ii) Briefly explain the reasons behind your selection.

8. *Class Discussion*: (i) How would you describe the condition of Walcott's faith before he reads the letter? (ii) 'I believe it all, and for no man's death I grieve.' What does this line tell you about Walcott's faith after he reads the letter?

9. *Individual Writing*: Using your work on Questions 6, 7, 8 and 9, write the letter that you think Walcott would have written in reply to the old lady. When you have finished you might like to share your work with the class.

Third reading

10. 'Walcott's skilful use of vivid images gradually reveals the theme of this poem'. Respond to this statement, using quotations from the poem to support your viewpoint.

11. *Class Presentation*: 'Walcott uses ordinary language in extraordinary combinations.' Using examples from this poem prepare a brief presentation for your class with this title.

Endings

Things do not explode,
they fail, they fade,

as sunlight fades from the flesh,
as the foam drains quick in the sand,

even love's lightning flash   5
has no thunderous end,

it dies with the sound
of flowers fading like the flesh

from sweating pumice stone,
everything shapes this   10

till we are left
with the silence that surrounds Beethoven's head.

Note

[9] **pumice stone:** porous volcanic rock useful for polishing and cleaning. Also used to remove hard skin.

Explorations

First reading

1. *Class Discussion*: Do you think that one long sentence made up of 59 words should be classed as a poem? Before you can decide on the answer to this question, you need to think about what makes a poem. Gather suggestions from your class on what makes a poem and agree on from four to six points that will be used as criteria in your discussion to arrive at an answer to the question.

2. *A. Class Discusssion*:
'Things do not explode, they fail, they fade,'.
(i) Do you think this is a successful opening to the poem? (ii) Is there a clear connection between these lines and the title of the poem?
B. Individual Writing:
Using the points that arose in the discussion, answer the following question. Imagine that Walcott has just read this poem to you and he asks you: 'What do you think of the first two lines?' Write your response to him.

3. *Group Discussion and Writing*: Most of the poem is made up of a series of vivid images. As a group, write out the way that you would film this poem. You could include notes on camera angles and movements, sound effects, music, named actors, set details. You might like to present your piece to the class.

Second reading

4. *A. Class Discussion*:
'till we are left
with the silence that surrounds Beethoven's head.'
In dealing with the following questions you might find it helpful to know that Beethoven's hearing began to deteriorate when he was thirty until, finally, he became profoundly deaf. (i) How do you think Beethoven, as a musician, felt about his loss of hearing? (ii) What is the connection between the image of Beethoven and the images in lines 1–7?
B. Individual Writing: In your own words, explain how the image of Beethoven is connected to the title of the poem?

5. *A Short Presentation to the Class*: (i) Do you feel that the final two lines of the poem provide a successful ending to the poem? Write a short piece for presentation to the class explaining your answer to this question. (ii) When all the presentations have been heard,

the class might like to vote on whether it is a good ending or not.

6. (i) Choose **one image** where you find the sounds of the words really help you to visualise the picture, and explain the reasons for your choice. (ii) Consider how Walcott uses the sounds of the words, as in alliteration and assonance, to make his images more 'real'.

7. *A. Paired Discussion*: (i) Given that Walcott uses only 59 words in the poem, do you think that his use of repetition is accidental or deliberate? (ii) Why do you think that he repeats the image of flesh fading?

    B. Individual Writing: Using the points that were discussed, answer the following question. Explain, in your own words, the theme of this poem. Your work on this question and Questions 2 and 4 should prove helpful.

Third reading

8. (i) How would you describe the tone of this poem? (ii) What does the tone reveal about Walcott's attitude towards this 'fading away' of things?

9. Do you think that Walcott's use of the 'stream of consciousness' is a successful method, or is this largely unstructured presentation of his inner thoughts and feelings simply confusing?

10. 'In Walcott's poetry, Nature is celebrated as a positive force.' Discuss this statement with reference to 'For Adrian' and 'Endings'.

The Sailor Sings Back to the Casuarinas (from The Schooner Flight)

You see them on the low hills of Barbados
bracing like windbreaks, needles for hurricanes,
trailing, like masts, the cirrus of torn sails;
when I was green like them, I used to think
those cypresses, leaning against the sea,   5
that take the sea-noise up into their branches,
are not real cypresses but casuarinas.
Now captain just call them Canadian cedars.
But cedars, cypresses, or casuarinas,
whoever called them so had a good cause,   10
watching their bending bodies wail like women
after a storm, when some schooner came home
with news of one more sailor drowned again.
Once the sound 'cypress' used to make more sense
than the green 'casuarinas', though, to the wind   15
whatever grief bent them was all the same,
since they were trees with nothing else in mind
but heavenly leaping or to guard a grave;
but we live like our names and you would have
to be colonial to know the difference,   20
to know the pain of history words contain,
to love those trees with an inferior love,
and to believe: 'Those casuarinas bend
like cypresses, their hair hangs down in rain
like sailors' wives. They're classic trees, and we,   25
if we live like the names our masters please,
by careful mimicry might become men.'

Notes

This extract comes from a long poem entitled *'The Schooner Flight'*. It tells the story of Shabine, a West Indian who is forced to leave Trinidad. He becomes a sailor on a schooner called *Flight*. The course the schooner takes follows the route taken by his African ancestors who were brought as slaves to the West Indies.

Casuarinas: a tropical tree with branches of long needles that look rather like birds' feathers or horsetails. The wind blowing through the needles makes a haunting, pleasant sound.

[3] **cirrus:** high-altitude clouds with a wispy appearance

[20] **colonial:** involved in a colony, that is a country fully or partly subject to another country

[27] **mimicry:** to copy in a slavish manner

Casuarinas

Explorations

First reading

1. *A. Group Discussion*: Divide into groups. Each group takes one of the following sections from the poem to use in their discussion: lines 1–3; lines 4–7; lines 8–10. (i) Do you think that these words are being spoken by an Irish or a West Indian person? (ii) What is it about the lines that you are considering that made you realise this? You might like to look at rhythm and syntax (the order of the words). (iii) Look up the word 'vernacular' in the dictionary. Is it relevant to your discussion?

   B. Individual Writing: Write a short report for presentation to the class that summarises your group's discussion about the passage that you considered.

2. Walcott creates a series of images to describe the Casuarina trees. (i) Choose **one** image that appeals to you and explain what you imagine when you read it. (ii) Does Walcott's use of similes make it easier for you to visualise the tree? Refer to the poem to support your views.

3. *A. Class Discussion*: (i) Why do you think the speaker is so concerned about the name that the trees are called by? (ii)

What do you think he means when he writes, 'we live like our names'?

   B. Individual Writing: Using the points that were discussed, answer the following question. (i) How does Walcott suggest that the names we use have powerful effects? (ii) Do you agree with him?

Second reading

4. *A. Class Discussion*:
   '. . . you would have to be colonial to know the difference,'.
   (i) Bearing in mind that the speaker, Shabine, is descended from African slaves, how could being 'colonial' make a person more sensitive to names? (ii) Given our Irish history, do you think that we can more readily understand what Shabine feels?

   B. Individual Writing: Using the points that arose in the discussion, answer the following question. Explain, in your own words, how Walcott sees language as a tool used by one group to keep control of another group. Use quotations from the poem to support your explanation.

5. *A. Paired Discussion and Writing*: In lines 19–22, Shabine tells us how he feels

about being 'colonial'. (i) What do the words 'pain' and 'inferior' suggest to you about his feelings? (ii) How would you describe the tone of these lines?

B. *Paired Writing*: Using the points that were discussed, answer the following question. With one of you as Shabine and one of you as a reporter, write a television interview between the two of you about Shabine's view of being 'colonial'. Present your interview to the class.

6. *A Class Debate*: Using your work on Questions 3 and 4 as a starting point, prepare a speech for or against the motion: 'Language has the power to make or break people.'

Third reading

7. Walcott once said: 'By vernacular I do not mean the diction, the language; I mean the immediacy of the voice.' In your view, is Walcott successful in creating 'immediacy of the voice' in this extract? Support your answer with relevant quotations.

8. 'For Walcott, landscape is more than just a setting for his poems.' Discuss, with reference to **this poem and two other poems by Walcott** that you have considered.

9. 'Dear Derek Walcott . . .' Write a letter to Derek Walcott telling him how you feel about his poetry. Use quotations or references from the poems that you have studied to illustrate your point of view.

10. 'Walcott's love of drama is evident in his ability to create "flesh and blood" characters in his poetry.' With reference to **three poems** by Walcott, respond to this statement.

To Norline

this poem is also prescribed for Ordinary Level exams in 2009 and 2010

This beach will remain empty
for more slate-coloured dawns
of lines the surf continually
erases with its sponge,

and someone else will come   5
from the still-sleeping house,
a coffee mug warming his palm
as my body once cupped yours,

to memorize this passage
of a salt-sipping tern,   10
like when some line on a page
is loved, and it's hard to turn.

Notes

This poem is made up of three groups of four lines of poetry, known as quatrains.

[10] **tern:** a seabird

Derek Walcott: 'Preparing the Net'

Explorations

Pre-reading

1. Have you a particular place that you remember because of who you were with? Take a moment to think about this place. Can you remember how you felt when the time came to leave the place?

First reading

2. *Class Discussion*: (i) Can you suggest a piece of music that should be played while this poem is being read? (ii) Try to agree on three pieces. Perhaps you might like to bring in the three pieces and see which one works the best.

3. A. *Group Discussion*: (i) Describe the setting for this poem. (ii) Are there any clues in the poem that indicate the type of relationship shared by Norline and Walcott? (iii) Is the beach special to Walcott purely because of its beauty?
   B. *Individual Writing*: Using the points that were discussed, answer the following question. Imagine that you are on the beach in the poem. Write a short descriptive passage conveying the sights, sounds, smells, textures and tastes of your experience. You might like to share your work with the class when you have finished.

Second reading

4. A. *Paired Discussion*:
   'The beach will remain empty for more slate-coloured dawns
   of lines the surf continually erases with its sponge,'.
   (i) Can you suggest a connection between the image of the 'dawns' and the image of the 'surf'? (ii) How could these two images be related to the idea of Time?
   B. *Individual Writing*: Using the points that arose in the discussion, answer the following question. Does Time have any effect on the beach described in the first quatrain?

5. A. *Paired Discussion*: (i) What is the first change that occurs on the beach in the second quatrain? (ii) Why do you think Walcott introduces this person into the poem? (iii) Do you think that he and Norline will still be on the beach at this time?
   B. *Individual Writing*: Using the points that were discussed, answer the following question. How is the idea of things changing conveyed in the second quatrain?

6. A. *Class Discussion*: Bearing in mind your thoughts on the first and second quatrain,

consider the final quatrain of the poem. (i) Why do you think Walcott tries to 'memorize' the seabird's flight across the beach? (ii) Can you suggest a connection between the tern's flight and the image of being unwilling to move on from a 'line' that is 'loved'? (iii) Are the emotions that Walcott feels about the tern and the line the same?

B. *Individual Writing*: Using the points that arose in the discussion, answer the following question. In the final quatrain, what is Walcott trying to communicate about his feelings concerning his time on the beach with Norline?

7. *Individual Writing*: Imagine you are Norline and Walcott has just given you this poem. Write a piece describing your reactions.

Third reading

8. 'Walcott uses tenses in a deliberate way so that they reinforce the feeling of standing in a moment on the edge of the present and the future.' Consider this statement, using quotations from 'To Norline' to support your view.

9. Derek Walcott once commented, 'A life that is here and now is timeless.' Discuss with reference to this poem.

10. *A Presentation to the Class*: 'A Precious Moment in Time'. Prepare a speech about your thoughts and feelings on this topic. You may refer to 'To Norline' if you wish.

11. 'The vividness of Walcott's images lies in their appeal not only to the sense of sight but also to hearing, touch and taste.' Discuss this statement, using references from **at least three** of Walcott's poems to illustrate your answer.

Summer Elegies

this poem is also prescribed for Ordinary Level exams in 2009 and 2010

I

Cynthia, the things we did,
our hands growing more bold as
the unhooked halter slithered
from sunburnt shoulders!

Tremblingly I unfixed it   5
and two white quarter-moons
unpeeled there like a frisket,
and burnt for afternoons.

We made one shape in water
while in sea grapes a dove   10
gurgled astonished 'Ooos' at
the changing shapes of love.

Time lent us the whole island,
now heat and image fade
like foam lace, like the tan   15
on a striped shoulder blade.

Salt dried in every fissure,
and, from each sun-struck day,
I peeled the papery tissue
of my dead flesh away;   20

it feathered as I blew it
from reanointed skin,
feeling love could renew itself, and a new life begin.

A halcyon day. No sail.   25
The sea like cigarette paper
smoothed by a red thumbnail,
then creased to a small square.

Derek Walcott: 'Setting the Bait'

The bay shines like tinfoil,
crimps like excelsior;   30
All the beach chairs are full,
but the beach is emptier.

The snake hangs its old question
on almond or apple tree;
I had her breast to rest on,   35
the rest is History.

Notes

[7] **frisket:** a metal frame used in hand printing that is placed over the paper to protect areas that are not to be printed.

[10] **sea grapes:** a coastal plant with leaves, flowers and fruit that resemble grapes

[17] **fissure:** a narrow opening

[25] **halcyon:** calm, peaceful

[30] **crimps:** presses into ridges or waves

[30] **excelsior:** slender, curved wood-shavings

Explorations

First reading

1. (i) Think of one word to describe this poem. (ii) Write each person's contribution on the board. (iii) Are the responses generally positive or negative?

2. *Class Discussion*: (i) Do you think that this is a surprising piece of writing to find on the Leaving Certificate course? Why? (ii) Did the first quatrain make you want to read on? Why?

3. *Individual Writing*: (i) What is the mood created in the first and second stanzas? (ii) Choose two phrases that you feel express this mood.

4. A. *Class Discussion*: How does Walcott suggest an emotional intensity in the third stanza?
   B. *Individual Writing*: Using the points that arose in the discussion, answer the following question. The first three quatrains are filled with a heady eroticism. What images and sounds does Walcott use to convey this eroticism?

5. *Class Discussion*: (i) Does the intensity of emotion carry on into the fourth quatrain? (ii) Walcott introduces the word 'fade' at this point. What effect does it have on the mood of the poem?

6. A. *Class Discussion*: (i) How would you describe the mood of the final five quatrains? What images and sounds do you feel suggest this change in mood?
   B. *Individual Writing*: Using the points that arose in the discussion, answer the following question. Discuss the ways in which Walcott creates a change of mood in the second half of the poem. Use quotations to illustrate your points.

Second reading

7. (i) Why do you think Walcott introduces a snake into the final quatrain? (ii) Do the lovers seem particularly disturbed by the snake? (iii) Do you think that they should be? Why? (iv) Do you feel that this quatrain suggests a happy or unhappy ending to the poem?

8. You have been asked to choose a poem for an anthology of poetry for young adults entitled 'Great Love Poems'. You decide to choose 'Summer Elegies'. Write out the letter that you would send to the publishers explaining the reasons for your choice.

Third reading

9. 'Walcott's ability to vividly create a moment and a place means that we do not simply read his work: we live it.' Respond to this comment, using references from 'Summer Elegies' and 'To Norline'.

10. Walcott once wrote that the strength of the West Indian psyche (that is, the soul, the spirit and the mind) was its 'fusion of formalism with exuberance'. Discuss how Walcott fuses formalism with exuberance in three of his poems. You might like to consider his use of structural elements such as rhyme, rhythm, assonance and alliteration in connection with 'formalism'; while tone, mood, imagery and language might be examined for 'exuberance'.

For Adrian

April 14, 1986

(To Grace, Ben, Judy, Junior, Norline,
Katryn, Gem, Stanley and Diana)

Look, and you will see that the furniture is fading,
that a wardrobe is as unsubstantial as a sunset,

that I can see through you, the tissue of your leaves,
the light behind your veins; why do you keep sobbing?

The days run through the light's fingers like dust   5
or a child's in a sandpit. When you see the stars

do you burst into tears? When you look at the sea
isn't your heart full? Do you think your shadow

can be as long as the desert? I am a child, listen,
I did not invite or invent angels. It is easy   10

to be an angel, to speak now beyond my eight years,
to have more vestal authority, and to know,

because I have now entered a wisdom, not a silence.
Why do you miss me? I am not missing you, sisters,

neither Judith, whose hair will banner like the leopard's   15
in the pride of her young bearing, nor Katryn, not Gem

sitting in a corner of her pain, nor my aunt, the one
with the soft eyes that have soothed the one who writes
        this,

I would not break your heart, and you should know it;
I would not make you suffer, and you should know it;   20

and I am not suffering, but it is hard to know it.
I am wiser, I share the secret that is only a silence,

with the tyrants of the earth, with the man who piles
    rags
in a creaking cart, and goes around a corner

of a square at dusk. You measure my age wrongly,   25
I am not young now, nor old, not a child, nor a bud

snipped before it flowered, I am part of the muscle
of a galloping lion, or a bird keeping low over

dark canes; and what, in your sorrow, in our faces
howling like statues, you call a goodbye   30

is – I wish you would listen to me – a different welcome,
which you will share with me, and see that it is true.

All this the child spoke inside me, so I wrote it down.
As if his closing grave were the smile of the earth.

Notes

[2] **insubstantial:** lacking solidity
[12] **vestal:** pure
[23] **tyrants:** cruel rulers

Explorations

Pre-reading

1. Think of something dissolving or melting away. It could be a small patch of snow on grass, or a small pool of water on sand, or perhaps you might like to come up with your own idea. (i) Take a moment to think about how it happens, then write a short piece describing in words what you saw in your imagination. When you have finished, try reading the piece. How does it sound? Is it slow or fast? Does the pace match the 'melting-away' feeling you want to convey? (ii) Rewrite your piece so that after every two sentences you leave a gap of one line in your copy. Now try reading it again. What effect has leaving the gaps had on the pace of your passage? Which piece do you think works best at communicating your picture? Why?

First reading

2. Think of one word to describe this poem. Write the word on the board. (i) Is there a common response in the class to the poem, or are there a variety of responses? (ii) Why do you think this is?

3. *Paired Discussion*: (i) Choose one image from lines 1–5 that you feel is particularly successful in suggesting the idea of something melting away. (ii) Explain to your partner how and why you think it works.

4. A. *Class Discussion*: (i) How old would you say the speaker in the poem is? (ii) What clues in the poem led you to this view? (iii) Who is he addressing in lines 14–18? What is the connection between them all?
   B. *Individual Writing*: Using the points that were discussed, answer the following question. What do we learn about the relationship between the speaker of the poem and those he is addressing?

5. A. *Paired Discussion*: (i) What images does the child use to suggest that he is now part of a different world? (ii) What qualities do the 'galloping lion' and the 'bird keeping low' suggest to you?
   B. *Individual Writing*: Using the points that arose in the discussion, answer the following question. In your own words, describe how you imagine the other world from the little boy's descriptions.

Second reading

6. *Class Discussion*: (i) The title of the poem is 'For Adrian'. Can you work out where Adrian is in the poem? (ii) What impression do you get of the type of child that Adrian was from the poem?

7. (i) How would you describe the mood conveyed in the lines where Adrian is speaking? (ii) How does his mood contrast with his family's mood? (iii) Why do you think there is this contrast?

8. *Group Discussion and Writing*: Discuss the following questions, then agree on a common answer to be written into your copies. (i) How do alliteration and assonance help to convey the 'melting-away' sensation in lines 1–6? (ii) Lines 1–10 are filled with 's' sounds. Do you think that this sound suggests that Adrian is speaking loudly or quietly? Give reasons for your answer.

9. *Individual Writing*: Imagine that you are a member of Adrian's family. Write a letter to Derek Walcott telling him what the poem meant to the family.

Third reading

9. 'An Elegy is usually defined as a poem that
   - is written to lament the death of someone of importance;
   - usually involves some thoughts on the transient and passing nature of Life.'

   (i) Taking each part of this statement, discuss how it may or may not be applied to 'For Adrian'. (ii) Do you feel that this poem could, indeed, be classified as an Elegy? Why?

10. 'Walcott writes as a poet who is also a dramatist and a painter.' Discuss this statement with reference to **three** poems that you have studied by Derek Walcott.

The Young Wife

(For Nigel)

this poem is also prescribed for Ordinary Level exams in 2010

Make all your sorrow neat.
Plump pillows, soothe the corners
of her favourite coverlet.
Write to her mourners.

At dusk, after the office,   5
travel an armchair's ridge,
the valley of the shadow in the sofas,
the drapes' dead foliage.

Ah, but the mirror – the mirror
which you believe has seen   10
the traitor you feel you are –
clouds, though you wipe it clean!

The buds on the wallpaper
do not shake at the muffled sobbing
the children must not hear,   15
or the drawers you dare not open.

She has gone with that visitor
that sat beside her, like wind
clicking shut the bedroom door;
arm in arm they went,   20

leaving her wedding photograph in
its lace frame, a face smiling at
itself. And the telephone
without a voice. The weight

we bear on this heavier side   25
of the grave brings no comfort.
But the vow that was said
in white lace has brought

you now to the very edge
of that promise; now, for some,   30
the hooks in the hawthorn hedge
break happily into blossom

and the heart into grief.
The sun slants on a kitchen floor.
You keep setting a fork and knife   35
at her place for supper.

The children close in the space
made by a chair removed,
and nothing takes her place,
loved and now deeper loved.   40

The children accept your answer.
They startle you when they laugh.
She sits there smiling that cancer
kills everything but Love.

Notes

[8] **drapes:** curtains
[8] **foliage:** leaves

Derek Walcott: 'Still Life – The Desk'

 # Explorations

wife's death.

4. *Class Discussion*: (i) What is the mood created in the fifth quatrain? (ii) What image does Walcott use to convey the young wife's acceptance of death? (iii) Do you find this a surprising portrayal of death? Why?

5. (i) Why do you think Walcott uses images of the couple's wedding in the sixth, seventh and eighth quatrains? (ii) What effect is created by the contrast between the present and the past memory? (iii) Can you suggest what is meant by the husband being brought 'to the very edge | of that promise'? You might find it helpful to think of the words in the marriage promise.

6. *A. Paired Discussion*: (i) How do the young wife's children react to her death? (ii) Do you find their reaction surprising or do you think that it is realistic? (iii) Does their reaction have any effect on the husband?
   B. Individual Writing: Who do you think copes better with the young wife's death, her husband or her children? Use references to the poem to support your points.

7. *A. Class Discussion*: (i) What mood is created by the images in the final quatrain? (ii) What effect do these final four lines have on you? (iii)

Do you think that Walcott succeeds, in 'The Young Wife', in proving that Love cannot be killed?
B. Individual Writing: Using the points that arose in the discussion, answer the following question. Explain the theme of this poem in your own words.

Third reading

8. Walcott does not use a rigid, end-of-line rhyme scheme in this poem; instead, his rhymes are subtle and intermittent. Consider the links in meaning that are created between the pairs of words that do rhyme:
   corners, mourners;
   seen, clean;
   space, place;
   answer, cancer;
   laugh, Love.

9. You have been asked to make a short film based on this poem. Using the information in the poem: (i) Describe the sets that you would use. (ii) Suggest suitable music to complement the poem. Explain what camera shots and angles you would use to visually communicate the poem.

10. Do you think that poems such as 'The Young Wife' and 'For Adrian' should be subjected to the cold knife of critical analysis in pursuit of exam marks? Give reasons for your opinion.

Saint Lucia's First Communion

At dusk, on the edge of the asphalt's worn-out ribbon,
in white cotton frock, cotton stockings, a black child stands.
First her, then a small field of her. Ah, it's First Communion!
They hold pink ribboned missals in their hands,

the stiff plaits pinned with their white satin moths.   5
The caterpillar's accordion, still pumping out the myth
along twigs of cotton from whose parted mouths
the wafer pods in belief without an 'if'!

So, all across Saint Lucia thousands of innocents
were arranged on church steps, facing the sun's lens,   10
erect as candles between squinting parents,
before darkness came on like their blinded saint's.

But if it were possible to pull up on the verge
of the dimming asphalt, before its headlights lance
their eyes, to house each child in my hands,   15
to lower the window a crack, and delicately urge

the last moth delicately in, I'd let the dark car
enclose their blizzard, and on some black hill,
their pulsing wings undusted, loose them in thousands to stagger
heavenward before it came on: the prejudic, the evil!   20

Notes

Saint Lucia: Walcott's birthplace. An isolated island in the Lesser Antilles in the Caribbean, named after Saint Lucy, the virgin martyr of Syracuse who was put to death by the sword in AD 303

[1] **asphalt:** mix of pitch, sand and gravel used to surface roads

[4] **missals:** book containing texts of Mass and prayers

Procession for First Communion on St Lucia

Explorations

Pre-reading

1. This poem centres on 'First Communion': a religious ceremony within the Catholic Church, where children receive Holy Communion for the first time. Have you ever taken part in a religious ceremony? You might like to describe your memories of the ceremony and what it meant to you.

First reading

2. Did any image in the poem remind you of your own experience? Explain, in your own words, how it triggered your memories.

3. *Individual Writing*: Imagine that you are a reporter for the local newspaper in St Lucia. You have been asked to cover the First Communion. Write an article of no more than 150 words describing the occasion.

4. (i) What colours do the First Communion children wear? (ii) Can you suggest what these colours symbolise? (iii) Is there a connection between these colours and his use of the word 'innocents' in line 9 to describe the children?

5. A. *Paired Discussion*: (i) How do the parents react to the setting sun? (ii) What does the phrase 'erect as candles' suggest to you about how the children feel? (iii) Why do you think the children are not concerned about the sunlight while the adults are?

   B. *Individual Writing*: Using the points that arose in the discussion, answer the following question. What evidence is there in the poem that making their First Communion had an effect on the children?

6. A. *Class Discussion*: (i) In line 5, Walcott introduces the image of a moth. What is Walcott using the moth to describe in this line? (ii) What does the moth image in lines 17–20 suggest?

   B. *Individual Writing*: Using the points that were discussed, answer the following question. (i) What qualities do the moths and the children have in common? (ii) Do you think that Walcott's connection of the two helps you to understand the poem, or is it simply confusing?

Second reading

7. A. *Group Discussion*: (i) What does Walcott's use of the phrase 'belief without an "if"' suggest to you about the children's attitude to religion?

   B. *Individual Writing*: Imagine

that you are one of the children in the poem. Explain your thoughts and feelings.

8. *A. Group Discussion*: (i) What does Walcott's desire to take the children to 'some black hill' and 'loose them' suggest about his attitude to religion? (ii) Using the other clues in the poem, decide whether Walcott sees religion as a positive or negative force.
B. Individual Writing: Using the points that arose in the discussion, answer the following question. (i) Summarise Walcott's attitude to religion as it is revealed in this poem. (ii) Which attitude do you feel closer to: the children's or Walcott's?

9. 'their pulsing wings undusted, loose them in thousands to stagger
heavenward before it came on: the prejudice and evil!'.
(i) Do you find this image easy to visualise? (ii) In your own words, describe what you 'see'. (iii) Do these lines help you to understand the theme of this poem? (iv) Explain the theme of the poem in your own words.

Third reading

9. The imagery in the poem is stunning. Choose **two images** that you particularly like and try to tease out the different layers that are in each of them. You might like to begin with the visual level, perhaps considering what you 'see' when you read the words; then move on to the way that the line structure, rhythm or sounds of the words reinforce the image so that you can 'feel' it; and, finally, examine the metaphorical level where the image represents something more than just a vivid description.

11. Children feature in a number of Walcott's poems. With reference to **three** of his poems, discuss whether or not he depicts them in a realistic manner.

Pentecost

Better a jungle in the head
than rootless concrete.
Better to stand bewildered
by the fireflies' crooked street;

winter lamps do not show   5
where the sidewalk is lost,
nor can these tongues of snow
speak for the Holy Ghost;

the self-increasing silence
of words dropped from a roof   10
points along iron railings,
direction, if not proof.

But best is this night surf
with slow scriptures of sand,
that sends, not quite a seraph,   15
but a late cormorant,

whose fading cry propels
through phosphorescent shoal
what, in my childhood gospels,
used to be called the Soul.   20

Notes

Pentecost: Ten days after Jesus ascended into Heaven the disciples gathered in Jerusalem. The Holy Ghost came to the apostles in the form of tongues of fire resting over their heads. They began to preach the gospel and they were able to speak in the language of the person who was listening to them.

[14] **scriptures:** sacred writings

[15] **seraph:** an angel

[16] **cormorant:** a black, diving seabird

[18] **phosphorescent:** luminous, full of glowing light

[18] **shoal:** a group of fish, a multitude

Explorations

Pre-reading

1. Have you ever been outside in a heavy snowfall? Think about what you saw around you and as you looked up. What sounds did you hear? How did the snow feel as it brushed your skin? Write a short descriptive piece based on your thoughts.

First reading

2. *Class Discussion*: (i) Is the theme of this poem clear to you on a first reading? (ii) How do you feel about this? (iii) Do you like poems to have a simple, clear theme, or do you prefer having to work your way through layers to arrive at an understanding? (iv) Might your attitude be influenced by the fact that you are studying poetry for an examination?

3. Walcott uses the images 'tongues of snow' and 'night surf' to describe the snow. (i) Which of these images do you like better? (ii) Explain the reasons for your choice.

4. A. *Class Discussion*: (i) What feelings does the phrase 'a jungle in the head' suggest to you? Is it connected to 'bewildered' in line 3? (ii) Bearing this in mind, what feelings does the phrase

'rootless concrete' suggest to you? (iii) Walcott prefers the 'jungle'. Why do you think he feels this? (iv) Which would you prefer inside your head? B. *Individual Writing*: What do the first two lines of the poem suggest about Walcott's state of mind?

Second reading

5. A. *Group Discussion*: (i) 'Trying to find the right way' is an important concept in the poem. In line 12 Walcott finds 'direction, if not proof'. What is the difference between 'direction' and 'proof'? (ii) Which would be of more help in 'trying to find the right way'? B. *Individual Writing*: Using the points that were discussed, answer the following question. Explain, in your own words, how Walcott explores the idea of 'finding the right way' in this poem.

6. A. *Group Discussion*: (i) Walcott uses a number of 'religious' words in this poem. List these words. (ii) Is there a connection between his concern with 'finding the right way' and these religious words? B. *Individual Writing*: How could Walcott's concern with

'finding the right way' be interpreted in a religious sense?

7. A. *Class Discussion*: (i) What creature appears in line 16? (ii) What effect does the cormorant have on Walcott? (ii) How does Walcott's use of the word 'propels' help you to understand what this effect is?
    B. *Individual Writing*: Using the points that arose in the discussion, answer the following question. Do you think the cormorant's arrival helps Walcott in his search for 'the right way'?

8. A. *Class Discussion*: Walcott does not get all that he would like – he gets direction but not proof; he gets a cormorant, but not a seraph. (i) Do you think that he is unhappy because he has to settle for direction and a cormorant?
    B. *Individual Writing*: Using the points that were discussed, answer the following question. Walcott begins the poem with a 'jungle' in his head. Do you think that he has untangled this 'jungle' a little by the end

of the poem? Give reasons for your view. Share your answers with the class with a view to further discussion.

Third reading

9. Do you find Walcott's use of the 'stream of consciousness' method successful in helping you to understand the poem or do you find it confusing? Use quotations from 'Pentecost' to support your viewpoint.

10. Is Walcott's attitude to religion, as expressed in 'Pentecost', contradictory to the attitude that he expresses in 'Saint Lucia's First Communion'? Support your argument by reference to the two poems.

11. A lyric is a poem that does not tell a story, but rather features a single speaker who wishes to share a mood, attitude or state of mind with the reader. Discuss Walcott's use of the lyric form with regard to **two poems** that you have studied. Support your answer by relevant quotations.

From Omeros

Chapter XXX, I, lines 1–65

He yawned and watched the lilac horns of his island
lift the horizon.
         'I know you ain't like to talk,'
the mate said, 'but this morning I could use a hand.
Where your mind was whole night?'   5
            'Africa.'
                'Oh? You walk?'
The mate held up his T-shirt, mainly a red hole,
and wriggled it on. He tested the bamboo pole

that trawled the skipping lure from the fast-shearing hull   10
with the Trade behind them.
            'Mackerel running,' he said.
'Africa, right! You get sunstroke chief. That is all.

You best put that damn captain-cap back on your head.'
All night he had worked the rods without any sleep,   15
watching Achille cradled in the bow; he had read

the stars and known how far out they were and how deep
the black troughs were and how long it took them to lift,
but he owed it to his captain, who took him on

when he was stale-drunk. He had not noticed the swift.   20
'You know what we ketch last night? One *mako* size "ton,"'
using the patois for kingfish, blue albacore.

'Look by your foot.'
          The kingfish, steel-blue and silver,
lay fresh at his feet, its eye like a globed window   25
ringing with cold, its rim the circular river

of the current that had carried him back, with the spoon
bait in its jaw, the ton was his deliverer,
now its cold eye in sunlight was blind as the moon.

A grey lens clouded the gaze of the albacore   30

that the mate had gaffed and clubbed. It lay there, gaping,
its blue flakes yielding the oceanic colour

of the steel-cold depth from which it had shot, leaping,
stronger than a stallion's neck tugging its stake,
sounding, then bursting its trough, yawning at the lure   35

of a fishhook moon that was reeled in at daybreak
round the horizon's wrist. Tired of slapping water,
the tail's wedge had drifted into docility.

Achille had slept through the fight. Cradled at the bow
like a foetus, like a sea-horse, his memory   40
dimmed in the sun with the scales of the albacore.

'Look, land!' the mate said. Achille altered the rudder
to keep sideways in the deep troughs without riding
the crests, then he looked up at an old man-o'-war

tracing the herring-gulls with that endless gliding   45
that made it the sea-king.
                         'Them stupid gulls does fish
for him every morning. He himself don't catch none,

white slaves for a black king.'
                         'When?' the mate said. 'You wish.'   50
'Look at him dropping.' Achille pointed. 'Look at that son-
of-a-bitch stealing his fish for the whole focking week!'

A herring-gull climbed with silver bent in its beak
and the black magnificent frigate met the gull
halfway with the tribute; the gull dropped the mackerel   55

but the frigate-bird caught it before it could break
the water and soared.
                    'The black bugger beautiful,
though!' The mate nodded, and Achille felt the phrase lift

his heart as high as the bird whose wings wrote the word   60
'Afolabe,' in the letters of the sea-swift.
'The king going home,' he said as he and the mate

watched the frigate steer into that immensity
of seraphic space whose cumuli were a gate
dividing for a monarch entering his city.   65

Notes

This extract comes from Walcott's 325-page poem 'Omeros'. In this work, Walcott takes the
epic world of Homer and places it in his Caribbean world. So, Homer's Achilles becomes
Achille the West Indian seaman. Journeys, both real and spiritual, are at the heart of the
poem.

[10] **lure:** item of fishing equipment used to attract fish

[10] **shearing:** cutting

[11] **Trade:** The Trade Winds blow continually towards the equator

[21] **mako:** a large bluish-coloured shark

[21–22] **ton / kingfish / albacore:** a long-finned tuna

[22] **patois:** a regional dialect based on a standard language often used by illiterate classes
and usually considered substandard. In the West Indies, French Creole and English Creole.

[31] **gaffed:** seized using a stick with an iron hook

[38] **docility:** becoming submissive, easily managed

[44] **man-o'-war:** also called the frigate-bird. A type of tropical seabird with a large
wingspan and a forked tail.

[55] **tribute:** a payment made to a ruler as a mark of respect

[61] **Afolabe:** Achille's African ancestor

[64] **seraphic:** serene, angelic

[64] **cumuli:** large rounded clouds with flat bases

Painting by Derek Walcott used as the cover of *Omeros*.

Explorations

First reading

1. *Class Discussion*: Derek Walcott has always wanted to film parts of 'Omeros'. Choose one descriptive passage from the poem and explain why you find it particularly film-like.

2. *Class Discussion*:
   'He yawned and watched the lilac horns of his island lift the horizon.'
   (i) How do you rate this as an opening to a piece of writing? (ii) Does it catch your interest? Why?

3. (i) Where is this extract set? (ii) What time of day is it? (iii) Who are the people involved? (iv) What did each of them do during the night? (v) What do they see happening in the sky?

Second reading

4. A. *Paired Discussion*: (i) What physical details do we learn about the Mate? (ii) From the evidence in the poem, what sort of a person do you think the Mate is? (iii) How does the Mate feel about Achille?
   B. *Individual Writing*: Describe the Mate in your own words.

5. A. *Paired Discussion*: (i) What physical details de we learn about Achille? (ii) From the evidence in the poem, what

sort of person do you think Achille is? (iii) How does Achille feel about the Mate?
   B. *Individual Writing*: Describe Achille in your own words.

6. A. *Class Discussion*: (i) What are Achille's feelings towards the man-o'-war? (ii) Achille compares the bird to his African ancestor, Afolabe. Can you suggest what it is about the bird that reminds him of his ancestor?
   B. *Individual Writing*: Describe the reactions that the appearance of the man-o'-war cause in Achille. Use quotations to support your points.

7. A. *Individual Writing*: 'Walcott shapes his images not only in words that create mind pictures but in sounds and rhythms that make us feel what is happening.' Discuss this statement with reference to lines 24–38 or lines 53–65. Your discussion should include comments on his use of metaphor, colour, assonance, alliteration and rhythm.

8. A. *Paired Discussion*: Rhythm plays a very important part in this extract, particularly in the conversation between Achille and the Mate in lines

3–14. (i) Does the rhythm of their speech sound real and convincing to you? (ii) Choose one line or phrase that you feel is particularly effective in conveying West Indian speech.

B. *Paired Writing*: Using the points that arose in the discussion, answer the following question. Take the conversation in lines 3–14 and rewrite it the way that you would say it. As a class, compare examples of the two passages and decide which of the two sounds more 'alive'.

Third reading

9. Journeys, both real and spiritual, pervade 'Omeros'. Consider the concept of 'journeying' in any two of Walcott's poems. Use references to support your consideration.

10. In many ways Ireland and the West Indies share a common bond,, in that both experienced the imposition of a language by an outside power. In her book 'The Flight of the Vernacular', Maria Cristina Fumagalli comments, 'Walcott seems to suggest that belief in the power of language to signify is a kind of "religious" faith . . . '. Discuss this statement with regard to **three** poems by Walcott, using quotations to support your argument.

12 Sylvia PLATH

prescribed for Higher Level exams in 2007 and 2008

Sylvia Plath was born in Boston, Massachusetts on 27 October 1932, to Aurelia Schober Plath and Otto Plath, professor of Biology and German at Boston University. In 1940 Otto died after a long illness, a tragedy which haunted Sylvia throughout her life. From a young age, Sylvia wanted above all else to be a writer. Already writing at the age of five, she had her first poem published in the children's section of the *Boston Herald* at the age of eight. She was a brilliant high-school student, consistently earning A grades, and also led a busy social life. She had a number of stories and poems published – and also got many rejection slips; this pattern recurred throughout her writing life. In 1950 she entered the prestigious women's university, Smith College, Massachusetts.

In 1952 Plath was selected to work as one of twenty 'guest editors' with *Mademoiselle* magazine in New York City. On her return to Wellesley, she suffered a serious bout of depression for which she was given electric-shock treatment. However, this seems to have deepened her depression and she attempted suicide in August, leading to a four-month spell in a psychiatric hospital. She resumed her studies in Smith College in

1932–1963

January 1953, graduating with honours in 1955, and winning a Fulbright scholarship to study in Cambridge, England. There she met Ted Hughes, a young English poet, whom she married in June 1956.

Sylvia and Ted worked and wrote in the US for two years and returned to London in December 1959. 'Black Rook in Rainy Weather' and 'The Times Are Tidy' date from this period. Her first book, *The Colossus and Other Poems*, was published in February 1960, but received disappointing reviews. April 1960 saw the birth of their daughter, Frieda. The following year they moved to Devon where their son, Nicholas, was born in January 1962. Throughout this time, Sylvia was writing poetry, (including 'Morning Song', 'Finisterre', 'Mirror', 'Pheasant' and 'Elm') some of which was published in magazines in Britain and the US. Her semi-autobiographical novel, *The Bell Jar,* was published in 1963.

Shortly after Nicholas's birth, Ted and Sylvia separated. She remained in Devon, caring for her children and writing, despite poor health and recurring depression. She

Sylvia Plath

completed most of the poems which made up her second book, *Ariel* (published posthumously), among them 'Poppies in July' and 'The Arrival of the Bee Box'. In mid-December 1962, she moved to London with her children. The poems she wrote at this time include 'Child', written on 28 January 1963. However, unable to cope with the many difficulties facing her, she took her own life on 11 February 1963. Since her death her writing has received wide acclaim, including the prestigious Pulitzer Prize, an award rarely bestowed posthumously.

Black Rook in Rainy Weather

On the stiff twig up there
Hunches a wet black rook
Arranging and rearranging its feathers in the rain.
I do not expect a miracle
Or an accident   5

To set the sight on fire
In my eye, nor seek
Any more in the desultory weather some design,
But let spotted leaves fall as they fall,
Without ceremony, or portent.   10

Although, I admit, I desire,
Occasionally, some backtalk
From the mute sky, I can't honestly complain:
A certain minor light may still
Lean incandescent   15

Out of kitchen table or chair
As if a celestial burning took
Possession of the most obtuse objects now and then –
Thus hallowing an interval
Otherwise inconsequent   20

By bestowing largesse, honour,
One might say love. At any rate, I now walk
Wary (for it could happen
Even in this dull, ruinous landscape); sceptical,
Yet politic; ignorant   25

Of whatever angel may choose to flare
Suddenly at my elbow. I only know that a rook
Ordering its black feathers can so shine
As to seize my senses, haul
My eyelids up, and grant   30

A brief respite from fear
Of total neutrality. With luck,
Trekking stubborn through this season
Of fatigue, I shall
Patch together a content   35

Of sorts. Miracles occur,
If you care to call those spasmodic
Tricks of radiance miracles. The wait's begun again
The long wait for the angel,
For that rare, random descent.   40

Notes

[2] **rook:** crow

[8] **desultory:** without method, disjointed

[10] **portent:** omen of some possibly calamitous event

[15] **incandescent:** glowing, brilliant

[19] **hallowing:** making sacred

[21] **largesse:** generously given present

[25] **politic:** prudent

[31] **respite:** brief period of relief

Explorations

Before reading

1. What picture does the title create for you? Does it suggest a particular mood?

First reading

2. The poem is set against a very definite landscape: read the poem and describe the scene as accurately as you can. Build your picture from the poet's words and phrases.

3. What does the narrator seem to be doing in this poem? What thoughts does this lead to?

4. Describe the atmosphere the poem creates for you. What details are most important in setting this atmosphere?

Second reading

5. There is an abrupt change between lines 3 and 4. What is it?

6. The narrator claims that 'I do not expect . . . nor seek . . .'. What does she neither expect nor seek? (Lines 4–10.)

7. What does she 'admit' to desiring? How does she convey the idea that it may not be possible to get what she desires?

8. Can you find other places in the poem where she makes a statement, and then qualifies it – 'neutralises' it? What do such

statements tell us about the narrator's frame of mind?

9. The 'minor light' of line 14 'may' have an extraordinary effect: read lines 14–22 carefully and explain this effect in your own words.

10. Can you explain how the 'rook | Ordering its black feathers can . . . grant | A brief respite' to the speaker? A brief respite from what?

11. In the final lines, she is waiting for the 'rare, random descent' of the angel. What might the angel bring? What examples of this has she already given?

12. The angel's 'rare, random descent' is a metaphor: what do you think it represents? Look at references to other heavenly phenomena before answering.

Third reading

13. Comment on the effect of the repetition of the sound 'rain' in line 3.

14. Look through the poem again, and pick out words connected with darkness and light. Compare the images or words used. Can you find any pattern?

15. The narrator does not 'seek . . . design' in things around her. How does the language reflect that lack of design, the

accidental nature of what happens? A good starting point might be to identify the words associated with time or chance.

16. There is a mixture of the everyday/earthly and the extraordinary/miraculous here. How is this effect achieved? You might find it helpful to contrast concrete descriptions with references to the sacred.

Fourth reading

17. Examine the rhyme scheme. What pattern do you find? What is the effect of this careful sound pattern?

18. Write a note on the style of the poem, looking at tone, language, imagery, structure.

19. Throughout her life, Plath was preoccupied with the conflict between her ambitions to be a poet and the expectations of a society which defined women as home-makers. Reread this poem with this in mind. Would you agree that this could be one theme of the poem? Are there other possibilities? Write about what you consider to be the main themes of this poem.

The Times Are Tidy

Unlucky the hero born
In this province of the stuck record
Where the most watchful cooks go jobless
And the mayor's rôtisserie turns
Round of its own accord.   5

There's no career in the venture
Of riding against the lizard,
Himself withered these latter-days
To leaf-size from lack of action:
History's beaten the hazard.   10

The last crone got burnt up
More than eight decades back
With the love-hot herb, the talking cat,
But the children are better for it
The cow milks cream an inch thick.   15

Notes

[4] **rôtisserie:** A rotating spit, traditionally used to roast whole animals.
Often a communal service used by peasants who would not own an oven
or a spit.

[11] **crone:** witch

Explorations

Before reading

1. Think back to folk-tales or legends you have read or heard involving knights in armour, witches and monsters. What can you remember about their world, the adventures described?

2. Jot down whatever comes into your mind when you hear the word 'tidy'.

First reading

3. The poem puts two eras side by side. What can you learn from the poem about each of them?

4. Which era sounds more appealing to you? Why? Which does the author seem to favour? Refer to the poem to support your impression.

Second reading

5. Try to mentally recapture the effect of listening to a stuck record. What do you think the poet is telling you about 'this province' when she uses this image? Do you think this links in any way with 'tidy'?

6. The poem was written about a particular phase in American political life. Suggest then what the 'mayor's rôtisserie' might represent? Who might the 'cooks' be?

7. We are told that the jobless cooks are the 'most watchful': why then are they jobless? By choice? Because they have been sacked?

8. What mythical creature does the lizard resemble? Think of medieval knights and the creatures they did battle with. What is there in this stanza to show that the poet intends this connection to be made?

9. In what way has 'history' beaten the hazard?

10. What association exists between the crone and the 'love-hot herb', the 'talking cat' and the 'cream an inch thick'?

11. What do the crone, the hero and the lizard have in common? How does their absence affect the 'times'?

12. Most of the poem focuses on what this age has lost: the last two lines suggest a gain. What is this? Do you think the poet is being serious here, or is she being ironic? Explain your answer.

Third reading

13. Two eras are contrasted in the poem. How do they differ? Be precise – refer to the text for each point you make.

14. Choose the image(s) you consider to be most effective. Explain your choice.

15. Keeping in mind the title, the images used and the comparisons made, write a note on the tone of the poem.

General question
16. 'This poem is an ironic commentary on an era of smug, self-satisfied complacency in American life.' Discuss this statement, referring to imagery, language and tone.

Morning Song

Love set you going like a fat gold watch.
The midwife slapped your footsoles, and your bald cry
Took its place among the elements.

Our voices echo, magnifying your arrival. New statue.
In a drafty museum, your nakedness   5
Shadows our safety. We stand round blankly as walls.

I'm no more your mother
Than the cloud that distils a mirror to reflect its own slow
Effacement at the wind's hand.

All night your moth-breath   10
Flickers among the flat pink roses. I wake to listen:
A far sea moves in my ear.

One cry, and I stumble from bed, cow-heavy and floral
In my Victorian nightgown.
Your mouth opens clean as a cat's. The window square   15

Whitens and swallows its dull stars. And now you try
Your handful of notes;
The clear vowels rise like balloons.

Explorations

Before reading

1. Look at the title of this poem: jot down the ideas you associate with both words. What mood do they evoke?

First reading

2. Stanzas 1–3 centre on the infant taking her place in the world: how do others respond to her? Which emotions come across most clearly?

3. How do you understand the image of the baby as a 'New statue' taking its place in a 'drafty museum'? How does nakedness 'shadow' the safety of the onlookers? (There are a number of possibilities.)

4. Explain in your own words what happens in stanzas 4–6. Do you find the description realistic?

Second reading

5. What emotions does the opening line suggest to you? Look at the first word, the image, the rhythm. Do you think it is an effective opening line? Why?

6. Identify the noises named in the poem. Name the source of each sound. Who is listening to them? What impression do they create? How do they contribute to the texture of the poem?

Third reading

7. This poem is rich in vivid imagery and word-pictures. Identify these.

8. Say what each image or word-picture suggests about the baby, about the mother, about the world they inhabit. How is this suggested? Refer to the language, the juxtaposition of images, the associations implied.

9. Explain the cloud/mirror/wind image used in stanza 3. What does the comparison suggest about the narrator's feelings about motherhood?

General questions

10. 'Morning Song' is a tender evocation of a simple, daily event. Examine how the writer conveys the mood of tenderness, while avoiding sentimentality.

11. Compare this poem with 'Child' in terms of theme, tone, language and imagery. Which of the two poems do you prefer? Why?

Finisterre

This was the land's end: the last fingers, knuckled and rheumatic,
Cramped on nothing. Black
Admonitory cliffs, and the sea exploding
With no bottom, or anything on the other side of it,
Whitened by the faces of the drowned.   5
Now it is only gloomy, a dump of rocks –
Leftover soldiers from old, messy wars.
The sea cannons into their ear, but they don't budge.
Other rocks hide their grudges under the water.

The cliffs are edged with trefoils, stars and bells   10
Such as fingers might embroider, close to death,
Almost too small for the mists to bother with.
The mists are part of the ancient paraphernalia –
Souls, rolled in the doom-noise of the sea.
They bruise the rocks out of existence, then resurrect them.   15
They go up without hope, like sighs.
I walk among them, and they stuff my mouth with cotton.
When they free me, I am beaded with tears.

Our Lady of the Shipwrecked is striding toward the horizon,
Her marble skirts blown back in two pink wings.   20
A marble sailor kneels at her foot distractedly, and at his foot
A peasant woman in black
Is praying to the monument of the sailor praying.
Our Lady of the Shipwrecked is three times life size,
Her lips sweet with divinity.   25
She does not hear what the sailor or the peasant is saying –
She is in love with the beautiful formlessness of the sea.

Gull-colored laces flap in the sea drafts
Beside the postcard stalls.
The peasants anchor them with conches. One is told: 30
'These are the pretty trinkets the sea hides,
Little shells made up into necklaces and toy ladies.
They do not come from the Bay of the Dead down there,
But from another place, tropical and blue,
We have never been to.   35
These are our crêpes. Eat them before they blow cold.'

Finisterre: the westernmost tip of Brittany – literally 'land's end'

[3] **admonitory:** giving a warning

[10] **trefoils:** three-leaved plants

[13] **paraphernalia:** belongings, bits and pieces, ornaments

[14] **doom:** judgement, punishment

[30] **conches:** spiral shells

[36] **crêpes:** light, lacy, crispy pancakes – speciality of Brittany

 # Explorations

Before reading
1. What kind of landscape/ seascape do the place names 'Finisterre' and 'land's end' suggest? How do you visualize it – colours, shapes, sounds, weather . . .?

First reading
Stanza 1
2. Read stanza 1. What overall picture do you form of the scene? What words or images do you find most striking? Is the personification effective?
3. How is language used to create the impression of an attack, a battle? Does this description of a headland create a familiar picture for you?
Stanza 2
4. What does stanza 2 describe? How does it connect with stanza 1? Notice how language and imagery are used to create links.
5. What qualities do you usually associate with mist? Which of these qualities does this mist share? What other qualities does the narrator attribute to it? Do these add anything new?
6. What is your impression of the atmosphere in this place? How is it created?

Second reading
Stanza 3
7. Describe in your own words the scene depicted in stanza 3. What connection is there with the first two stanzas?
8. The perspective in this stanza has changed: the poet is showing us things from a different angle. How is this indicated?

9. This stanza tells a little story within the poem. Tell it in your own words.

Stanza 4

10. The stalls in stanza 4 are suggested through a few precise details: look at the description – can you picture them?

11. This stanza differs remarkably from the preceding stanzas. In what way?

12. Identify the ideas/words/images which link stanza 4 with the earlier stanzas. Explain the connection.

13. We now learn that the bay is named the 'Bay of the Dead': does the name fit, in your opinion? Why do you think the poet did not name it until the end of the poem?

Third reading

14. Comment on the effect of the image in lines 1 and 2. How is this image developed in the rest of this stanza and in stanza 2?

15. Stanza 3 opens with a description of the monument. Contrast the 'I' of stanza 2 with Our Lady of the Shipwrecked. What is the impact of the contrast? What is the narrator's attitude to Our Lady?

16. Comment on the language used to describe the scene – the details given, the intentions or qualities attributed to each figure. Where does the narrator fit into this scene? What does she seem to be saying about prayer?

17. The author broadens the scope of the poem through the stall-keeper's comments, which reflect quite a different response to the bay. How? What is the effect of the wider canvas?

18. How does the final line strike you? Would you agree that there is a slightly ironic note here? What effect does this have on your reading of the poem?

General questions

19. Write a note on the tone of the poem. Be aware of the gradual change in tone, reflected in the language and imagery; note the differences between the narrator's attitude, and that of the other figures in the poem.

20. Trace the progress of thought from the opening line to the end of the poem. Focus on how the author moves from the inner thoughts of the narrator to a more objective view. Note where the changes occur.

21. Plath once commented: '. . . a poem, by its own system of illusions, can set up a rich and apparently living world within its particular limits.' Write about 'Finisterre' in the light of this comment, looking at her choice of words, images, sound effects and point of view.

Coastal landscape of Finisterre

Mirror

I am silver and exact. I have no preconceptions.
Whatever I see I swallow immediately
Just as it is, unmisted by love or dislike.
I am not cruel, only truthful –
The eye of a little god, four-cornered.   5
Most of the time I meditate on the opposite wall.
It is pink, with speckles. I have looked at it so long
I think it is a part of my heart. But it flickers.
Faces and darkness separate us over and over.

Now I am a lake. A woman bends over me,   10
Searching my reaches for what she really is.
Then she turns to those liars, the candles or the moon.
I see her back, and reflect it faithfully.
She rewards me with tears and an agitation of hands.
I am important to her. She comes and goes.   15
Each morning it is her face that replaces the darkness.
In me she has drowned a young girl, and in me an old woman
Rises toward her day after day, like a terrible fish.

Note

[11] **reaches:** stretch of water, depths

Explorations

Before reading

1. Think for a minute about a mirror. Write down quickly all the words, ideas and associations that come to mind.

First reading

2. Listen to this poem a number of times. What is it saying?
3. Write a note on the form of the poem: number of stanzas, number of lines, etc.
4. Pick out all the 'I' statements. How many are there? What effect do they have?
5. Identify the qualities the mirror claims to possess. What overall impression is created by these attributes?
6. Notice the position of the words 'a little god': they are at the exact centre of stanza 1. Can you suggest why the poet placed them just there?
7. What impression is created by the description of 'the opposite wall'?
8. In stanza 2, the mirror states that it is now 'a lake': what similarities are there between a lake and a mirror? What differences are there? How does this new image expand the mirror image?
9. Why do you think the narrator describes the candles and the moon as 'liars'?

10. What might cause the woman's tears and agitation? How does this point broaden the scope of the poem?
11. The mirror/lake contains three phases of the woman's life: what are these?

Second reading

12. The focus – the point of view – changes between stanzas 1 and 2. How has the centre of consciousness changed? What is the effect of this?
13. Write a note about what you think the 'terrible fish' may be.
14. 'I am important to her': this is a very strong statement. How could a mirror be important to her? What do you think the mirror may represent to the narrator? (Try to move beyond the most obvious points.)

Third reading

15. Compare the opening lines (1–3) with the final lines. Trace the progress of thought through the poem, showing how the narrator moves from the opening statement to the conclusion. Note the changes in tone which occur.
16. The poem concludes on a note of desperation. How is this prepared for in the poem as a whole?
17. Do you agree that the narrator

has 'no preconceptions' as stated in line 1? What evidence can you find to support your opinion? Look especially at phrases like 'I think', 'those liars', etc.

18. While the poem is unrhymed, Plath uses a variety of sound effects. Identify some of these, and say what effect they create.

General questions

19. Many writers and artists use the mirror as a symbol – for example, of the self, the alter ego, the 'dark side of the soul'. Reread the poem with this idea in mind. How does it colour your reading of the poem? Does it fit the poem?

20. It has been argued that in this poem Plath is addressing the conflict between what a woman was expected to be (smooth, unruffled, reflecting the image the world wanted to see), and her true nature (struggling to be heard, seen for what it is: the 'terrible fish'). Reread the poem in the light of this comment, and write your response.

Pheasant

You said you would kill it this morning.
Do not kill it. It startles me still,
The jut of that odd, dark head, pacing

Through the uncut grass on the elm's hill.
It is something to own a pheasant,   5
Or just to be visited at all.

I am not mystical: it isn't
As if I thought it had a spirit.
It is simply in its element.

That gives it a kingliness, a right.   10
The print of its big foot last winter,
The tail-track, on the snow in our court –

The wonder of it, in that pallor,
Through crosshatch of sparrow and starling.
Is it its rareness, then? It is rare.   15

But a dozen would be worth having,
A hundred, on that hill – green and red,
Crossing and recrossing: a fine thing!

It is such a good shape, so vivid.
It's a little cornucopia.   20
It unclaps, brown as a leaf, and loud,

Settles in the elm, and is easy.
It was sunning in the narcissi.
I trespass stupidly. Let be, let be.

Notes   [14] **crosshatch:** criss-cross pattern
         [20] **cornucopia:** A mythical horn, always full of flowers and
              fruit. A symbol of plenty.

 # Explorations

First reading

1. The poem opens very abruptly:
   it plunges the reader right into
   the narrator's preoccupation.
   What is this? Why do you
   think she repeats the word
   'kill'?
2. Lines 3 and 4 present a graphic
   picture. What scene is evoked?
3. The speaker's attitude toward
   the pheasant is clearly signalled
   in lines 5 and 6. What is it?
   Can you find any further echo
   of this feeling in the poem?
4. In stanzas 4 and 5 the poet
   pictures the pheasant: how
   does she underline its
   difference to the other birds
   that visit her yard?
5. Stanza 7 moves back to the
   present: the pheasant's 'clap'
   draws her attention. What was
   it doing before it flew up into
   the elm?
6. She loves the colour, the shape,
   the sound of the pheasant.
   Identify where each of these is
   praised.

Second reading

7. In verse 3 the narrator explains
   why she feels so honoured by
   the visit of the pheasant:
   identify what 'it is' and what
   'it isn't' that touches her. Why
   do you think she tells us that
   she is 'not mystical'?
8. In what sense is she
   trespassing? What does this
   word suggest about her

attitude to the pheasant?

9. How do the final words link back to the opening statement and request? Do you feel the narrator has got her way at the end? Explain.

10. What is the tone/mood of the poem? Use the text to support your points, paying attention to the narrator's relationship with 'you'.

General question

11. Plath describes the pheasant as 'vivid'. The same word could apply to this poem: it is strong, vigorous and sinewy. Write about this quality of the poem. Look at language – verbs, nouns, adjectives – as well as imagery, structure, rhythm and rhyme.

Elm

For Ruth Fainlight

I know the bottom, she says. I know it with my great tap root:
It is what you fear.
I do not fear it: I have been there.

Is it the sea you hear in me,
Its dissatisfactions?   5
Or the voice of nothing, that was your madness?

Love is a shadow.
How you lie and cry after it
Listen: these are its hooves: it has gone off, like a horse.

All night I shall gallop thus, impetuously,   10
Till your head is a stone, your pillow a little turf,
Echoing, echoing.

Or shall I bring you the sound of poisons?
This is rain now, this big hush.
And this is the fruit of it: tin-white, like arsenic.   15

I have suffered the atrocity of sunsets.
Scorched to the root
My red filaments burn and stand, a hand of wires.

Now I break up in pieces that fly about like clubs
A wind of such violence   20
Will tolerate no bystanding: I must shriek.

The moon, also, is merciless: she would drag me
Cruelly, being barren.
Her radiance scathes me. Or perhaps I have caught her.

I let her go. I let her go   25
Diminished and flat, as after radical surgery.
How your bad dreams possess and endow me.

I am inhabited by a cry.
Nightly it flaps out
Looking, with its hooks, for something to love.   30

I am terrified by this dark thing
That sleeps in me;
All day I feel its soft, feathery turnings, its malignity.

Clouds pass and disperse.
Are those the faces of love, those pale irretrievables?   35
Is it for such I agitate my heart?

I am incapable of more knowledge.
What is this, this face
So murderous in its strangle of branches? –

Its snaky acids hiss.   40
It petrifies the will. These are the isolate, slow faults
That kill, that kill, that kill.

Notes   [15] **arsenic:** lethal poison

[18] **filaments:** thread-like conductors of electrical current

[24] **scathe:** to hurt or injure, especially by scorching

[35] **irretrievables:** cannot be recovered or won back

Explorations

First reading

1. Listen to the poem a number of times. What sounds are most striking? Which words stay in your mind? Jot down your impressions.
2. What attitude does 'I' seem to adopt toward 'you' in stanza 3?
3. Stanzas 5–8 introduce rain, sunset, wind and moon: how is each one presented? How do they affect 'I'?
4. What change seems to occur in 'I' in stanzas 9–14? Can you identify at what point the change began?
5. Would you agree that the latter half of the poem powerfully conveys a nightmare world? Which images and phrases are most effective in building this impression?

Second reading

6. 'Elm' opens on a confident, objective note, as if the narrator is quite detached from 'you'. How is this achieved?
7. Trace the references to love in the poem. How does the narrator view love? Is it important to her?
8. There are several references to violence, both physical and mental. Select those you consider most powerful. What is the source of the violence?
9. Compare the force of love with the force of evil. Which comes across as the more powerful? Explain how this is achieved.

Third reading

10. Plath uses many rich and powerful images. The central image is the elm, the 'I' persona. (*a*) Trace the elm's feelings, mood through the poem. (*b*) What do you think the elm may symbolise to the poet? In answering this, reflect on the tone, the utter weariness, the feelings of anguish, the growing terror and the role 'you' plays in generating these feelings.
11. The moon is another important image in the poem. Reread the stanzas describing it (8, 9, 13). What qualities are attributed to it? What do you think it symbolises? Can you explain the seeming contradictions?

Fourth reading

12. The poet uses rich sound effects throughout the poem. Note where she uses rhyme, assonance, repetition, cacophony and soft sounds. How do these affect the reader/listener?
13. The poem opens with a calm

confident voice, a sense of control: 'I know . . . I I do not fear . . .'. It closes on a note of hysterical despair, total loss of control: 'It petrifies the will. These are the isolate, slow faults I That kill, that kill, that kill.' Trace the change through the poem. Describe how this transformation is achieved.

General questions

14. 'Plath infuses this poem with a strong sense of vulnerability pitted against destructive energy.' What is your response to this statement? Use detailed reference to the poem in support of each point you make.

15. '"Elm" is a powerful urgent statement spoken by a narrator who has been abandoned by the person she loves.' Discuss this view of the poem.

16. 'This poem has the surreal quality of a nightmare in which the smallest objects seem fraught with hidden significance.' Discuss how this effect is achieved, basing each point you make on specific reference to the poem.

Poppies in July

Little poppies, little hell flames,
Do you do no harm?

You flicker. I cannot touch you.
I put my hands among the flames. Nothing burns.

And it exhausts me to watch you   5
Flickering like that, wrinkly and clear red, like the skin of a mouth.

A mouth just bloodied.
Little bloody skirts!

There are fumes that I cannot touch.
Where are your opiates, your nauseous capsules?   10

If I could bleed, or sleep! –
If my mouth could marry a hurt like that!

Or your liquors seep to me, in this glass capsule,
Dulling and stilling.

But colorless. Colorless.   15

Notes   [10] **opiates:** narcotics, drugs which induce sleep, dull feelings
            [10] **nauseous:** causing vomiting or illness

 # Explorations

Before reading	**First reading**
1. Imagine a poppy: what qualities do you associate with it? Think of colour, texture and shape.	2. The poem opens with a question. What does it suggest to you? 3. Describe what the narrator is doing in this poem. What

thoughts are triggered by her actions?

4. Identify the words associated with fire in lines 1–6. What is the narrator's feeling about this fire/these poppies? What does fire symbolise? Do you see any of these qualities reflected here?

5. Which qualities of the poppies might make the narrator think of a mouth?

6. What could 'bloody' a mouth? Do any of the other words suggest violence?

7. Lines 9–13 focus on another aspect of poppies: what is this?

8. Looking at the various descriptions of the poppies, try to explain the author's attitude to them.

Second reading

9. What feelings does the narrator convey in this poem? Say how each feeling is suggested, referring to specific words and images.

10. There is a strong contrast between lines 1–8 and lines 9–15. How is this effected? Look at how words, images and tone contribute to the contrast.

11. The narrator seems to imply an answer to the question posed in stanza 1. How does she answer it?

Third reading

12. While there is no end rhyme in this poem, the poet uses quite intricate sound effects, including repetition. Trace these, noting the effect they have.

13. Write a paragraph about the poet's use of colour in the poem, noting how she moves from the vividness of the early stanzas to the final repeated 'colorless'. What might the loss of colour say about the narrator's feelings?

14. The poem moves from the outside world to the inner world of the narrator. Chart this movement through the poem. How does she connect one to the other?

Fourth reading

15. Do you consider the intensity of the feeling conveyed is consistent with a simple description of poppies? What underlying emotion do you think might cause such intense anguish? Discuss this point, referring to the text in support of your arguments.

16. In both 'Poppies in July' and 'Elm', Plath takes a simple natural object and invests it with intense feelings, creating a metaphor for personal suffering – the inner struggle to come to terms with an overwhelming problem. Write a comparison of the two poems.

The Arrival of the Bee Box

this poem is also prescribed for Ordinary Level exams in 2007 and 2008

I ordered this, this clean wood box
Square as a chair and almost too heavy to lift.
I would say it was the coffin of a midget
Or a square baby
Were there not such a din in it.   5

The box is locked, it is dangerous.
I have to live with it overnight
And I can't keep away from it.
There are no windows, so I can't see what is in there.
There is only a little grid, no exit.   10

I put my eye to the grid.
It is dark, dark,
With the swarmy feeling of African hands
Minute and shrunk for export,
Black on black, angrily clambering.   15

How can I let them out?
It is the noise that appals me most of all,
The unintelligible syllables.
It is like a Roman mob,
Small, taken one by one, but my god, together!   20

I lay my ear to furious Latin.
I am not a Caesar.
I have simply ordered a box of maniacs.
They can be sent back.
They can die, I need feed them nothing, I am the owner.   25

I wonder how hungry they are.
I wonder if they would forget me
If I just undid the locks and stood back and turned into a tree.
There is the laburnum, its blond colonnades,
And the petticoats of the cherry.   30

They might ignore me immediately
In my moon suit and funeral veil.
I am no source of honey

So why should they turn on me?
Tomorrow I will be sweet God, I will set them free.   35

The box is only temporary.

Notes

[22] **Caesar:** Roman emperor

[28] **turned into a tree:** A reference to the Greek myth of Daphne who was chased by Apollo. She pleaded with the gods to help her escape, and they changed her into a tree.

[32] **moon suit and funeral veil:** protective clothing worn by beekeepers

 # Explorations

First reading

1. Stanza 1 gives the background to the arrival of the bee box and the narrator's reaction. Which feeling is most obvious? Have you ever felt this way about bees, wasps . . .?

2. How does she seem to relate to the bees in stanzas 3–5?

3. Stanza 5 concludes with the statement 'They can die'. Do you actually believe she means this? How does she undermine her statement? Be precise.

4. How does she propose to escape the bees' wrath if she releases them?

5. She describes her clothing as a 'moon suit': what ideas does this image suggest?

6. Comment on the contradiction between 'I am no source of honey' and 'I will be sweet God'. Note the play on words – what is the tone of these lines? How can she be 'sweet God' to the bees?

7. What happens in this poem? What part does the 'I' of the poem play in the event?

Second reading

8. The language used to describe the bee box is strong, suggesting something sinister and dangerous. Select the words or images that help to create this impression.

9. There is a contradiction between the image of a coffin and the intense life within the box. Which idea – death or life – is implied with more strength in the rest of the poem? Be precise.

10. In stanza 3, the writer creates a graphic metaphor for the bees and their sound. Identify these

and note the common link between them. What do they tell us about the narrator?

11. In stanzas 4 and 5, the bees have become a metaphor for the narrator's words. Explain the image, trying to convey some of the feeling she captures. What relationship is suggested between the narrator and her words in these two stanzas?

12. The image of turning into a tree is associated with the Greek myth of the god Apollo and Daphne: she turned into a tree to escape his attentions. What does this association say about the narrator's attitude to the bees?

13. Write a detailed description of the changes in the narrator's attitude between stanza 1 and stanza 7.

14. The final line stands alone, separated from the rest of the poem which is arranged in five-line stanzas. What does the line suggest? How does it colour the reader's response to the poem as a whole?

Third reading

15. Plath makes extensive use of internal rhyme, assonance and word play. One example is 'square as a chair'. Here, 'chair' suggests the homely and ordinary, while 'square' implies honest, straightforward, exact. The rhyme almost echoes the box's shape – its regularity and squareness. Identify other examples of sound effects and word-play in the poem. Comment on their use.

16. This poem moves between the real and familiar world, and the symbolic. Can you identify what is real and ordinary, what happens on the surface?

17. On the symbolic level, what is suggested by the poem? Look at the metaphors used for the bee box, the bees, the 'I' persona. Be aware of the feelings conveyed throughout.

18. There is a touch of dark humour, self-mockery, running through the poem. Where is this most obvious? What effect does it have on the reader?

General question

19. What do you consider to be the central theme of the poem? In answering, refer to the writer's tone and the images used. Look also at your answers to Questions 16 and 17.

Child

this poem is also prescribed for Ordinary Level exams in 2007 and 2008

Your clear eye is the one absolutely beautiful thing.
I want to fill it with color and ducks,
The zoo of the new

Whose names you meditate –
April snowdrop, Indian pipe,   5
Little

Stalk without wrinkle,
Pool in which images
Should be grand and classical

Not this troublous   10
Wringing of hands, this dark
Ceiling without a star.

Explorations

First reading

1. Read this poem aloud and listen to its lyrical tone. What is your first impression of the speaker's feeling for her child? Try to imagine the speaker and child – what image do you see?
2. What pictures does she create for the child's 'eye'?
3. Which words here remind you of childlike things? What mood is usually associated with these?
4. How do you interpret the final stanza? Does it affect your reading of the rest of the poem?

Second reading

5. What feelings does the narrator display toward the child in the opening stanzas?
6. Does the narrator's focus remain consistent through the poem? Where do you think the change occurs? Look at the verb tenses used when answering this.
7. How is the adult/narrator/ mother contrasted with the child?

Third reading

8. What is the effect of line 1 on the reader? Examine how this is achieved.
9. Write a paragraph showing how this contrasts with the final lines. Look at language, imagery, tone.
10. The language of the poem is fresh, clear and simple. What is the effect of this?
11. Write a note about the impressions created by this poem for you.

13 *Michael* LONGLEY

prescribed for Higher Level exams in 2009 and 2010

Michael Longley was born in Belfast on 27 July 1939, of English parents. His father, Richard, who features in the poems 'Wounds', 'Wreaths' and 'Last Requests', fought in the trenches in the First World War and was gassed, wounded, decorated, and promoted to the rank of captain. In *Tuppenny Stung*, a short collection of autobiographical chapters published in 1994, Longley describes his family, primary and secondary education and the forces of his early cultural formation: Protestant schoolboys' fears of the dark savageries supposedly practised by Catholics, an English education system dismissive of Irish culture and history, and Protestant Belfast's fear and resentment of the Republic. His early education and local socialisation made him aware of conflicting classes and religions, and of the duality of Irish identity.

Later he was educated at the Royal Belfast Academical Institution. In 1958 he went to Trinity College, Dublin, where the student population at the time consisted mainly of southern and northern Protestants, middle- and upper-class English, and a scattering of southern Catholics. He studied classics and wrote poetry but felt very under-read in English literature until taken in

1939–

hand by his friend and young fellow-poet Derek Mahon.

Longley worked for the Arts Council of Northern Ireland in the period 1970–91, when he took early retirement. His work for the arts was driven by a number of guiding principles, among which were the nurturing of indigenous talent; support for the artists, not just the arts; allied to the need to transcend class barriers and bring the arts, at an affordable price, to the working class. He was a champion of cultural pluralism, fostering the artistic expression of both sides of the religious and political divide. His vision of Ulster culture has always sought to include its many different strands and influences and so to encourage a unique hybrid rather than separate, antagonistic cultures.

No Continuing City (1969), Longley's first collection, is known for its technically accomplished and learned poetry – among its concerns are poets, poetry and nature. It is best known for the erudite, witty and sophisticated love poetry, almost in the metaphysical tradition. *An Exploded View* (1973) continues to deal with poetry and poetic issues.

MICHAEL LONGLEY 377

Nature is also a major preoccupation. ('Badger' is from this volume.) The collection does respond briefly to the upsurge of violence in Northern Ireland around this time. In 'Wounds' the violence is seen in the broad perspective of international conflict. A great number of the poems focus on an alternative life in the west of Ireland. 'Carrigskeewaun' and 'Poteen' are among these.

Michael Longley

The Echo Gate (1979) demonstrates Longley's now-established bifocal view: on Belfast and Mayo. He confronts the political violence in its stark everyday settings in 'Wreaths' and explores the war experiences of his father as a perspective on this violence in 'Last Requests'. He also explores the folklore, ethos and culture of the west of Ireland and finds a bleak, unconscious parallel between its crude violence and that of Belfast in 'Self-Heal'. *Gorse Fires* (1991) is centred on Longley's adopted second home of Carrigskeewaun in Co. Mayo; but it also includes poems on the Holocaust, the Second World War and the Spanish Civil War. Interspersed with these are some free translations from Homer's *Odyssey*, focusing on Odysseus's return to his home and interpreted by some critics as having strong (if oblique) relevance to Longley's own home province. 'Laertes' is from this sequence.

Michael Longley is a fellow of the Royal Society of Literature and a member of Aosdána. He is married to the critic and academic Edna Longley.

Badger

For Raymond Piper

I

Pushing the wedge of his body
Between cromlech and stone circle,
He excavates down mine shafts
And back into the depths of the hill.

His path straight and narrow   5
And not like the fox's zig-zags,
The arc of the hare who leaves
A silhouette on the sky line.

Night's silence around his shoulders,
His face lit by the moon, he   10
Manages the earth with his paws,
Returns underground to die.

II

An intestine taking in
patches of dog's-mercury,
brambles, the bluebell wood;   15
a heel revolving acorns;
a head with a price on it
brushing cuckoo-spit, goose-grass;
a name that parishes borrow.

III

For the digger, the earth-dog   20
It is a difficult delivery
Once the tongs take hold,
Vulnerable his pig's snout
That lifted cow-pats for beetles,
Hedgehogs for the soft meat,   25

His limbs dragging after them
So many stones turned over,
The trees they tilted.

CD Track 11

Notes

[2] **cromlech:** a name formerly used for the remains of a portal tomb; here the poet uses it to mean the horizontal slab on top of the upright stones

[14] **dog's mercury:** a herbaceous woodland plant, usually regarded as toxic

[19] **a name that parishes borrow:** The poet refers to *broc*, the Irish for 'badger' (in fact the element Broc found in place-names – for example *Domhnach Broc*, anglicised Donnybrook – is the man's name Broc.

Explorations

First reading: section I

1. Think of section I as a picture or painting. What do you see? Consider the setting described, the background, the lighting, and the main subject.

2. What do you notice about the badger? How do you visualise the animal? Examine the connotations of descriptive words and phrases, such as 'the wedge of his body'; 'Night's silence around his shoulders'; 'he | Manages the earth'. How do the badgers' paths differ from those of other animals, and what might this suggest about the nature of the badger?

3. What is suggested here about the animal's relationship with the earth? Consider his association with cromlech and stone circle; how he 'manages' the earth; how he 'Returns underground to die.'

4. Do you think the badger has particular significance for the poet? Explain.

5. How would you describe the atmosphere of section I? What words or phrases help to create it?

Second reading: section II

6. What do you notice about the badger's diet?

7. What other aspects of the badger's environmental function are referred to in section II?

8. 'a head with a price on it . . . a name that parishes borrow.' What do these lines suggest about human attitudes to the badger?

Third reading: section III

9. What do you think is happening in section III?

10. Contrast the humans' treatment of the environment in section III with the badger's management of the earth in sections I and II.

11. Do you think the poet has some sympathy for the animal in this section? Which phrases or images might suggest this?

12. Explore the ironies in the first stanza of this section.

Fourth reading

13. What point is the poet making about humankind's interaction with the environment?

14. What other themes do you notice in the poem?

15. Would you agree that 'Longley displays the scientific assurance of a naturalist'?

16. 'Longley's view of the west of Ireland is a realistic rather than a romantic one.' On the evidence of the poem 'Badger' would you agree with this

statement? Refer to the text to support your argument.

17. Summarise your thoughts and feelings on this poem.

Wounds

CD Track 12

this poem is also prescribed for Ordinary Level exams in 2010

Here are two pictures from my father's head –
I have kept them like secrets until now:
First, the Ulster Division at the Somme
Going over the top with 'Fuck the Pope!'
'No Surrender!': a boy about to die,   5
Screaming 'Give 'em one for the Shankill!'
'Wilder than Gurkhas' were my father's words
Of admiration and bewilderment.
Next comes the London-Scottish padre
Resettling kilts with his swagger-stick,   10
With a stylish backhand and a prayer.
Over a landscape of dead buttocks
My father followed him for fifty years.
At last, a belated casualty,
He said – lead traces flaring till they hurt –   15
'I am dying for King and Country, slowly.'
I touched his hand, his thin head I touched.

Now, with military honours of a kind,
With his badges, his medals like rainbows,
His spinning compass, I bury beside him   20
Three teenage soldiers, bellies full of
Bullets and Irish beer, their flies undone.
A packet of Woodbines I throw in,
A lucifer, the Sacred Heart of Jesus
Paralysed as heavy guns put out   25
The night-light in a nursery for ever;
Also a bus-conductor's uniform –
He collapsed beside his carpet-slippers
Without a murmur, shot through the head
By a shivering boy who wandered in   30
Before they could turn the television down
Or tidy away the supper dishes.
To the children, to a bewildered wife,
I think 'Sorry Missus' was what he said.

Notes

[3] **Ulster Division:** a division of the British army in the First World War

[3] **Somme:** a river in north-eastern France, the scene of continuous heavy fighting during the First World War, particularly from July to November 1916

[4] **Going over the top:** an infantry attack, with soldiers climbing out of the trenches

[6] **Shankill:** an area of west Belfast around the Shankill Road, inhabited mainly by Protestants

[9] **London-Scottish padre:** the regimental chaplain; 'London-Scottish' refers to his father's regiment. He seems preoccupied with flicking down the dead soldiers' kilts in order to allow them some dignity in death.

[24] **lucifer:** an old name for a match

 # Explorations

First reading

(Focus on the first half of the poem.)

1. The first part of the poem is taken up with the 'two pictures from my father's head'. Explore the first picture – lines 3–8. What are your thoughts about this?

2. Interpret the father's reaction – lines 7–8.

Or

3. Compose a brief diary extract that the father might have written on the evening following the attack.

4. Explore the second picture – lines 9–11. What are your thoughts on this?

5. Reflect on the two images. What do they suggest to you about people at war? Jot down all the ideas suggested by these pictures.

6. Read lines 12–15. What do you discover about the effects of war on the father?

7. From a reading of the first part of this poem, what do you discover about Longley's father?

8. Comment on the relationship between father and son. Refer to specific words and phrases.

Second reading

(Focus on the second half of the poem.)

9. What is happening in the second part of this poem? Read it a number of times. If you are still confused, examine the first three lines very carefully.

10. At this surreal burial ceremony the poet interns an odd collection of objects and images. (*a*) Comment on the significance of the objects directly connected with the father. What is revealed about the father and about the

relationship between father and son? (*b*) Explore the images of violence. What do you see? What do they suggest to you about the society?

11. 'A shivering boy who wandered in': compose an interior monologue of the imagined thoughts of this boy.

Third reading

12. Examine the structure or division of this poem into two parts. How do the two parts relate? What point is the poet making here?

13. Comment on the themes explored in this poem. What view of life is presented?

14. Do you think the poet is angry, saddened, depressed or what by these happenings? Refer to specific phrases and lines.

15. Would you agree that this poem shows the ordinary human being as insignificant and powerless in the face of violence? Refer to specific incidents in the text.

16. Comment on any feature of the poet's style you consider significant. You might consider the impact of the imagery; the humour; the tone of the piece; the surreal nightmarish effects; the realism; or any other.

Soldiers from the Royal Irish Rifles during a break from fighting at the Battle of the Somme in 1916

Poteen

Enough running water
To cool the copper worm,
The veins at the wrist,
Vitriol to scorch the throat –

And the brimming hogshead,   5
Reduced by one noggin-full
Sprinkled on the ground,
Becomes an affair of

Remembered souterrains,
Sunk workshops, out-backs,   10
The back of the mind –
The whole bog an outhouse

Where, alongside cudgels,
Guns, the informer's ear
We have buried it –   15
Blood-money, treasure-trove.

Notes **Poteen:** illegally produced alcohol, [poitín]

[2] **copper worm:** a spiral of copper piping, part of the
     equipment used in the still that produces alcohol

[4] **vitriol:** sulphuric acid; used metaphorically it means
     caustic speech or criticism

[5] **hogshead:** a large cask or barrel

[6] **noggin:** a measure of spirits

[9] **souterrains:** underground chambers

Explorations

First reading

1. What is happening in the first two stanzas? What do you see? Which words and phrases create the most striking images for you? What particular quality of the poitín is emphasised?

2. Why do you think they might sprinkle 'one noggin-full . . . on the ground'? Explore all possibilities, both practical and symbolic.

Second reading

3. If we interpret the sprinkling as a superstitious gesture and agree that this primitive action casts the speaker's mind back in time, what does he recall or imagine? Explore stanzas 3 and 4.

4. What have these imagined locations in common with the setting of the present activity?

5. What is suggested to you by the line 'The whole bog an outhouse'?

6. What atmosphere is conjured up by this catalogue of images in the two final stanzas?

7. How are they connected to 'the back of the mind'?

Third reading

8. How would you describe the culture or way of life that is imaginatively unearthed by the speaker?

9. What statement about Irishness is made by the poem?

10. What part does the imagery play in the impact of the poem? Refer to specific examples.

11. Consider the shape of the poem, the length of the lines and the number of sentences used. Do these enhance and complement the subject matter and activity in the poem? Explain how the form contributes to this poem.

Carrigskeewaun

For Penny and David Cabot

The Mountain
This is ravens' territory, skulls, bones,
The marrow of these boulders supervised
From the upper air: I stand alone here
And seem to gather children about me,
A collection of picnic things, my voice   5
Filling the district as I call their names.

The Path
With my first step I dislodge the mallards
Whose necks strain over the bog to where
Kittiwakes scrape the waves: then, the circle
Widening, lapwings, curlews, snipe until   10
I am left with only one swan to nudge
To the far side of its gradual disdain.

The Strand
I discover, remaindered from yesterday,
Cattle tracks, a sanderling's tiny trail,
The footprints of the children and my own   15
Linking the dunes to the water's edge,
Reducing to sand the dry shells, the toe-
And fingernail parings of the sea.

The Wall
I join all the men who have squatted here
This lichened side of the dry-stone wall   20
And notice how smoke from our turf fire
Recalls in the cool air above the lake
Steam from a kettle, a tablecloth and
A table she might have already set.

The Lake
Though it will duplicate at any time   25
The sheep and cattle that wander there,
For a few minutes every evening
Its surface seems tilted to receive
The sun perfectly, the mare and her foal,
The heron, all such special visitors.   30

Notes

Carrigskeewaun: a townland in the parish of Kilgeever, Co. Mayo; the name means 'rock of the wall ferns'

[1] **raven:** a large black bird that feeds chiefly on carrion

[7] **mallard:** a wild duck

[9] **kittiwake:** small marine gull

[10] **lapwing:** bird of the plover family

[10, 14] **curlew, snipe, sanderling:** types of wading bird, usually found in marshy places or by the seashore

Explorations

First reading

The Mountain

1. What is the poet's first impression of this landscape? Of what does it remind him? What is the significance of the raven?

2. How does the speaker react to the bleak landscape? Explore the contrast between his thoughts and the nature of the terrain.

The Path

3. What is happening in this section? What do you see? How do you picture the poet in the scene?

4. How would you describe the poet's relationship with the local fauna? Where is this indicated in the language?

Second reading

The Strand

5. What absorbs the poet's attention here?

6. What aspects of the cycle of nature does he find fascinating?

7. How would you describe the atmosphere of this section? How is this achieved by the language and imagery?

The Wall

8. How does he portray his feelings of a sense of continuity?

9. Do you think he feels at all lonely here? Explain.

The Lake

10. If this were a painting, what would it show? What colours would you use?

11. What aspects of nature are emphasised in this section?

Third reading

12. In general, how do you think Longley feels about Carrigskeewaun? Explore the evidence for this.

Whooper swans on the lake at Carrigskeewaun, a drawing by Michael Viney

13. Explain how the imagery conveys the atmosphere of the place.
14. What particular significance do you think Carrigskeewaun might have for Longley? Explain your views, with reference to this and other poems by Longley.

Fourth reading

15. Alan Peacock writes about the notion of escape to elemental places found among some urban writers: 'The dangers of course in this view of writing are well known: sentimentality, a penchant for the picturesque and a tendency towards idealisation which masks realities.' Examine 'Carrigskeewaun' from the point of view of his general reservations on this type of poem.
16. Peacock also mentions Longley's 'genuinely sympathetic and at the same time coolly scientific engagement with the particularities of the environment'. Do you think this statement could be applied to 'Carrigskeewaun'? Explain, with reference to the text.
17. Do you think this poem shows 'a man at ease with himself and his fellows' (Brown)?
18. What did you discover about the poet from a reading of this poem?

Wreaths

The Civil Servant
He was preparing an Ulster fry for breakfast
When someone walked into the kitchen and shot him:
A bullet entered his mouth and pierced his skull,
The books he had read, the music he could play.

He lay in his dressing gown and pyjamas   5
While they dusted the dresser for fingerprints
And then shuffled backwards across the garden
With notebooks, cameras and measuring tapes.

They rolled him up like a red carpet and left
Only a bullet hole in the cutlery drawer: 10
Later his widow took a hammer and chisel
And removed the black keys from his piano.

The Greengrocer
He ran a good shop, and he died
Serving even the death-dealers
Who found him busy as usual   15
Behind the counter, organised
With holly wreaths for Christmas,
Fir trees on the pavement outside.

Astrologers or three wise men
Who may shortly be setting out   20
For a small house up the Shankill
Or the Falls, should pause on their way
To buy gifts at Jim Gibson's shop,
Dates and chestnuts and tangerines.

The Linen Workers
Christ's teeth ascended with him into heaven: 25
Through a cavity in one of his molars
The wind whistles: he is fastened for ever
By his exposed canines to a wintry sky.

I am blinded by the blaze of that smile
And by the memory of my father's false teeth   30

Brimming in their tumbler: they wore bubbles
And, outside of his body, a deadly grin.

When they massacred the ten linen workers
There fell on the road beside them spectacles,
Wallets, small change, and a set of dentures: 35
Blood, food particles, the bread, the wine.

Before I can bury my father once again
I must polish the spectacles, balance them
Upon his nose, fill his pockets with money
And into his dead mouth slip the set of teeth.   40

 # Explorations

The Civil Servant
First reading

1. What do you notice about the incident?

2. Ponder the description of the killing: 'A bullet entered his mouth and pierced his skull'. How do you think the line should be read? Explain the tone you would employ.

3. What kind of man was the victim? Examine the details.

4. What is your reaction to the treatment of the victim after death?

Second reading

5. What does the poem say to you about violence and about the value and significance of human life?

6. Comment on the tone of the writing. Examine the descriptions, the choice of words, the style of speech. Is there any evidence of emotional reaction to this killing?

The Greengrocer
First reading

7. What do you find most incongruous about this killing?

8. What is your understanding of the reference to 'Astrologers or three wise men'?

9. How do you read the tone of this piece?

The Linen Workers
First reading

10. Explore each of the three main images developed here – the Christ figure, the father and the massacre – in stanzas 1, 2, 3. (*a*) How are they linked? What have the Christ figure

and the father to do with the massacre? (*b*) Comment on the quality and nature of the images. Are they everyday, realistic, unusual, or what?

11. In what ways does the treatment of violence here differ from that in the other poems?

Overall reading

12. Record your thoughts on a final reading of the three pieces.

13. What aspects of violence engage Longley's imagination?

14. Comment on the poet's style of imagery and on the tone of the narration.

15. 'Violence is unblinkingly looked at in its graphic, but strangely intimate, everyday actuality' (Alan Peacock). Do you think Peacock's view of Longley's work could be applied to this poem? Explain, with reference to the detail of the poem.

Last Requests

this poem is also prescribed for Ordinary Level exams in 2009 and 2010

I

Your batman thought you were buried alive,
Left you for dead and stole your pocket watch
And cigarette case, all he could salvage
From the grave you so nearly had to share
With an unexploded shell. But your lungs   5
Surfaced to take a long remembered drag,
Heart contradicting as an epitaph
The two initials you had scratched on gold.

II

I thought you blew a kiss before you died,
But the bony fingers that waved to and fro   10
Were asking for a Woodbine, the last request
Of many soldiers in your company,
The brand you chose to smoke for forty years
Thoughtfully, each one like a sacrament.
I who brought peppermints and grapes only   15
Couldn't reach you through the oxygen tent.

Explorations

First reading: part I

1. What do you notice about the episode described here?
2. What does it convey of the poet's view of war? Explain, with reference to the text.
3. Is there a certain light-heartedness about this, despite the topic? Explain.

Second reading: part II

4. In your own words, describe the death-bed scene as you see it from a reading of this section.
5. Is the scene as you imagine a death-bed scene might be?

6. Is there a sense of sadness behind the humour? Where?
7. Write about the poet's view of his father. (*a*) What are his significant memories of him? (*b*) Do you suppose father and son were close? Explain.
8. Which lines created most impact for you? Explain.

Third reading

9. What impression of the poet did you form from reading this poem? Refer to the text.
10. What view of life informs or inspires this poem? Refer to the text.

Mayo Monologues – Self-Heal

I wanted to teach him the names of flowers,
Self-heal and centaury; on the long acre
Where cattle never graze, bog asphodel.
Could I love someone so gone in the head
And, as they say, was I leading him on?   5
He'd slept in the cot until he was twelve
Because of his babyish ways, I suppose,
Or the lack of a bed: hadn't his father
Gambled away all but rushy pasture?
His skull seemed to be hammered like a wedge   10
Into his shoulders, and his back was hunched,
Which gave him an almost scholarly air.
But he couldn't remember the things I taught:
Each name would hover above its flower
Like a butterfly unable to alight.   15
That day I pulled a cuckoo-pint apart
To release the giddy insects from their cell.
Gently he slipped his hand between my thighs.
I wasn't frightened; and still I don't know why,
But I ran from him in tears to tell them.   20
I heard how every day for one whole week
He was flogged with a blackthorn, then tethered
In the hayfield. I might have been the cow
Whose tail he would later dock with shears,
And he the ram tangled in barbed wire   25
That he stoned to death when they set him free.

Notes

[2] **Self-heal:** any of various plants believed to have healing properties

[2] **centaury:** a plant said to have been discovered by Chiron the centaur

[3] **bog asphodel:** Asphodel is a lily-type plant, common on moorlands, considered an immortal flower in mythology and said to cover the Elysian meadows (Homer's *Odyssey*).

[16] **cuckoo-pint:** A plant commonly called 'lords and ladies'; it has sexual connotations because of its appearance.

Explorations

First reading: lines 1–15

1. 'I wanted to teach him'. Who are the two people involved?
2. What do we learn of 'him' in the first fifteen lines? Consider physical appearance, mental ability and the manner of his treatment. Why do you think he is not named?
3. Explore the speaker's motivation in this. Is it clear-cut? Is she herself clear about it?

Second reading: lines 16 to end

4. Explore the speaker's reaction to the incident – lines 16–20. Can she explain it? Can you understand her reaction?
5. Examine the consequent treatment of the man. Can you understand any possible reasons for it? What are the long-term consequences?

Third reading

6. What are your thoughts on finishing this poem? What are your feelings?
7. Who is the victim here? Could this be read as a poem on victims?
8. What view of society is advanced by this poem?
9. 'Beauty and violence and sexuality are reflected in the imagery.' Comment, with reference to the text.
10. Do you think Longley is angered by this episode? Comment on the tone of the poem.

An Amish Rug

this poem is also prescribed for Ordinary Level exams in 2009 and 2010

As if a one-room schoolhouse were all we knew
And our clothes were black, our underclothes black,
Marriage a horse and buggy going to church
And the children silhouettes in a snowy field,

I bring you this patchwork like a smallholding   5
Where I served as the hired boy behind the harrow,
Its threads the colour of cantaloupe and cherry
Securing hay bales, corn cobs, tobacco leaves.

You may hang it on the wall, a cathedral window,
Or lay it out on the floor beside our bed   10
So that whenever we undress for sleep or love
We shall step over it as over a flowerbed.

Notes

Amish: A group of conservative Mennonite Christians in the United States characterised by distinctive dress (plain black clothes, no jewellery) and non-conformist way of life (agriculture, simple living, shunning motor vehicles); plainness and naturalness characterise their architecture and artwork. In stark contrast, this colourful rug was made for tourists.

[6] **harrow:** agricultural implement consisting of a frame with downward-pointing spikes dragged over a field to break up the earth

[7] **cantaloupe:** small, delicately flavoured melon with red and orange flesh

Explorations

First reading

1. What did you learn of the Amish way of life from a reading of this poem?
2. Describe the rug from the clues provided in the second stanza.
3. How might it be displayed? Refer to the text.

Second reading

4. What do you think is the poet's attitude to the Amish values and way of life? Refer to specific words and phrases.
5. Do you think the poet is happy in his relationship?
6. What do you consider to be the main theme of this poem?

Third reading

7. Comment on the significance of colours in the poem.
8. Do you think the poem displays a naïve, romantic view of life?
9. Consider this as a love poem. Do you like it? Outline your thinking.

Fourth reading

10. 'Longley's international perspective lends depth to his poetry.' Examine 'An Amish Rug' from the point of view of this statement.

Laertes

When he found Laertes alone on the tidy terrace, hoeing
Around a vine, disreputable in his gardening duds,
Patched and grubby, leather gaiters protecting his shins
Against brambles, gloves as well, and to cap it all,
Sure sign of his deep depression, a goatskin duncher,   5
Odysseus sobbed in the shade of a pear-tree for his father
So old and pathetic that all he wanted then and there
Was to kiss him and hug him and blurt out the whole story,
But the whole story is one catalogue and then another,
So he waited for images from that formal garden,   10
Evidence of a childhood spent traipsing after his father
And asking for everything he saw, the thirteen pear-trees,
Ten apple-trees, forty fig-trees, the fifty rows of vines
Ripening at different times for a continuous supply,
Until Laertes recognised his son and, weak at the knees,   15
Dizzy, flung his arms around the neck of great Odysseus
Who drew the old man fainting to his breast and held him there
And cradled like driftwood the bones of his dwindling father.

CD Track 19

Note

[5] **duncher:** dialect term for a hat or cap

 # Explorations

First reading

1. Examine the portrait of Laertes in the first five lines of this poem. What do you notice about him? What is his state of mind?

2. What is Odysseus's first reaction on seeing his father?

3. What does he actually do? Explore lines 10–14. Why do you think he acts in this way?

Second reading

4. Explore in detail the relationship between father and son depicted in this poem.

5. What other themes do you find submerged in the poem? Explain.

6. Do you think Longley's eye for detail contributes to the success of the poem?

7. Is there a sense of dramatic excitement in the poem? How is it created? Examine the sentence structure of the poem.

Third reading

8. Do you think this poem communicates any significant truths? Comment.

Ceasefire

I

Put in mind of his own father and moved to tears
Achilles took him by the hand and pushed the old king
Gently away, but Priam curled up at his feet and
Wept with him until their sadness filled the building.

II

Taking Hector's corpse into his hands Achilles   5
Made sure it was washed and, for the old king's sake,
Laid out in uniform, ready for Priam to carry
Wrapped like a present home to Troy at daybreak.

III

When they had eaten together, it pleased them both
To stare at each other's beauty as lovers might,   10
Achilles built like a god, Priam good-looking still
And full of conversation, who earlier had sighed:

IV

'I get down on my knees and do what must be done
And kiss Achilles' hand, the killer of my son.'

Notes

[2] **Achilles:** one of the legendary Greek heroes

[3] **Priam:** King Priam of Troy was father of the princes Hector and Paris; it was Paris who brought about the war by abducting Helen from Sparta in Greece.

[5] **Hector:** see above

Explorations

First reading

1. Examine the first stanza. What is happening here? What do you see? Describe the scene. If you are unclear, read also stanza 4.
2. In the first stanza, what detail did you find most moving? Explain.
3. Why does Achilles relent?
4. In the first stanza, what do the postures reveal of the different roles of the two men?
5. How would you describe the mood of the first stanza? What words or images help to create this?
6. What do his actions in the second stanza reveal about Achilles?
7. Comment on the description 'to carry | Wrapped like a present home to Troy'?

Second reading

8. What do you think is the significance of the fact that they 'had eaten together'? Do you think there is a change of mood in the third stanza? Is there a noticeable shift in power between the two characters?
9. The third stanza reflects a growing respect and mutual admiration. How is this communicated? Do you find this unexpected, even uncomfortable? What is the effect here?
10. What does the third stanza reveal of classical Greek culture? What qualities were valued in the society?

Third reading

11. Briefly outline the theme of this piece as you understand it.
12. Do you think that Homer's themes are of universal significance? Explain.
13. Could you read this as one of Longley's father–son poems? What does it add to that theme?
14. Could you read this as a 'political' poem? Explore that aspect of it.

14 Derek MAHON

prescribed for Higher Level exams in 2008 and 2009

Mahon is a retiring man who shuns publicity and literary politics. Born in 1941, he was the only child of a Church of Ireland family. He grew up in Glengormley, a north-side suburb of Belfast. His father worked in the Harland and Wolff shipyard, where the *Titanic* was built, and his mother in the Flax Spinning Company. His earliest memories are of the bomb raids of Belfast during the Second World War. He spent much of his school holidays cycling, often to the seaside town of Portrush and sometimes even to Donegal. He was a choirboy in St Peter's Church, and says that this experience fostered his interest in language. While at school he discovered poetry but that did not deter him from being, in his own words, a 'fairly nifty' scrum half. Cinema also attracted him, especially war movies and *A Night to Remember*, a film about the *Titanic*. He attended Royal Belfast Academical Institution, a grammar school. When he failed the eyesight test for the Merchant Navy he entered Trinity College, Dublin, where he studied French, English and Philosophy, and began writing poetry in earnest. Later he studied at the Sorbonne in Paris. On leaving university Mahon earned a living from freelance journalism and

1941–

teaching, as well as radio and television work. For years his humorous, insightful literary reviews in *The Irish Times* attracted a regular following. In addition to Dylan Thomas, the first modern poets he encountered were Robert Graves, W.B. Yeats and Louis MacNeice (another Northern Irish poet). He claims a cultural affinity with Dublin-born writer Samuel Beckett that relates to their shared Protestantism and mordant humour. Other poets whom he admires include the Americans Robert Lowell, Elizabeth Bishop and Hart Crane. French and Russian poetry also interest him, and he has been awarded numerous prizes for his translations.

He has lived in Canada, the US, London, Kinsale Co. Cork and briefly in Northern Ireland. His relationship with his home place is complex. He found it impossible to settle there, yet admits to feelings of guilt for having abandoned it. He recognises that his middle-class, urban background is uninspiring and unlike its rural counterpart, has little mythology or symbolism to nurture his imagination. His raw materials are the unresolved tensions and ironies of harsh, intolerant Belfast. If he does have a hidden myth, it is what Terence Brown describes as 'the Protestant Planter's historical myth of conquest, and careful, puritan self-dependence frozen to vicious, stupid bigotry'. Mahon has rejected the idea that poetry should be socially or politically relevant. Poetry 'may appear to be about history or politics or autobiography, but [it] is essentially an artistic activity', he writes. He believes that it is about shape and form, about taking the formless and making it interesting. Notice the spareness of his poems: the few, precise details; the limited palette of colour; the controlled tone; the unyielding landscape; all fastidiously chosen. That technical virtuosity is matched by inspiration. 'You need soul, song and formal necessity,' he has written. Yet he recognises that a life spent pursuing perfect form and technique carries the danger of isolating the poet from fellow humans. His interest in form is evident in his versions of classic dramas. He has adapted French plays by Molière and Racine as well as Euripides' *The Bacchae*. You will encounter Mahon's early poetry in the selection here – the most recent poem included was published in 1985. In later poems he has adopted a less tense and less minimalist style, using a more relaxed and contemporary conversational idiom – characterised by an informal candour, longer lines and playful lists. The autobiographical, intimate form of the verse letter, in particular, attracts him. Nowadays Mahon lives in Dublin and is a member of Aosdána, an elected group of Irish artists who receive pensions from the state. He has two adult children.

Derek Mahon

Grandfather

this poem is also prescribed for Ordinary Level exams in 2008 and 2009

CD Track 21

They brought him in on a stretcher from the world,
Wounded but humorous; and he soon recovered.
Boiler-rooms, row upon row of gantries rolled
Away to reveal the landscape of a childhood
Only he can recapture. Even on cold   5
Mornings he is up at six with a block of wood
Or a box of nails, discreetly up to no good
Or banging round the house like a four-year-old –

Never there when you call. But after dark
You hear his great boots thumping in the hall   10
And in he comes, as cute as they come. Each night
His shrewd eyes bolt the door and set the clock
Against the future, then his light goes out.
Nothing escapes him; he escapes us all.

Notes

[3] **gantries:** overhead structures with a platform supporting a travelling crane, an essential tool of shipbuilding

[11] **cute:** The word means attractive and also shrewd, cunning or crafty.

 # Explorations

First reading

1. Who is the subject of the poem?
2. Where did grandfather work?
3. Describe grandfather's working life and contrast it with his present-day activities.

Second reading

4. Describe grandfather's conduct.
5. Do you think that the members of his community would approve of his behaviour?

6. Note the adjectives used to describe grandfather. What do they suggest about his personality?
7. Outline his bedtime ritual.
8. What do the first two lines of the poem tell us about the old man?

Third reading

9. How does he relate to the outside world?
10. What is the speaker's attitude towards grandfather? What evidence is there to support your view?
11. Why do you think that grandfather is described as 'cute'?
12. What is revealed about his attitude to the future?
13. Describe the mood of the poem. Is it serious, playful, dark, or a combination of these and other moods?
14. Look at the three prepositions in the first line, 'in', 'on' and 'from'. What do they convey about grandfather's relationship with the world?
15. Comment on the diction of the poem.

Fourth reading

16. Would you consider this a nostalgic poem? Why?

17. What is the effect of the repetition in the poem? Examine these examples: 'row upon row of gantries rolled'; '. . . he is up at six with a block of wood | Or a box of nails, discreetly up to no good'; 'You hear his great boots thumping in the hall | And in he comes, as cute as they come.'
18. In what ways might grandfather be a role model for the speaker of the poem?
19. What values are underwritten and questioned in this poem?
20. What characteristics of the sonnet do you discern in this poem? How does it differ from the Shakespearean sonnet? You might take account of the rhyming scheme, the irregular use of the iambic pentameter (the metre most common to the sonnet), the 'turn' or volta.
21. Examine the treatment of time in this poem. Consider, for example, the implicit contrast between the old man and the speaker, two generations younger. Think about the childhood memories to which only he has access. Note the poem's treatment of seasonal change and the ebb and flow of days. What does the future hold for grandfather?

Day Trip to Donegal

We reached the sea in early afternoon,
Climbed stiffly out; there were things to be done,
Clothes to be picked up, friends to be seen.
As ever, the nearby hills were a deeper green
Than anywhere in the world, and the grave   5
Grey of the sea the grimmer in that enclave.

Down at the pier the boats gave up their catch,
A writhing glimmer of fish; they fetch
Ten times as much in the city as here,
And still the fish come in year after year –   10
Herring and mackerel, flopping about the deck
In attitudes of agony and heartbreak.

We left at eight, drove back the way we came,
The sea receding down each muddy lane.
Around midnight we changed-down into suburbs   15
Sunk in a sleep no gale-force wind disturbs.
The time of year had left its mark
On frosty pavements glistening in the dark.

Give me a ring, goodnight, and so to bed . . .
That night the slow sea washed against my head,   20
Performing its immeasurable erosions –
Spilling into the skull, marbling the stones
That spine the very harbour wall,
Muttering its threat to villages of landfall.

At dawn I was alone far out at sea   25
Without skill or reassurance – nobody
To show me how, no promise of rescue –
Cursing my constant failure to take due
Forethought for this; contriving vain
Overtures to the vindictive wind and rain.   30

Notes

[6] **enclave:** a part of one state surrounded by another, but viewed by the surrounding territory. It can also mean a group of people who are culturally, intellectually or socially distinct from those surrounding them.

[29] **vain:** Both meanings, proud and conceited, and worthless and futile, apply here.

[30] **vindictive:** vengeful, spiteful, unforgiving

 # Explorations

First reading

1. Generally, what kind of experiences are day trips?
2. Discuss the significance of the title of this poem.
3. What does the speaker see on the pier?
4. Where does the speaker go in stanza three?
5. Briefly paraphrase each stanza.

Second reading

6. The encounter with the sea has a profound effect on the speaker. What is it about the sea that makes it so profoundly different from the land?
7. What is the most telling image in the poem for you?
8. Note where the plural 'we' gives way to the singular 'I'. What does this shift convey?
9. Discuss the contrasts that abound in this poem. In addition to the oppositions of land and sea already mentioned, you might consider the antitheses of suburban and rural landscape, isolation and camaraderie, night and day. Note the contrast in stanza four between the desultory goodbyes and the experience that follows.
10. Having read the poem, do you detect an irony in the term 'day trip'?

Third reading

11. How is the speaker's thinking and feeling altered by the sight of the dying fish?
12. Describe the movement in the poem.
13. Alliteration is widely used in this poem – for example, in stanza one there is an accumulation of 'gr' sounds: 'green | . . . grave | Grey . . .

grimmer'. Find other examples of alliteration in the poem. Why is this and how effective is it?

14. Consider some of the distinctive features of stanza three. Comment on sentence length, the change of setting, the pace of the third line and how this is achieved.

15. What does the speaker mean when he says he is 'far out to sea'?

Fourth reading

16. In what ways could the erosion of the sea be compared to the effects of history?

17. What change is brought about in the speaker as a result of his day trip?

18. What political significance might be read into the greenness of Donegal, the fact that the speaker sees it as an enclave, and the grim greyness of its sea?

After the Titanic

this poem is also prescribed for Ordinary Level exams in 2008 and 2009

They said I got away in a boat
And humbled me at the inquiry. I tell you
    I sank as far that night as any
Hero. As I sat shivering on the dark water
    I turned to ice to hear my costly   5
Life go thundering down in a pandemonium of
    Prams, pianos, sideboards, winches,
Boilers bursting and shredded ragtime. Now I hide
    In a lonely house behind the sea
Where the tide leaves broken toys and hatboxes   10
    Silently at my door. The showers of
April, flowers of May mean nothing to me, nor the
    Late light of June, when my gardener
Describes to strangers how the old man stays in bed
    On seaward mornings after nights of   15
Wind, takes his cocaine and will see no one. Then it is
    I drown again with all those dim
Lost faces I never understood, my poor soul
    Screams out in the starlight, heart
Breaks loose and rolls down like a stone.   20
    Include me in your lamentations.

Notes

Titanic: The *Titanic* was a ship built in Belfast. It was completed in 1912 and was described as 'the latest thing in the art of shipbuilding'. The word 'titanic' has come to mean colossal, and indeed, the ship was immense. That it was built in Belfast placed the city at the very leading edge of the Industrial Revolution. However, it sank dramatically when it collided with an iceberg on its maiden voyage to America, with the loss of 1,500 lives, the greatest tragedy in maritime history. This catastrophe has entered the global imagination as a major disaster, and was a mortal blow to the self-confidence of the age.

[1] **They said I got away in a boat:** The speaker of the poem is Bruce Ismay (1892–1937), manager of the White Star Line for which the *Titanic* sailed. He was one of the relatively few men to have escaped from the sinking *Titanic*, and he was strongly criticised for failing to help the drowning passengers.

[6] **pandemonium:** meaning chaos, confusion, turmoil. In John Milton's poem, 'Paradise Lost', it is the place of all demons.

[7] **winches:** plural of a windlass, the crank of a wheel or axle (singular is 'winch')

[8] **ragtime:** a type of jazz music, a syncopated musical rhythm developed by American black musicians in the 1890s and usually played on the piano

[15] **seaward:** going or facing toward the sea

[16] **cocaine:** a drug used as both a local anaesthetic and a stimulant

[21] **lamentations:** At one level, 'Include me in your lamentations' is the plea of the poem's speaker, Bruce Ismay, for inclusion in the community's mourning of the victims of the *Titanic* disaster. However, it is also a reference to the Old Testament book containing five poems that constitute the 'Lamentations of Jeremiah'.

Explorations

First reading

1. What does the title suggest to you?
2. Describe the persona that speaks in this poem.
3. Why and at what inquiry was he humbled?
4. How does the speaker spend his time?
5. What does he remember of the Titanic disaster?

Second reading

6. What has the persona of the poem in mind when he refers to his 'costly life'?
7. How would you describe his mood?
8. How does the speaker convey his isolation?
9. 'Prams, pianos, sideboards, winches,
   Boilers bursting and shredded ragtime.'
   Describe the effect of this list.
10. In what way is the speaker's suffering indicated?
11. How does he deal with the pain?

Third reading

12. How would you describe the diction of the following three lines? '. . . my poor soul I Screams out in the starlight, heart I Breaks loose and rolls down like a stone.'
    What effect does this style have on the reader?
13. In your opinion, what causes the greatest distress to Ismay?
14. What does the speaker finally demand of his listeners?
15. In your opinion, should the persona Ismay be included in the mourning?

Fourth reading

16. '. . . Then it is I I drown again with all those dim I Lost faces I never understood . . .'
    What does the speaker mean by the three lines above?
17. Is there a resemblance between his response to catastrophe and that of society to its victims?
18. How does Ismay deal with the tragedy of the *Titanic*, the burden of the episode in history in which he is implicated?

Workers leaving the Belfast Shipyard in 1911 with the half-finished *Titanic* in the background

Ecclesiastes

God, you could grow to love it, God-fearing, God-
    chosen purist little puritan that,
for all your wiles and smiles, you are (the
    dank churches, the empty streets,
the shipyard silence, the tied-up swings) and   5
    shelter your cold heart from the heat
of the world, from woman-inquisition, from the
    bright eyes of children. Yes, you could
wear black, drink water, nourish a fierce zeal
    with locusts and wild honey, and not   10
feel called upon to understand and forgive
    but only to speak with a bleak
afflatus, and love the January rains when they
    darken the dark doors and sink hard
into the Antrim hills, the bog meadows, the heaped   15
    graves of your fathers. Bury that red
bandana and stick, that banjo; this is your
    country, close one eye and be king.
Your people await you, their heavy washing
    flaps for you in the housing estates –   20
a credulous people. God, you could do it, God
    help you, stand on a corner stiff
with rhetoric, promising nothing under the sun.

Notes

Ecclesiastes: the title of an Old Testament book of the Bible, but also a person who addresses an assembly, a preacher

[2] **purist:** a person who scrupulously advocates rigid precision and formality, especially in the field of language or art

[2] **puritan:** In its historical meaning, the term refers to a member of a group of English protestants who regarded the Reformation as incomplete and refused to subscribe to the established church, that is, the Church of Ireland or the Church of England. They sought to simplify and regulate forms of worship. However, a puritan is also a distinct character type, a person who practises extreme strictness in matters of religion and morals. The term could be applied in both senses to the person addressed in the poem.

[5] **the tied-up swings:** It was customary for many local authorities in Northern Ireland to close public parks on Sundays.

[9] **zeal:** fervour and earnestness in furthering a cause; uncompromising partisanship; fanaticism; indefatigable enthusiasm

[10] **locusts and wild honey:** In the Bible, this was often the only food available to penitents who fasted in the desert.

[13] **afflatus:** a divine creative impulse; inspiration
[16–17] **red | bandana ... stick ... banjo:** emblems of non-conformity, wanderlust and art
[18] **close one eye:** Closing one eye may sharpen the focus, but it restricts the range of vision and is a metaphor for narrow-mindedness.
[21] **credulous:** gullible
[23] **rhetoric:** The discipline, or art, of persuasive writing or speaking. It often implies exaggeration or insincerity.

 # Explorations

First reading

1. What does the word 'Ecclesiastes' mean?
2. Where is the poem set?
3. Who is the speaker in this poem?
4. Describe the ecclesiastes to whom this poem is addressed. What kind of person is he or she?
5. Describe the place in which this preacher's community lives.

Second reading

6. Is the title a good one? Why?
7. What does the preacher promise his or her people?
8. Find some positive and negative images of Belfast in this poem.
9. Find some references to the Bible and to religion in this poem.
10. Are the speaker and the ecclesiastes one and the same person? Why do you think that?
11. What colours predominate in this poem?
12. What kind of atmosphere pervades the place described?
13. What groups of people tend to wear black and why?

Third reading

14. Discuss the mood of the poem.
15. What tone does the speaker use?
16. Why must the ecclesiastes leave behind the 'red | bandana . . . stick . . . banjo'?
17. What is the effect of the repetition of the word 'God'?
18. In what does the preacher take pleasure?

Fourth reading

19. Explore some of the rhetorical devices employed in the poem. These might include the declamatory tone, the fluency and formality, the repetitions of sentence structure and the amplitude of the first two sentences.
20. Discuss the irony of this poem. At whom is it directed?
21. Can you identify any parallels between the preacher depicted here and the poet-speaker?
22. Show how the first and last sentences of the poem are similar. Consider the sentence structure, the sentiments expressed and the repetition of words. What purpose does this form serve?

As It Should Be

We hunted the mad bastard
Through bog, moorland, rock, to the starlit west
And gunned him down in a blind yard
Between ten sleeping lorries
And an electricity generator.   5

Let us hear no idle talk
Of the moon in the Yellow River;
The air blows softer since his departure.

Since his tide-burial during school hours
Our children have known no bad dreams.   10
Their cries echo lightly along the coast.

This is as it should be.
They will thank us for it when they grow up
To a world with method in it.

Notes

[1] **We hunted the mad bastard:** The persona of the poem is a spokesman for the Irish Free State, which condones the murder of the revolutionary, the dreamer.

[3] **blind:** in this case, walled up, closed at one end; also lacking foresight and understanding

[5] **an electricity generator:** a machine for converting mechanical energy into electrical energy

[7] **the moon in the Yellow River:** This is the title of a play by Denis Johnston written in 1931. Johnston took the phrase from Ezra Pound's image of a drunken poet, Li-Po, who grasped at illusory ideals and was drowned while trying 'to embrace the moon in the yellow river'. The play's story is set in Ireland in 1927, and one of the new Irish State's projects intended to modernise the country is a hydroelectric scheme. When a revolutionary called Blake tries to blow up its generator, Lanigan, an officer of the Free State, shoots him. In this poem, a revolutionary is shot among lorries beside an electricity generator, monuments to progress. Material improvement comes at a price, in this case brutal murder.

[9] **tide-burial:** the body is cast into the water and carried away on the tide

[14] **method:** implies orderliness, regular habits, procedure, pattern, system

Explorations

First reading

1. On what incident is this poem based?
2. In what part of the country was the fugitive pursued?
3. Would it be easy to hide in bog, moorland or rock?
4. Where was he found?
5. What did his pursuers do when they found him?

Second reading

6. How did they dispose of his body?
7. Whom does the 'we' of the poem represent?
8. Why does the speaker say that the children no longer have bad dreams?

Third reading

9. What is the effect of the obscenity in the first line?
10. What image of themselves do the speakers present in the first stanza?
11. What values do the speakers wish to pass on to their children?
12. Show how the poem suggests that violence is implicated in the fabric of the state from its foundation.
13. Describe the speaker's tone.

Fourth reading

14. Comment on the variations in line and stanza length.
15. What is it that the speakers wish to suppress? With what will they replace it?
16. Compare the ironic tone of this poem with that of other poems by Mahon.
17. In what sense are the speakers making history?
18. Examine this poem's links to other literary works.

A Disused Shed in Co. Wexford

CD Track 26

Let them not forget us, the weak souls among the asphodels.
– Seferis, *Mythistorema*

(for J.G. Farrell)

Even now there are places where a thought might grow –
Peruvian mines, worked out and abandoned
To a slow clock of condensation,
An echo trapped for ever, and a flutter
Of wild flowers in the lift-shaft,   5
Indian compounds where the wind dances
And a door bangs with diminished confidence,
Lime crevices behind rippling rain-barrels,
Dog corners for bone burials;
And in a disused shed in Co. Wexford,   10

Deep in the grounds of a burnt-out hotel,
Among the bathtubs and washbasins
A thousand mushrooms crowd to a keyhole.
This is the one star in their firmament
Or frames a star within a star.   15
What should they do there but desire?
So many days beyond the rhododendrons
With the world waltzing in its bowl of cloud,
They have learnt patience and silence
Listening to the rooks querulous in the high wood.   20

They have been waiting for us in a foetor
Of vegetable sweat since civil war days,
Since the gravel-crunching, interminable departure
Of the expropriated mycologist.
He never came back, and light since then   25
Is a keyhole rusting gently after rain.
Spiders have spun, flies dusted to mildew
And once a day, perhaps, they have heard something –
A trickle of masonry, a shout from the blue
Or a lorry changing gear at the end of the lane.   30

Notes

asphodels: A type of lily. It has been represented in literature as an immortal flower growing in the fields of Elysium, the place where, in Greek mythology, the blessed go after death.

Seferis: George Seferis (1900–71), a Greek poet and ambassador to Britain, whose poetry draws on Greek mythology.

There have been deaths, the pale flesh flaking
Into the earth that nourished it;
And nightmares, born of these and the grim
Dominion of stale air and rank moisture.
Those nearest the door grow strong –   35
'Elbow room! Elbow room!'
The rest, dim in a twilight of crumbling
Utensils and broken pitchers, groaning
For their deliverance, have been so long
Expectant that there is left only the posture.   40

A half century, without visitors, in the dark –
Poor preparation for the cracking lock
And creak of hinges; magi, moonmen,
Powdery prisoners of the old regime,
Web-throated, stalked like triffids, racked by drought 45
And insomnia, only the ghost of a scream
At the flash-bulb firing-squad we wake them with
Shows there is life yet in their feverish forms.
Grown beyond nature now, soft food for worms,
They lift frail heads in gravity and good faith.   50

They are begging us, you see, in their wordless way,
To do something, to speak on their behalf
Or at least not to close the door again.
Lost people of Treblinka and Pompeii!
'Save us, save us,' they seem to say,   55
'Let the god not abandon us
Who have come so far in darkness and in pain.
We too had our lives to live.
You with your light meter and relaxed itinerary,
Let not our naive labours have been in vain!'   60

J.G. Farrell: This poem had its source in Farrell's novel *Troubles*. Farrell, a good friend of Mahon, was drowned while fishing in 1979. 'I'd read *Troubles* and I was convinced that there was a shed in it, with mushrooms,' Mahon has written. 'But when I went back and re-read it, the shed with the mushrooms was missing. I must have imagined it.'

[6] **compounds:** large open enclosures for housing workers

[14] **firmament:** the sky

[17] **rhododendrons:** evergreen shrubs with large flowers that grow profusely in some parts of Ireland

Notes *continued*

[20] **querulous:** complaining, fractious

[21] **foetor:** stench

[22] **civil war days:** This is probably a reference to the civil war fought in Ireland in 1922–23. It began when some members of nationalist movements rejected the treaty that brought an end to the War of Independence fought with Britain. Although the actual death toll was not high, it left a legacy of bitterness and a lasting influence on the shape of party politics in Ireland. J.G. Farrell's novel *Troubles*, which inspired this poem, is set in civil war Ireland.

[24] **expropriated mycologist:** an expert on fungi or mushrooms who has been dispossessed, especially one whose property has been taken away by the state

[43] **magi:** the 'wise men' who brought gifts to the infant Jesus; the plural of 'magus', a word that means a sorcerer; also priests in ancient Persia

[43] **moonmen:** They are moonmen because they have been denied the light of the sun for so long.

[45] **triffids:** These are monstrous, lethal plants from outer space that can propel themselves about, originally in John Wyndham's science fiction novel, *The Day of the Triffids*. This book describes the contrast between a comfortable setting and a sudden invasion that is a metaphysical catastrophe. The term has now come to describe any hostile plant.

[45] **racked by drought:** tortured by thirst

[46] **insomnia:** sleeplessness

[54] **Treblinka:** a Nazi concentration camp in Poland where Jews were put to death during the Second World War

[54] **Pompeii:** a city in south-east Italy which was buried after Mount Vesuvius erupted in 79 B.C.

[59] **itinerary:** a detailed route, often mapped out for tourists by travel consultants

 # Explorations

First reading

1. Name some of the places where 'a thought might grow'.
2. Describe in detail the mushrooms' surroundings.
3. How have they spent their existence?
4. Describe the horrors endured by the forgotten mushrooms in stanza four.
5. How long have they been behind locks?
6. Describe the effect of their confinement on the mushrooms.
7. How do they respond to the garish light of 'the flash-bulb firing-squad'?

Second reading

8. What is distinctive about the places 'where a thought might grow'?
9. What is the mushrooms' plea?

---

10. How do the mushrooms communicate?
11. Discuss the title of the poem.

Third reading

12. What is the significance of the opening phrase 'Even now'?
13. Describe the tone, or range of tones, of this poem. How does the poem represent the strong emotions aroused by the plight of the abandoned?
14. Why do you think Mahon chose to nominate mushrooms as his central characters?
15. Why does the poet delay before introducing the mushrooms, around which the poem is centred?
16. What is the effect of the rhetorical question 'What should they do there but desire'?
17. What does the poet mean when he writes 'the world waltzing in its bowl of cloud'?
18. Discuss who or what you think the 'expropriated mycologist' represents.

Fourth reading

19. How does Mahon achieve the effect of time passing in stanzas two and three?
20. Identify the specific historic references in the poem and discuss their significance.
21. What is the speaker's reaction to the plight of the mushrooms?
22. Would the liberation of the mushrooms resolve all their difficulties? Does being part of history offer a solution to the agonies described in the poem?
23. In what way is this poem a meditation on the legacy of war?
24. What difficulties confront the speaker of this poem? You might refer to the problem of speaking on behalf of the voiceless, representing them rather than enabling them to speak for themselves.
25. Show how this poem depicts the manner in which the powerful abandon and ignore the helpless.
26. What in your opinion, is significant about the epigram and dedication?
27. How do the themes of this poem relate to those in other poems by Mahon that you have read?
28. Consider the use of the past tense in 'We too had our lives to live' (stanza six).
29. Does this poem suggest that Mahon is 'through with history', as he has twice suggested in other poems? What evidence is there to support your opinion?
30. In what ways is the speaker of the poem involved in the present exploitation of the victims of history?
31. Show how Mahon achieves a local and global context. What does this double focus suggest?

The Chinese Restaurant in Portrush

Before the first visitor comes the spring
Softening the sharp air of the coast
In time for the first seasonal 'invasion'.
Today the place is as it might have been,
Gentle and almost hospitable. A girl   5
Strides past the Northern Counties Hotel,
Light-footed, swinging a book-bag,
And the doors that were shut all winter
Against the north wind and the sea-mist
Lie open to the street, where one   10
By one the gulls go window-shopping
And an old wolfhound dozes in the sun.

While I sit with my paper and prawn chow mein
Under a framed photograph of Hong Kong
The proprietor of the Chinese restaurant   15
Stands at the door as if the world were young,
Watching the first yacht hoist a sail
– An ideogram on sea-cloud – and the light
Of heaven upon the hills of Donegal;
And whistles a little tune, dreaming of home.   20

Notes

Portrush: a seaside town in north Antrim, to which the young Mahon would cycle at weekends

[12] **wolfhound:** This is perhaps an oblique reference to the bloody Ulster cycle of heroic tales. When the young mythical champion Cuculann killed a wolfhound owned by Culann, a blacksmith, he replaced the animal as Culann's guardian, and became known as the hound of Ulster. In one of his exploits, he single-handedly defended Ulster from the army of Queen Maeve of Connaught. Here the hound is sleeping, suggesting that ancient aggressions are temporarily laid aside.

[18] **ideogram:** a character symbolising or representing the idea of a thing without indicating the sequence of sounds in its name. Ideograms are used in Chinese writing.

Background

This elegy is taken from *Cymbeline* (act IV, scene ii), one of Shakespeare's later comedies (*c.* 1609–10). Set in Roman Britain, it is a play of uneven quality, full of sinister scheming, gratuitous horror, and a great deal of confusion. Innogen (the daughter of Cymbeline, king of Britain), while travelling in disguise through the forest has fainted and is presumed dead by her companions (really her disguised half-brothers, Guiderius and Arviragus), who are moved to sing this dirge.

 # Explorations

First reading

1. Can you imagine the setting, the positions of the speakers, and the position of the person addressed? Describe what you see.

2. In what tone of voice should this be spoken or sung? Why?

Second reading

3. What categories of things are no longer to be feared by the dead person?

4. What view of death is conveyed in this song?

Third reading

5. What picture of society comes across in this song?

Fourth reading

6. How would you describe the mood of this poem? What words or images help create it? What effect has the metre on the mood of the poem?

7. Briefly, set down the main idea of this song.

John Milton (1608–1674)

John Milton was born in London of well-to-do parents who appear to have given him a good basic education, especially in music and literature. He attended St Paul's School and graduated with BA and MA degrees from Cambridge. Milton was appointed 'Latin secretary of the council of state' by Oliver Cromwell in 1649, because of his fluency in Latin, the language of diplomacy at that time. He wrote extensively on religious and political matters as well as writing poetry in Latin and English. His eyesight, which had been failing for some time, failed him completely when he was aged forty-four. From then on he dictated his work to his secretaries and family members. Milton's masterpiece, the epic *Paradise Lost*, was published in 1667; in it he attempted 'to justify the ways of God to men'. The restoration of the monarchy briefly threatened Milton with execution for regicide, and brought an end to

his political career in 1660. Having been granted a royal pardon he retired to concentrate on writing and published the sequel to *Paradise Lost*, called *Paradise Regained*, as well as a drama called *Samson Agonistes* in 1671. A revised volume of his collected poetry appeared the following year. Milton died of gout in 1674.

When I Consider

prescribed for the Ordinary Level exam in 2010

When I consider how my light is spent,
E're half my days, in this dark world and wide,
And that one Talent which is death to hide,
Lodg'd with me useless, though my Soul more bent
To serve therewith my Maker, and present 5
My true account, least he returning chide,
Doth God exact day-labour, light deny'd,
I fondly ask; But patience to prevent
That murmur, soon replies, God doth not need
Either man's work or his own gifts, who best 10
Bear his milde yoak, they serve him best, his State
Is Kingly. Thousands at his bidding speed
And post o're Land and Ocean without rest:
They also serve who only stand and waite.

Notes

[3] **Talent:** gift, faculty, also a unit of currency in New Testament times

[4] **bent:** determined

[8] **fondly:** foolishly

[11] **yoak:** yoke, burden

 # Explorations

First reading

1. What is Milton saying about his blindness in the opening three lines? How do you imagine 'this dark world'?

2. Does Milton take the parable of the Talents seriously? What is the implication of 'which is death to hide'?

3. What does Milton's soul incline to do? What does this tell us about him?

4. 'Doth God exact day-labour, light deny'd'
   What is your understanding of this line? What does the question tell us about Milton's attitude to God?

5. What does 'Patience' reply to the question posed in the first eight lines? According to Milton, does God need man's work? Does he need man's gifts?

6. According to Milton, how do people best serve God? How can God be served passively?

Second reading

7. Read the poem aloud. What do you notice about its sounds and rhythm? How many full stops appear in the text? Does this affect how you read the poem? What tone of voice should you adopt?

8. Comment on the financial terminology, 'spent'; 'Talent'; 'Lodg'd'; 'account'. What is Milton saying with this choice of words?

9. How do you see John Milton on the evidence of the poem? What kind of person do you think he was? Does he display any self-pity or sense of injustice? What comment would you make on how he deals with his disability?

10. How would you summarise the octet?

11. Describe how Milton resolves his difficulties in the sestet. Do you find his conclusion convincing?

12. How does Milton feel toward God in the poem? What words and images convey his emotions?

Third reading

13. Examine how images of light and darkness are used in the first eight lines. Do you consider such imagery to be appropriate?

14. How is the majesty of God conveyed in the final six lines?

15. Would you agree that this poem's language has a biblical quality? What words or phrases would you highlight for comment?

16. What do you think of Milton's portrayal of God? Is this interpretation of God one you are comfortable with?

17. How would you describe the mood of the final line? Has the conclusion been anticipated in the poem?

18. Write a paragraph giving your personal response to the poem.

Henry Vaughan (1622–1695)

Henry Vaughan was born in Wales. He studied in Oxford but left without taking a degree; he went on to study law and later medicine. Vaughan practised as a doctor in Breconshire, after fighting in The English Civil War on the Royalist side. His first poems were secular in nature and dealt with love and the fashionable concerns of the age. Some profound spiritual experience prompted him to more sacred and serious themes and he repudiated frivolous verse. He was influenced by George Herbert 'whose holy life and verse gained many pious Converts, (of whom I am the least)' and Platonic philosophy. Vaughan's best religious poetry in *Silex Scintillans* has a mystical quality which is quite distinctive.

Peace

prescribed for Ordinary Level exams in 2007 and 2010

My Soul, there is a Countrie
Far beyond the stars,
Where stands a winged Centrie
All skilfull in the wars,
There above noise, and danger   5
Sweet peace sits crown'd with smiles,
And one born in a Manger
Commands the Beauteous files,
He is thy gracious friend,
And (O my Soul awake!)   10
Did in pure love descend
To die here for thy sake,
If thou canst get but thither,
There growes the flowre of peace,
The Rose that cannot wither,   15
Thy fortresse, and thy ease;
Leave then thy foolish ranges;
For none can thee secure,
But one, who never changes,
Thy God, thy life, thy Cure.   20

Notes

[3] **Centrie:** sentry
[8] **files:** ranks, as in soldiers
[17] **ranges:** wanderings

Explorations

First reading

1. How do you visualise the 'Countrie | Far beyond the stars'? What kind of heaven is suggested by Vaughan's description?

2. 'And one born in a Manger Commands the Beauteous files' What is your impression of Christ from these lines? Are you surprised by the image of Christ as a military commander?

3. According to the speaker, how is the flower of peace to be grasped? Look at line 13 carefully.

4. What do you understand by 'Thy fortresse, and thy ease'? What qualities are highlighted here?

5. Why must the listener 'Leave then thy foolish ranges'? What reward is on offer?

Second reading

6. Read the poem aloud. What do you notice about the sound and rhythm of the poem? Note how Vaughan punctuates the poem. Read the last two lines again, paying particular attention to the pauses after the commas. What effect is achieved?

7. Make a list of the military vocabulary used in the poem. How are such warlike terms appropriate in a poem about peace?

8. What is the tone of this poem? What words and images convey the tone?

Third reading

9. 'The Rose that cannot wither' Do you think this is an effective image? Does this metaphor blend with the other patterns of imagery that Vaughan explores?

10. What do you think was the writer's intention in writing this poem? Discuss this in your group or class.

11. Do you find this poem convincing? Explore your personal response to the text.

12. 'The search for permanence in a changing world is characteristic of Henry Vaughan.' Discuss this statement with reference to 'Peace'.

13. How would you describe Vaughan's concept of peace? Would your personal view of peace be different?

William Wordsworth (1770–1850)

William Wordsworth was born in Cumberland, England, on 7 April 1770. He and his younger sister, Dorothy, became orphans at an early age. As a result, the two developed a close relationship that was to last throughout their lives.

Wordsworth's early writing was not particularly popular, although it was admired by the literary set. Working with another poet, Samuel Taylor Coleridge, Wordsworth produced a book of poems entitled 'The Lyrical Ballads'. This book, expressing the importance of Man's relationship with Nature in everyday language, is seen as marking the beginning of the Romantic Movement in English poetry.

Towards the end of his life Wordsworth's work became more popular, and he received a state pension when he was appointed Poet Laureate. Wordsworth died in 1850 at the age of eighty.

Composed Upon Westminster Bridge

prescribed for the Ordinary Level exam in 2009

Earth has not anything to show more fair:
Dull would he be of soul who could pass by
A sight so touching in its majesty:
This City now doth, like a garment, wear
The beauty of the morning: silent, bare,   5
Ships, towers, domes, theatres, and temples lie
Open unto the fields, and to the sky;
All bright and glittering in the smokeless air.
Never did sun more beautifully steep
In his first splendour, valley, rock or hill;   10
Ne'er saw I, never felt, a calm so deep!

Notes
(4) **doth:** does
(11) **Ne'er:** never

The river glideth at his own sweet will:
Dear God! the very houses seem asleep;
And all that mighty heart is lying still!

 # Explorations

First reading

1. (a) What two words would you use to describe the mood created in this poem? (b) What lines or phrases in the poem suggest these words to you?

2. Choose one image, or picture, in the poem that you find particularly easy to imagine and, in your own words, describe what you can 'see'.

3. What is the setting for this poem? In your answer use clues from the poem to work out where Wordsworth is standing and what he is looking at.

Second reading

4. (a) What time of day is it when Wordsworth sees the city? (b) How does this affect the way that the city appears?

5. 'The City now doth, like a garment, wear
The beauty of the morning'
Explain in your own words what you think Wordsworth is trying to suggest about the city's beauty by using the simile of 'a garment' to describe it.

6. (a) How does the scene affect Wordsworth? (b) What emotion does his use of three exclamation marks in the final four lines of the poem suggest to you?

7. 'And all that mighty heart is lying still!'
Do you find this a successful final line to the poem? Why?

8. Explain the theme, or central message, of this poem in one or two sentences.

Third reading

9. Imagine that you are rushing across Westminster Bridge to school with your friend William Wordsworth, when suddenly he stops to look at the view. In one page, write the conversation that you would have with him.

10. The Romantic poets were particularly fond of the Lyric form of poem because this form allows the poet to express his own emotional and psychological reactions to a situation. Do you think that 'Composed Upon Westminster Bridge' could be classed as a Lyric? Give reasons for your answer.

Percy Bysshe Shelley (1792–1822)

The son of an English country gentleman, Shelley was educated at Eton and Oxford, where he spent a rebellious and unhappy youth. Revolutionary in thought, he was anti-religious and anti-monarchy and wrote and spoke publicly on the need for radical social and political reforms. He felt it was the role of the poet to be prophetic and visionary. He lived a fairly unconventional family life, much of it in Italy, where the Shelleys seemed dogged by illness and death. It was here that he wrote some of his best-known poems, such as 'Stanzas Written in Dejection Near Naples', 'Ode to the West Wind', 'Ode to a Skylark', and 'Prometheus Unbound'.

Ozymandias

prescribed for the Ordinary Level exam in 2008

I met a traveller from an antique land
Who said: Two vast and trunkless legs of stone
Stand in the desert . . . Near them, on the sand,
Half sunk, a shattered visage lies, whose frown,
And wrinkled lip, and sneer of cold command,   5
Tell that its sculptor well those passions read
Which yet survive, stamped on these lifeless things,
The hand that mocked them, and the heart that fed:
And on the pedestal these words appear:
'My name is Ozymandias, king of kings: 10
Look on my works, ye Mighty, and despair!'
Nothing beside remains. Round the decay
Of that colossal wreck, boundless and bare
The lone and level sands stretch far away.

Notes

Ozymandias: another name for the Pharaoh Rameses II of Egypt (thirteenth century B.C.), whose great tomb at Thebes was shaped like a sphinx. It was the great historian Diodorus the Sicilian who first referred to it as the tomb of Ozymandias

[1] **antique:** ancient
[4] **visage:** face
[8] **The hand that mocked:** the hand that imitated, referring to the hand of the sculptor
[8] **the heart that fed:** the king's heart which gave life to these qualities and passions that were captured in stone by the sculptor

 # Explorations

First reading

1. The poem is in the form of a narrative or story told by a traveller who had been to 'an antique land'. What suggestions and pictures does this phrase conjure up for you?

2. What did the traveller actually see, as reported in lines 2–4? What is your first reaction to this scene: interesting, pathetic, grotesque, or what? Why do you think he might consider this worth reporting?

3. Where is this scene? What impressions of the land do we get?

4. Does the poet tell us the name of the place? Why do you think this is?

Second reading

5. What do we learn of the king from this sculpture: qualities, character traits, etc.?

6. Do you think Shelley appreciates the sculptor's skill? Explain.

7. Relate lines 4–8 in your own words and as simply as possible.

Third reading: the sestet etc.

8. What was your own reflection on reading the words on the pedestal?

9. Explore the final two and a half lines. What do you see? Really look. What atmosphere is created here? What statement do you think is being made?

10. What do you think this poem is saying about human endeavour and about power? Explain with reference to specific phrases etc.

11. Consider the imagery. Do you think the imagery appropriate to the theme? Explain. What pictures do you find most effective?

Fourth reading

12. How does the poet make use of irony to communicate his theme? Do you find this effective?

13. Would you agree that this poem embodies Shelley's view that the poet should really be a kind of prophet or wise person in society? Discuss this with reference to the text.

14. What features of the sonnet do you notice in the poem? Do you think it is a good sonnet?

15. Do you think this poem was worth reading? Why, or why not?

Christina Rossetti 1830–1894

Christina Rossetti was born in London on 5 December 1830 into a prosperous and creative family. Her Italian father was professor of Italian at King's College, London and her mother was half-Italian. So, along with her sister and two brothers, Christina grew up speaking both Italian and English.

Christina showed a talent for writing from an early age. During her life she wrote approximately eleven hundred poems, both for children and adults, along with numerous short stories. However, as a woman in Victorian England she was restricted in her activities and it took some time before her work became widely known.

Along with her mother and sister, Christina had a very strong religious faith. Indeed, it was difficulties with religion that caused her to reject two offers of marriage. Christina died of cancer on 29 December 1894.

Remember

prescribed for Ordinary Level exams in 2007 and 2008

Remember me when I am gone away,
Gone far away into the silent land;
When you can no more hold me by the hand,
Nor I half turn to go, yet turning stay.
Remember me when no more day by day   5
You tell me of our future that you plann'd:
Only remember me; you understand
It will be late to counsel then or pray.
Yet if you should forget me for a while
And afterwards remember, do not grieve: 10
For if the darkness and corruption leave
A vestige of the thoughts that once I had,
Better by far you should forget and smile
Than that you should remember and be sad.

Notes

(8) **counsel:** to give advice
(10) **grieve:** to be distressed
(11) **corruption:** physical disintegration
(12) **vestige:** a trace

Explorations

First reading

1. (a) How would you describe the tone, or the emotion, expressed in Rossetti's words? (b) Choose a line or a phrase from the poem that you feel reveals this tone.

2. (a) What images does Rossetti use in the first four lines of the poem to convey the idea of two people parting from each other? (b) Can you suggest a connection between the idea of parting and the title of the poem 'Remember'?

3. 'Gone far away into the silent land;'
   Would you like to go to this 'land'? Why?

Second reading

4. What indications are there in lines 5–8 that the two people have a close and caring relationship?

5. (a) In your own words, describe the picture that you imagine when you read the phrase 'darkness and corruption'. (b) Is it a pleasant or unpleasant picture?

6. (a) What do you think will cause the poet to leave her companion? (b) From your reading of the poem do you feel that she is eager or reluctant to leave? Refer to the poem in your answers.

7. (a) What emotion does the poet not want her companion to feel when they are parted? (b) Why do you think that she feels this way?

8. Which do you think is more important to the poet, that her companion remembers her after she is gone, or that her companion is not sad? Use quotations from the poem to support your view.

Third reading

9. This poem is written in the Sonnet form so it can have only 14 lines. Do you feel that Rossetti expresses her theme, or message, well in this number of lines, or do you think that she should have written a longer poem? Give reasons for your answer.

10. Imagine that you are the person for whom this poem is meant. Write a letter to the poet describing your reactions to what she has written.

Edward Thomas (1878–1917)

At the outbreak of the First World War, Thomas was thirty-six years old, married with two children. His decision to enlist came from a sense of idealism. He was killed on Easter Monday 1917. The encouragement of his friend, the American poet Robert Frost, brought him to write poetry and his war poems reflect not just his experience of war, but his love of the English countryside. His language shows a deceptive strength and his work artistic integrity.

Adlestrop

prescribed for the Ordinary Level exam in 2007

Yes, I remember Adlestrop –
The name, because one afternoon
Of heat the express-train drew up there
Unwontedly. It was late June.

The steam hissed. Someone cleared his throat.   5
No one left and no one came
On the bare platform. What I saw
Was Adlestrop – only the name

And willows, willow-herb, and grass,
And meadowsweet, and haycocks dry,   10
No whit less still and lonely fair
Than the high cloudlets in the sky.

And for that minute a blackbird sang
Close by, and round him, mistier,
Farther and farther, all the birds   15
Of Oxfordshire and Gloucestershire.

Notes

[4] **Unwontedly:** unusually
[10] **haycocks:** small haystacks
[11] **whit:** the least possible amount

Explorations

First reading

1. Have you ever stopped briefly on a car or train journey? Can you describe the scene you saw? Are there any similarities between your experience and the one described in this poem?

2. What does the poet notice about Adlestrop in the first two stanzas?

3. 'No one left and no one came On the bare platform.' Can you find the word in the poem that explains why this happened?

4. Describe in your own words the picture that the poet creates in the third and fourth stanzas of the poem. Is it a pleasant one?

5. How is the scene in stanzas 1 and 2 different from the scene in stanzas 3 and 4? Can you explain why this change takes place?

Second reading

6. Consider the senses that the poet appeals to in this poem. How do they contribute to the overall effect?

7. What sort of mood do you think the poet was trying to create? Are there any words that are especially important in suggesting this mood?

8. How does the poet suggest a sense of distance in the poem? Choose two phrases that you feel are important in creating this effect.

Third reading

9. Do you think that the poet was on his own or travelling with a friend? Use the poem to support your opinion.

10. Why do you think the poet remembers this scene? Was it because he spent a long time looking at it or can you suggest another reason?

William Carlos Williams (1883–1963)

The early poetic work of William Carlos Williams shows the influence of two of the major poets of the twentieth century, Ezra Pound and T.S. Eliot. However, he eventually felt limited by this, and searched for an authentic American expression in poetry. He found this in writing about commonplace objects and the lives of ordinary people. In this way, he managed to bring out the significance of people and things we might otherwise take for granted. He has proved an inspiration for accepted major poets, in particular Ginsberg. His output includes stories and plays besides his five well-known books of poetry.

The Red Wheelbarrow

prescribed for the Ordinary Level exam in 2010

so much depends
upon

a red wheel
barrow

glazed with rain   5
water

beside the white
chickens

Explorations

First reading

1. Write down three words to describe your first reaction to this poem. Discuss these in your group or class. Is it possible to agree on three words to describe the reaction of the whole class or are there a number of different reactions in the group?

2. Where do you think this poem is set, in the city or in the country? What words in the poem support your view?

3. In your own words, write down what this poem is about. Did you find it easy or difficult to do this? Why?

Second reading

4. Can you suggest a connection between the wheelbarrow and the chickens?

5. How do you feel when it rains? Is the fact that it is raining important in the poem? Why?

6. Do the first four words of the poem tell you anything about the poet's reaction to what he sees? Do you empathise with his feelings? Why?

Third reading

7. Does this poem create a mood? How would you describe it? Use the piece to support your view.

8. Consider which is more important in the poem, what the poet sees or what he feels. Is it more than just a simple description?

9. In your own words, write down what you now think this poem is about. Compare it with your answer to Question 3. Has your opinion changed in any way?

10. Is it the way that words are arranged, or how they sound, or the feelings they express, that turns them into poetry? What do you expect to see in a poem? How does this piece go against your expectations? Can sixteen words be classed as a poem? Why? Discuss these issues in your group or class.

Siegfried Sassoon (1886–1967)

Sassoon enlisted in the British army on the first day of the First World War and was one of the few poets to survive the fighting. He is best known for his satirical poems of disillusionment with the war, such as 'The Hero', 'Base Details' and 'The General'. In 1919 Sassoon became literary editor of the *Daily Herald* and achieved notice for his semi-autobiographical writings, beginning with *Memoirs of a Fox-Hunting Man* (1928) and *Memories of an Infantry Officer* (1930).

On Passing the New Menin Gate

prescribed for Ordinary Level exams in 2008 and 2009

Who will remember, passing through this Gate,
The unheroic Dead who fed the guns?
Who shall absolve the foulness of their fate, –
Those doomed, conscripted, unvictorious ones?
       Crudely renewed, the Salient holds its own.   5
       Paid are its dim defenders by this pomp;
       Paid, with a pile of peace-complacent stone,
       The armies who endured that sullen swamp.

Here was the world's worst wound. And here with pride
'Their name liveth for ever,' the Gateway claims.   10
Was ever an immolation so belied
As these intolerably nameless names?
Well might the Dead who struggled in the slime
Rise and deride this sepulchre of crime.

Notes:

the New Menin Gate: a large memorial in Belgium inscribed with the names of over 50,000 Allied soldiers who died in the Ypres area in the First World War. Either their remains could not be identified or they were never found.

(3) **absolve:** pardon

(4) **conscripted:** compulsory enlistment into the armed forces

(5) **Salient:** a network of fortifications and trenches. The 'Salient' at Ypres was the focus of intense fighting.

(6) **pomp:** splendid display

(7) **complacent:** smugly self-satisfied

(10) **'Their name liveth for ever,':** taken from a book of biblical writings known as Ecclesiasticus.

(11) **immolation:** a sacrifice often of a valued thing and involving killing

(11) **belied:** to give a false notion; to fail to justify or to fulfil

(12) **intolerably:** cannot be endured

(14) **deride:** ridicule

(14) **sepulchre:** a tomb

 # Explorations

First reading

1. Siegfrid Sassoon fought bravely in the First World War. What images in the poem reveal that Sassoon had experienced the horrible reality of war?

Second reading

2. (a) What were the lives of the 'Dead' like before they died? (b) Can you suggest who the 'Dead' are?

3. Why is Sassoon concerned about the 'Dead' in the first four lines of the poem?

4. (a) What words and phrases does Sassoon use to describe the New Menin Gate? (b) Do they tell you anything about his attitude to this memorial?

5. 'Paid are its dim defenders by this pomp;'
   Do you feel that Sassoon really believes that this monument is full payment for the sacrifice of the soldiers' lives, or is he being ironic? Why?

6. '"Their name liveth for ever,"'
   (a) How does Sassoon react to this inscription? (b) Can you suggest why he feels this way?

Third reading

7. 'Who shall absolve the foulness of their fate,–'

'Paid are its dim defenders by this pomp;
Paid, with a pile of peace-complacent stone,'
How does Sassoon use alliteration to suggest his emotions in these lines?

8. What three words would you use to describe the tone of this poem? Use quotations from the poem to support your three words.

9. How do you think this poem should be read aloud:
i. softly and calmly or
ii. loudly and passionately?
Give reasons for your choice.

10. Imagine that you are one of the soldiers in this poem and you are keeping a diary of your experiences. Based on Sassoon's images of war, write a page of your diary entries.

W.H. Auden (1907–1973)

Wystan Hugh Auden was born at York on 21 February 1907 and educated at Oxford and Berlin. He is considered one of the most important English poets of the 1930s, writing on political and social themes. A prolific poet, he wrote in a variety of verse forms, composing both humorous and serious poetry. 'Funeral Blues', originally a song in one of his plays, is taken from the volume *Another Time* (1940), which contains many of his best-known poems, such as 'September 1939' and 'Lullaby'. Auden spent much of his life in the United States, becoming an American citizen in 1946.

Funeral Blues

prescribed for the Ordinary Level exam in 2007

Stop all the clocks, cut off the telephone,
Prevent the dog from barking with a juicy bone,
Silence the pianos and with muffled drum
Bring out the coffin, let the mourners come.

Let aeroplanes circle moaning overhead   5
Scribbling on the sky the message He Is Dead,
Put the crêpe bows round the white necks of the public doves,
Let the traffic policemen wear black cotton gloves.

He was my North, my South, my East and West,
My working week and my Sunday rest,   10
My noon, my midnight, my talk, my song;
I thought that love would last for ever: I was wrong.

The stars are not wanted now: put out every one;
Pack up the moon and dismantle the sun;
Pour away the ocean and sweep up the wood.   15
For nothing now can ever come to any good.

 # Explorations

First reading

1. What images grab your attention?
2. What do you think is happening in this poem?
3. Do you find it unusual in any way? Explain.

Second reading

4. The first two stanzas create the atmosphere of a funeral. What sights and sounds of a funeral do you notice?
5. It used to be a custom that clocks were stopped in a house where a death had occurred: as well as marking the time of death, this signified that time stood still for the grieving family. Do you think that the signs of mourning have been carried to extremes in the first

two stanzas? Examine the
actions called for.

6. How do you think the first
stanza should be read: in a
low, defeated tone, or semi-
hysterical, or what? Read it
aloud.

7. Read the second stanza aloud.

8. Do you think there might be a
change of tone from the third
stanza on? Read aloud stanzas
3 and 4.

9. Are you sympathetic to the
speaker in this poem?

Third reading

10. What does the third stanza
suggest about the relationship
between the speaker and the
person mourned? Examine
each line in detail for the
kernel of truth behind the
clichés.

11. How do you understand the
speaker's state of mind,
particularly in the last verse?

12. Do you take this poem to be a
serious statement about loss
and bereavement, or do you
find it exaggerated and 'over
the top'? Explain your opinion.
Do you think it could be read
as a satire, that is, a poem
ridiculing, in this case, the
public outpouring of emotion
at the funerals of famous
people? Read the poem again.

Fourth reading

13. What do you think the poem is
saying?

14. Look at the imagery again.
How does it fit in with what
the poem is saying?

15. Find out what you can about
blues music and lyrics. What
elements of a blues song do
you find in the poem?

16. What do you like about this
poem?

Dylan Thomas (1914–1953)

Dylan Thomas was born in Swansea where his father was an English teacher. After attending the local grammar school he went to work as a journalist on a local newspaper, *The South Wales Daily Post*. In 1934 he went to London where he worked as a journalist and reviewer, as well as doing other jobs for newspapers and magazines. During the Second World War he came to work as a scriptwriter for the BBC and a number of film companies. In the postwar years he began broadcasting, featuring his own poems and stories. Thomas published four volumes of poetry and two prose works. His 'play for voices' *Under Milk Wood*, which evokes the spirit of a Welsh village from early morning to night, was published after his death. Thomas said of his poetry 'I wrote my poems for the glory of God and the love of man'.

He married Caitlin Macnamara in 1937, and after much wandering eventually settled in Wales in 1949. He went to America on a lecture and poetry-reading tour the following year and made a great deal of money. Unfortunately Thomas found life as a literary celebrity a strain, which he relieved by heavy drinking. In 1953 he died in America after a heavy drinking bout.

The Hunchback in the Park

prescribed for Ordinary Level exams in 2009 and 2010

The hunchback in the park
A solitary mister
Propped between trees and water
From the opening of the garden lock
That lets the trees and water enter   5
Until the Sunday sombre bell at dark

Eating bread from a newspaper
Drinking water from the chained cup
That the children filled with gravel
In the fountain basin where I sailed my ship   10
Slept at night in a dog kennel
But nobody chained him up.

Like the park birds he came early
Like the water he sat down
And Mister they called Hey mister   15
The truant boys from the town
Running when he heard them clearly
On out of sound

Past lake the rockery
Laughing when he shook his paper   20
Hunchbacked in mockery
Through the loud zoo of the willow groves
Dodging the park keeper
With his stick that picked up leaves.

And the old dog sleeper   25
Alone between nurses and swans
While the boys among willows
Made the tigers jump out of their eyes
To roar on the rockery stones
And the groves were blue with sailors   30

Made all day until bell time
A woman figure without fault
Straight as a young elm
Straight and tall from his crooked bones
That she might stand in the night   35
After the locks and the chains

All night in the unmade park
After the railings and shrubberies
The birds the grass the trees the lake
And the wild boys innocent as strawberries   40
Had followed the hunchback
To his kennel in the dark.

Notes:

(6) **sombre:** gloomy

(16) **truant:** a child who is absent from school without permission

 # Explorations

First reading

1. (a) In your own words, describe the life of the hunchback. (b) Choose one image from the poem that helps you to picture the way that he lives.

2. (a) How do the boys behave towards the hunchback? (b) Why do you think that they behave in this way?

Second reading

3. From the details given in the poem, describe the park as you imagine it.

4. (a) Apart from the hunchback and the 'truant boys', who are the other people in the park? (b) Can you suggest reasons why each of the different people go there?

5. (a) Who does the hunchback imagine in the sixth stanza? (b) Do you think that there is a connection between his fantasy and the fact that he is described as being 'solitary' and 'alone'?

Third reading

6. Would you agree that the images of the park and the dog kennel suggest the idea of being confined or imprisoned? Refer to the poem to support your view.

7. 'But nobody chained him up.' (a) Bearing in mind your answer to Question 6, could the hunchback be said to live a freer type of life than the rest of the people in the poem? (b) Does this freedom make him happy?

8. Using your work on Questions 6 and 7, explain the theme, or central message, of this poem in two or three sentences.

9. 'And Mister they called Hey mister'
    'With his stick that picked up leaves.'
    As a Welshman, Thomas was very aware of the musical sounds of language. How does Thomas use the sounds of the words in the two lines above to help us to imagine what he is describing?

10. Imagine that the hunchback has been found dead in the park and you are a reporter on the local newspaper who has been sent to ask the people who use the park how they feel about his death. Write a short newspaper article giving their reactions.

Judith Wright (1915–2000)

Judith Wright was one of the most important Australian poets of the twentieth century. Her first volume of poetry, *The Moving Image* (1946), dealt with the Aboriginal and convict history of Australia and made an immediate impact. She also wrote about the Australian landscape and the solitary figures of Australian rural life, and she was interested in conservationist issues. She also explored the theme of love, and particularly maternal experience, in *Woman to Man* (1949). Her *Collected Poems, 1942–1970* was published in 1972. She died in 2000.

Request to a Year

prescribed for Ordinary Level exams in 2009 and 2010

If the year is meditating a suitable gift,
I should like it to be the attitude
of my great-great-grandmother,
legendary devotee of the arts,

who, having had eight children   5
and little opportunity for painting pictures,
sat one day on a high rock
beside a river in Switzerland

and from a difficult distance viewed
her second son, balanced on a small ice-floe,   10
drift down the current towards a waterfall
that struck rock-bottom eighty feet below,

while her second daughter, impeded,
no doubt, by the petticoats of the day,
stretched out a last-hope alpenstock   15
(which luckily later caught him on his way).

Nothing, it was evident, could be done;
and with the artist's isolating eye
my great-great-grandmother hastily sketched the scene.
The sketch survives to prove the story by.   20

Year, if you have no Mother's Day present planned;
reach back and bring me the firmness of her hand.

 # Explorations

First reading

1. Picture the drama in this scene. What do you see? Roughly sketch the outline of the scene and describe what you see. What is happening? Where is each character? Imagine the expression on the face of each.

2. What was the reaction of the great-great-grandmother to the incident? Can you explain her reaction? What is your impression of her?

3. Do you think this poem is meant to be taken seriously? Explain your view.

Second reading

4. Does the poet realise that this scenario is incredible? Where is this indicated?

5. Explore the poet's reaction to the great-great-grandmother. Is it one of horror, indifference, admiration, or what? What quality of the great-great-grandmother's does she respect?

6. Explain the title of the poem.

Third reading

7. How is the humour created? Explore the effect of exaggeration, unexpected behaviour, the language used, and irony. Do you consider this light humour or bleak humour? Why?

8. What statements do you think the poem is making about motherhood, about art, or about childhood?

Edwin Morgan (1920–)

Morgan was born in Glasgow, was first published in 1952 and was still being published in 1996. Such a long career is marked by an ability and vision to write poetry inspired by a wide and varied list of subjects, from space travel to mythological goddesses. His prolific output includes libretti, plays, criticism and translations from Anglo-Saxon and Russian. His poems are as varied in form as they are in material, showing, for example, similarities to medieval Latin writing on the one hand and e. e. cummings on the other.

Strawberries

prescribed for the Ordinary Level exam in 2007

There were never strawberries
like the ones we had
that sultry afternoon
sitting on the step
of the open french window   5
facing each other
your knees held in mine
the blue plates in our laps
the strawberries glistening
in the hot sunlight   10
we dipped them in sugar
looking at each other
not hurrying the feast
for one to come
the empty plates   15
laid on the stone together
with the two forks crossed

and I bent towards you
sweet in that air
in my arms   20
abandoned like a child
from your eager mouth
the taste of strawberries
in my memory
lean back again let me love you   25

let the sun beat
on our forgetfulness
one hour of all
the heat intense
and summer lightening   30
on the Kilpatrick hills

let the storm wash the plates

Explorations

First reading

1. The poet suggests that food connected with special moments has a special taste. Would you agree with him? Have you any special memories where the food seemed to taste especially good?
2. What impression do you get of the setting for this poem? Do you find it a surprising setting for a poem? Why?
3. What sort of a relationship do you think these two people have? Choose two phrases from the poem to support your view.

Second reading

4. What is the weather like as the couple eat the strawberries? Does it tell you anything about their feelings?
5. 'the empty plates
    laid on the stone together
    with the two forks crossed'
    Why do you think the poet introduces this image into the poem at this point? Does it have any connection with the couple?
6. How does the poet use the weather to suggest the intensifying of their emotions? Do you think that this is a

successful device or is it rather over-dramatic?

Third reading

7. 'not hurrying the feast
    for one to come'
    Eating is a sensual experience. Can the 'feast' of strawberries be seen as a preparation for another equally sensual 'feast'? What is your reaction to this connection of ideas?
8. Eating is also an important social activity. Can you think of occasions where sharing food has a special significance perhaps even suggesting a change in the nature of a relationship? How would you feel if you had to share a table in a restaurant with a stranger, or if you were invited to a friend's home for a meal?
9. Why do you think the poet chose to write this poem without any punctuation? Was he trying to suggest something about the moment, or perhaps about the way that he remembers the moment?
10. This is a remembered moment. Do you think that this affects the way in which the poet views the scene? Can memories be trusted? Does it matter if they are unreliable?

Howard Nemerov (1920–1991)

Howard Nemerov was born in 1920 in New York. After he graduated from Harvard in 1941, he served as a pilot in the Royal Canadian unit of the US Army Air Force. He flew throughout World War II and he became a first lieutenant. He married in 1944.

Following the war, Nemerov taught in a number of American universities while writing poetry, novels, short stories, essays and criticism. He was awarded numerous prizes for his poetry, including the prestigious Pulitzer Prize for Poetry in 1978 for 'The Collected Poems of Howard Nemerov'.

Nemerov became the third Poet Laureate of the United States of America in 1988. He died in 1991.

Wolves in the Zoo

prescribed for Ordinary Level exams in 2007 and 2010

They look like big dogs badly drawn, drawn wrong.
A legend on their cage tells us there is
No evidence that any of their kind
Has ever attacked man, woman, or child.

Now it turns out there were no babies dropped   5
In sacrifice, delaying tactics, from
Siberian sleds; now it turns out, so late,
That Little Red Ridinghood and her Gran

Were the agressors with the slavering fangs
And tell-tale tails; now it turns out at last   10
That grey wolf and timber wolf are near extinct,
Done out of being by the tales we tell

Told us by Nanny in the nursery;
Young sparks we were, to set such forest fires
As blazed from story into history   15
And put such bounty on their wolvish heads

As brought the few survivors to our terms,
Surrendered in happy Babylon among
The peacock dusting off the path of dust,
The tiger pacing in the stripéd shade.   20

Notes:

(2) **legend:** an inscription, a traditional unauthenticated story

(7) **Siberian:** of Siberia in the north-eastern part of Russia

(9) **aggressors:** attackers

(9) **slavering:** dribbling

(16) **bounty:** reward

(18) **Babylon:** one of the most important cities of the ancient world. The Hanging
     Gardens of Babylon were one of the Seven Wonders of the Ancient World.

 # Explorations

First reading

1. (a) In the first line of the
    poem, Nemerov describes the
    wolves as 'big dogs badly
    drawn'. How do you picture
    the wolves from this
    description? (b) Do you find it
    a surprising image to use about
    the wolves? Why?

2. (a) What does the notice on
    the wolves' cage say? (b) Why
    do you think Nemerov decided
    to put this piece of information
    at the very beginning of his
    poem?

Second reading

3. (a) How is the wolf usually
    portrayed in the 'Little Red
    Riding Hood' story? (b) What
    does Nemerov have to say
    about this portrayal? (c) What
    other untrue story was told
    about wolves?

4. What effect did these untrue
    stories have on (a) the young
    children who heard them and
    (b) the world's wolf
    population?

5. 'As blazed from story into
    history'
    (a) Explain the difference

between a 'story' and 'history'? (b) What is Nemerov suggesting happened to the untrue tales told about wolves?

Third reading

6. (a) What type of scene can you picture from the images in the final stanza of the poem? (b) Do you think that the wolves, the peacock and the tiger are really 'happy'? Why?

7. 'now it turns out, so late,
    That Little Red Ridinghood
    and her Gran
    Were the aggressors'
    'Done out of being by the tales
    we tell'
    'As brought the few survivors
    to our terms,
    Surrendered in happy Babylon'
    (a) What do these lines suggest about the way that humans have treated the wolves? (b) Do you agree with this point of view? Why?

8. The forming of people's attitudes and the consequences of those attitudes are ideas that occur in this poem. (a) Did thinking about this poem make you reconsider your attitude to wolves? (b) Might this poem encourage you to reconsider some of your other attitudes?

9. Explain the theme, or central message, of this poem in your own words. Use quotations from the poem to support your explanation.

10. Write a letter to the newspaper either in favour of or against the practice of keeping animals in zoos.

Richard Wilbur (1921–)

Richard Wilbur was born in New York and educated at Amherst College and Harvard University. He served in the American army during the Second World War and has been a teacher at Harvard and other universities. Among his collections of poetry are *The Beautiful Changes and Other Poems* (1947); *Ceremony and Other Poems* (1950) (from which 'The Pardon' is taken); *Things of This World: Poems,* which won a Pulitzer Prize in 1956; and *New and Collected Poems* (1988). Wilbur believed that one of the main functions of poetry was to examine the inconsistencies and disharmony

of modern life. He was made Poet Laureate of the United States in 1987.

The Pardon

prescribed for the Ordinary Level exam in 2008

My dog lay dead five days without a grave
In the thick of summer, hid in a clump of pine
And a jungle of grass and honeysuckle-vine.
I who had loved him while he kept alive

Went only close enough to where he was   5
To sniff the heavy honeysuckle-smell
Twined with another odour heavier still
And hear the flies' intolerable buzz.

Well, I was ten and very much afraid.
In my kind world the dead were out of range   10
And I could not forgive the sad or strange
In beast or man. My father took the spade

And buried him. Last night I saw the grass
Slowly divide (it was the same scene
But now it glowed a fierce and mortal green)   15
And saw the dog emerging. I confess
I felt afraid again, but still he came
In the carnal sun, clothed in a hymn of flies,
And death was breeding in his lively eyes.
I started in to cry and call his name,   20

Asking forgiveness of his tongueless head.
... I dreamt the past was never past redeeming:
But whether this was false or honest dreaming
I beg death's pardon now. And mourn the dead.

Explorations

First reading

1. Briefly outline the story of this poem.
2. How did the boy first discover that his dog was dead? What did he do then? Can you understand his reaction? Have you any experience of a similar situation?
3. How does he himself rationalise or explain his reaction? Examine stanza 3 in some detail. Can you understand his response? Explain.

Second reading

4. The boy is haunted by this experience. What elements of nightmare do you find in the dream?
5. How is the frightening effect of the dream created? Examine stanzas 4 and 5 in detail. 'But still he came': what is the effect of this? What is suggested by 'the carnal sun'? What does the image 'a hymn of flies' suggest? Do you find this contradictory? Explain your immediate reaction to the phrase. 'And death was breeding in his lively eyes.' Why 'lively'? What does the line mean to you?
6. How does he comprehend death at first – rationally or sensually? Does 'the carnal sun' fit in with his experience of death and of nature generally?
7. In the final stanza he talks about 'asking forgiveness' and begs 'death's pardon'. Can you

explain his feelings? What are
the thoughts inside his head at
this point?
8. Explain the title of the poem.
9. 'False or honest dreaming': do
you think Wilbur considers
that dreams have an important
function? Explain.

Third reading

10. What does the speaker of this
poem learn about himself and
about life? Refer to specific
phrases to support your
assertions.
11. 'Wilbur apprehends the world
mainly through the senses.'
Could this statement be
justified from the evidence of
this poem? Explain.

12. Do you think Wilbur's power
of description is particularly
effective? Examine two
examples and say why you
think them effective or not.
13. Would you agree that this is a
dramatic poem? Explain two
ways in which you think this
effect is created. Examine the
subject matter; the pace of the
narration; the depth of feelings
involved; the descriptions.

Fourth reading

14. Outline the main themes you
find in the poem.
15. What do you think is the most
effective aspect of Wilbur's
style of writing? Explain.

Denise Levertov (1923–1997)

Denise Levertov was born in Essex in England. Her father had converted from Judaism to become an Anglican parson. She was educated completely at home and at five years old decided that she would become a writer. At the age of twelve she sent her poetry to T.S. Eliot, who responded very positively to her work. She published her first poem at seventeen and her first collection in 1946. During World War Two she worked as a civilian nurse during the bombing of London.

In 1947 she married an American and soon after moved to the US with him. By 1956 she had become an American citizen. Her poetry became much less formal and she was heavily influenced by poets such as William Carlos Williams. Her second American volume, *With Eyes at the Back of Our Heads*, in 1959 established her as one of the great American poets, and her British roots were by now a thing of the past. During the 1960s she became very involved in activism and feminism. She was strongly opposed to the Vietnam War. *The Sorrow Dance*, which emphasised her feelings to the Vietnam War and to the death of her sister, was a passionate, angry collection. In all she published more than twenty volumes of poetry. She died in December 1997.

What Were They Like?

prescribed for the Ordinary Level exam in 2007

1. Did the people of Vietnam
   use lanterns of stone?
2. Did they hold ceremonies
   to reverence the opening of buds?
3. Were they inclined to laughter?   5
4. Did they use bone and ivory,
   jade and silver, for ornament?
5. Had they an epic poem?
6. Did they distinguish between speech and singing?

1. Sir, their light hearts turned to stone.   10
   It is not remembered whether in gardens
   stone lanterns illumined pleasant ways.
2. Perhaps they gathered once to delight in blossom,
   but after the children were killed
   there were no more buds.   15
3. Sir, laughter is bitter to the burned mouth.
4. A dream ago, perhaps. Ornament is for joy.
   All the bones were charred.
5. It is not remembered. Remember,
   most were peasants; their life   20
   was in rice and bamboo.
   When peaceful clouds were reflected in the paddies
   and the water buffalo stepped surely along terraces,
   maybe fathers told their sons old tales.
   When bombs smashed those mirrors   25
   there was time only to scream.
6. There is an echo yet
   of their speech which was like a song.
   It was reported their singing resembled
   the flight of moths in moonlight.   30
   Who can say? It is silent now.

Explorations

Before reading

1. What do you know about the Vietnam War? Find out about it and discuss it.

First reading (lines 1–9)

2. Read the questions. What does the questioner want to find out?
3. What do these questions tell us about the questioner – for example: what preconceptions does s/he have about the Vietnamese; what is his/her profession – journalist, historian, archaeologist or what?
4. Read the questions aloud in the tone of voice you would expect the questioner to ask them. Discuss the tone and manner of the questioning.
5. What responses would you expect to each of these questions? Suggest sample answers.

Second reading (lines 10–31)

6. Are the answers as you expected? What do you find surprising or unexpected? Do you think the answers might have surprised the questioner? Why?
7. From the answers, what do we learn about the way of life of the Vietnamese?
8. What is the chief preoccupation of the person who replies – what preys on his/her mind and colours all the replies?
9. Do you think the tone of the answers differs from that of the questions? Explain your views on this and discuss them in your group or class.

Third reading

10. What is your favourite image or phrase in the poem?
11. Examine each of the metaphors individually: the light, the bud, laughter, decoration, heritage and culture. What is suggested by each metaphor? What do they contribute to the atmosphere of the poem?
12. What impression is given of the attitude to life of Vietnamese people after the war? Where is this suggested?
13. Are there any signs of hope for the future in this poem?

Fourth reading

14. Were you moved by the poem? Discuss your reaction with your group or class.
15. What do you think the poem is saying? Write two or three paragraphs on this.
16. Have you previously read a poem that took the format of a 'question and answer' sequence? What do you think of this format? Is it effective in this case? Explain your views.

Patricia Beer (1924–1999)

Patricia Beer was born in Exmouth, Devon, into a Plymouth Brethren family. Her father was a railway clerk and her mother a teacher; Beer wrote a vivid account of her stern upbringing in *Mrs Beer's House* (1968). Patricia won a scholarship to Exmouth Grammar School and achieved a first-class honours degree at Exeter University. She went on to St Hugh's College, Oxford, and lived in Italy teaching English during the period 1947–53. After a succession of temporary jobs Beer was appointed lecturer in English at Goldsmiths' College in London in 1962, where she remained for six years. In 1964 she married an architect, John Damien Parsons with whom she refurbished a Tudor farmhouse in Up Ottery, Devon, where she lived the rest of her life. Patricia Beer left teaching to become a full-time writer four years later.

In all, Beer published nine volumes of poetry, one novel and an academic study *Reader I Married Him* – an analysis of the major nineteenth-century women novelists and their female characters. Patricia Beer makes her poems out of the ordinary events of daily life with a wry humour and a sharp eye for detail.

The Voice

prescribed for the Ordinary Level exam in 2007

When God took my aunt's baby boy, a merciful neighbour
Gave her a parrot. She could not have afforded one
But now bought a new cage as brilliant as the bird,
And turned her back on the idea of other babies.

He looked unlikely. In her house his scarlet feathers   5
Stuck out like a jungle, though his blue ones blended
With the local pottery which carried messages
Like 'Du ee help yerself to crame, me handsome.'

He said nothing when he arrived, not a quotation
From pet-shop gossip or a sailor's oath, no sound   10
From someone's home: the telephone or car-door slamming,
And none from his: tom-tom, war-cry or wild beast roaring.

He came from silence but was ready to become noise.
My aunt taught him nursery rhymes morning after morning.
He learnt Miss Muffett, Jack and Jill, Little Jack Horner,   15
Including her jokes; she used to say turds and whey.

A genuine Devon accent is not easy. Actors
Cannot do it. He could though. In his court clothes
He sounded like a farmer, as her son might have.
He sounded like our family. He fitted in.   20

Years went by. We came and went. A day or two
Before he died, he got confused, and muddled up
His rhymes. Jack Horner ate his pail of water.
The spider said what a good boy he was. I wept.

He had never seemed puzzled by the bizarre events   25
He spoke of. But that last day he turned his head towards us
With the bewilderment of death upon him. Said
'Broke his crown' and 'Christmas pie'. And tumbled after.

My aunt died the next winter, widowed, childless, pitied
And patronised. I cannot summon up her voice at all.   30
She would not have expected it to be remembered
After so long. But I can still hear his.

 # Explorations

First reading

1. What impression of the aunt do you get from the first stanza? How do you visualise her?

2. 'He looked unlikely.' What do you think the author means by this?

3. How do you imagine the aunt's home looked? Examine the detail in the two opening stanzas.

4. Why do you think the aunt taught the parrot nursery rhymes? Is there a connection with the loss of her baby son?

5. 'He fitted in.' How did the parrot fit in?

6. Why do you think the author 'wept'? How does she feel about the parrot?

7. What do you think the poet means by 'pitied | And patronised'? What does this tell us about how people perceived the aunt?

Second reading

8. Read the poem aloud. Jot down what you notice about its sounds and rhythms.

9. How do you react to the first sentence? Is it an effective opening?

10. Comment on the 'jungle' simile in the second stanza.

11. Do you get a sense of place from the references to Devon and the local pottery? Does this enrich the poem?

12. 'With the bewilderment of death upon him. Said | "Broke his crown" and "Christmas pie". And tumbled after.'
Comment on these lines. Do you think the lines work well? Can you detect some humour in the clever phrasing?

13. What evidence is there in the poem that the parrot was regarded more as a family member than as a mere household pet?

14. How do you feel about the aunt's life? Can you suggest why we are not told her name?

Third reading

15. Briefly state what the theme of the poem is.

16. Would you agree that there is genuine warmth of feeling in this poem?

17. How do you react to the style in which the poem is written? Comment on any three features. You might consider the poet's conversational language, her wry humour, her eye for detail and her use of imagery.

18. What is the mood of this poem? What choice of words and images suggest the mood? Look closely at the final stanza.

19. What have you learned about the character of the author from reading the poem?

Fourth reading

20. Write a paragraph giving your personal reaction to 'The Voice'. Would you recommend it?

Elizabeth Jennings (1926–2001)

Elizabeth Jennings was born in Lincolnshire, England and was educated at Oxford University. In the famous poetry anthology *The New Lines* she was the only woman poet. This placed her alongside many of the writers of 'The Movement' which included Kingsley Amis, Philip Larkin and others. Her poetry is often interested in finding order in experience. It often searches for answers rather than giving a message. It concerns itself with the chase as much as the beast.

The Ladybird's Story

prescribed for the Ordinary Level exam in 2008

It was a roadway to me.
So many meeting-places and directions.
It was smooth, polished, sometimes it shook a little
But I did not tumble off.
I heard you say, and it was like a siren,   5
'A ladybird. Good luck. Perhaps some money.'
I did not understand.
Suddenly I was frightened, fearful of falling
Because you lifted your hand.

And then I saw your eyes,   10
Glassy moons always changing shape,
Sometimes suns in eclipse.
I watched the beak, the peak of your huge nose
And the island of your lips.
I was afraid but you were not. I have   15
No sting. I do not wound.
I carry a brittle coat. It does not protect.
I thought you would blow me away but superstition

Saved me. You held your hand now in one position,
Gentled me over the veins and arteries.   20
But it was not I you cared about but money.
You see I have watched you with flies.

Notes:

(5) **siren:** a device for making a loud prolonged noise
(12) **eclipse:** where light is obscured from one celestial body by another

 # Explorations

First reading

1. In your own words, explain the situation that the ladybird is in, in this poem.
2. (*a*) What three words would you use to describe the ladybird? (*b*) What phrases or lines in the poem made you think of your chosen words?

Second reading

3. (*a*) What image does the ladybird use to describe the human hand in the first two lines of the poem? (*b*) Do you think that this is an effective metaphor? Why?
4. 'Suddenly I was frightened, fearful of falling'
   How does Jennings' use of alliteration in this line help to suggest that the ladybird was afraid?
5. What metaphors does Jennings use to suggest the huge size of the human face looming over the ladybird in lines 10–14?
6. (*a*) How does the human being treat the ladybird? (*b*) What reason does the ladybird give for this behaviour?

Third reading

7. ' You see I have watched you with flies.'
   Can you suggest what the ladybird might have seen the human doing to flies?
8. (*a*) In what way is the human being portrayed in this poem? (*b*) Do you think that this is a fair portrayal? Why?
9. Examine how the tone, or emotion, changes in the ladybird's words in the course of this poem.
10. Imagine that you are the human being in this poem. Describe the incident from your point of view.

One Flesh

prescribed for the Ordinary Level exam in 2010

Lying apart now, each in a separate bed,
He with a book, keeping the light on late,
She like a girl dreaming of childhood,
All men elsewhere – it is as if they wait
Some new event: the book he holds unread,   5
Her eyes fixed on the shadows overhead.

Tossed up like flotsam from a former passion,
How cool they lie. They hardly ever touch,
Or if they do it is like a confession
Of having little feeling – or too much.   10
Chastity faces them, a destination
For which their whole lives were a preparation.

Strangely apart, yet strangely close together,
Silence between them like a thread to hold
And not wind in. And time itself's a feather   15
Touching them gently. Do they know they're old,
These two who are my father and my mother
Whose fire from which I came, has now grown cold?

Explorations

First reading

Stanza 1

1. The scene is described with all the clarity of a photograph. What do you notice about the picture? Describe the scene exactly.

2. Write out three questions you would like to ask the couple.

3. 'It is as if they wait | Some new event'. What does this suggest? Explore possible meanings.

Second reading

Stanza 2

4. Their relationship now is different from their former one. Explain the difference as we learn about it from the second stanza.

5. 'Tossed up like flotsam from a former passion'. What does this suggest about the condition of their lives? Explore all the possible. connotations of this image.

6. What do you imagine they are thinking, as they lie there? Draft a 'thoughts-inside-the-head' sequence for each person.

Third reading

Entire poem

7. 'Strangely apart, yet strangely close together'. How can this be?

8. There is a sense in this poem that neither parent can be complete without the other. Do you agree? Where is this evident?

9. Do you think they know that they are old?

10. If you had only read the first two verses, would you have known that the poem was about the poet's parents? What effect did this information have on you?

11. How do you think the poet feels about her parents?

Fourth reading

12. What particular images do you think contribute most to the atmosphere in this poem? Explain.

13. Explain the 'thread' simile.

14. Trace the rhyming scheme the poet uses. What is the effect of the sounds of these words?

15. What is the poem saying about age, love and families? Write three paragraphs on this.

Richard Murphy (1927–)

Richard Murphy was born in Mayo in 1927. His poetry collections include: *The Archaeology of Love* (Dolmen, 1955); *Sailing to an Island* (Faber, 1963); *The Battle of Aughrim* (Knopf and Faber, 1968; LP recording 1969); *High Island* (Faber, 1974); *High Island: New and Selected Poems* (Harper and Row, 1975); *Selected Poems* (Faber, 1979); *The Price of Stone* (Faber, 1985); *The Price of Stone and Earlier Poems* (Wake Forrest, 1985); *New Selected Poems* (Faber, 1989); *The Mirror Wall* (Bloodaxe, 1989) and *In the Heart of the Country: Collected Poems*, (Oldcastle, Co. Meath, Gallery Press, 2000). His awards include the Æ Memorial Award (1951); first prize, Guinness Awards, Cheltenham (1962); British Arts Council Awards (1967 and 1976); Marten Toonder Award (1980); Fellow of the Royal Society

of Literature (1969); American-Irish Foundation Award (1983). He lives in Co. Dublin.

His poetry is often concerned with issues of history. He is renowned as a crafter of poems who has been overlooked in recent years because of the fascination with Northern poetry.

The Reading Lesson

prescribed for Ordinary Level exams in 2007 and 2008

Fourteen years old, learning the alphabet,
He finds letters harder to catch than hares
Without a greyhound. Can't I give him a dog
To track them down, or put them in a cage?
He's caught in a trap, until I let him go,   5
Pinioned by 'Don't you want to learn to read?'
'I'll be the same man whatever I do.'
He looks at a page as a mule balks at a gap
From which a goat may hobble out and bleat.

His eyes jink from a sentence like flushed snipe   10
Escaping shot. A sharp word, and he'll mooch
Back to his piebald mare and bantam cock.
Our purpose is as tricky to retrieve
As mercury from a smashed thermometer.

'I'll not read anymore.' Should I give up?   15
His hands, long-fingered as a Celtic scribe's,
Will grow callous, gathering sticks or scrap;
Exploring pockets of the horny drunk
Loiterers at the fairs, giving them lice.
A neighbour chuckles. 'You can never tame   20
The wild duck: when his wings grow, he'll fly off.'

If books resembled roads, he'd quickly read:
But they're small farms to him, fenced by the page,
Ploughed into lines with letters drilled like oats:
A field of tasks he'll always be outside.   25
If words were bank-notes, he would filch a wad;
If they were pheasants, they'd be in his pot
For breakfast, or if wrens he'd make them king.

 # Explorations

First reading

1. What's the boy's background? Can you tell from the evidence in the poem?
2. Does the boy fit a stereotype?
3. What is the relationship between the two in the poem? Is it equal?

Second reading

4. Do you think the boy will give up?
5. Do you think the narrator will give up?

6. Will learning to read really change his life?
7. How does the narrator feel about the exercise?

Third reading

8. Why do you think the poet uses so many nature-related metaphors in the poem? Suggest a possible reason.
9. What do you think of the dialogue that is used in the poem? Is it realistic? Explain your thinking.

10. How does the last verse change the tone of the poem?
11. In the second verse the boy's reactions are compared to 'animals'. Do you think these descriptions are delivered well? Are they fair?

Fourth reading
12. Do you think the neighbour is right?
13. Do you think a wild duck should be tamed?
14. With whom of the two main characters in the poem do you empathise most? Why?

Maya Angelou (1928–)

Maya Angelou, originally Marguerite Johnson, was born on 4 April 1928 in St Louis, Missouri. Her older brother gave her the name 'Maya'. Her early life was unsettled and traumatic and for many years Maya had to struggle to overcome her childhood experiences.

Maya's parents divorced when she was three and Maya and her brother lived for five years with their grandmother in Arkansas, a state where racial segregation was practised. When Maya was eight she and her brother went back to their mother. During this time, Maya was raped by her mother's boyfriend. Deeply traumatised, Maya withdrew into herself, speaking only to her brother. Once again, the children returned to Arkansas and through the loving support of her grandmother and her study of literature and music, Maya rediscovered full speech by the age of twelve.

Maya had a son at the age of sixteen and embarked on a series of jobs that ranged from being the first female streetcar conductor to dancing in musicals. In the late 1950s, Maya moved to New York to pursue her singing and acting careers. This proved to be a turning point in her life and Maya Angelou has since developed into a playwright, a civil-rights activist, a lecturer and a director, amongst other occupations. In 1993, she read one of her poems at the inauguration of President Bill Clinton and she has developed a close friendship with Oprah Winfrey.

Phenomenal Woman

prescribed for Ordinary Level exams in 2008 and 2009

Pretty women wonder where my secret lies.
I'm not cute or built to suit a fashion model's size
But when I start to tell them,
They think I'm telling lies.
I say,   5
It's in the reach of my arms
The span of my hips
The stride of my step,
The curl of my lips.
I'm a woman   10
Phenomenally.
Phenomenal woman,
That's me.

I walk into a room
Just as cool as you please,   15
And to a man,
The fellows stand or
Fall down on their knees.
Then they swarm around me,
A hive of honey bees.   20
I say,
It's the fire in my eyes,
And the flash of my teeth,
The swing in my waist,
And the joy in my feet.   25
I'm a woman
Phenomenally.
Phenomenal woman,
That's me.

Men themselves have wondered   30
What they see in me.
They try so much
But they can't touch
My inner mystery.
When I try to show them,   35

They say they still can't see.
I say,
It's in the arch of my back,
The sun of my smile,
The ride of my breasts,   40
The grace of my style.
I'm a woman

Phenomenally.
Phenomenal woman,
That's me.   45

Now you understand
Just why my head's not bowed.
I don't shout or jump about
Or have to talk real loud.
When you see me passing   50
It ought to make you proud.
I say,
It's in the click of my heels,
The bend of my hair,
The palm of my hand   55
The need of my care,
'Cause I'm a woman
Phenomenally.
Phenomenal woman,
That's me.   60

Notes:

Phenomenal: extraordinary, exceptional

(8) **stride:** to walk with firm, long steps

Explorations

First reading

1. (a) Having read this poem for the first time, would you describe your overall reaction to it as a positive or a negative one? (b) Choose a particular extract from the poem that really triggers this response in you and try to explain why it affects you in this way.

Second reading

2. What effect does Angelou have on men when she goes into a room?

3. Why do you think that the 'Pretty women' want to know her 'secret'?

4. How do (a) the 'Pretty women' and (b) the 'Men' react when Maya tries to reveal her secret to them?

5. 'The stride of my step,'
'The swing in my waist'
'The sun of my smile,'
Which of the following words would you use to describe the tone, or emotion, expressed in the quotations above: positive, confident, assured, happy?

Third reading

6. Angelou explains where her secret lies in lines 6–9; 22–25; 37–45 and 53–56. Can you suggest a connection between these lines and her repetition of the phrase 'I'm a woman'?

7. 'When you see me passing It ought to make you proud.' Bearing in mind the difficulties that Angelou has faced in her life, why do you think that she feels that we should be 'proud' when we see her 'passing'?

8. (a) From your reading of the poem, sum up, in your own words, the qualities that Angelou feels make her a 'Phenomenal Woman'. (b) Do you agree with her that she is, indeed, a 'Phenomenal Woman'?

9. (a) What is the theme, or central message, of this poem? (b) In your opinion, could this theme apply to both males and females?

10. Write a short passage of prose, or a poem, entitled 'Phenomenal Man' or 'Phenomenal Person', outlining the characteristics and qualities that you find admirable.

Fleur Adcock (1934–)

Fleur Adcock was born in New Zealand and lived there at various times, but has spent much of her life in England. Her volumes of poetry include *The Eye of the Hurricane* (1964), *Tigers* (1967), *High Tide in the Garden* (1971), *The Inner Harbour* (1979), *The Incident Book* (1986), and *Time Zones* (1991). She is considered one of the foremost feminist poets of the age, famous for her 'anti-erotic' style of love poems. 'For Heidi with Blue Hair' is taken from *The Incident Book* and is dedicated to her god-daughter, Heidi Jackson.

For Heidi with Blue Hair

prescribed for Ordinary Level exams in 2007 and 2010

When you dyed your hair blue
(or, at least, ultramarine
for the clipped sides, with a crest
of jet-black spikes on top)
you were sent home from school   5

because, as the headmistress put it,
although dyed hair was not
specifically forbidden, yours
was, apart from anything else,
not done in the school colours.   10

Tears in the kitchen, telephone-calls
to school from your freedom-loving father:
'She's not a punk in her behaviour;
it's just a style.' (You wiped your eyes,
also not in a school colour.)   15
'She discussed it with me first –

we checked the rules.' 'And anyway, Dad,
it cost twenty-five dollars.
Tell them it won't wash out –
not even if I wanted to try.'   20

It would have been unfair to mention
your mother's death, but that
shimmered behind the arguments.
The school had nothing else against you;
the teachers twittered and gave in.   25

Next day your black friend had hers done
in grey, white and flaxen yellow –
the school colours precisely:
an act of solidarity, a witty
tease. The battle was already won.   30

 # Explorations

First reading

1. What details of the story stand out? What in particular do you notice on a first reading?
2. Visualise the scene in the kitchen. What details do you notice? How do you hear the voices? Comment on the tones of voice, or say the words aloud as you imagine them.
3. Read the second stanza aloud as you imagine the headmistress would say it. How would you describe the tone? What kind of person do you think she is? Explain.
4. What kind of person do you think the father is?

Second reading

5. Why do you think Heidi dyed her hair?
6. Why did Heidi's black friend have hers done? Explore the last stanza for clues.
7. 'It would have been unfair to mention | your mother's death, but that | shimmered behind the arguments.' What do you imagine people were thinking? Write out the thoughts that the father, or the headmistress or the teachers, might have had. What might Heidi herself have thought? Comment on the word 'shimmer'.
8. What kind of school do you suppose it was? Comment on

the school's attitude and outlook as revealed in the poem. Do you think it was strict, 'stuffy', 'posh', reasonable, or what? Read the entire poem again before committing yourself.

9. Do you think the poem accurately reflects the demand for conformity found in school life? Do you find it true? Explain.

Third reading

10. Would you consider the father's attitude usual or unusual for a parent? Explain.

11. What truths about the life of a teenager do you find in this poem?

12. Do you think the poem is humorous? Mention two ways in which this humour is created. Is this note of humour maintained all the way through?

13. Make notes on the main themes and issues you find dealt with in the poem.

Brendan Kennelly (1936–)

Brendan Kennelly was born in 1936 in Kerry. He was educated at Trinity College and Leeds University. He is currently Professor of Modern Literature at Trinity College, Dublin. He has always published a lot of poetry and is a well-known personality, something which is unusual for a poet and an academic. He was featured in an ad for a high-profile car manufacturer, even though he doesn't drive.

Kennelly is fascinated with the past and the way in which the past re-emerges in contemporary society. He is also interested in giving voice to historical characters who were cast as villains. The best examples of this are in his two long sequences 'Cromwell' and the 'Book of Judas'.

He has also worked on translations from the French as well as updating classical works of Greek drama. He has published a novel too, and his selected criticism is contained in *Journey into Joy* (1994).

Night Drive

prescribed for the Ordinary Level exam in 2010

I

The rain hammered as we drove
Along the road to Limerick
'Jesus what a night' Alan breathed
And – 'I wonder how he is, the last account
Was poor.'   5
I couldn't speak.

The windscreen fumed and blurred, the rain's spit
Lashing the glass. Once or twice
The wind's fist seemed to lift the car
And pitch it hard against the ditch.   10
Alan straightened out in time,
Silent. Glimpses of the Shannon –
A boiling madhouse roaring for its life
Or any life too near its gaping maw,
White shreds flaring in the waste   15
Of insane murderous black;
Trees bending in grotesque humility,
Branches scattered on the road, smashed
Beneath the wheels.
Then, ghastly under headlights,   20
Frogs bellied everywhere, driven
From the swampy fields and meadows,
Bewildered refugees, gorged with terror.
We killed them because we had to,
Their fatness crunched and flattened in the dark.   25
'How is he now?' Alan whispered
To himself. Behind us,
Carnage of broken frogs.

II

His head
Sweated on the pillow of the white hospital bed.   30
He spoke a little, said
Outrageously, 'I think I'll make it.'
Another time, he'd rail against the weather,
(Such a night would make him eloquent)

But now, quiet, he gathered his fierce will   35
To live.

III

Coming home
Alan saw the frogs.
'Look at them, they're everywhere,
Dozens of the bastards dead.'   40

Minutes later –
'I think he might pull through now.'
Alan, thoughtful at the wheel, was picking out
The homeroad in the flailing rain
Nighthedges closed on either side.   45
In the suffocating darkness
I heard the heavy breathing
Of my father's pain.

 # Explorations

First reading
1. What is the relationship between Alan and the narrator?
2. What is the purpose of their journey?
3. How do you think the two men feel as they go on their journey?
4. How do their reactions differ?

Second reading
5. What is the relationship between the two men and nature?
6. How is the night described?
7. Describe your reaction to the frogs. What do you think is their significance in the poem?

Third reading
8. How does the tone change in the second stanza?
9. Do you get any impression of what type of man the father was?
10. How is the journey home different?
11. Does the road seem different to the narrator?

Fourth reading
12. Why do you think the poet seems to put more emphasis on the journey than on his father's ill health? Suggest a possible

13. How does the pace of the poem change throughout?
14. It is rare to see dialogue in poems; what effect does it have?
15. Compare Alan's attitude to the frogs and his attitude to the father.

Fifth reading

16. 'Kennelly succeeds in building tension expertly.' Do you agree?
17. Kennelly has been criticised for being too sentimental in his poems. Does this poem make you agree with those critics?

Roger McGough (1937–)

Roger McGough was born in Liverpool and studied modern languages at Hull University. Along with Adrian Henri and Brian Patten, he popularised poetry in the 1960s as part of the MerseyBeat poets based in Liverpool. Their poetry put heavy emphasis on live performance and was therefore funny and accessible. It dealt with real concerns for ordinary working-class people. His poetry has been used a lot in schools and he continues to be as popular today as he was in the 60s. He is often used to promote poetry for events such as National Poetry Day. These days his poetry has become more conventional and he uses it for promoting social and human rights issues.

Bearhugs

prescribed for Ordinary Level exams in 2008 and 2010

Whenever my sons call round we hug each other.
Bearhugs. Both bigger than me and stronger
They lift me off my feet, crushing the life out of me.

They smell of oil paint and aftershave, of beer
Sometimes and tobacco, and of women   5
Whose memory they seem reluctant to wash away.

They haven't lived with me for years,
Since they were tiny, and so each visit
Is an assessment, a reassurance of love unspoken.

I look for some resemblance to my family.   10
Seize on an expression, a lifted eyebrow,
A tilt of the head, but cannot see myself.

Though like each other, they are not like me.
But I can see in them something of my father.
Uncles, home on leave during the war.   15

At three or four, I loved throse straightbacked men
Towering above me, smiling and confident.
The whole world before them. Or so it seemed.

I look at my boys, slouched in armchairs
They have outgrown. See Tom in army uniform   20
And Finn in air force blue. Time is up.

Bearhugs. They lift me off my feet
And fifty years fall away. One son
After another, crushing the life into me.

 # Explorations

First reading
1. (a) How would you explain
    the word 'Bearhugs'? (b) Did
    this title make you want to
    read the poem? Why?
2. McGough recalls his sons
    coming to visit him. Choose
    one image that helps you to
    picture the scene and explain
    why you chose it.
3. Using the information in the
    poem, describe McGough's
    two sons.

Second reading
4. What does the first stanza tell

you about the type of relationship that the poet has with his sons?

5. 'They haven't lived with me for years,
Since they were tiny, and so each visit
Is an assessment, a reassurance of love unspoken.'
(a) Why are his sons' visits very special to McGough? (b) Do you think that he might feel differently if he had lived with them when they were growing up? Why?

6. (a) Who do his two sons remind him of? (b) In McGough's view, what characteristics and qualities do his sons share with his father and uncles?

7. (a) Compare the way that McGough, as a boy, felt about his father and uncles with the way that he, as an adult, feels about his sons. (b) Are there any similarities between his feelings?

Third reading

8. 'I look for some resemblance to my family.'
(a) Can you suggest why the poet wants to see if his sons look like him or the rest of his family? (b) Might this desire have anything to do with the fact that he did not live with them during their childhood?

9. Although McGough does not directly describe himself in the poem, there are clues about his physical appearance and his personality. Try to find as many of these clues as possible and then use them to write a description of how you picture him.

10. Imagine that you are one of McGough's sons. Write a diary entry of one of your meetings with your Dad, including what happened and your feelings.

Seamus Heaney (1939–)

Seamus Heaney was born on 13 April 1939 in Co. Derry. He attended Queen's University, Belfast, where he received a First Class degree in English Language and Literature. From there, he went to St. Joseph's College of Education in Belfast, where he studied to be a teacher. He married Marie Devlin in 1965 and she has played a pivotal role in his life, both on an emotional and creative level. In 1966, he was appointed lecturer in English at Queen's University and he also published his first book of poetry. In 1969, the political tensions in Northern Ireland escalated into riots, bombings, sectarian killings and the appearance of the British army on the streets. Heaney was invited to the University of California in Berkeley as a guest lecturer from 1970 to 1971. The ideas that he encountered during his time away from Northern Ireland led Heaney to resign from his lectureship at Queen's University and to move his family to Dublin. While he continued with his writing, he was Head of the English Department at Carysfort Teacher Training College until 1984. From there, Heaney went to lecture at Harvard and Oxford University. He was awarded the Nobel Prize for Poetry in 1995.

Seamus Heaney has never limited his exploration of the world of words to poetry alone. He has also written numerous prose essays and his most recent work, an acclaimed translation of the Greek drama 'Antigone' by Sophocles, was presented at the Abbey Theatre in 2004.

Postscript

prescribed for Ordinary Level exams in 2008 and 2009

And some time make the time to drive out west
Into County Clare, along the Flaggy Shore,
In September or October, when the wind

And the light are working off each other
So that the ocean on the one side is wild   5
With foam and glitter, and inland among stones
The surface of a slate-grey lake is lit
By the earthed lightning of a flock of swans,
Their feathers roughed and ruffling, white on white,
Their fully grown headstrong-looking heads   10
Tucked or cresting or busy underwater.
Useless to think you'll park and capture it
More thoroughly. You are neither here nor there,
A hurry through which known and strange things pass
As big soft buffetings come at the car sideways   15
And catch the heart off guard and blow it open.

Explorations

First reading:

1. (a) Have you ever seen flashes of scenery on a car journey that you can still remember, even though you only saw them for a moment? (b) Does this poem in any way remind you of your experience?

Second reading

2. This poem is set in County Clare in 'September or October'. What images are there in lines 3–7 that help you to picture what Co. Clare is like at this time of the year?

3. 'The surface of a slate-grey lake is lit
By the earthed lightning of a flock of swans,
Their feathers roughed and ruffling, white on white,'.
Can you suggest why Heaney describes the swans as 'earthed lightning'? You might find it helpful to consider the colour and texture of the lake and the swans.

4. Do you find Heaney's description of the swans a realistic one? Why? Use quotations from the poem to support your answer.

5. Heaney decided not to use any full stops until line 11 of this poem. (a) What effect does this have on the way that you read the poem? (b) Does the effect that he is trying to create have anything to do with the fact that he is describing a car journey?

6. 'You are neither here nor there,
A hurry through which known and strange things pass'

What do you think Heaney is
trying to suggest about
travelling in a car when he uses
the phrases 'neither here nor
there' and 'A hurry through'?

Third reading

7. What do the final two lines of
the poem reveal about how the
glimpses of the scenery affected
Heaney?

8. From your readings of the
poem, can you work out how
Seamus Heaney feels about Co.
Clare? You will find it useful
to consider the tone, or the
emotion, of his words.

9. (a) Why do you think Heaney
decided to give this poem the
title 'Postscript'? (b) Do you
think that it is a successful title
or can you suggest another
title that you would consider
to be more suitable?

10. Imagine that you have been
asked to prepare a short film
to be shown as Seamus Heaney
reads this poem. Describe the
images that you would show
and the camera angles that you
would use to capture how you
'see' this poem.

Eamonn Grennan (1941–)

Eamonn Grennan was born in
1941 in Dublin. He was
educated at University College,
Dublin and eventually at Harvard
where he did his PhD. He has taught
at City University, New York and
then at Vassar College. He is now
professor of English at Vassar. He
has written a lot of criticism on
contemporary Irish poetry as well as
on Shakespeare, Spenser and
Chaucer. He is very influenced by
Kavanagh. His poetry aims to tell of
'the miracle of the actual'. He is
interested in showing things as they
are but focusing on the detail like a
painter would. His books include
What Light There Is, So It Goes, As

If It Matters, translations of
Leopoldi and most recently his
selected poems, *Relations*.

Taking My Son to School

prescribed for Ordinary Level exams in 2009 and 2010

His first day. Waiting, he plays
By himself in the garden.
I take a photo he clowns for,
Catching him, as it were, in flight.

All the way there in the car he chatters   5
and sings, giving me directions.
There are no maps for this journey:
It is the wilderness we enter.

Around their tall bespectacled teacher,
A gaggle of young ones in summer colours.   10
Silent, he stands on their border,
Clutching a bunch of purple dahlias.

Shyly he offers them up to her.
Distracted she holds them upside down.
He teeters on the rim of the circle,   15
Head drooping, a flower after rain.

I kiss him goodbye and leave him:
Stiff, he won't meet my eye.
I drive by him but he doesn't wave.
In my mind I rush to his rescue.   20

The distance bleeding between us,
I steal a last look back:
From a thicket of blondes, brunettes,
His red hair blazes.

It is done. I have handed him over.   25
I remember him wildly dancing
Naked and shining, shining
In the empty garden.

Notes:

(15) **teeters:** to stand unsteadily; to be uncertain

Explorations

First reading

1. (a) How do you feel about the little boy in this poem? (b) Choose one image that you found particularly affecting and explain why it touched your feelings.

2. (a) List the verbs that Grennan uses to describe his son's actions in lines 1–6, before he arrives at the school. (b) What do these verbs suggest to you about the child's feelings and mood?

3. (a) Now, list the verbs that are used about the boy's actions in lines 11–18, when he arrives at the school. (b) How do these verbs convey a change in his emotions and mood?

4. What picture do you get of the little boy from the metaphor 'Head drooping, a flower after rain'?

Second reading

5. 'There are no maps for this journey:
    It is the wilderness we enter.'
    (a) Can you explain how the little boy's first day at school could be seen as a journey without a map for him and his father? (b) What does Grennan's use of the word 'wilderness' suggest about his attitude as a father to this journey?

6. (a) In your own words, explain how Grennan feels in lines 19–25, when he leaves his son in the classroom. (b) Pick one line from this section that you feel sums up his feelings.

7. Which of the following words would you use to describe the tone, or the emotion, in the phrase 'I have handed him over': guilt; sadness; regret? Explain the reasons behind your choice.

8. 'I remember him wildly dancing
    Naked and shining, shining
    In the empty garden.'
    (a) How does this image of the little boy contrast with the images of him in the classroom? (b) Which image of his son do you think Grennan prefers? Give reasons for your answer.

Third reading

9. (a) What does this poem reveal about Grennan's attitude to young children being sent to school? (b) Do you agree or disagree with his opinion? Why?

10. Imagine that you are the 'tall bespectacled teacher'. Using the information in the poem, write a short e-mail to a friend describing your first day with your class of new school-goers.

Sharon Olds (1942–)

Sharon Olds is the author of seven volumes of poetry. Her latest work, *The Wellspring* (1996), shares with her previous work the use of raw language and startling images to convey truths about domestic and political violence, sexuality, family relationships and the body. A reviewer of this book for the *New York Times* hailed Olds's poetry for its vision: 'Like Whitman, Ms Olds sings the body in celebration of a power stronger than political oppression.'

Olds is currently an Associate Professor at New York University. She also conducts a number of workshops across the country including at The Omega Institute, The Squaw Valley Writers

Workshop, and the 'In the Wilderness' programme. Olds helped to found NYU's creative writing programme for the physically disabled at Goldwater Hospital in New York City.

The Present Moment

prescribed for the Ordinary Level exam in 2007

Now that he cannot sit up,
now that he just lies there
looking at the wall, I forget the one
who sat up and put on his reading glasses
and the lights in the room multiplied in the lenses.   5
Once he entered the hospital
I forgot the man who lay full length
on the couch, with the blanket folded around him,
that huge, crushed bud, and I have
long forgotten the man who ate food –   10
not dense, earthen food, like liver, but
things like pineapple, wedges of light,
the skeiny nature of light made visible.
It's as if I abandoned that ruddy man

with the swollen puckered mouth of a sweet-eater,   15
the torso packed with extra matter
like a planet a handful of which weighs as much as the earth, I have
left behind forever that young man my father,
that smooth-skinned, dark-haired boy,
and my father long before I knew him, when he could   20
only sleep, or drink from a woman's
body, a baby who stared with a steady
gaze the way he lies there, now, with his
eyes open, then the lids start down
and the milky crescent of the other world   25
shines, in there, for a moment, before sleep.
I stay beside him, like someone in a rowboat
staying abreast of a Channel swimmer,
you are not allowed to touch them, their limbs
glow, faintly, in the night water.   30

 # Explorations

First reading

1. Who are the people in the poem?
2. What is their relationship?
3. What condition is the man in?
4. Was he always this way? What was he like before this?

Second reading

5. Describe each phase of his life as described in the poem.
6. How does the narrator feel about her father now?
7. Did she always feel this way?
8. How does she feel about their relationship?
9. Why does she feel that she is 'not allowed to touch'?

Third reading

10. There are many impressions of him given. Which strikes you most?
11. Of which impression is she fondest?
12. 'S' sounds dominate the poem. Why is this sound used? What effect does it have?
13. Examine the effectiveness of each metaphor: the glasses, the band, the food, the planet, the swimmer, etc.

Fourth reading

14. This poem is about regret. Do you agree?
15. Who do you think the poet wrote this poem for?
16. Is there an overall theme in this poem or is the poet just describing a situation?

Looking at Them Asleep

prescribed for Ordinary Level exams in 2008 and 2009

When I come home late at night and go in to kiss the children,
I see my girl with her arm curled around her head,
her face deep in unconsciousness – so
deeply centered she is in her dark self,
her mouth slightly puffed like one sated but   5
slightly pouted like one who hasn't had enough,
her eyes so closed you would think they have rolled the
iris around to face the back of her head,
the eyeball marble-naked under that
thick satisfied desiring lid,   10
she lies on her back in abandon and sealed completion,
and the son in his room, oh the son he is sideways in his bed,
one knee up if he is climbing
sharp stairs up into the night,
and under his thin quivering eyelids you   15
know his eyes are wide open and
staring and glazed, the blue in them so
anxious and crystally in all this darkness, and his
mouth is open, he is breathing hard from the climb
and panting a bit, his brow is crumpled   20
and pale, his long fingers curved,
his hand open, and in the center of each hand
the dry dirty boyish palm
resting like a cookie. I look at him in his
quest, the thin muscles of his arms   25
passionate and tense, I look at her with her
face like the face of a snake who has swallowed a deer,
content, content – and I know if I wake her she'll
smile and turn her face toward me though
half asleep and open her eyes and I   30
know if I wake him he'll jerk and say Don't and sit
up and stare about him in blue
unrecognition, oh my Lord how I
know these two. When love comes to me and says
Who do you know, I say This girl, this boy.   35

Notes:

(5) **sated:** totally pleased or satisfied

(6) **pouted:** with lips pushed forward

(8) **iris:** the circular coloured part of the eye

(15) **quivering:** trembling

Explorations

First reading

1. Do you think that two children asleep is a surprising subject for a poem, or do you feel that poetry can be written about any topic?

2. Would you agree or disagree with Olds' view that the way we sleep reveals something of our personality? Why?

Second reading

3. In lines 2–11, Olds draws a word picture of her daughter asleep. In your own words, describe the type of sleep suggested to you by the following words and phrases: 'curled', 'unconsciousness', 'deeply centred' and 'eyes so closed'.

4. 'her mouth slightly puffed like one sated but
   slightly pouted like one who hasn't had enough,'
   'under that
   thick satisfied desiring lid,'
   What is Olds trying to suggest about her daughter's personality in these lines? You might find it helpful to discuss the way that the poet repeats the idea of being satisfied but still wanting more in both of the quotations above.

5. 'she lies on her back in abandon and sealed completion,'
   In your own words, describe how this line makes you picture the little girl asleep.

6. In lines 12–24, Olds writes about her son asleep. What type of sleep do you think that he is experiencing from the following words and phrases: 'climbing', 'quivering eyelids', 'breathing hard' and 'brow is crumpled'?

7. 'and under his thin quivering eyelids you
   know his eyes are wide open
   and staring and glazed, the blue in them so anxious'
   'his brow is crumpled and pale'
   In your own words, describe the impression that you get from these lines of the son's character.

8. The son is 'sideways in his bed' with 'one knee up'. How does his sleeping contrast with that of his sister? Refer to the poem to support your viewpoint.

Third reading

9. Olds sums up the differences in her children's personalities in lines 24–28. Explain what these differences are.

10. Do you agree with the theme, or central message, of this poem, expressed in the final two lines: when you truly love someone you truly know and accept them, faults and all? Why?

Paul Durcan (1944–)

Among the more notable of Paul Durcan's many collections are *The Berlin Wall Café* (1985), *Daddy Daddy* (1990), *A Snail in My Prime* (1993), *Christmas Day* (1996) and *Greetings to Our Friends in Brazil* (1999). He focuses on contemporary Ireland, particularly the west, and also on themes of political violence, love and marriage, and religion. He is well known for his satires directed at church and state and for his zany wit. But much of his most moving poetry springs from his own life experience, for example the breaking up of his marriage in *The Berlin Wall Café* and the love–hate relationship

with his father in *Daddy, Daddy*. 'Going Home to Mayo, Winter 1949' is taken from the collection *Sam's Cross* (1978).

Going Home to Mayo, Winter 1949

Prescribed for Ordinary Level exams in 2007 and 2008

Leaving behind us the alien, foreign city of Dublin
My father drove through the night in an old Ford Anglia,
His five-year-old son in the seat beside him,
The rexine seat of red leatherette,
And a yellow moon peered in through the windscreen.   5
'Daddy, Daddy,' I cried, 'Pass out the moon,'
But no matter how hard he drove he could not pass out the moon.
Each town we passed through was another milestone
And their names were magic passwords into eternity:
Kilcock, Kinnegad, Strokestown, Elphin,   10
Tarmonbarry, Tulsk, Ballaghaderreen, Ballavarry;
Now we were in Mayo and the next stop was Turlough,
The village of Turlough in the heartland of Mayo,
And my father's mother's house, all oil-lamps and women,

And my bedroom over the public bar below,   15
And in the morning cattle-cries and cock-crows:
Life's seemingly seamless garment gorgeously rent.

Notes

[4] **Rexine:** the brand name of a type of artificial leather used in upholstery

Explorations

First reading

1. In the first part of the poem, what does the child notice about the journey? What aspects give it a magical quality for him?

2. What does the young boy like, in particular, about the family home in Turlough? What do you notice about the atmosphere of the place and how is it created? Look at the sights and sounds.

3. In the first part of the poem what evidence is there that the child is unhappy in Dublin?

Second reading

4. What do you think he means by the phrases 'But home was not home' and 'the moon could be no more outflanked'?

5. What images are used to signify the city, and what atmosphere is created? Describe the city as you think the speaker sees it.

6. In the poem, how does life in the city contrast with life in the country?

7. How do you think the poet feels about both the country and the city? What exactly leads you to say this?

Third reading

8. What do you discover about the relationship between father and son in this poem?

9. Do you think Durcan captures well the child's view of the world? Refer to specific images or phrases of dialogue to support your views.

10 How do you understand the final three lines of the poem?

Fourth reading

11. Briefly explain the main themes you find in the poem. What has it to say about the country versus the city; one's place of origin; holidays; dreams and reality; a child's view of the world?

12. On the evidence of this poem, would you consider Durcan to be an idealist, a nostalgic person, or what?

13. Do you find this to be a sad or a happy poem? Comment.

Bernard O'Donoghue (1945–)

Bernard O'Donoghue was born in Cullen, Co. Cork in 1945. Although he now lives in England, O'Donoghue readily acknowledges that his fascination with the sound of language is rooted in his early life in Cork.

In 1965, he moved to Oxford and attended University there. By his own admission, he did not begin to write poetry 'in any concerted sort of way' until after his mother's death in 1979. His father had died some years previously, and O'Donoghue found that the loss of his parents released him 'into a kind of honesty and openness' that found expression in poetry. His first volume of poetry was published in 1984.

O'Donoghue regards himself primarily as a teacher and he is a tutor in Old and Middle English, Linguistics and the History of the English Language at Wadham College, Oxford. He has published a number of books including collections of poetry, a critical study on Seamus Heaney and 'Oxford Irish Quotations'. In 1995, his collection of poetry entitled 'Gunpowder' won the Whitbread Prize for Poetry.

As well as his involvement in the literary and academic world, O'Donoghue also finds time to support Manchester City football club.

Gunpowder

prescribed for Ordinary Level exams in 2009 and 2010

In the weeks afterwards, his jacket hung
Behind the door in the room we called
His study, where the bikes and wellingtons
Were kept. No-one went near it, until
Late one evening I thought I'd throw it out.   5
The sleeves smelled of gunpowder, evoking . . .
Celebration – excitement – things like that,
Not destruction. What was it he shot at

And missed that time? A cock pheasant
That he hesitated too long over   10
In case it was a hen? The rat behind
The piggery that, startled by the bang,
Turned round to look before going home to its hole?

Once a neighbour who had winged a crow
Tied it to a pike thrust into the ground   15
To keep the others off the corn. It worked well,
Flapping and cawing, till my father
Cut it loose. Even more puzzlingly,
He once took a wounded rabbit off the dog
And pushed in back into the warren   20
Which undermined the wall. As for
Used cartridges, they stood well on desks,
Upright on their graven golden ends,
Supporting his fountain-pen so that
The ink wouldn't seep into his pocket.   25

Notes:

(15) **pike:** a weapon with a pointed iron or steel head on a top of a wooden shaft

(18) **undermined:** weakened the foundations

(23) **graven:** engraved, inscribed

(25) **seep:** ooze out

 # Explorations

First reading

1. Using the clues in this poem, can you say in what type of house and environment this poem is set?

2. O'Donoghue creates a number of vivid images depicting animals in this poem. Choose one image that you found particularly easy to picture and explain why you chose it.

Second reading

3. 'In the weeks afterwards, his jacket hung
Behind the door . . .'
What do you think had happened to the poet's father? Give reasons for your answer.

4. (a) Take a moment to list the words that you think of when you hear the word 'gunpowder'. (b) Based on your list, describe the character

and behaviour of a person who you would expect to have jacket sleeves that 'smelled of gunpowder'.

5. (a) Do the series of incidents that the poet recounts of his father's dealings with animals fit in with your description in Question 4? (b) What are the differences between the two?

6. O'Dononghue thought his father behaved 'puzzlingly' when he put the wounded rabbit back into the warren. (a) Why do you think he was puzzled by this action? (b) Do you also find it puzzling?

7. The final image of the poem is of O'Donoghue's father using shotgun cartridges to hold his pen 'so that | The ink wouldn't seep into his pocket.' What does this image tell you about his personality?

Third reading

8. What theme do you think lies at the heart of this poem? Is it simply about O'Donoghue's father, or does it express a more general message?

9. 'The sleeves smelled of gunpowder, evoking ...' (a) What experience is the poet trying to describe in this line? (b) What do you think he was trying to convey by his use of '. . .' at the end of this line?

10. Using your thoughts on this poem write an Obituary, an account of a dead person's life, for O'Donoghue's father.

Liz Lochhead (1947–)

Liz Lochhead was born in a Lanarkshire mining village in Scotland on 26 December 1947. As a child, she spent much of her time drawing and painting. She attended Glasgow School of Art from 1965 to 1970 and then taught art until 1979, when she became a full-time writer.

Although her early writing was mainly poetry, in the 1980s Lochhead also began to write for the stage. Much of her poetry explores what it is to be Scottish and what it is to be a woman, often in a humorous way; while her work as a playwright, featuring a number of adaptations of ancient Greek plays, explores what it is to be human.

Liz Lochhead has won many prizes for her work and in 1998 was listed among 'Scotland's Fifty Most Influential Women' in a Scottish Sunday newspaper. She now lives in Glasgow with her architect husband.

Kidspoem/Bairnsang

prescribed for Ordinary Level exams in 2009 and 2010

it wis January
and a gey dreich day
the first day Ah went to the school
so my Mum happed me up in ma
good navy-blue napp coat wi th rid tartan hood   5
birled a scarf aroon ma neck
pu'ed oan ma pixie an' my pawkies
it wis that bitter
said noo ye'll no starve
gie'd me a wee kiss and a kid-oan skelp oan the bum   10
and sent me aff across the playground
tae the place Ah'd learn to say
it was January
and a really dismal day
the first day I went to school   15
so my mother wrapped me up in my
best navy-blue top coat with the red tartan hood,
twirled a scarf around my neck,
pulled on my bobble-hat and mittens
it was so bitterly cold   20
said now you won't freeze to death
gave me a little kiss and a pretend slap on the bottom
and sent me off across the playground
to the place I'd learn to forget to say
it wis January   25
and a gey dreich day
the first day Ah went to the school
so my Mum happed me up in ma
good navy-blue napp coat wi th rid tartan hood,
birled a scarf aroon ma neck,   30
pu'ed oan ma pixie an' my pawkies
it wis that bitter.

Oh saying it was one thing
but when it came to writing it
in black and white   35
the way it had to be said
was as if you were posh, grown-up, male, English and dead.

 # Explorations

First reading

1. Explain, in your own words, what is happening between the little girl and her mother in this poem.
2. What picture do you get of the little girl from the images that Lochhead uses to describe her?

Second reading

3. Pick out two lines from the poem that you think sound very Scottish and explain why they sound Scottish to you.
4. (a) Find the same two lines that you chose for Question 2 in the English sounding version and explain why they sound English to you. (b) Which version do you prefer? Why?
5. From the clues in the poem can you guess where the little girl spoke with a Scottish accent and where she spoke with an English accent?
6. (a) Can you suggest which accent the little girl felt most comfortable with? Why do you think that she felt like this?

Third reading

7. 'but when it came to writing it in black and white
   the way it had to be said
   was as if you were posh,
   grown-up, male, English and dead.'
   What does the tone, or the emotion, of these lines tell you about the little girl's feelings when she was made to write in this way?
8. Do you feel that Lochhead is correct in her description of the way you are expected to write in school as 'posh, grown-up, male, English and dead'? Give reasons for your answer.
9. (a) Do you think that the lines 1–12 might put some readers off finishing this poem? Why? (b) Would you advise them to keep on reading? Why?
10. (a) Imagine that you have just come home from a shopping trip or from a match. Write out the description you would give of your experience to (i) a friend of your own age and (ii) an adult that you know. (b) In which piece were you most 'yourself'? Why do you think this was?

Paddy Bushe (1948–)

Paddy Bushe was born in Dublin in 1948. He lived in Australia for a number of years before returning to Waterville, Co. Kerry. He has published poetry in English and Irish. He won the 1990 Listowel Writers' Week Award and was a runner-up in the 1988 Patrick Kavanagh Award. His poems are full of a sense of immediacy and he seems to be conscious of finding a musical sound in his poems.

Jasmine

prescribed for the Ordinary Level exam in 2007

What colour is jasmine? you asked
out of the blue from your wheelchair.
And suddenly the ward was filled
with the scent of possibility, hints
of journeys to strange parts.   5

The question floored us. But the gulf
was not the colours that we couldn't name
but that we couldn't recognise the road
your question had travelled, nor sound the extent
of the blue void to which it would return.   10

The ward remade itself in a hum
of conscientious care. Outside, the usual
traffic jams. We took the long way home.
Father, jasmine is a climbing plant
whose flowers are normally white or yellow.   15

And may the fragrance of its blossoms twine
around the broken trellises of your mind.

Explorations

Before reading

1. What impression does the sound of the word 'jasmine' give you?

First reading

2. Where is the poem set? What gives this away?
3. Who are the two main characters in the poem?
4. What is their relationship?
5. Do you think there has been any recent change in their relationship?
6. Why did the question floor them?

Second reading

7. Why did they take the long way home? Suggest a possible reason.

8. Do you think this poem is too sentimental? Discuss this.

Third reading

9. Explain how the 'jasmine' metaphor develops in the last two lines.
10. How are the senses challenged throughout the poem?
11. What is the atmosphere created in the poem? How is this done?
12. Write about the main idea in this poem.

Fourth reading

13. Compare the poem to 'Night Drive' by Brendan Kennelly.
14. Is this a hopeful poem? Share your views.

Midwife
(for Ciairín)

prescribed for the Ordinary Level exam in 2009

Daughter, that time you fell
from the high bank, in slow
motion it seemed,
your two-year-old body turning
into the black and white   5
suddenly loud Caragh River,
and your wide eyes pleaded for breath
instead of that liquid burning :
that, indeed, was like a little death.
Daughter, after my stretched hand   10

had slipped – hair floating away –
and slipped again, grasped, pulled
you, gasping, from the heaving water,
you cried, you were not hurt,
and you were swaddled up   15
in someone's coat, while the whole earth
breathed again: o daughter,
that, indeed, was like another birth.

Notes:

(15) **swaddled:** a practice done in the past with newborn infants where they were
wrapped up in narrow bandages

 # Explorations

First reading

1. (a) Did you find this poem easy to imagine as you were reading it? (b) In your own words, describe the scene as you picture it.

2. Choose one line or image in the poem that you found particularly exciting and dramatic and explain why you chose it.

Second reading

3. (a) Why do you think Bushe describes his daughter falling 'in slow I motion'? (b) Have you ever had this feeling about some experience that you were involved in?

4. 'into the black and white suddenly loud Caragh River,' What impression do you get of the river from this description?

5. 'and your wide eyes pleaded for breath' What does this line tell you about the little girl's feelings as she fell into the river?

6. How does Bushe suggest his panic and desperation in lines 10–12? You might find it helpful to consider his use of commas, dashes and repetition.

7. 'while the whole earth breathed again' What emotion do you think the poet is trying to communicate in this image?

Third reading

8. Can you explain why the poet describes the little girl's accident as 'a little death' in the final line of the first stanza?

9. Do you think that 'Midwife' is a good title for this poem? Why?

10. Using the information given in the poem, describe this experience from the little girl's point of view.

Paul Muldoon (1951–)

Paul Muldoon was born in Co. Armagh and educated at Queen's University, Belfast. After leaving college he went to work as a producer for BBC radio in Belfast. He also lived in Dingle, Co. Kerry for a while. Since then he has worked mainly as an academic; much of his teaching has been in the creative writing programme at Princeton University in the US. Recently, he was appointed to the prestigious position of Professor of Poetry at Oxford University.

Muldoon is a brilliant technical poet. He is equally at ease writing sonnets and long poems, lyric or narrative poetry. Some of his poetry is written about the North, but often only incidentally. He is very conscious of using puns and word associations in a very deliberate way. His collections include: *Mules, New*

Weather, Why Brownlee Left, Quoof, Meeting the British, Madoc: A Mystery, The Annals Of Chile and most recently *Hay*. His *Selected Poems* (1968–94) is probably the best introduction to his work.

Anseo

prescribed for Ordinary Level exams in 2007 and 2008

When the Master was calling the roll
At the primary school in Collegelands,
You were meant to call back Anseo
And raise your hand
As your name occurred.   5
Anseo, meaning here, here and now,
All present and correct,
Was the first word of Irish I spoke.
The last name on the ledger

Belonged to Joseph Mary Plunkett Ward   10
And was followed, as often as not,
By silence, knowing looks,
A nod and a wink, the Master's droll
'And where's our little Ward-of-court?'

I remember the first time he came back   15
The Master had sent him out
Along the hedges
To weigh up for himself and cut
A stick with which he would be beaten.
After a while, nothing was spoken;   20
He would arrive as a matter of course
With an ash-plant, a salley-rod.
Or, finally, the hazel-wand
He had whittled down to a whip-lash,
Its twist of red and yellow lacquers   25
Sanded and polished,
And altogether so delicately wrought
That he had engraved his initials on it.

I last met Joseph Mary Plunkett Ward
In a pub just over the Irish border.   30
He was living in the open,
In a secret camp
On the other side of the mountain.
He was fighting for Ireland,
Making things happen.   35
And he told me, Joe Ward,
Of how he had risen through the ranks
To Quartermaster, Commandant:
How every morning at parade
His volunteers would call back Anseo   40
And raise their hands
As their names occurred.

Explorations

Before reading

1. What are your own memories of primary school, your teachers, friends and characters in your own class – especially the ones that got into a lot of trouble?

First reading

2. What does the word 'Anseo' mean? When was it used in school?
3. Describe the 'master'. What does his title say about him?
4. Why are Ward's forenames important?
5. What is Ward's life like at the end of the poem?
6. What do you imagine his soldiers' lives are like under his command?

Second reading

7. Why do you think Ward takes such care with the stick? Suggest reasons.
8. The narrator of the poem and the master use puns. Isolate each pun and explain what they are referring to.

Third reading

9. The tone in the first verse is very unemotional. What effect does this have on your reading of the poem? Does the tone change later on? If so, how?
10. What contradictions are in the poem?
11. How do the first and last verses mirror each other? What point do you think the poet is making here?

Fourth reading

12. 'What comes around goes around.' Do you think that this saying is relevant to the poem?
13. What is your own reaction to the life and experiences of Joseph Mary Plunkett Ward?
14. What do you think this poem is saying about life?

Kerry Hardie (1951–)

Kerry Hardie was born in Singapore in 1951. However, she spent her early years in Co. Down and then went to York University in England to study English. When she graduated, Hardie worked for BBC Northern Ireland as a researcher and radio interviewer. She now lives in Co. Kilkenny with her husband Sean, who is also a writer.

Unfortunately, Hardie has suffered from Chronic Fatigue Syndrome, ME, for a number of years. Nevertheless, she continues to write and to teach creative writing courses. She has won a number of awards for her poetry, including the Hennessy Award for Poetry in 1995.

Her first novel, 'A Winter Marriage' published in 2002, was very well received.

May
for Marian

prescribed for Ordinary Level exams in 2008 and 2009

The blessèd stretch and ease of it –
heart's ease. The hills blue. All the flowering weeds
bursting open. Balm in the air. The birdsong
bouncing back out of the sky. The cattle
lain down in the meadow, forgetting to feed.   5
The horses swishing their tails.
The yellow flare of furze on the near hill.
And the first cream splatters of blossom
high on the thorns where the day rests longest.

All hardship, hunger, treachery of winter forgotten.   10
This unfounded conviction: forgiveness, hope.

Notes:

(3) **balm:** a soothing and healing ointment

(7) **furze:** also known as gorse, a spiny shrub with yellow flowers

(10) **treachery:** betrayal

(12) **unfounded:** having no basis

(12) **conviction:** firm belief

 # Explorations

First reading

1. Pick out one image from the poem that really helps you to picture what happens to the countryside in May.

2. Which of the following senses does Hardie appeal to her in description of the effects that May has on Nature: sight; taste; touch; hearing; smell? Use quotations from the poem to support your choices.

Second reading

3. 'The blessèd stretch and ease of it –'
   What words and images does Hardie use to suggest that the countryside is, indeed, relaxing after the winter?

4. Do you think that the colours that Hardie refers to in the poem are suitable colours for the month of May? Why?

5. (a) How would you describe the mood, or the feeling, of lines 1–9? (b) What words or phrases in these lines convey this mood to you?

6. 'All hardship, hunger, treachery of winter'

(a) Can you suggest how winter could be seen as treacherous? (b) Do you think that the three words that Hardie uses give a fair description of winter? Why?

7. Does the appearance of May in the countryside have a positive or negative effect on the poet? Refer to the poem to support your views.

Third reading

8. In your own words, explain the theme of this poem.

9. 'All the flowering weeds bursting open. Balm in the air. The birdsong bouncing back out of the sky.'
   'The horses swishing their tails.'
   How does Hardy use alliteration and onomatopoeia in these lines to make her descriptions come alive for the reader?

10. You have been asked to choose a poem for a collection called 'Ireland's Most Beautiful Month'. Say why you would choose this poem.

Julie O'Callaghan (1954–)

Julie O' Callaghan was born in Chicago in 1954 and moved to Ireland in 1974. Her poetry for children is particularly popular and appears in a number of children's anthologies. Her poetry for adults is highly regarded and in 2001 she won the Michael Hartnett Poetry Award.

In April 2003, Julie O'Callaghan was made a member of Aosdana in recognition of the contribution that she has made to the arts in Ireland. She lives in Kildare with her husband, Dennis O'Driscoll, who is also a writer.

The Great Blasket Island

prescribed for Ordinary Level exams in 2009 and 2010

Six men born on this island
have come back after twenty-one years.
They climb up the overgrown roads
to their family houses
and come out shaking their heads.   5
The roofs have fallen in
and birds have nested in the rafters.
All the white-washed rooms
all the nagging and praying
and scolding and giggling   10
and crying and gossiping
are scattered in the memories of these men.
One says, 'Ten of us, blown to the winds –
some in England, some in America, some in Dublin.
Our whole way of life – extinct.'   15
He blinks back the tears
and looks across the island

past the ruined houses, the cliffs
and out to the horizon.

Listen, mister, most of us cry sooner or later   20
over a Great Blasket Island of our own.

Notes:
(15) **extinct:** has died out

 # Explorations

First reading

1. In your own words, describe
   the Great Blasket Island as you
   imagine it from the images in
   the poem.

Second reading

2. Can you suggest why the men
   come out of their family homes
   'shaking their heads'?
3. How have the houses changed
   since the men lived there
   twenty-one years previously?
4. 'all the nagging and praying
   and scolding and giggling
   and crying and gossiping'
   Do you think that this is a
   good summary of family life?
   Why?
5. Why did the young people
   have to leave the island to go
   to England, America and
   Dublin?
6. '"Our whole way of life –
   extinct."'

What tone, or emotion, is
expressed in this line?
7. 'He blinks back the tears'
   Why do you think one of the
   men reacts in this way?

Third reading

8. 'Listen, mister, most of us cry
   sooner or later | over a Great
   Blasket Island of our own.'
   Bearing in mind your work on
   the previous questions, can you
   suggest what the Great Blasket
   Island symbolises in the final
   two lines of the poem?
9. In your own words, explain
   the theme, or central message,
   of this poem.
10. Imagine you return to your
    home in twenty-one years'
    time. Write a description of
    what you find and how you
    feel.

Carol Ann Duffy (1955–)

Carol Ann Duffy was born in Glasgow of Irish parents but grew up in Staffordshire, England. She attended university in Liverpool, studying philosophy. Her poetry very often gives voice to the powerless or the mad. She is very adept at putting herself in somebody else's head and then writing from their perspective, be they psychopaths, maids or tabloid editors. Her poetry has a wry humour and a lot of people who would not regularly read poetry are comfortable with her style.

She has won many awards for her collections, which include *Standing Female Nude* (1985), *Selling Manhattan* (1987), *The*

Other Country (1990), *Mean Time* (1993) and *The World's Wife* (1998). This last collection featured a series of poems written from the perspective of the forgotten female: Mrs Midas, Queen Kong, Mrs Lazarus and others.

Valentine

prescribed for Ordinary Level exams in 2007 and 2008

Not a red rose or a satin heart.

I give you an onion.
It is a moon wrapped in brown paper.
It promises light
like the careful undressing of love.   5

Here.
It will blind you with tears
like a lover.
It will make your reflection
a wobbling photo of grief.   10

I am trying to be truthful.

Not a cute card or a kissogram.

I give you an onion.
Its fierce kiss will stay on your lips,
possessive and faithful   15
as we are,
for as long as we are.

Take it.
Its platinum loops shrink to a wedding-ring,
if you like.   20
Lethal.
Its scent will cling to your fingers,
cling to your knife.

 # Explorations

Before reading

1. What do you associate with Valentine's Day?

First reading

2. What is your first reaction on reading this poem? Discuss the various reactions.

3. The onion is given four times. With what is it associated each time?

4. Is there anything at all romantic about this poem?

Second reading

5. How long will the taste of onion stay on the lover's lips? How long will the couple last?

6. What type of relationship do the couple have? Have they been in love for long?

7. How does the onion promise light?

Third reading

8. How would you feel if you were given an onion for Valentine's Day?

9. The poet uses very short lines regularly in the poem. What effect do these short lines have?

10. Describe each metaphor that the speaker uses to describe the onion?

Fourth reading

11. Read 'My mistress's eyes . . .' by William Shakespeare and compare it with this poem.

12. This poem manages to be 'cold and passionate'. How?

13. Do you think that this is a good love poem? What makes it good or bad?

14. 'Love is particular to individuals and can't be represented by Love Hearts and Teddy Bears.' Does the poet agree? Do you?

Paula Meehan (1955–)

Paula Meehan was born in the Gardiner Street area of Dublin. She was thrown out of school yet managed to study and attended Trinity College, Dublin and Eastern Washington University. She made a huge impact with the publication of her third volume of poems *The Man Who was Marked by Winter* and then with *Pillow Talk*. Meehan's poetry should be read out loud. She is a mesmerising reader of her own work. Her poetry has harrowing lyrical intensity. She uses regular language confidently yet without making it seem ostentatious or over the top. Many of her poems such as 'The Pattern' or 'The Ghost of my Mother Comforts Me' celebrate women in adversity and give them a voice. She has also written a number of successful plays. The most recent of these was *Cell* (1999) which was written after the poet had spent time giving poetry workshops in women's prisons.

Buying Winkles

prescribed for the Ordinary Level exam in 2009

My mother would spare me sixpence and say,
'Hurry up now and don't be talking to strange
men on the way.' I'd dash from the ghosts
on the stairs where the bulb had blown
out into Gardiner Street, all relief.   5
A bonus if the moon was in the strip of sky
between the tall houses, or stars out,
but even in rain I was happy – the winkles
would be wet and glisten blue like little
night skies themselves. I'd hold the tanner tight   10
and jump every crack in the pavement,
I'd wave up to women at sills or those
lingering in doorways and weave a glad path through
men heading out for the night.

She'd be sitting outside the Rosebowl Bar	15
on an orange-crate, a pram loaded	
with pails of winkles before her.	
When the bar doors swung open they'd leak	
the smell of men together with drink	
and I'd see light in golden mirrors.	20
I envied each soul in the hot interior.	

I'd ask her again to show me the right way
to do it. She'd take a pin from her shawl –
'Open the eyelid. So. Stick it in
till you feel a grip, then slither him out.   25
Gently, mind.' The sweetest extra winkle
that brought the sea to me.
'Tell yer Ma I picked them fresh this morning.'

I'd bear the newspaper twists
bulging fat with winkles   30
proudly home, like torches.

Notes:

Winkles: small shellfish

(5) **Gardiner Street:** just off O'Connell Street, Dublin. Up to mid 20th Century, the fine Georgian houses were tenements housing many families.

(10) **tanner:** slang for 6 penny piece

 # Explorations

First reading

1. What details, given in the poem, tell you that it is set in the city rather than the countryside?
2. (a) Which of the five senses (taste, touch, smell, hearing and sight) does Meehan appeal to in her descriptions? (b) How does this technique help to make the poem come alive for her readers?
3. How do you know that the speaker in the poem is a child rather than an adult? Refer to the poem to support your answer.

Second reading

4. Choose your favourite image from Meehan's description of her trip to buy the winkles and explain the reasons for your choice.
5. (a) Which of the following words would you use to describe the child's feelings as she goes to buy the winkles: excited; important; happy; nervous? (b) Can you suggest why she has these feelings?
6. 'I'd ask her again to show me the right way to do it.'
(a) Why do you think the little girl asks the woman selling

winkles to show her how to open the winkles again? (*b*) Do you think that this is realistic behaviour for a child? Why?

7. In the final three lines of the poem Meehan compares the 'newspaper twists' to 'torches'. In your own words, explain how this simile works.

Third reading

8. Consider the ways in which the young girl behaves towards women and men. (*a*) Which gender do you think she feels more comfortable with? (*b*) Bearing in mind that Meehan was a young child in the 1950s and 60s, can you suggest why she feels like this?

9. (*a*) 'Hurry up now and don't be talking to strange | men on the way.'

What do we learn about Meehan's mother from what she says here?

(*b*) 'Open the eyelid. So. Stick it in
till you feel a grip, then slither him out.
Gently, mind.'

'Tell yer Ma I picked them fresh this morning.'

What do these quotations tell you about the winkle seller?

10. Try to remember back to when you were a young child. Were you ever sent on a message for an adult, perhaps to the shops, or to the staff-room for a teacher? Write a piece describing what happened and how you felt.

My Father Perceived as a Vision of St Francis

for Brendan Kennelly

prescribed for the Ordinary Level exam in 2010

It was the piebald horse in next door's garden
frightened me out of a dream
with her dawn whinny. I was back
in the boxroom of the house,
my brother's room now,   5
full of ties and sweaters and secrets.
Bottles chinked on the doorstep,
the first bus pulled up to the stop.
The rest of the house slept

except for my father. I heard   10
him rake the ash from the grate,
plug in the kettle, hum a snatch of a tune.
Then he unlocked the back door
and stepped out into the garden.

Autumn was nearly done, the first frost   15
whitened the slates of the estate.
He was older than I had reckoned,
his hair completely silver,
and for the first time I saw the stoop
of his shoulder, saw that   20
his leg was stiff. What's he at?
So early and still stars in the west?

They came then: birds
of every size, shape, colour; they came
from the hedges and shrubs,   25
from eaves and garden sheds,
from the industrial estate, outlying fields,
from Dubber Cross they came
and the ditches of the North Road.
The garden was a pandemonium   30
when my father threw up his hands
and tossed the crumbs to the air. The sun

cleared O'Reilly's chimney
and he was suddenly radiant
a perfect vision of St Francis,   35
made whole, made young again,
in a Finglas garden.

Notes:

St Francis: the patron saint of animals and the environment

Brendan Kennelly: a distinguished Irish poet

(1) **piebald:** marked with irregular patches of colour

(28) **Dubber Cross:** in Finglas, Dublin

(29) **the North Road:** in Finglas, Dublin

(30) **pandemonium:** a scene of uproar

(34) **radiant:** dazzling, beaming with joy

Explorations

First reading

1. (*a*) List the sounds that occur in lines 1–12 of the poem. (*b*) What time of day do these sounds suggest to you? Give reasons for your answer.

2. Pick one image from the poem that you found particularly memorable and explain why you like and remember it.

Second reading

3. 'He was older than I had reckoned,'
   How does Meehan describe her father in lines 17–21?

4. 'What's he at?'
   (*a*) What does this question tell you about Meehan's attitude towards her father when she hears him going out into the garden? (*b*) Why does her father go out into the garden?

5. Do you find it surprising that Meehan's elderly father feeds the birds? Why?

6. (*a*) How does Meehan describe her father in the final four lines of the poem? (*b*) Which of the following qualities do you think Paula Meehan sees in her father as he feeds the birds: kindness; gentleness; childlike innocence; concern? Refer to the poem to support your choice.

Third reading

7. In your own words, describe the changes that take place in (*a*) the way that Meehan sees her father and (*b*) her attitude towards him in the course of this poem.

8. 'Autumn was nearly done, the first frost
   whitened the slates of the estate.'
   'The sun
   cleared O'Reilly's chimney'
   How does Meehan use the change in the weather to symbolise the change in her attitude towards her father?

9. What does the tone, or the feeling, expressed in the words that Meehan uses in the poem tell you about the relationship that she had with her father?

10. Often it is hard to believe that our parents, or any other adults, were once young. Write a description of an incident where you suddenly saw something of the young person he or she once was in an older adult.

Simon Armitage (1963–)

Simon Armitage was born in Huddersfield and studied geography at Portsmouth Polytechnic. He is a very prolific poet, having published seven books since 1989: *Zoom!* (1989); *Kid* (1992); *Book of Matches* (1993); *The Dead Sea Poems* (1995); *Cloudcuckooland* (1996); a book about Iceland, *Moon Country* (1996); and a prose book about life in Northern England, *All Points North* (1998). Most recently he edited a major anthology of British and Irish poetry.

He is a very popular poet and is often the youngest writer in many anthologies. A lot of his poems have been influenced by his work as a probation officer. He provides good social observations into the thinking of people, especially young people, who are marginalised. Some of his poetry is said to have been influenced by the work of Paul Muldoon.

It Ain't What You Do, It's What It Does To You

prescribed for Ordinary Level exams in 2007 and 2008

I have not bummed across America
with only a dollar to spare, one pair
of busted Levi's and a bowie knife.
I have lived with thieves in Manchester.

I have not padded through the Taj Mahal,   5
barefoot, listening to the space between
each footfall picking up and putting down

its print against the marble floor. But I
skimmed flat stones across Black Moss on a day
so still I could hear each set of ripples   10
as they crossed. I felt each stone's inertia
spend itself against the water; then sink.

I have not toyed with a parachute chord
while perched on the lip of a light-aircraft;
but I held the wobbly head of a boy   15
at the day centre, and stroked his fat hands.
And I guess that the tightness in the throat
and the tiny cascading sensation
somewhere inside us are both part of that
sense of something else. That feeling, I mean.   20

 # Explorations

Before reading

1. What usually comes after the line 'It ain't what you do'? Would it have the same effect?

First reading

2. There are three things that the poet has not done and three things that he has. Compare them. Which is the more attractive to you?

3. What emotion does he get from living with thieves? How would this compare to the feeling that he would get if he was hiking across America?

4. How does he justify comparing a lake in Manchester to one of the 'seven wonders of the world'?

5. What would helping a boy at the day care centre make him feel?

6. How would the boy feel?

Second reading

7. Have you ever had the sensation that the poet has in the final verse? When? Describe it.

Third reading

8. How does the poet use repetition in the poem?

Fourth reading

9. Is the last sentence in the poem completely necessary?

10. What type of guy do you think the poet is?

Rosita Boland (1965–)

Rosita Boland was born in 1965 in Co. Clare. In 1990, she hitchhiked around the coast of Ireland on her own and wrote a book describing her experiences entitled 'Sea Legs: Hitchhiking Around the Coast of Ireland Alone'. She published her first collection of poems in 1991 and her second 'Dissecting the Heart' in 2003.

Rosita Boland won the Hennessy/Sunday Tribune First Fiction award in 1997. She now works as a journalist with *The Irish Times*.

Naming My Daughter

prescribed for Ordinary Level exams in 2009 and 2010

Beside my desk, I had pinned
A list of possible names for my unborn child,
Adding to it at intervals
As the months swelled slowly on.

She was born without colour   5
Among the yellow daffodils
And the greening trees of a wet March.

I chose none of those names for my daughter.
I gave her instead
The Caribbean name of Rain: 10
Wanting something soft, familiar and constant
To touch and touch again
Her thin coverlet of earth.

Explorations

First reading

1. What are your feelings having read this poem for the first time?

2. Did this poem develop in the way that the title 'Naming My Daughter' led you to expect?

Second reading

3. (a) How does Boland go about choosing her baby's name? (b) Do you think that she was right to take so much care? Why?

4. 'As the months swelled slowly on.'
   Can you suggest why Boland uses the word 'swelled' here?

5. How does Boland's use of colour words in lines 5–7 help you to understand that her daughter was born dead?

5. Boland decides to call her daughter 'Rain' because she considers rain to be 'soft, familiar and constant'. (a) Can you explain how each of these words applies to rain? (b) Might these three words also be applied to a particular person in a baby's life?

6. 'To touch and touch again Her thin coverlet of earth.'
   Does Boland's use of the words 'touch and touch again' and 'thin coverlet' remind you of anything that a mother might do for her baby?

7. Do you think that writing this poem helped Rosita Boland to come to terms with her daughter's death? Why?

Third reading

8. Although Boland uses simple conversational language in this poem, she still communicates intense emotions. Choose 1–3 lines that had a strong emotional impact on you and explain the reasons for your choice.

9. The Lyric is a poetic form where the poet expresses his own emotions and psychological reactions to a situation. Do you think that 'Naming My Daughter' could be classed as a Lyric? Why?

10. Imagine that you are a friend of Rosita Boland and she has just read this poem to you. Write out what you would say to her.

Unseen Poetry: Approaching the Question

An Approach to a Poem

Like any other work of art, such as a painting, sculpture, film or building, a poem needs many viewings or readings before we come to appreciate it fully. All the usual techniques we employ when viewing any new or unusual object can be of use here: first noticing the particularly striking or unusual features; then focusing in on a small area of it; drawing back and trying to see the whole structure; circling around it; finding words to describe it to ourselves; asking ourselves what we like about it; and so on. And so by circling the object and zooming in and out to examine interesting features, gradually we pick up more and more of the detail until the entire object makes sense for us. *Many readings are the key to understanding.*

Here are some questions you might ask yourself as you read and reread:

What do I notice on a first reading?

List any and every thing I notice on first reading the poem. This gives me the confidence to say something about it, even though I don't yet understand the full picture.

What do I see?

- Where is it set? What scene or scenes are featured?
- What pictures strike me as interesting? Focus on a setting or an image. What are my thoughts on it?
- Follow the images through the poem. Is there a sequence or a pattern? Have the images anything in common?
- Do the images or settings suggest anything about the themes or issues the poem might be dealing with?
- What atmosphere or mood is suggested by the visual aspects? Which words or images are most powerful in creating this atmosphere?

What is the poem doing, and how is it structured?

(1) Does it tell a story?

- Is there a narrative structure to this poem? If so, what is happening? What is the sequence of events? Am I clear about the story line?
- What is my reaction to this story?
- Is there a main idea behind the narrative? What is the poet's central concern?
- What do I notice about the shape of the poem?
- If a narrative poem, is it in the genre of a ballad, epic, allegory, etc.?
- Is it serious, humorous, satirical, or what?

(2) Is it a descriptive piece, re-creating a scene?

- Is its primary purpose to re-create the atmosphere of an event or the mood of a moment?
- Is it mainly decorative? Or has it a point to make, or a moral to transmit?
- How does the poet want me to feel? What mood is created in this poem? What words or phrases help to create this mood?
- If a lyric poem, is it in the form of a sonnet, ode, villanelle, sestina, or what?
- What is the poet's central concern (theme)?
- Leaving technical terms aside, how would I describe what the poem sets out to do?

The speaker

- Who is the speaker in the poem? What kind of person do I imagine him or her to be? What state of mind is the speaker in? What words or phrases reveal most about the attitude and state of mind of the speaker? Consider the tone of the poem and how it is created.
- What point of view is being put across in the poem? Am I in sympathy with it or not?
- Who is the speaker addressing in the poem?

What do I notice about the poet's style?

- Does the poet rely heavily on images? If so, what do I notice about them?
- Does the poet use the musical sounds of words to create effect: alliteration, assonance, onomatopoeia, etc.? Does he or she use rhyme? What is the effect? What do the sounds of words contribute to the atmosphere of the poem?
- What do I notice about the type of words (diction) most frequently used – ordinary, everyday, learned and scholarly, technical, or what?
- Does the poet use regular metre (rhythm or regular beat in the lines) or do the lines sound more like ordinary conversation or a piece of prose writing? What is the overall effect? Explore the rhythm of the language.
- Are any of these features particularly noticeable or effective? What do I like?

What is my reaction to it?

- Can I identify with the experience in this poem? Has there been any similar experience in my life?
- What are my feelings on reading this poem, and what words, phrases, images or ideas spark off these reactions in me?
- How do I react to it? Do I find it amusing, interesting, exciting, frightening, revolting, thought-provoking, or what?
- What seems to me most important about the piece?

- At a critical level, do I think it is a well-made poem? What in particular do I think is effective?

Some basic questions

A final line-by-line or stanza-by-stanza exploration should bring the poem into clearer focus and facilitate answers to the basic questions:

1. What is the poem about (theme)?
2. Is it an interesting treatment of this theme?
3. What is important about the poem?
4. How is the poem structured (form and genre: narrative or lyric, ballad, ode, sonnet, etc.)?
5. What are the poet's feelings and attitudes (tone)?
6. How would one describe the atmosphere or mood of the poem, and how is it created?
7. What features of poetic style are noticeable or effective?

8. What are my reactions to the poem?

Comparing a newly read poem with a prescribed poem

Which ideas are similar? Which are different?
Which poem made the greater impact on you, and why?
What insights did you get from each poem?
What is the attitude of the poet in each case? Are there similarities or differences in tone?
How does each poet differ in use of language, imagery, etc.?
Comment on the form and genre in each case.

Practice

To practise answering similar questions on unseen poems, use any of the poems in this anthology which are **not** on your prescribed course.

Past Examination Questions (Higher Level)

John Donne

'Why read the poetry of John Donne?'

Write out the text of a talk that you would give, or an article that you would submit to a journal, in response to the above title. Support the points you make by reference to the poetry of John Donne on your course.

(Higher Level 2003)

John Keats

Often we love a poet because of the feelings his/her poems create in us. Write about the feelings John Keats's poetry creates in you and the aspects of the poems (their content and/or style) that help to create those feelings. Support your points by reference to the poetry by Keats that you have studied.

(Higher Level 2001)

Robert Frost

'We enjoy poetry for its ideas and for its language.'

Using the above statement as your title, write an essay on the poetry of Robert Frost. Support your points by reference to the poetry by Robert Frost on your course.

(Higher Level 2003)

Patrick Kavanagh

Imagine you were asked to select one or more of Patrick Kavanagh's poems from your course for inclusion in a short anthology entitled, 'The Essential Kavanagh'.

Give reasons for your choice, quoting from or referring to the poem or poems you have chosen.

(Higher Level 2004)

Elizabeth Bishop

'Introducing Elizabeth Bishop'

Write out the text of a short presentation you would make to your friends or class group under the above title. Support your point of view by reference to or quotation from the poetry of Elizabeth Bishop that you have studied.

(Higher Level 2001)

'The poetry of Elizabeth Bishop appeals to the modern reader for many reasons.'
Write an essay in which you outline the reasons why poems by Elizabeth Bishop have this appeal.

(Higher Level 2002)

Philip Larkin

Write an essay in which you outline your reasons for liking and/or not liking the poetry of Philip Larkin. Support your points by reference to the poetry of Larkin that you have studied.

(Higher Level 2001)

Sylvia Plath

If you were asked to give a public reading of a small selection of Sylvia Plath's poems, which ones would you choose to read? Give reasons for your choices, supporting them by reference to the poems on your course.

(Higher Level 2003)

'I like (or do not like) to read the poetry of Sylvia Plath.'
Respond to this statement, referring to the poetry by Sylvia Plath on your course.

(Higher Level 2004)

Michael Longley

What impact did the poetry of Michael Longley make on you as a reader? In shaping your answer you might consider some of the following:
– *Your overall sense of the personality or outlook of the poet*
– *The poet's use of language and imagery*
– *Your favourite poem or poems.*

(Higher Level 2001)

Imagine you have invited Michael Longley to give a reading of his poems to your class or group. What poems would you ask him to read and why do you think they would appeal to your fellow students?

(Higher Level 2002)

Derek Mahon

'Speaking of Derek Mahon . . .'
Write out the text of a public talk you might give on the poetry of Derek Mahon. Your talk should make reference to the poetry on your course.

(Higher Level 2004)

Eavan Boland

Write a personal response to the poetry of Eavan Boland.
Support the points you make by reference to the poetry of Boland that you have studied.

Past Examination Questions (Ordinary Level)

Poems also prescribed for Higher Level

W.B. Yeats

An Irish Airman Foresees His Death (page 57)

1. (*a*) What, in your view, is the attitude of the airman to the war in which he is fighting? (10)
    (*b*) Write out the line or phrase from the poem that best shows his attitude.
    Give a reason for your choice. (10)
    (*c*) Write a short paragraph in which you outline your feelings towards the airman. Support your view by quotation from the poem. (10)

2. Answer **ONE** of the following. [Each part carries 20 marks.]
    (*a*) 'I balanced all, brought all to mind'
    What are the kinds of things the airman is referring to in this line from the poem?

    OR

    (*b*) Imagine the airman has to give a short speech to his fellow pilots as they prepare for battle. Write out the text of the speech he might give.

    OR

    (*c*) Suggest a different title for the above poem. Give reasons for your answer, supporting them by quotation from the poem.

The Lake Isle of Innisfree (page 49)

1. (*a*) How in the first two stanzas of the above poem does the poet

help us to imagine the kind of place Innisfree is? (10)

(b) In your opinion what qualities of the place are most important to the poet, W.B. Yeats? Support your answer by reference to the text of the poem. (10)

2. This poem by Yeats is very popular among readers of poetry. From the following list of reasons why it is so popular, choose the one that is closest to your own view and explain your choice. Support your answer by illustration from the text.
 – *The descriptions of the place are very appealing*
 – *The poem contains many beautiful sounds*
 – *The main idea in the poem is attractive to people.* (10)

3. Answer **ONE** of the following. [Each part carries 20 marks.]
(a) 'While I stand on the roadway, or on the pavements grey, I hear it in the deep heart's core.' What do you understand these last two lines of the poem to mean?

OR

(b) Write a paragraph outlining the reasons why you like or dislike the poems by W.B. Yeats on your course.

OR

(c) Would Innisfree appeal to you as a place to live? Support your answer by reference to the poem.

(Ordinary Level 2003)

Philip Larkin

The Explosion (page 228)

1. (a) What impression of the miners do you get from reading the opening four stanzas of the above poem? Support your view by reference to the text. (10)

(b) Stanza five ('At noon, there came a tremor . . .') describes the moment of the explosion. What effect does the poet achieve by describing the event in the manner in which he does? Give a reason in support of your view. (10)

2. Why, in your opinion, does Larkin end the poem with the image of the 'eggs unbroken'? Support your answer by reference to the poem.

3. Answer **ONE** of the following. [Each part carries 20 marks.]
(a) Compare *The Explosion* with any other poem by Philip Larkin that you have studied as part of your course.

OR

(b) What, in your opinion, can we learn about Philip Larkin himself, (the things he values or considers important) from reading this poem? Support your view by brief reference to the poem.

OR

(c) Imagine that the wife of one of the men killed in the explosion were to write an article describing the event for her local newspaper. Write out a paragraph that you think she might include in her article.

(Ordinary Level 2002)

Sylvia Plath

The Arrival of the Bee Box (page 372)

1. (a) What impression of the poet, Sylvia Plath, do you get from reading this poem? (10)
    (b) What words or phrases from the poem especially help to create that impression for you? (10)
2. The following list of phrases suggest some of the poet's attitudes to the bee box:
    - *She is fascinated by it*
    - *She is annoyed by it*
    - *She feels she has great power over it.*
    Choose the phrase from the above list that is closest to your own reading of the poem. Explain your choice, supporting your view by reference to the words of the poem.
3. Answer **ONE** of the following. [Each part carries 20 marks.]
    (a) Imagine you were asked to select music to accompany a public reading of this poem. Describe the kind of music you would choose and explain your choice clearly.

    OR

    (b) 'The box is only temporary.'
    What do you understand the last line of the poem to mean?

    OR

    (c) Write a paragraph in which you outline the similarities **and/or** differences between 'The Arrival of the Bee Box' and the other poem on your course by Sylvia Plath, 'Child'.

(Ordinary Level 2003)

Derek Mahon

After the Titanic (page 411)

1. (a) What effect did the sinking of the *Titanic* have on Bruce Ismay, the speaker in this poem? (10)
    (b) Do you sympathise with him after reading this poem? Give a reason. (10)
    (c) What details in the poem make you sympathise with him, or not sympathise with him? (10)
2. Answer **ONE** of the following. [Each part carries 20 marks.]

(a) 'This poem gives you a vivid picture of the disaster.'
Would you agree? Support your answer with reference to the poem.

OR

(b) 'Letter from a ghost'
Imagine you are one of the people who drowned on the *Titanic*. Write a letter to Bruce Ismay telling him about your memories of that night. Use details from the poem in your letter.

OR

(c) In this poem Mahon speaks *as if he is* Bruce Ismay. How well do you think he gets into Bruce Ismay's mind? Give reasons for your answer.

(Ordinary Level 2004)

Eavan Boland

This Moment (page 452)

1. (a) Why in your opinion does the poet call the poem, 'This Moment'? (10)

   (b) Write out two images from the poem that best help you to picture the neighbourhood at dusk. Give a reason for your choice in each case. (10)

   (c) Taken as a whole, does this poem give you a comforting or a threatening feeling about the neighbourhood? Explain your answer. (10)

2. Answer **ONE** of the following, (a) or (b) or (c). [Each part carries 20 marks.]

   (a) Imagine you were asked to make a short film based on the poem, 'This Moment'. Describe the sort of atmosphere you would try to create and say how you would use music, sound effects and images to create it.

OR

   (b) 'Stars rise.
   Moths flutter
   Apples sweeten in the dark.'
   Do you think these lines provide a good ending to the poem? Give reasons for your opinion.

OR

   (c) Write a short letter to Eavan Boland in which you tell her what her poems on your course mean to you.

(Ordinary Level 2001)

Alternative Poems for Ordinary Level

W.H. Auden

Funeral Blues (page 483)

1. (*a*) How did this poem make you feel?   (10)
    (*b*) Do you think that the poet really loves the one who has died?
         Explain your answer.   (10)
    (*c*) Do you like the way the poet expresses sadness at the death of
         his friend? Give a reason.   (10)

2. Answer **ONE** of the following. [Each part carries 20 marks.]
    (*a*) Imagine that the poet wanted to choose a line or two from the
         poem to be written on his lover's tombstone. Which line or lines
         would you advise him to choose? Write the lines and give
         reasons for your choice.

OR

    (*b*) Imagine you wanted to perform this poem to music with a group
         of musical friends. How would you perform it so that people
         would remember the experience?

OR

    (*c*) What things did you learn about the poet W.H. Auden from
         reading the poem? Refer to the poem in your answer.

(Ordinary Level 2003)

Richard Wilbur

The Pardon (Page 495)

1. (*a*) What impression of the young boy do you get from reading the
         first three stanzas of this poem?   (5)
         What words or phrases from the poem best convey that
         impression to you?   (10)
    (*b*) Choose two phrases from the poem that, in your view, describe
         the dead dog most powerfully. Write each phrase down and
         comment on why you have chosen it.   (10)
    (*c*) In an overall way, how does this poem make you feel? Give one
         reason for your answer.   (5)

2. Answer **ONE** of the following, (*a*) or (*b*) or (*c*). [Each part carries 20
    marks.]
    (*a*) How, in your opinion, does the father's reaction to the death of
         the dog compare with that of the young boy's? Support your
         view by reference to the poem.

OR

(b) 'Well, I was ten and very much afraid.'

Write a short letter to the poet, Richard Wilbur, in which you show how this poem reminds you of a childhood experience of your own.

OR

(c) Why, in your view, did Richard Wilbur choose the title 'The Pardon' for this poem? Illustrate your answer by reference to the poem.

(Ordinary Level 2001)

Fleur Adcock

For Heidi with Blue Hair (page 514)

1. (a) What impression of Heidi do you get from the above poem? (5)
   (b) Where does the language used by the poet especially create that impression for you? (10)

2. (a) From the following list, choose the phrase that is closest to your own reading of the poem:
   - *a funny and clever poem*
   - *an important poem about people's rights*
   - *a sad poem.*

   Explain your choice, supporting your view by reference to the words of the poem. (10)

   (b) 'The battle was already won.'
   What do you understand the last line of the poem to mean? (5)

3. Answer **ONE** of the following, (a) or (b) of (c). [Each part carries 20 marks.]

   (a) 'It would have been unfair to mention your mother's death, but that shimmered behind the arguments,'
   How do these lines from the fifth stanza affect your attitude to Heidi and what she had done? Give reasons for your answer.

OR

   (b) Does Heidi remind you of anyone you know in real life? Write a short paragraph that shows how that person is most like Heidi. [**N.B.** You should not give the person's real name.]

OR

   (c) What impression of Heidi's father emerges from the poem? Support your answer by reference to the text.

(Ordinary Level 2001)

Carol Ann Duffy

Valentine (page 548)

1. (*a*) 'I am trying to be truthful.'
    In your opinion, what is the speaker of the poem trying to tell her
    lover about her feelings?   (10)
    (*b*) Write down one line or phrase from the poem that tells you most
    about the kind of relationship the lovers have. Say why you
    think it is an important line.   (10)
    (*c*) How do you imagine a lover would feel if he or she received this
    poem on St Valentine's Day? Explain your answer.   (10)
2. Answer **ONE** of the following. [Each part carries 20 marks.]
    (*a*) In what way is this poem different from the normal poems or
    rhymes that lovers send to each other on Valentine's Day?

    OR

    (*b*) In your opinion, what reply might the lover write to this
    Valentine? You may, if you wish, write your reply in verse.

    OR

    (*c*) 'Lethal.
    Its scent will cling to your anger,
    cling to your knife.'
    Do you think that this is a good ending to the poem? Explain
    your view.

                                                          (Ordinary Level 2003)

Simon Armitage

It Ain't What You Do, It's What It Does To You (page 555)

1. (*a*) What kind of life does the poet say he has not lived?   (10)
    (*b*) What do the things he has done tell you about him? Refer to the
    poem in your response.   (10)
    (*c*) Do you think he creates a feeling of stillness in the following
    lines?
    'But I
    skimmed flat stones across Black Moss on a day
    so still I could hear each set of ripples
    as they crossed. I felt each stone's inertia
    spend itself against the water; then sink'.
    Give a reason for your answer.   (10)
2. Answer **ONE** of the following. [Each part carries 20 marks.]
    (*a*) Armitage thinks that titles are very important. Do you think he
    has chosen a good title for this poem? Refer to the poem in your
    response.

    OR

(*b*) Someone asks you to suggest a poem to be included in a collection for young people. You recommend this one. Explain why.

OR

(*c*) 'That feeling, I mean.'
What kind of feeling do you think Armitage is describing in the last stanza? Do you think he describes it well? Explain your view.

Acknowledgments

The author and publisher are grateful to the following for permission to reproduce copyrighted material:

The poems by **W.B. Yeats** are reproduced by kind permission of A P Watt Ltd on behalf of Michael B. Yeats; The poems by **Robert Frost** are reproduced by kind permission of Henry Holt and Company; The poems by **T.S. Eliot** are reproduced by kind permission of Faber and Faber Ltd.; The poems by **Patrick Kavanagh** are reprinted from *Collected Poems*, edited by Antoinette Quinn (Allen Lane, 2004), by kind permission of the Trustees of the Estate of the late Katherine B. Kavanagh, through the Jonathan Williams Literary Agency; 'The Armadillo', 'At the Fishhouses', 'The Blight', 'Filling Station', 'First Death in Nova Scotia', 'In the Waiting Room', 'The Prodigal', 'Questions of Travel', and 'Sestina' from *The Complete Poems: 1927–1979* by **Elizabeth Bishop.** Copyright © 1979, 1983 by Alice Helen Methfessel. Reprinted by permission of Farrar, Straus and Giroux, LLC; 'At Grass', 'Wedding-Wind' and 'Church Going' by **Philip Larkin** are reprinted from *The Less Deceived* by permission of The Marvell Press, England and Australia; 'An Arundel Tomb', 'The Whitsun Weddings', 'MCMXIV', 'Ambulances', 'The Trees', 'The Explosion' and 'Cut Grass' are reproduced by kind permission of Faber and Faber Ltd.; The poems by **John Montague** are reproduced by kind permission of the author and The Gallery Press, Loughcrew, Oldcastle, County Meath, Ireland. From *Collected Poems* (1995); 'Aunt Jennifer's Tigers'. Copyright © 2002, 1951 by **Adrienne Rich**, 'Power'. Copyright © 2002 by Adrienne Rich. Copyright © 1978 by W.W. Norton & Company, Inc., 'Storm Warnings'. Copyright © 2002, 1951 by Adrienne Rich, from *The Fact of a Doorframe: Selected Poems 1950–2001* by Adrienne Rich. Used by permission of the author and W.W. Norton & Company, Inc.; 'The Uncle Speaks in the Drawing Room', 'Living in Sin', 'The Roofwalker', 'Our Whole Life', 'Trying to Talk with a Man', 'Diving into the Wreck' and 'From a Survivor' Copyright © Adrienne Rich; The poems by **Derek Walcott** are reproduced by kind permission of Faber and Faber Ltd.; The poems by

Sylvia Plath are reproduced by kind permission of Faber and Faber Ltd.; Poems by Michael Longley reproduced by kind permission of Michael Longley; The poems by Derek Mahon are reproduced by kind permission of the author and The Gallery Press, Loughcrew, Oldcastle, County Meath, Ireland. From *Collected Poems* (1999); The poems by Eavan Boland published by Carcanet Press Limited reproduced by kind permission of Carcanet Press Limited; 'For Heidi with Blue Hair' by Fleur Adcock, *Poems 1960–2000* (Bloodaxe Books, 2000); 'Phenomenal Woman' by Maya Angelou reproduced from *The Complete Collected Poems* by Maya Angelou, by permission of Virago Books, a division of Time Warner Book Group UK; 'It Ain't What You Do, It's What It Does To You' by Simon Armitage, *Zoom!* (Bloodaxe Books, 1989); 'Funeral Blues' by W.H. Auden is reproduced by kind permission of Faber and Faber Ltd.; 'The Voice' by Patricia Beer published by Carcanet Press Limited reproduced by kind permission of Carcanet Press Limited; 'Naming My Daughter' by Rosita Boland reproduced by kind permission of the author; 'Jasmine' and 'Midwife' by Paddy Bushe reproduced by kind permission of Paddy Bushe and Dedalus Press; 'Valentine' by Carol Ann Duffy is reproduced by kind permission of Faber and Faber Ltd.; 'Going Home to Mayo, Winter 1949' by Paul Durcan is reproduced by kind permission of Paul Durcan; 'Taking My Son to School' by Eamon Grennan reproduced by kind permission of the author and The Gallery Press, Loughcrew, Oldcastle, County Meath, Ireland. From *Wildly for Days* (1983); 'May' by Kerry Hardie reproduced by kind permission of the author and The Gallery Press, Loughcrew, Oldcastle, County Meath, Ireland. From *A Furious Place* (1996); 'Postscript' by Seamus Heaney is reproduced by kind permission of Faber and Faber Ltd.; 'One Flesh' and 'The Ladybird's Song' by Elizabeth Jennings published by Carcanet from *New Collected Poems* reproduced by kind permission of David Higham Associates; 'Night Drive' by Brendan Kennelly, *Familiar Strangers: New & Selected Poems 1960–2004* (Bloodaxe Books, 2004); 'What Were They Like?' by Denise Levertov reproduced by permission of Pollinger Limited and the proprietor; 'Kidspoem/Bairnsang' by Liz Lochhead reproduced by kind permission of Birlinn Limited; 'Bearhugs' by Roger McGough from *Defying Gravity* (Copyright © Roger McGough 1993) is reproduced by permission of PFD (www.pfd.co.uk) on behalf of Roger McGough; 'Buying Winkles' and 'My Father Perceived as a Vision of St Francis' by Paula Meehan reproduced by kind permission of the author and The Gallery Press, Loughcrew, Oldcastle, County Meath, Ireland. From *The Man Who Was Marked by Winter* (1991) and *Pillow Talk* (1994); 'Strawberries' by Edwin Morgan published by Carcanet Press Limited; 'Anseo' by Paul Muldoon is reproduced by kind permission of Faber and Faber Ltd.; 'The Reading Lesson' by Richard Murphy reproduced by kind permission of the author and The Gallery Press, Loughcrew, Oldcastle, County Meath, Ireland. From *Collected Poems* (2000); 'Wolves in the Zoo' by Howard Nemerov reproduced by kind permission of Mrs Margaret Nemerov; 'The Great Blasket Island' by Julie O'Callaghan, *What's What* (Bloodaxe Books, 1991); 'Gunpowder' from *Gunpowder* by Bernard O'Donoghue published by Chatto & Windus. Used by permission of the Random House Group Limited; 'Looking at Them Asleep' and 'The

Present Moment' from *The Unswept Room* by **Sharon Olds** published by Jonathan Cape. Used by permission of The Random House Group Limited; Barbara Levy Literary Agency for permission to reproduce 'On Passing the New Menin Gate' by **Siegfried Sassoon**; Copyright Siegfried Sassoon by kind permission of George Sassoon; 'The Hunchback in the Park' by **Dylan Thomas** from *Collected Poems* published by Dent reproduced by kind permission of David Higham Associates; 'The Pardon' from *Ceremony and Other Poems*, copyright 1950 and renewed 1978 by **Richard Wilbur**, reprinted by permission of Harcourt, Inc.; 'The Red Wheelbarrow' by **William Carlos Williams** published by Carcanet Press Limited; 'Request to a Year' by **Judith Wright** published by Carcanet Press Limited.

Compact Disk

CD recordings are by permission of The Gallery Press (Montague and Mahon), Lucas Alexander Whitely (Longley) and Carcanet Press (Boland). The kind co-operation of John Montague, Derek Mahon, Michael Longley and Eavan Boland in recording their poems is gratefully acknowledged.

Illustrations

For permission to reproduce photographs and other material, the author and publisher gratefully acknowledge the following:

pp.1, 22, 114, 464, 471 National Portrait Gallery, London; **p.20** Bridgeman Art Library/Guildhall Library, Corporation of London; **p.23** Art Archive/Royal Holloway College; **p.25** Wellcome Institute Library, London; **p.32** Bridgeman Art Library/City of Bristol Museum and Art Gallery; **p.39** Keats-Shelley Memorial House, Rome/Christopher Warde-Jones (photographer); **p.40** Parthenon frieze section (British Museum)/Michael Holford; **p.43** National Gallery, London/E.T. Archive; **p.48** Hugh Lane Municipal Gallery of Modern Art, Dublin; **pp.56, 79, 87 (B), 168** Bord Fáilte; **p.57** Dúchas: The Heritage Service; **p.65** Hugh Lane Municipal Gallery of Modern Art, Dublin/Sarah Purser copyright holders; **p.71** Art Archive/Dagli Orti; **p.77** National Library of Ireland; **pp.87 (T), 163** The Slide File; **p.89** Corbis/E.O. Hoppé; **pp.93, 97, 100** Bridgeman Art Library; **p.122** Art Archive/Museé du Louvre/Dagli Orti; **p.127** Staatsgalerie Stuttgart/© DACS 2001; **p.140** Bridgeman Art Library/Philips Fine Art Auctioneers; **p.144** Bridgeman Art Library/Prado, Madrid; **p.146** Gerard Burns Photography Services; **p.148** John Skelton/Patrick Kavanagh Rural and Literary Resource Centre, Inniskeen; **p.164** Professor Connolly, St James' Hospital; **p.166** Helen Mulkerns; **p.170** Elizabeth Bishop – Special Collections, Vassar College Libraries, Ploughkeepsie, New York; **p.171** 'Cabin with Porthole' and **p.180** 'Nova Scotia Landscape' and **p.187** 'Brazilian Landscape' – all undated paintings by Elizabeth Bishop (whereabouts unknown) reproduced from *Changing Hats: Elizabeth Bishop Paintings*, ed with an introduction by William Benton, published by Farrar, Straus and Giroux